Legal Philosophy

KT-465-466

Legal Philosophy

Stephen Riley

Sheffield Hallam University

PEARSON

Harlow • England • London • New York • Boston • San Francisco • Toronto • Sydney
Auckland • Singapore • Hong Kong • Tokyo • Seoul • Taipei • New Delhi
Cape Town • São Paulo • Mexico City • Madrid • Amsterdam • Munich • Paris • Milan

Pearson Education Limited
Edinburgh Gate
Harlow
Essex CM20 2JE
England

and Associated Companies throughout the world

Visit us on the World Wide Web at:
www.pearson.com/uk

First published 2013 (print and electronic)

ISBN 978-1-4082-7734-8 (print)
     978-1-4082-7888-8 (e Text)

British Library Cataloguing-in-Publication Data
A catalogue record for this book is available from the British Library

Library of Congress Cataloging-in-Publication Data
A catalog record for this book is available from the Library of Congress

10 9 8 7 6 5 4 3 2 1
16 15 14 13 12

Typeset in 10/14 pt Giovanni by 75
Printed and bound by in Great Britain by Henry Ling Ltd, Dorchester, Dorset

Contents

CONTENTS

Preface

This book is an analysis of seven concepts crucial to philosophical discussion of law. It presumes no knowledge of existing philosophical debates. It begins discussion at a fundamental and, it is hoped, immediately intelligible level. By understanding the meaning of these seven concepts and the work they can do in analysis of law, major texts in the jurisprudential tradition should become accessible, and the relevance of philosophy for law should become clearer.

Using this book

This book reflects the belief that law is suffused with philosophy, and it serves as an introduction to the most important ideas shared by law and philosophy. A range of legal instruments and legal sources are used to illustrate the presence of philosophical ideas within law's raw materials.

The text is intended to cover a considerable amount of scholarly ground and be accessible to those without a philosophical background who will nonetheless be asked to use legal theories. It contains questions to draw out ideas discussed in the text, along with suggestions for further reading. Common philosophical terms, distinctions and tools are highlighted in the 'concepts and methods' sections. A glossary provides definitions of some philosophical 'terms of art' used in the text.

In short, the book is a starting-point for some difficult ideas and texts, and, accordingly, it ends where other texts in the philosophy of law begin: with discussion of the meaning of 'law'. The chapters can be read in any order according to the needs and requirements of different courses. Nonetheless, there is a logical development of ideas and analytical tools across the chapters, starting with intuitive ideas about justice in the first, through to a synthesis of ideas and arguments concerning law in the last. The book's unifying themes are outlined in the introduction.

The book reflects the interests and tastes of the author, namely both Anglo-American and Continental philosophy, and both domestic and international law. It is hoped this will not disadvantage the reader but, on the contrary, expose them to the breadth of approaches used by legal researchers and philosophers today. The legal materials are from the United Kingdom unless otherwise stated. They are for illustrative purposes and should not be treated as law in force.

I would like to thank Owen Knight at Pearson for his initial enthusiasm for the project and unflagging support thereafter. My colleagues (past and present) at Sheffield Hallam University – especially the stalwarts of the staff reading group, Miroslav Baros, Sam Burton, Cathy Morse, Martin O'Boyle, Phil Rumney and Chalen Westaby – have been unwitting accomplices. I am particularly grateful to Lesley Klaff for sharing her passion for the subject and for allowing me to experiment with her Legal Theory syllabus. Many of the ideas in the book were introduced to me by Professor Paul Roberts (University of Nottingham), Dr David Seymour and Professor Peter Rowe (Lancaster University): my thanks to them. Dr Phil Riley kindly read, commented on, and improved, the drafts. All remaining faults are my own. It would not have been possible without Ruth's patience, while she herself worked on significant outputs: the book is dedicated to her.

Introduction

Law and philosophy

If myths are to be believed, being a philosopher and being a lawyer are two very different ways of living, working and thinking. Lawyers use their time getting things done. Philosophers think about thinking. These two different vocations – one active, one contemplative – have nothing in common. These caricatures are false (although, like any caricatures, they contain a grain of truth). Even where they are in conflict – when lawyers want to get things done and philosophers want to get things right – both are working on similar problems.

What problems do law and philosophy share? They are concerned with how people live their lives; they are concerned with justice in human affairs. Both demand clarity in discussing human life; both want to determine how we can, and should, order ourselves as a society. In short, lawyers and philosophers face the same problems: clarifying ideas and putting ideas into practice.

This book is an introduction to those ideas shared by philosophy and law, and it is ideas that give the book its structure. Understanding the concepts 'person', 'good', 'right', 'rule', 'norm' and 'justice' requires more than checking a dictionary. It is to ask what these words have meant, are used to mean and should mean; and with clarity on these ideas we have a better sense of what is at stake in both law and philosophy. However, this book does not seek to define these ideas exhaustively or definitively. In a more limited way it seeks to show that there are concepts, problems and practices shared by lawyers and philosophers, not least the idea of being critical.

Critical concepts

Philosophy *is* critical because it is a discipline with no unassailable assumptions, no 'orthodoxy', other than that its practitioners should be critical of ideas. Philosophers are committed to criticism because the problems that fall within its scope – multifarious questions from the organisation of society to the relationship between the world and language – are worthy of the most rigorous analysis necessary to find rational solutions.

Law is critical because it has to make judgments and decisions, on the basis of general rules, about what people are entitled to. Lawyers are critical with a purpose: to realise justice, or as close to justice as is humanly possible. Drawing both

1

together, law needs answers to social problems, while philosophy needs answers to perplexing human problems. In both cases they need the *right* answers. Therefore, criticism as practised by lawyers and philosophers is not cynicism. It is insistence on finding what is true, right or just.

Getting to the right answer is not something that we have to struggle with every time there is a problem. There are ways of getting to answers that are reliable, that are useful or that are socially agreed upon. Everyone, including lawyers and philosophers, have traditions. However, while law and philosophy have long traditions, they have only qualified respect for tradition. Without criticism of our inheritance from the past, our ideas and practices stagnate. Lawyers and philosophers, perhaps more than other scholars, have a responsibility to criticise their traditions. Being critical with a purpose is not only to take a position on other people's problems, but requires being critical about the perspective with which we ourselves begin. Without law and philosophy being critical about themselves they would not be useful or interesting parts of people's lives, they would be historical curiosities.

This gives us a first meaning of critical – probing other people's ideas and one's own – and lawyers and philosophers, in different ways, are specialists in this field. Dealing with specialists of any kind, particularly specialists in criticism, means dealing with terminology, abstractions and complexities. Human life is a complicated thing, and we have to 'abstract' from that complexity simpler ideas. Simple ideas are the life-blood of philosophy because philosophy aims to 'state the obvious' as clearly as possible in order to show where 'the obvious' hides problems and imprecision (Hacker, 1997). Law has a habit of taking simple ideas, like 'right' or 'responsibility', and making them complex through debate and refinement (Katz, 2011). Here is a second meaning of 'critical': some ideas are essential, critical for getting things done. It is critical for lawyers to have a clear understanding of certain ideas, and critical for philosophers that they do not settle for anything less than perfect clarity in these ideas.

Some debates between law and philosophy

While law and philosophy have some broad areas of agreement on critical problems, and the tools needed to solve those problems, there are nonetheless tensions, not least the practising lawyer's desire to have a stable set of concepts (rules, principles and a shared vocabulary) which are not called into question every time legal discussion takes place. The philosopher, conversely, views these concepts with suspicion. Taking one example, all legal systems contain the idea 'adult person' (it is a status that is granted to a person once they reach a certain age). Philosophy considers 'person', along with 'adult', to be words enmeshed within a web of debates about language, meaning and the rights and responsibilities of an individual.

Legal institutions have to make decisions without constant dissection of their vocabulary. And, as a consequence of the need to cut away some 'purely' philosophical debates and prioritise those ideas central to law's functioning, a specialised discipline of 'jurisprudence' – lawyers' own distinctive philosophical tradition – has emerged where the practice of law is set aside in the pursuit of clarifying basic legal ideas. In jurisprudence, 'law' itself quickly becomes a core object of enquiry, and the discipline of jurisprudence is predominantly a forum for discussion of the word, the idea and the ideal of, law (Hart, 1994; Ross, 2004). This is an argument fought primarily between two schools of thought – legal positivism and natural law – schools who disagree over the fundamental, starting, assumptions. Positivists insist that the sources of law are primary; the natural lawyers insist that the ideals giving rise to law are the proper foundation for philosophical debate. This is the framework within which jurisprudence is still conducted and taught today, albeit with developments in both schools (and other rival schools) allowing a more nuanced, less monumental, clash over where debate should begin and go (Del Mar (ed.), 2011).

The relationship between law and philosophy is wider than this debate suggests. Not least because there are common questions about law that generate philosophically interesting answers. For instance, why do many people not *like* lawyers? It cannot be that they make money out of people's misfortunes. If that were the case people would dislike surgeons with equal ferocity. The answer is, perhaps, that we see lawyers falling short of an ideal: the pursuit of justice. In courtrooms, manipulation and rhetoric seem more abundant than noble ideals. In learning law we find it 'replete with loopholes [and] the teaching of their exploitation is a mainstay of legal training' (Katz, 2011: 10).

Another question: why, if we want to understand our fellow human beings, would we turn to literature, psychology or history, but are unlikely to turn to law? Despite centuries of experience being distilled in legal texts and legal practices it is assumed that humans are poorly or inaccurately understood by law (Shklar, 1986). Perhaps because law is as much an instrument of power as it is a reflection of the human condition. Perhaps because law seems to simplify human action and human existence in a way that misses vital, interior, aspects of our lives. These are just two of the kinds of questions that lead into philosophical reflection on justice, persons and other critical terms that law uses, but has no authority to monopolise.

For these reasons, this text assumes that there is no strict division between 'legal philosophy', 'legal theory', 'jurisprudence' and general philosophy. There is enough overlap between these disciplinary categories to make distinction unnecessary. An argument could be made to insist that law is a social *institution* and as such generates specific questions about how that institution exists and how it should function. However, the assumption of this text is that law – as an institution, as a set of rules and as an ideal – provokes questions concerning knowledge, obligation and authority that are part of the wider philosophical tradition. Consequently, while the text addresses a limited number of concepts, it covers an extremely wide range of ideas, schools and concepts in pursuit of clarifying fundamental ideas.

Why concepts?

The format and structure of the book requires further comment and justification. Texts in the philosophy of law tend to adopt a 'canonical' approach, setting out a number of well established schools of thought (principally positivism, natural law and realism) and then explain the ideas of the schools' main exponents. This text does not seek to do this. There are many books already available that do this well, and these are highlighted in the 'further reading' sections of the chapters.

The approach taken here is to begin with concepts shared by law and philosophy and demonstrate that these concepts cut across schools and traditions. This encompasses the traditional canons of jurisprudential thought, but it is not driven by the – different and sometimes incompatible – starting assumptions of those schools. Nor does it seek to chart the development of, and relationships between, key thinkers in these schools. Rather, it is concerned with the extent to which these schools and thinkers contribute to explaining core concepts. Structuring enquiry around concepts shared by law and philosophy is not a new idea and is broadly in line with the approach of Critical Legal Studies (see Chapter 6). This school of thought insists, among other things, that law and philosophy must reconnect with one another after a long period in which they functioned in isolation from one another, to neither discipline's advantage (Douzinas and Gearey, 2005).

Seven concepts are major battlegrounds of argument; they are concepts necessary for accurate, critical and reflective understanding of law. They account for how law could be said to have a foundation (justice or persons), a justification (the good or the right) or a particular structure (rules or norms). It is suggested that for each of these concepts there is a central area of debate and disagreement which can be stated as follows. Discussion of *justice* can be divided between positions that argue law has a unique relationship with justice, and positions that see a close relationship between legal and political justice. The idea of the *person* lies somewhere between 'human' as a factual category and 'personhood' as a value. The idea of the *good* is split in its meaning between a narrow idea of usefulness, and a complex idea of human happiness. The idea of *right*, as an adjective, points to law producing 'right answers'; *right*, as a noun, is a possession (my rights) or something granted by a lawgiver (legal rights). The idea of a legal *rule* can be understood either as a command or as something accepted as an obligation. The idea of a *norm* is located somewhere between a rule and a pattern of behaviour. Finally, the idea of *law* is itself divided between being something real and something ideal.

These are philosophical debates because looking at what lawyers *do* in order to clarify them would be to assume that legal institutions must possess a settled and authoritative insight into law. This assumption is challenged because it does not capture the creative responsibilities of judges (Dworkin, 1998) or the social practices that allow law to exist at all (Delacroix, 2006). Furthermore, we should not assume that the schools of legal philosophy have the right starting-point. These schools should be *questioned*, not allowed to define the questions. In short, the benefit of starting with these concepts is sustained engagement with ideas that are fundamental across schools and disciplines.

The underlying argument of the book

This book can be read as constituting an argument about law as an object of philosophical enquiry. The following line of argument, while it does not have to be accepted in order for the book to be intelligible, makes this explicit.

The objectives of the philosophy of law are two-fold. First, to give an account of what 'law' means to those inside and outside legal institutions. Second, to engage with philosophical questions generated by legal rules, practices and institutions. The first is a focused conceptual enquiry into meaning; the second draws legal debates out of the courtroom and into a philosophical forum. Accordingly, the best place to commence the philosophy of law is with our intuitions about 'justice': justice weaves through both the narrow conceptual question of the meaning of 'law' and wider discussions about rules and practices. In other words, understanding 'justice' demands that we map out *where* justice applies and what *forms* justice could take. More specifically, theories of justice often need further justification in the needs and interests of persons, singularly or collectively.

Persons can be understood in a range of ways, but each frame of reference generates a question with respect to the division between facts and values. However much we can know (scientifically or psychologically) about humans, there is still a further step needed to turn these facts into the values (obligations, duties or expectations) associated with personhood. This stark division between fact and value can be bridged with the idea of 'the good' and its various manifestations in legal and moral philosophy. What is good for us as persons must create values. However, this also raises suspicions about how appropriate the (predominantly moral and ethical vocabulary) of goodness is in capturing the concept of *law*. Thus, 'the good' is contrasted with 'the right' understood as the prioritisation of a certain kind of *coherence* closely related to law and legality.

The coherence demanded by 'right answers' and 'legal rights' lends weight to the idea of law being best captured in its rules, rules which are capable of generating right answers in logically defensible, and rights-preserving, ways. But scepticism about the efficacy of rules alone – given their close relationship with habitual behaviour and the *sense* of obligation – demands their partial dissolution into 'norms'. Norms are sets of expectations, practices and obligations that give order to our world without necessarily taking the form of rules.

These lines of enquiry, together, leave us marginally closer to where we aimed. That is, a philosophical relationship with the word 'law' which encompasses an 'internal' point of view (the practices and institutions of law) and an 'external' point of view (law as a dimension of our social practices and social ideals). We should be left with an idea of law which is far from a 'brooding omnipresence in the sky'. Rather, we should understand 'law' as denoting certain ideas and practices – ideas and practices with distinctive sources, forms and functions. We should also be left with a clearer idea of where and why the practice of law gives rise to philosophically significant debates, along with philosophical techniques with which to analyse these debates.

1 Justice

Introduction

This chapter is intended to be an example of philosophical analysis. It is structured around common or intuitive ideas about how law and justice are connected. But it concludes with fundamental debates about meaning, knowledge and ethics. How do common or intuitive ideas lead into fundamental philosophical debates? Collecting intuitive ideas and then classifying them is a necessary first step in philosophical analysis. It is precisely this classification that leads to more fundamental types of philosophical questioning: what to classify and how to classify.

The remainder of this introduction provides an overview of the ideas and categories adopted in the chapter. It also sketches a basic opposition within which questions about justice can be contextualised. On the one hand, an insistence that justice and law have a unique relationship; on the other, the belief that justice is something sought by all individuals and institutions.

Justice is among the most important philosophical terms associated with law. However, there are no uncontested accounts of justice and no single idea is denoted by 'legal justice'. Its meaning is historically variable, contested and arguably dependent on our perspective. For instance, justice stands outside law: law can meet, or fail to meet, the standard of justice. Justice is also within law: law is the aspiration to achieve, or to deliver, justice. This standard, or aspiration, demands clarification. Is justice a standard which applies to legal decisions, legal procedures, or all and any social institutions? And, if justice has a special relationship with law, do different fields of law possess their own standards of justice, or does one standard apply across all legal activities?

Could 'legal justice' represent the *same* standard in *every* field of legal activity? The following line of enquiry suggests some problems with such a proposition. The idea of a court coming to 'the right legal answer' might be common to all fields of legal activity, but law is more than the activity of courts, because courts can only function where there are rules. Therefore, legal justice must, at the very least, combine a concern with rules and with decisions. The idea of 'giving people what they deserve' might better capture this combination. However, note that 'giving people what they deserve' is also provided by non-legal institutions and practices, through arbitration processes and political policies. For this reason we might choose a slightly narrower definition of justice, for example 'holding people to account for their actions'. But while this would hold good for criminal or administrative law, it would seem less appropriate for family or contract law. Clearly, defining the relationship between law and justice requires prior analysis and classification in order to yield clear answers. Are we only concerned with legal practices (and what do we mean by 'legal'?) and how general, or specific, do we need our definition of justice to be?

Without having to decide in advance exactly *what* we want to find, we can classify our ideas of justice under general categories. This chapter uses four broad categories. The first is 'ends', meaning goals or objectives. The second is 'means', i.e. instruments by which we bring about ends. Third, 'collectives' denotes collections of people. Fourth, 'individual' denotes any single person within a collection of people. These categories begin to draw some distinctions without presuming too much about the kind of answer we want to find.

The category 'individual' captures the fact that law, and social life as a whole, is made up of individual actions and individual needs. But individuals also form collectives. Collectives encompass nations, groups, communities or families who have joint interests which sometimes override the preferences, or even the interests, of the individuals that form them. We also have to consider goals, what it is activities aim to achieve. Law is goal-oriented: it intervenes in social life in particular ways for particular reasons. But it does so with a unique set of means, i.e. the tools, practices and decisions which allow it to fulfil certain kinds of goals but also limit the kinds of goals it seeks. Law can seek to resolve conflicts but does not have the means to solve all social problems. This chapter begins with some important debates about what is distinctive in law's ends and its means, and by questioning what the relationship between the two might be.

The difference between ends and means also plays a large role in drawing a crucial distinction: the difference between law and politics. Law seems to have a closer, more intimate, relationship with justice than any other social practice because, not only legal outcomes are assessed as just or unjust, the very *practice* of law, regardless of its outcomes, seeks to be just. Politics, 'the art of the possible' or 'the science of government', is judged less by its practices than by its immediate outcomes. Law has to seek and demonstrate justice *at all times*. It is not enough for laws to 'look good on paper', or for judges to choose good outcomes at whim. Justice must be done and be seen to be done through the use of legal means. That is, everyone, at all stages in a legal process, should see that just practices are being maintained.

However, isolation of what exactly is being demanded here is difficult. Many of the things we want a legal system to aspire to – for example, equality or fairness – are not distinctively legal virtues at all but are generally good and desirable. Moreover, legal justice could be said to ultimately *serve* social ends (such as the resolution of conflicts or social stability) rather than being an 'end in itself': law is not just, but many of things that it seeks to bring about are. In short, as a *means* to social or political justice, law might be seen as merely a 'handmaiden' to more fundamental aspirations such as economic justice or the common good. We must decide whether law's aspiration to maintain just practices is enough to make its claim to justice superior to that of politics. Or whether, on the contrary, law is squarely a part of, and dependent upon, wider social and political objectives and aspirations.

A different way to consider law's claim to a special relationship with justice is to ask whether they have a *necessary* relationship or a *contingent* relationship. That is, does justice always *necessarily accompany* law? Or, is law associated with justice because our traditions, our language and our culture, have taught us to link the words law and justice? There are strong currents of thought, flowing from Ancient philosophy, that grant only a contingent link between law and justice. This denies that there is a necessary relationship between 'legal' and 'just', not least because many things can be labelled 'legal' without having a special claim to our approval. In fact, there is much philosophy, to this day, which is sceptical of a necessary relationship between law and justice.

From the perspective of the lawyer, such scepticism might well appear wrongheaded. Everyone, it could be argued, would rather have their disputes settled by a court than a duel, and would rather have their interests protected by the state than through their own resources. Law's special kind of dispute settlement, and its assurance of equality between parties, is enough to make the link between law and justice necessary, not contingent.

Clearly, ideas look different from different perspectives, and this 'common sense' intervention by lawyers should encourage us to contrast perspectives inside and outside law. Oliver Wendel Holmes (1841–1935) sought a viewpoint outside law in order to be 'realistic' about what law does in our society. He imagined the perspective of the 'bad man'. For the bad man law is, above all, a threat (Holmes, 1897). Conversely, Ronald Dworkin (b.1931), in order to make sense of how law can be said to provide right answers to difficult disputes, finds an ideal point of view inside law, the judge 'Hercules' (Dworkin, 1977). For Hercules, law is a story of society's self-creation. Drawing upon both perspectives, law is both a threat and the story of our society's evolution.

By the same token, the meaning of *justice* depends upon whether we are inside or outside law. From a social or political perspective outside legal institutions, legal systems offer a distinct form of justice: law provides the best means for adjudicating disputes. From within a legal system, justice is often found in what is *beyond* legal procedures, processes and adjudication, namely individual *needs*, *moral* rights or *political* principles. Put this way, the question of law's relationship with justice does not demand isolating a certain *property* that law possesses. It demands determining what the word 'justice' means, and whether it is owned by any one group: lawyers, politicians or ethicists. If one group offers the definitive meaning of 'justice' we have a single answer to what justice is. If it is not owned by any particular group we might, perhaps, have to treat justice as a complex concept that will always have different, and competing, meanings.

One common philosophical means to widen the range of perspectives brought to bear on a complex debate is to return to historical discussions. The philosophical works of the Ancient world offer us familiar problems in an unfamiliar context. We find ideas that are sometimes wildly different from own, but also familiar concerns and interests. Significantly, we also find a sustained effort to provide definitions of important ideas. The Ancients – Greek and Roman thinkers stretching from, roughly, 500BCE to 500CE – often (though not uniformly) agreed that justice should be defined as a virtue. A virtue is an ideal, or a tendency to act in a certain way. Such ideals provide a template or aspiration for both institutions and individuals (Winthrop, 1978; Cicero, 1998).

By treating justice as a virtue, justice is held to be independent of the state and its legal system. It is a standard by which collective decisions *and* personal actions can be judged. This reflects, in part, the fact that Ancient social institutions were on a smaller scale and more integrated into social life. The individual is not 'set against' the state; free individuals participated in every aspect of the state. For this reason, Ancient philosophers were far more attuned to the fact that courts are a human creation – and susceptible to the same vices of weakness and corruption – and for that reason should be judged by the same standards by which we judge individuals.

Put another way, the Ancients are far from assuming that law has a special status superior to politics. Both concern governing a body of people, and both are arenas where persuasion can be as important as truth (Carey, 2012). In contrast, our own, modern, understanding of justice is coloured by the assumption that legal systems have already proven their worth (their fairness, their independence or their usefulness) and that our only task is to successfully isolate which property (fairness, independence or usefulness) is the ultimate source of that worth.

We now have two approaches to justice to compare. The modern assumption that law is a distinct social institution and any theory of justice must take account of this independence, and the Ancient assumption that justice is equally the measure of law, politics and the individual. The modern assumption, that law is an *independent* set of procedures to arbitrate between disputing parties, suggests that law and justice are related precisely because law is aloof from wider social forces. The Ancient philosophers have a critical standard, a virtue, by which to judge a range of practices of institutions; they caution us against being too quick to separate law from other social forces. From this perspective we have yet to prove that a division between law and society, or law and politics, captures everything we mean by 'justice'.

1 Ends

Introduction

We begin with 'ends' because, whatever else we can say about it, law surely seeks to achieve something. That 'something' may be complex but, like any other organised human activity, law is purposive, i.e. goal-driven.

'Ends' are goals, end-points or objectives. A person's goals and objectives may be monumental or trivial. Either way, 'goal-oriented activity' is the most fundamental aspect of human practices. Humans do not simply react to their environment like animals. Humans choose courses of action in order to fulfil ends such as their happiness, their well-being or their survival.

Law's ends could be said to be both practical ('solving problems') and ideal ('realising our potential as a society'). At the practical level, we could treat justice as the outcomes of trials and courts. Using established courts of law solves problems that cannot be solved in any other way: courts produce decisions that are acceptable to two otherwise opposed parties, and they produce a public record of how disputes are likely to be settled. These ends are important. Conflicts between individuals that are not settled by law can escalate into revenge; law offers remedies to problems that close a chapter in people's lives. In addition, a public record of the actions of courts allows people to know what remedies are available to them and when to try to avoid the courts.

A conflict being arbitrated by a third party is no guarantee of a good decision; and this indicates a second broad set of goals: realising certain kinds of ideals. Law is not simply aiming to reduce the overall conflict in the world, it is seeking to bring about particular kinds of solutions to particular problems. One candidate for the specific objective of legal decisions is the idea of *giving people what they are owed*. This seems to capture much of what is delivered by law, and where law fails to do this we feel that an injustice has taken place. If I have been denied what I am owed (for example payment for work) I could seek some kind of political change to ensure that this does not happen again, but I am more likely to seek a legal remedy to ensure *I* get what I am owed. While self-serving, this is also *just*, as the remedying of a wrong through a public (authorised and transparent) process of putting it right. However, in order to ascertain what people are owed there needs to be fair examination of the facts of the case, the submissions of two parties. Consequently, law must seek judgment based on truth and facts: law is not simply about judgment, but about judgment on the basis of the fullest available evidence. Accordingly, among the ideals towards which law aims, we must consider truth and truth-finding.

1a Judgment

Judgment is central to human life and activity. In the broadest sense we exercise judgment all the time from choosing what to wear or when to cross the road. Legal judgment clearly has a special status. It is an *authorised* form of judgment with an especially *authoritative* status. Whatever the society we inhabit, only specific people in specific (institutional or ritualised) contexts will be authorised to make legal judgments, and because of this their judgment is especially authoritative. Common law legal systems give such authoritative weight to judgments that judges and courts are said to 'make the law' and not just interpret or apply it. At the same time, in modern legal systems legal judgment will be constrained by the rules of procedure governing courts and officials. For this reason we are unlikely to treat a judgment as authoritative ('expert' or 'definitive') unless it is authorised (originating from a duly constituted court).

Judgment in every context is a process of taking the particular (particular people, circumstances, needs and relationships) and bringing the particular under a general rule. The particular is treated as failing within general – public and universal – categories. This is true whether we are judging a work of art, a sporting event or a case: does *this* action fulfil our *general standards* of a good, justified or reasonable action? Law is distinctive in possessing an extensive set of general rules for public conduct under which particular instances and circumstances can be brought. Law's judgments do not always take the form of commands, but are also generalisations about the rights and duties of individuals (see Chapter 5). So, legal judgment can be said to concern, on the one hand, the context and authority of the people making the judgment. On the other, judgment concerns the rules – the public and generalisations about conduct – that legal professionals are called upon to use in judgment. These two elements of judgment will be considered at greater length.

Legal judgments are uniquely authorised judgments made by uniquely authorised people. Why are they *authorised* judgments? We, as an electorate, authorise laws because they are made by our representatives. In this sense the authority of legal decisions flows directly from the authority possessed by democratic institutions and practices. But legal institutions and legal officials seem to have their own independent authority to make judgments. Those who make judgment on law are uniquely authorised people; authorised to make decisions and trusted to use the right methods of judgment. As such we can understand legal justice as the considered judgment of a qualified legal professional (West, 1998).

This discussion of the *authorisation* to judge can be contrasted with a focus on the *process* of judgment itself. This, as suggested, can be understood as the particular brought under the general. Law has many general rules and the task of lawyers is to give the best account of how a particular set of actions can be encompassed within general rules (Schauer, 1991). The outcome of a legal process might be said to be the successful joining of the general (rules) with the particular (facts). The best 'fit' between the two is the objective of any court and this may well be part of what is articulated by legal justice: the careful matching of public generalisations (rules) and particular events (facts). Much more could be said about this, not least because it presumes a great deal about the value and justification of those general rules and about what facts are to be considered relevant. Some general rules are bad rules; some facts about the world are always excluded by legal decision-making (see Chapters 5 and 6).

For this reason, it can be concluded – provisionally – that judgment is important because of its relationship with authority, less its relationship with rules and processes. Rules run out (law does not anticipate every possible state of affairs), not all facts need to be brought under rules (law 'does not concern itself with trivialities'), and because 'hard cases make bad law' (Coval and Smith, 1982: 457; see also Chapter 5). In other words, legal judgment may have to be, in some instances, a moral decision, a policy decision, or a pragmatic decision (see Chapter 6). It will, nonetheless, be an authorised judgment.

EXAMPLE

Sweezy v New Hampshire 354 US 234 (1957) (US Supreme Court)

Sweezy had been prosecuted under a New Hampshire law prohibiting 'subversive activity'. He had delivered a lecture that appeared to align him with the Communist Party and was therefore 'subversive'. Other than to insist that he was a member of the Progressive Party, not the Communist Party, he refused to cooperate with police questioning and was convicted of contempt of court. Here the United States Supreme Court is considering whether the law prohibiting 'subversive activity' was unconstitutional given that the standard of proof needed to establish it was vague. It is a question of judgment, here understood as a kind of balancing, rather than the simple application of a rule.

> To be sure, this is a conclusion based on a judicial judgment in balancing two contending principles – the right [. . .] of a citizen to political privacy, as protected by the Fourteenth Amendment, and the right of the State to self-protection. And striking the balance implies the exercise of judgment. This is the inescapable judicial task [of] this Court. It must not be an exercise of whim or will. It must be an overriding judgment founded on something much deeper and more justifiable than personal preference. As far as it lies within human limitations, it must be an impersonal judgment. It must rest on fundamental presuppositions rooted in history to which widespread acceptance may fairly be attributed. Such a judgment must be arrived at in a spirit of humility when it counters the judgment of the State's highest court. But, in the end, judgment cannot be escaped [. . .].

1b Desert

Desert, i.e. what is *deserved* by someone, can be understood as that which a person is entitled to on the basis of their rights, their needs or their interests. Desert is not what a particular person wants, rather what they are entitled to, and law is clearly more concerned with the latter than the former. Law will usually entail a loser as well as a winner, and involves duties as much as rights. While 'getting a good outcome' might be what we want from law, it is an incomplete account of legal justice. Getting what you want is achievable by many means. 'Getting what you are entitled to', in contrast, looks more like a *just* outcome.

If we were pushed to clarify what constitutes the 'right legal outcome' we might be tempted to say that it is not simply one or more parties being made happy, but rather the outcome delivering what the parties deserved. In other words, desert and 'the right outcome' are closely related: law determines what is owed, whether in financial terms, or in terms of recognising an individual's value or status. The latter is not unlike being 'owed an apology' or 'owed an explanation', it concerns having the right to be treated in a particular way (Marmor, 2004). While none of us has an obvious right to be rich, or famous, or happy, it seems true, by definition, that we have a right to what is owed to us.

How we determine what is owed to us is contested because it invokes both ideas of property and, in more abstract terms, our 'rights'. The 'corrective' capacity of law (see discussion of Aristotle, below) is not only its ability to compel the return of property, but to correct an 'imbalance' between two parties. Where there is conflict over a contract or a duty, what is owed is less a distribution of property from one party to another than a determination of 'what judges owe it to the parties to consider'. This may include how we deserve to be treated as consumers or as individuals expecting the discharge of a duty of care.

> 'To give everyone his own' sounds splendid. Who will dispute it? The only trouble is that this formula presupposes that I know what is due to each person as 'his' (i.e. as his *right*). The formula is thus devoid of meaning, since it presupposes the legal position for which it should be the basis. (Ross, 2004: 276)

Being 'owed' can therefore possess at least two meanings. First, what someone is entitled to given the particular facts of the case and applicable general rules. Second, being owed certain rights and responsibilities given our specific status or legal relationships.

These two ideas were turned against one another by Plato (c.438–c.348BCE). In his *Republic* (Book I) he examines the view that justice is giving to a person what they are owed. Plato raises the objection that we might owe our neighbour weapons that we borrowed from them, but that it would not be just to return them if the neighbour had gone mad and would harm themselves and others (1997: 975). The neighbour may be *owed* their property under law, but there might be a more general rule that we do not *deserve* to have our legal rights respected when we are likely to abuse them. Plato's argument asks *why* we should strive to give people what they are owed, and demands further clarification of the general rules of *when* and *where* people deserve things. Plato seeks, ultimately, to argue that desert takes second place to certain things that are intrinsically desirable (see Chapter 3), and that we must determine desert on moral, psychological, and political grounds prior to determining its legal meaning.

EXAMPLE

Cowan v Cowan [2001] EWCA Civ 679

This case discussed the controversial, and now largely defunct, idea of 'reasonable requirements' in divorce settlements under the Matrimonial Causes Act 1973. 'Reasonable' is a slippery idea that allows judges to look outside legal rules to the broad context of a case in order to decide whether something is justified; 'requirements' roughly denotes living expenses. Here the court has to determine a divorce settlement (involving substantial assets) and the extent to which 'reasonable requirements' is something constant ('objective') or a more nuanced question of desert relative to the wealth of a partner ('subjective').

Perhaps ['reasonable requirements'] could be criticised for masking what was in effect a judicial attempt to achieve the applicant's or the respondent's deserts. But the statute nowhere speaks of deserts or entitlement as being within the judicial objective. So to lodge deserts within the permissible evaluation of respective needs was unjustifiable. But lodging it solely within the permissible evaluation of respective contributions also seems to stretch the bounds of that concept beyond what Parliament intended. The evaluation of deserts is at the core of the court's quest for a fair outcome. [On the basis of another similar case, the law has now moved] the basis of the award firmly away from a subjective evaluation of desert to a more objective assessment of entitlement.

1c Truth

Truth and knowledge are the objectives of philosophy. Philosophy is a discipline concerned with the most basic questions of what we know, how we know and whether *knowing* something is the same as it being *true* (see Baggini and Fosl, 2010: 167–70). Philosophers can set the bar of truth high, demanding a perfect correspondence between our ideas and reality; where the standard is this high, many claims to knowledge will be met with scepticism. Conversely, a more 'deflationary' approach to truth allows for different kinds of certainty in difference spheres of human activity. This allows for a more flexible understanding of truth as something important, but potentially dependent on the context in which the word 'truth' is being used.

Courts need to find truth among facts submitted by two parties; justice cannot be achieved if judgment is founded on falsehoods and lies. However, the relationship of truth and law is complex, not least because a legal judgment has to be justified on the basis of proof: a combination of evidence (which may be contested) and judicial use of rules (which is a doubly difficult task of deciding *which* rules should be applied and *how* they should be applied). Law's relationship with justice is not always articulated in the language of truth, but it can be found in the pursuit of proof as the means of reaching judgment.

Another way to express this difference is to return to authorised and authoritative accounts of judgment. In historical research and in the social sciences, scholars bring together as much information as they can to create an authoritative picture of an event or historical epoch. This involves studying and synthesising a substantial range of sources. The more information used, the more authoritative the account. Fully authoritative judgments require objectivity (distance from the events and the actors) and should generate consensus in judgment. Legal tribunals use a more limited range of sources to bring the particular under specific general rules, namely those rules recognised to be legal rules. Courts are *authorised* to do this, and only this. They are authorised to draw conclusions (of guilt or of liability) *only* on the basis of specific kinds of information and with specific rules. The conclusions that they draw are therefore uniquely authorised judgments based on proof. But they are not *authoritative* judgments about an event or events (see Luban, 1989: 2156f). They exclude the kinds of general rules necessary for complete historical narratives (e.g. theories about psychology, culture and wider historical forces and trends) and they do not aspire to give an account of events which receives universal approval.

In the spheres in which it functions – human actions, human affairs, human conflicts – law has created and refined a mass of general rules and particular examples of how answers to questions can be sought. In private law, dealing with disputes between individuals, these answers may be found on the balance of probabilities, i.e. likelihoods. In criminal law, where proof beyond reasonable doubt is required, we have a standard that aspires to be as close to the truth as is humanly possible to the exclusion only of radical, sceptical, doubts based on the uncertainty of everything or the impossibility of any truth. This may not be enough to satisfy philosophical scepticism, but it is a far more stringent standard of truth than we normally bring to bear when we evaluate other people's actions and desert. So, while philosophy could puncture many of law's claims to the truth by stressing how difficult it is to call something 'true' or 'certain', law, because of its analysis of proof and tiers of

EXAMPLE

R v *B* [2010] EWCA Crim 4

This case involved evidence from a four-year-old victim of a sexual abuse. It was important for the prosecution that the child's evidence be given to the Court; the original prosecution succeeded, in large measure, because of the child's testimony. The defendant appealed against the conviction on the basis that the witness did not understand truth.

> *The conviction is upheld because the child could distinguish truth from falsity. For similar reasons, philosophical ideals of truth can be distinguished from the opposition 'true and false' which is a normal, rarely problematic, part of our vocabulary.*
>
> The question in each case is whether the individual witness, or, as in this case, the individual child, is competent to give evidence in the particular trial. The question is entirely witness or child specific. There are no presumptions or preconceptions. The witness need not understand the special importance that the truth should be told in court, and the witness need not understand every single question or give a readily understood answer to every question. Many competent adult witnesses would fail such a competency test. Dealing with it broadly and fairly, provided the witness can understand the questions put to him and can also provide understandable answers, he or she is competent.

judicial scrutiny, has a strong claim to being the best means of finding truth within the complex arena of human affairs.

2 Means

Introduction

'Means' are the tools, the instruments, and the intermediary steps, that are used in order to achieve ends. The means employed by law serve to distinguish it from other social activities. These means could be said to include the evaluation of evidence and arguments, the use of rules, or the use of reasonable and logical arguments. These means can be separated from specific ends becoming 'ends in themselves'. The outcome of evaluating evidence, using rules or framing arguments may, or may not, lead to a good outcome for the parties. But the very use of these legal tools is justified and desirable. Without them, judgment, desert and the discovery of truth could only be realised through force or fate. For this reason law is often described as the 'administration of justice': legal institutions administer, through their processes, justice. At the same time we can ask whether the distinctive procedures used by a legal system are actually a means to further political and social ends such as happiness, social stability or progress.

2a Adjudication

While the outcome of a legal process will be a judgment, the *process* of coming to a decision is adjudication between two competing parties. Note that law and courts have not always had the close relationship that we find now. In pre-modern Europe, law 'merchants' would have toured the land offering legal remedies at a price, and legal decisions were either not recorded, or recorded in a way that was only accessible to educated specialists (Twining, 2009: 282–3). 'Law' would not be treated as a body of rules, or an institutional tradition, but as a problem-solving tool. Nonetheless, this is recognisably legal because a third party adjudicated between the disputants, allowing outcomes that the two parties, alone, could not have reached.

A common shorthand for legal justice is 'having one's day in court'; here justice is nothing more, and nothing less than, having one's perspective heard in a courtroom (Marmor, 2004). Implicit in this is the assumption that one's views and 'side of the story' will be heard and respected, and that a judge or jury will have ample opportunity to hear one's position fully and fairly articulated. It says nothing about winning the case or any other kind of remedy. Justice is, rather, access to the legal process and being subject to the means that a legal process employs.

> If one cannot participate, then one is denied one's day in court. The principle contributes to dispute resolution, because parties that have been able to participate are more likely to accept a decision; although they might not agree with the decision, they are more likely to comply with it. (Bayles, 1986: 54)

This leaves much to explain as an account of legal justice. It does not specify what needs to happen in court or, rather, it already presupposes that there will be a *fair* hearing. Being convicted by a court established to imprison anyone undesirable to a tyrannical regime might, literally, mean a day in court, but not justice. It might be possible, in rejoinder, to say that 'a court that does not provide justice is not a real court', but this is only to defer the question of what means are employed by a 'properly constituted court'.

Having a *fair hearing* is part of what is captured in the idea of 'natural justice': that we should hear the other side of the argument and that we should be able to proffer whatever evidence is material to our case. Fairness is here related to certain procedural and institutional arrangements. What makes particular institutional arrangements fair? It is significant that courts around the world demonstrate significant variation in *who* has to be in a court (many courts do not require juries) and *what* can be done in them (spoken evidence is by no means a requirement of every trial). Note also that in many instances we would still want to argue that outcome is important. A well conducted trial still fails to deliver justice if the ultimate decision is wrong-headed or perverse; sometimes we can identify what the 'just outcome' should have been, in moral terms, even if we think a legal procedure was fair.

Adjudication is, in other words, a rather sparse understanding of legal justice. No specific procedure is identified and no kind of outcome is required. It is simply a question of having access to legal procedure and being heard by a court. However, even in these general terms, 'having one's day in court' does imply that one has a right to dispute settlement *on an equal footing* with other parties or with one's opponent. Adjudication is no justice at all if it involves being treated cursorily or arbitrarily or if there is clear imbalance between the parties. Nonetheless, beyond minimum expectations of fairness, this conception of legal justice leaves much unsaid. It may well also be a reflection of an attitude found in particular jurisdictions, jurisdictions with long-standing legal and constitutional arrangements, where it is assumed that courts themselves are, in the main, fair institutions.

EXAMPLE

'ICSID Convention: Regulations and Rules', International Centre for Settlement of Investment Disputes (2006)

The 'International Convention on the Settlement of Investment Disputes between States and Nationals of Other States' (the ICSID Convention) was created by the World Bank to resolve complex trade disputes concerning nationals of one country trading with, or invest-ing in, a state that is not their own. Such disputes are made difficult by differences in legal systems and by suspicions that the courts of one country may favour their own nationals. Given that these arbitration processes can involve large multinational entities they can involve high financial stakes. Nonetheless, these adjudications are outside the normal structures of national and international law and do not create precedent for other similar cases. Note the problems created when parties themselves are allowed to influence the means by which their dispute is adjudicated.

Article 34: (1) It shall be the duty of the Commission to clarify the issues in dispute between the parties and to endeavour to bring about agreement between them upon mutually acceptable terms. To that end, the Commission may at any stage of the proceed-ings and from time to time recommend terms of settlement to the parties. [. . .]. (2) If the parties reach agreement, the Commission shall draw up a report noting the issues in dispute and recording that the parties have reached agreement. If, at any stage of the proceedings, it appears to the Commission that there is no likelihood of agreement between the parties, it shall close the proceedings and shall draw up a report noting the submission of the dispute and recording the failure of the parties to reach agreement.

2b Impartiality

Having one's day in court clearly presumes certain minimum procedural standards will be fulfilled, foremost among them being that the parties will be treated with impartiality. This idea is often embodied in the image of Justice as a blindfolded judge who weighs up the arguments of two parties while ignorant of their personali-ties, i.e. their characteristics beyond their basic standing and rights as legal persons (see Chapter 2). Impartiality requires adjudication on the merit of the parties' evi-dence rather than on the status of the party offering it. Furthermore, this is necessary for *just* adjudication of conflicts because we assume that that rights and wrongs of the dispute are independent of the character or status of the disputants.

Blindness to the identities of the parties might fall short of legal justice if a judge or adjudicator paid *no* attention whatsoever to the needs or personalities of the par-ties to the case. For instance, law has been rightly criticised for failing to acknowledge imbalances of bargaining power between private individuals and the businesses that they form contracts with (Caudill and Gold, 1995: 141f). It is a recurrent criticism of law that it seeks to come to decisions in spite of, or in opposition to, the needs and particularity of individual human beings (see Chapter 7).

Having one's case judged impartially is articulated by lawyers themselves as 'natural justice' (the phrase 'natural justice' can be traced to Aristotle (1987: 412)). These are the basic structural characteristics of legal decision-making, including the employment of judges who do not have a direct interest in the outcome of their decision. It also recalls the Ancient conception of justice as a personal virtue rather than a public duty. If legal justice is reducible to impartiality, such impartiality is achieved in part through the skill and authority of judges. As Judith Shklar puts it:

> To pursue impartiality, fair-mindedness, an impersonal state of mind, the self-control to recognize and curb one's prejudices – all this surely is qualitative, a matter of content and character. Since all of this is done in the service of only one ethical ideal [justice] and since this ethical ideal includes the formal attributes of law, the distinction [between ethics and law] becomes insignificant. (1986: 115)

This is not yet to specify what impartiality consists of. It is clear, in general terms, that law should attend to certain things and ignore others, but this requires making a decision on what counts as legally relevant characteristics. In a criminal case, an individual may have a character that is morally objectionable, but we assume that the law will attend only to how and where their actions are relevant for the case at hand. Otherwise law becomes a way of punishing people for their character rather than finding what they deserve. Conversely, character is sometimes relevant as evidence of a 'propensity', and courts makes generalisations about what 'reasonable' people are likely to do in certain circumstances. Those appeals to 'character' and 'reasonableness' are themselves governed by general rules, ensuring that everyone is judged by the same standard. It is, therefore, through law's general *rules* and, by extension, its *abstractions* that impartiality is maintained. Law 'judges us i/ not in all our particularity but as identical *abstract beings*; ii/ by reference to *general and objective standards equally* applicable to all such beings' (Lucy, 2009: 482, emphasis in original).

Thus, the idea of reducing impartiality to 'giving weight only to legally relevant characteristics' is more complex than we might have hoped. Not only does this entail abstraction (and therefore a certain blindness to our particularity as individuals, see Chapter 2), but in most legal contexts the two parties are in a position to contest the other's assertion about what is 'legally relevant' in that context. We could claim that legal justice amounts to those procedures and rights that allow two parties to have a fair contest in court without irrelevant questions of identity and status coming into play. However, those procedures and rights do not prevent *ad hominem* arguments being used in courts. *Ad hominem* arguments are where the person, as the origin of an argument, is attacked rather than the argument itself. Such arguments are common in politics (where, for example, a politician is criticised not on their policies but on the basis of their track-record or personal life), but fall short of rigorous standards of rational argumentation and rarely have a place in philosophy. Law falls somewhere between politics and philosophy in this respect: it is impossible to conduct a case simply by attacking someone else's character in court, but equally an opponent's actions, conduct, reliability or reasonableness may be relevant to the facts or the findings. Again, law, especially through the idea of reasonableness, makes assumptions about how individuals should have acted. So, impartiality is opposed to rank injustice through prejudice, but it can mean being judged on the basis of generalisations.

EXAMPLE

Commonwealth v Nicola Sacco & another (1926) 255 Mass. 369 (United States)

This is from Judge Thayer's speech to the jury in the case of Sacco and Vanzetti, a notorious US case where two Italian-American anarchists were (in all likelihood) wrongly convicted of a robbery and first-degree murder and sentenced to death. The case involved much rhetoric about justice as well as blatant manipulation of racial fears. Here Thayer articulates the ideal that was fallen well short of in the case.

> Let me repeat to you what I said to another jury in a similar case: Let your eyes be blinded to every ray of sympathy or prejudice but let them ever be willing to receive the beautiful sunshine of truth, of reason and sound judgment, and let your ears be deaf to every sound of public opinion or public clamor, if there be any, in favor or against these defendants. Let them always be listening for the sweet voices of conscience and of sacred and solemn duty efficiently and fearlessly performed. [. . .] In the administration of our laws, criminal or civil, there is and should be no distinction between parties. For if it ever should so appear in some cases, this, gentlemen, is not the fault of the integrity of the law but rather due to the weakness of human beings in the administration of the law, all classes of society, the poor and the rich, the learned and the ignorant, the most powerful citizen as well as the most humble, the believer as well as the unbeliever, the radical as well as the conservative, the foreign-born as well as the native-born, are entitled to and should receive in all trials under our laws the same rights, privileges and consideration as the logic of law, reason, sound judgment, justice and common sense demand. I therefore beseech you not to allow the fact that the defendants are Italians to influence on prejudice you in the least degree. They are entitled, under the law, to the same rights and consideration as though their ancestors came over in the Mayflower.

2c Equality

If impartiality is related to law's tendency to work with abstractions, those abstractions have to be justified, not simply on the basis of legal convenience, but also as a contribution to the best possible outcomes. This may well be achieved through tying impartiality to equality: law should use only those abstractions which serve to ensure equality between the parties. Equality is the basic assumption that persons are equal, not because this is a convenient generalisation but because they should be treated as equal to ensure just outcomes.

A saying by Anatole France captures the problem in this idea of equality: 'the majestic equality of the laws [. . .] forbid[s] rich and poor alike to sleep under [. . .] bridges, to beg in the streets, and to steal [. . .] bread' (quoted in Oldfield, 2003: 452). In other words, law provides a certain kind of equality isolated from *social* facts and *social* problems. There are different kinds of equality – social equality, equality in outcomes, equality in treatment – and this makes unequivocal claims about equality difficult to make. The equality achieved through law's abstractions is not the equality of 'equal resources', 'equal pay' or 'equal opportunity'.

Equality is simultaneously a metaphor, a fiction and one of our most important ethical and legal ideas. It is a metaphor based on the mathematical principle of abstract quantities being entirely exchangeable; two numbers are equal if they can be exchanged for one another in every calculation. This helps to explain the 'fiction' of equality: no two people are mathematically equal, people are never exchangeable with one another, and no two people are equal in their properties and capabilities. Nevertheless, out of this abstraction arises the powerful idea that people should be *treated* as equals. Equal treatment is therefore an *obligation* placed on those with power. This suggests that particular caution is needed in discussion of equality.

The claim 'people are equal' is true only if we have a specific, legal and moral, understanding of personhood (see Chapter 2). The equality of *persons* exists in spite of the fact that *humans* are born with different talents and abilities and have, accidentally or deliberately, different social statuses. It is legally and morally defensible to say that differences in status and ability should be treated as unimportant. A more basic, and more universal, set of duties, rights or actions should be the only aspect of our lives of concern to law.

Equality, then, underpins both the value of having one's day in court (we are all equally entitled to a legal remedy) and impartiality (we should be treated as equals so far as our claim to a legal remedy is concerned). We remain, nonetheless, in the realm of *means*, the means by which we have our claims heard and the means by which a court approaches our claims; law's relationships with equality lies in the treatment of people, not the nature of people. Equality, and the difficulty of making sense of its application to otherwise unequal humans, will be returned to in later chapters, but it is significant that legal justice should be associated with so complex and shifting a term. This goes some way towards allowing us to say that justice has changed through time as humans' defence of equality has increased. It also encourages us to ask more difficult questions about the foundational assumptions at work in law, politics and morality. If as crucial an ideal as equality is premised on metaphor (and in some respects a contradiction of reality) can law be said to be founded upon convenient, if valuable, fictions rather than incontestable insights into truth and reality?

EXAMPLE

UN Committee on Economic, Social and Cultural Rights, 'General Comment 16: Article 3' UN Doc. E/C.12/2005/3 (2005)

This is an analysis of the meaning of Article 3 of the International Covenant on Economic, Social and Cultural Rights: the equal right of men and women to the enjoyment of all economic, social and cultural rights. It offers different but nonetheless powerful meanings of 'equality'. Law's equality is formal – it is an abstraction – and can be contrasted with substantive – or real – equality in people's lives.

Guarantees of non-discrimination and equality in international human rights treaties mandate both *de facto* and *de jure* equality. *De jure* (or formal) equality and *de facto* (or substantive) equality are different but interconnected concepts. Formal equality assumes that equality is achieved if a law or policy treats men and women in a neutral manner. Substantive equality is concerned, in addition, with the effects of laws, policies and practices and with ensuring that they do not maintain, but rather alleviate, the inherent disadvantage that particular groups experience. [. . .] Substantive equality for men and women will not be achieved simply through the enactment of laws or the adoption of policies that are gender-neutral on their face. In implementing Article 3, States parties should take into account that such laws, policies and practice can fail to address or even perpetuate inequality between men and women, because they do not take account of existing economic, social and cultural inequalities, particularly those experienced by women.

---

3 Individuals

Introduction

The ends and the means associated with law can be said to protect or give value to the individual. Activities and processes which protect the status and value of the individual (having one's day in court, or equality) contribute to the moral and legal acceptability of a state as a whole. Any state or society that failed, systematically, to protect individuals in the pursuit of wider social, economic or political goals would be considered objectionable or illegitimate. The extent to which a state should be considered to be nothing more than the sum of the individuals within it, or as, conversely, more than the sum of its parts, is principally a question for political and social philosophy. But it is one that we will encounter again in different guises: law's relationship with utilitarianism (Chapter 3), and how it is that a 'right legal answer' could be said to be an answer corresponding to a 'society's principles' (Chapter 4).

Our present concern is with the extent to which justice is dependent upon protecting or advancing the interests of the individual. Any system or process that ignored the needs of individuals would make a questionable contribution to justice, but it is difficult to state categorically that law's claim to justice is its systematic contribution to the well-being, the welfare, or the flourishing, of every individual. We could argue that this contribution to the well-being of the individual is a by-product of a more general contribution to the overall interests of the collective (the state or society). It may also be the case that the essence of law and legal processes is a synthesis of both of these kinds of priorities, the individual and the collective.

3a The individual's good

Legal systems protect and prioritise individuals to varying degrees. Some emphasise the interests of the collective; some seem to favour the individual over the collective. These priorities generate important problems for moral and political philosophy; the priority of one or the other depends upon assumptions about what is good, what is right and what is possible. In addition, there seems to be no way to say one has priority without easily identifying counter-examples of where the other is important. One illustrative debate concerns the expense of criminal justice systems. Criminal justice systems are expensive because they afford protections and rights to those suspected of crimes. If those individuals are guilty of crimes then it looks as though society is lavishing great expense on *anti*-social individuals. In addition, prioritisations often achieve the opposite of what they are aiming at. If we prioritise the individual at all costs we might give rise to a society so focussed on the individual that it loses all collective bonds and duties; this may be damaging to individuals within that society. Conversely, a state which prioritises the collective to the detriment of the individual has to explain how it is that the state can have any legitimacy if it is wholly tailored to the benefit of an abstract thing (state or society) with limited concern for the real individuals within it.

It is not the task of a legal *system* to make final statements on the ultimate prioritisation of individual and collective; any such prioritisation is likely to generate 'antinomies', contradictory obligations that cannot be fulfilled or resolved (see Spragens, 1993). However, in its day-to-day functioning law is called upon adjudicate between the claims of collective and individual in countless ways. For example, when building projects harm the interests of individuals but would bring wider social benefits (Dworkin, 1998: 20f). Or where decisions are made in the light of a 'floodgate problem' that a different outcome might create (Bix, 2004: 199). Or where a suspect is not prosecuted because they are unlikely (on a balance of probabilities) to be convicted, therefore time and money can be saved by avoiding prosecution.

There are good reasons to say that, despite the problems and paradoxes generated by the interplay within law of individual and collective, the individual's good should take priority. This is not to say that the interests of the individual should always and everywhere over-ride collective goals; rather that any legal system needs to make decisions based on the fundamental interests of human beings. This could be said to be trivially true in the sense that any social institutions must have *some* justification in human interests at some point or they would have no justification whatsoever. It might also be said to be the more substantial moral claim that, in social and legal conflicts, the fundamental tenet of decision-making should be the basic needs and requirements of the human being. For example, Finnis' natural law position (Chapter 3) roots the common good in the reasonable demands of the individual; Marx's materialism (Chapter 4) stresses the priority of real human needs over ownership. Finnis and Marx have very different views of what a state is and what it is for, but both agree that the good of the individual is the building block of any just social system.

EXAMPLE

Legal Consequences of the Construction of a Wall in the Occupied Palestinian Territory, International Court of Justice, 9 July 2004 (Separate Opinion of Judge Kooijmans)

Much international law created in the last 50 years protects the interests of the individual, not just the state of which they are a citizen. However, the enforcement of international treaties is problematic because the rules may run counter to a state's wider social and political commitments, including the safety and security of citizens. Israel is party to a number of international treaties but faces problems implementing them because of internal security problems.

The situation in and around Palestine has been for a number of decades not only a virtually continuous threat to international peace and security but also a human tragedy which in many respects is mind-boggling. How can a society like the Palestinian one get used to and live with a situation where the victims of violence are often innocent men, women and children? How can a society like the Israeli society get used to and live with a situation where attacks against a political opponent are targeted at innocent civilians, men, women and children, in an indiscriminate way? [. . .] Every State, including Israel, has the right and even the duty [. . .] to respond to [terrorist] acts in order to protect the life of its citizens, albeit the choice of means in doing so is limited by the norms and rules of international law.

3b Rights

'Right' is arguably the most ambiguous word in the legal lexicon. We can describe a legal decision as 'right'; we can also use 'right' to name something that is possessed by an individual and grants them various powers. In other words, we can distinguish a *right decision* (i.e. describing a decision), and a general respect for legal *rights* within the legal process. We also find, in other jurisdictions, description of law as a whole as 'right': this combines the very idea of *legality* with right decisions and legal rights. Here the word law has stronger moral connotations than it possesses in English, and 'law', 'right' and 'justice' become virtually synonymous.

We normally conceive of rights as possessed by, or accruing to, individuals. The exercise of rights is considered to be one of the crucial dimensions of being human, and a *person* can be said to be a 'rights-holding human' (Ohlin, 2002; see Chapter 2). While many philosophers stress the priority of duties over rights, it can be argued that rights have a more important role to play in our thinking about law. Law is not only called upon to adjudicate between individuals but to mediate conflicts between the individual and the collective. Often a state or society may have good reasons for prioritising the needs of many over the needs of a minority. For instance, tort law imposes liability for acts which are accidental but which have to be deterred for everyone's good. There is some claim to justice in this kind of 'social engineering', namely seeking to ensure benefits or protections for as many people as possible. Nonetheless, law ensures through rights that individuals' interests are not routinely sacrificed in favour of the demands of a larger group of people or of efficiency. Law is better characterised as a set of rights than it is as a form of social engineering (Dworkin, 1998: 93–4).

Many problems remain with the idea of, and the functioning of, rights. They are inefficient from a social perspective because they prevent easy or uncontested social or economic decisions. They have an unclear foundation: do they arise from the ability to control the actions of others or from the 'interests' of the possessor? More specifically, they have an unclear relationship with law: are they the 'possession' of the individual or are they the creation of legal language and legal processes alone? This is discussed further in Chapter 4, but their function in discussion of *justice* is clear: they are an assertion that law should respect the individual not simply serve social and political ends.

EXAMPLE

Teixeira de Castro v *Portugal* ECHR (Application no. 25829/94) 1999

Rights are cast in a poor light when they are granted to suspects in police investigations. Even where the police have strong evidence, they may be prevented from certain kinds of policing because of suspects' rights. Here a known drug dealer was encouraged by undercover police to deal harder drugs. This enticement amounted to the absence of a fair trial under Article 6 of the European Convention on Human Rights (1950).

The use of undercover agents must be restricted and safeguards put in place even in cases concerning the fight against drug-trafficking. While the rise in organised crime undoubtedly requires that appropriate measures be taken, the right to a fair administration of justice nevertheless holds such a prominent place that it cannot be sacrificed for the sake of expedience. The general requirements of fairness embodied in Article 6 apply to proceedings concerning all types of criminal offence, from the most straightforward to the most complex. The public interest cannot justify the use of evidence obtained as a result of police incitement.

3c Status

Legal rights emphasise that when the state and individuals are in conflict 'might does not make right'. The state is capable of side-lining or overriding the interests of the individual, but the granting of rights to individuals promotes their interests even at the expense of collective losses. The importance and status of individuals has not always been assured, and it remains the case in many political contexts that individuals are treated as secondary to collective needs. However, any legal system where rights are powerful and peremptory (see Chapter 4) is a system which respects the individual, and this respect itself has a claim to being justice.

Where a legal system (as opposed to authoritarian rule) exists, the state has no absolute right to act as it wishes, and the needs of the collective never automatically outweigh the needs of minorities. This is evidenced by administrative decisions where the actions of the state are assessed by their reasonableness, and in criminal justice where time and expense is expended ensuring that innocent people are not wrongly convicted of crimes. The status that we afford to the individual – as a 'rights-holder' or as a person worthy of respect – ensures that our legal system is expensive and inefficient. Such inefficiency is a reflection of the status we attribute to every individual regardless of their actions or their social status. Before the law, individuals are equal and have a fundamental status that cannot be revoked arbitrarily.

Another way of articulating the idea of status is as 'recognition'. Recognition is the other side of status: the demand that the state recognises individuals as having a particular status. Recognition can be achieved through the attribution of rights, but recognition is also afforded through the just practices that we expect from legal institutions. Criminal law is a cumbersome way of controlling crime, but the state recognises the status and rights of suspects, not just victims; by avoiding inhumane punishments the state is extending basic recognition to the convicted. While this is a minimal relationship (the state recognises all persons as possessing certain basic rights) it nonetheless indicates a fundamental orientation towards the individual, rather than the demands of the majority. Indeed, it has been argued that such recognition is the foundation of the modern state and modern legal systems. Such systems do not simply exercise authority, they are the necessary for us to be treated as fully human (Honneth, 1995).

EXAMPLE

N v Sweden ECHR (Application no. 23505/09) 2010

Individuals seek asylum for a number of reasons, most commonly an experience of, and fear of further, persecution. Difficult decisions have to be made by states who wish to respect the interests of these individuals, but face collective demands for control on immigration. The rights and status of asylum seekers is determined by assessments of risk and threat, rather than the more complete status ensured by nationality. Here the Court is required to make an assessment of the potential for, and significance of, 'ill-treatment'.

The Court firstly observes that women are at particular risk of ill-treatment in Afghanistan if perceived as not conforming to the gender roles ascribed to them by society, tradition and even the legal system. The UNHCR thus observed that Afghan women, who have adopted a less culturally conservative lifestyle, such as those returning from exile in Iran or Europe, continue to be perceived as transgressing entrenched social and religious norms and may, as a result, be subjected to domestic violence and other forms of punishment ranging from isolation and stigmatisation to honour crimes for those accused of bringing shame to their families, communities or tribes. Actual or perceived transgressions of the social behavioural code include not only social behaviour in the context of a family or a community, but also sexual orientation, the pursuit of a professional career, and mere disagreements as to the way family life is conducted.

---

4 Collectives

Introduction

By 'collective' we can indicate any collection of individuals. It is possible to conceive of collectives in a number of different ways. A state is a legal entity, the totality of individuals within a defined territory. A society is a cultural entity within which individuals have shared values and, to a greater or lesser extent, an interest in the welfare of people beyond their immediate friends and families. A nation is a historical entity wherein individuals are thought to have a bond of a shared past and, growing from this, common values. A community is a group of individuals, smaller than a state or society, which has the most clearly defined bonds of culture and value. The Roman philosopher Cicero (106-43BCE), whose work is an important source of ideas in the natural law school of legal philosophy (Chapter 3) is one of many philosophers to see such bonds, and their maintenance through law, as the essence of justice: 'men have a single way of living with one another which is shared equally by everyone, and [. . .] all are held together by a natural goodwill and kindliness and also by a fellowship in justice' (1998: 109).

The extent to which these 'entities' have any clear being or existence is a moot point. We are talking meaningfully, but also metaphorically, when we talk of the 'will of the nation', the 'desires of the state' or the 'demands of the community'. However, it is clear that with the ideas of *nation* and of *community* the whole is to be treated as more than the sum of the parts, that individuals must sometimes put their own interests second to those of their collectives, and that common bonds and common identity brings at least as many duties as it does rights. Conversely, it is generally, though not always, assumed that in *states* and *societies* individuals are to be considered rights-holders with interests that may diverge from the interests of the whole.

Law is clearly at the heart of state and society. The state promulgates law, while society demands law. Nations and communities tend to have a more ambivalent relationship with law. Law is secondary to the more basic, more organic, bonds that are at the heart of groups with shared values. Accordingly, the conception of legal justice related to collectives is not simple and depends upon what kind of social grouping is considered primary. This is not to say that law is always secondary to political conceptions of the good of the community, state or nation. Communities make rules, have a 'scheme of principles' (Dworkin, 1998: 211), or can share a 'morality of duty' (Fuller, 1969: 15).

4a The common good

The phrase 'the common good' encompasses different positions all pointing to the idea of the collective (state, society or nation) having its own set of interests, needs or demands over and above the interests of particular individuals within that collective. This could be wealth (the 'commonwealth'), but it may also be the more abstract ideas of stability or security (the 'national interest'). Law and legal justice may well contribute to this common good. Without good legal outcomes and fair legal institutions it might be that collective practices such as honesty, fair-dealing or promise-keeping lose their value and, thereafter, wealth, stability and security would be threatened.

In essence, law underpins a crucial aspect of social life: stable expectations between individuals. This can be understood as law being a resource in the background of social life waiting to correct problems generated by its political ordering. It can also be a more substantial idea, expressed by Aquinas and others (Chapter 3) that law has a role in determining social roles and responsibilities:

> [Laws] only command things that can be ordered to the common good, whether immediately, as when things are done directly for that good, or mediately, as when lawmakers ordain things belonging to good training, which trains citizens to preserve the common good of justice and peace. (Aquinas, 2002: 63)

This 'mediate' contribution to the common good finds expression in communitarian philosophies and in modern natural law. Communitarianism holds the common good to be more than the sum of the happiness of individual members (Taylor, 1992).

29

It is a natural or organic relationship – be it common history or solidarity – which prioritises responsibilities over the immediate interests of individuals. A different, but compatible, approach is offered by Finnis' modern natural law position (see Chapter 3) where both individual and collective harmonise in pursuit of the reasonable. The governance of a state, like the choices in our lives, should conform to certain basic – reasonable – assumptions about what shape human lives should take (Finnis, 2011: 164). However, because we cannot expect unanimity in every social decision, political leadership is necessary:

> The greater the intelligence and skill of a group's members, and the greater their commitment and dedication to common purposes and common good [. . .], the *more* authority and regulation may be required, to enable that group to achieve its common purpose, common good. (Finnis, 2011: 231, emphasis in original)

There is an attempt to place determination of the common good on scientific footing in utilitarianism (Bentham, 2007). This stresses the role of law in ensuring that social institutions and practices work towards maximising happiness for the greatest number of people (Chapter 3), and some elements of the communitarian, natural law and utilitarian positions can be found in 'historical jurisprudence'. This movement, at its peak in the eighteenth and nineteenth centuries, sought to justify the value and authority of legal systems on the basis of their historical origins (Chapter 6). It did not simply chart the beginnings of legal systems, but rather sought to find value, explanation and justification in those origins. Distinctive legal systems have developed in response to the values of different social groups. Accordingly, national legal systems should not seek to harmonise with one another (for instance on the model of the European Union), but should respect the particularity of different legal cultures, acknowledging the intimate relationships between national laws and social values. This is communitarian to the extent that law has a role in maintaining strong bonds and shared values. It is also utilitarian in so far as the individual is subsumed into the needs of the majority.

In contradistinction to such 'localised' (national or regional) ideas of the common good, there are universalising approaches which stress the commonalities between humans, within humanity and across national and territorial divides. Chapter 2 unpacks some of the assumptions and philosophical questions at work in these claims associated with humanism and liberalism. Suffice it to say, there are – philosophical and legal – tensions between seeking commonalities between people *and* respecting difference, a tension frequently manifest in international law. Through treaties, international law seeks harmony, and to a degree uniformity, between states. It also, through the principle of self-determination, defends the creation of wholly new social entities on the basis that *groups themselves* best determine what their common good is.

EXAMPLE

Hevra Kadisha [Burial Society] of the Jerusalem Community v *Lionel Aryeh Kastenbaum* **Supreme Court of Israel (Civil Appeal 294/91 (P.D. 46(2) 464)) (1992)**

The common good does not demand uniformity from individuals. It means reasonable – rational and fair – settlement of disputes for everyone's benefit. Here an individual sought to modify the prevailing burial rituals of Israel in order to respect his wife's wishes and culture. The Court identifies the common good with a balance between individual expression, prevention of harm and respect for familial bonds.

> The question is predominantly one of public law. In a free society there is room for various opinions, and the existence of liberty is proven by the creation of the correct balance in which we strive to allow every individual to achieve personal expression in the manner which he shall choose. This is the essence of tolerance, in that it allows a variety of opinions, liberty in argument, and freedom of conscience, so long as they pose no danger to the general public or other individuals. Individual liberty extends until the point that it abrogates law or significantly harms others; the degree of harm is measured with respect to the 'reasonable man', and not in accordance with subjective sentiments. [. . .] Every person has the right to properly respect his deceased loved ones [. . .], in accordance with his lifestyle and tradition, so long as this does not infringe upon the legitimate feelings and interests of others. A cemetery is not only a place to bury the dead; but also a place for the expression of love and honor, that those living bestow upon the dead.

4b The rule of law

One recurrent and powerful idea concerning the justice of law is that there can be rule by law. Such a rule by law is, in positive terms, a social order organised under rules, rules providing impartiality, fairness and stability. A rule of law is also, in more negative terms, social ordering which rejects the interests and prejudices of individuals, particularly those with power, and exchanges subjectivity for order and predictability. The significance of the rule of law is to separate law from other social forms of force, compulsion or authority and make rules themselves an objective and fair basis for conducting social affairs. Rules of law are dispassionate and non-arbitrary guidelines with which a society can gain its social, economic and political bearings.

This ideal is potent one, foreshadowed by Greek and Roman thought, and it gives law a fundamental place in our understanding of social existence. While it is paradoxical that humans would want to exchange the rule of humans for impersonal and mechanical rules, this is intelligible as a counter-weight to the dangers that we find in rule by humans. Humans are self-interested and corruptible, rules are disinterested and incorruptible. If we conjoin this idea with natural law ideas of a divine (or at least non-human) origin of law, law becomes a powerful force external to humans and which rightly governs our activities (Chapter 7). The rule of law demands the independence of legality from the pragmatism of politics, and gives impetus to, among other things, an insistence on a separation of powers between the legislature, executive and judiciary. Wieacker sees this separation of powers as part of an even wider process of 'legalism' which makes rules a safeguard against the arbitrary and irrational:

> [L]egalism has bestowed upon Europe an immeasurable gain in rationality in the external world. [L]egalism has unburdened social conflicts from the force, emotions, interests, and prejudices which [. . .] has more frequently produced emancipatory rather than repressive results. As against public authorities, legalism assures the individual of greater legal certainty, and in criminal and civil procedure it has always signified freedom from the arbitrariness of irrational forms of proof and proceedings, and later, above all, greater strategic equality in litigation. (Wieacker, 1990: 24)

However, even allowing that rule by law is synonymous with rational governance of human affairs, a number of conceptual problems render it difficult to substitute for *justice*. First, and most obviously, law is made by people and as such is never wholly excluded from the vicissitudes of politics. Second, the rule of law itself seems compatible with any form of legislation, good, bad or indifferent. A law that serves immoral ends may share all the same legislative characteristics with one that is morally acceptable; the ideal of a rule of law gives us no grounds for distinguishing the two. Finally, the rule of law seems to synthesise two more fundamental ideas. The idea of order: a society can be governed by rules in a way which is desirable and sustainable; and the idea of consent: a society can be governed by rules that are not simply created by whim, but which 'we the people' would choose. Both order and consent are, in their own ways, valuable collective goals and principles. However, it is not always possible to say that the rule of law provides both. The rule of law might provide social order without social consent, and we consent to rules that may be contrary to good social order. In short, the idea of the rule of law may well be a way of brushing aside difficult questions about the basis of consent, and the kind of order that should be pursued by a collective (Unger, 1986: 44–9).

EXAMPLE

'Rule of Law Indicators: Implementation Guide and Project Tools' (The United Nations) 2011

Jointly published by the United Nations Department of Peacekeeping Operations and the Office of the United Nations High Commissioner for Human Rights, this is the United Nations' first systematic account of the basic criteria for 'the rule of law' and how it can be measured in post-conflict states. Here the four basic criteria of the rule of law are outlined. They are not binding international law, but would constitute persuasive material in international political and legal discussions.

Performance: Institutions provide efficient and effective services that are accessible and responsive to the needs of the people. *Integrity, transparency and accountability*: Institutions operate transparently and with integrity, and are held accountable to rules and standards of conduct. *Treatment of members of vulnerable groups*: How criminal justice institutions treat minorities, victims, children in need of protection or in conflict with the law, and internally displaced persons, asylum-seekers, refugees, returnees, and stateless and mentally ill individuals. *Capacity*: Institutions have the human and material resources necessary to perform their functions, and the administrative and management capacity, to deploy these resources effectively.

4c Authority

The relationship a collective has with authority is a good gauge of its fundamental values and its perception of justice. All collectives need authorities – people and bodies with power – to make decisions on behalf of the group as a whole. However, perceptions of human, legal, authority can range from natural, necessary and incontestable (Aquinas, 2002: 185), to oppressive, illegitimate and dangerous (Paine, 1969: 63–4). Authority, implying as it does the ability to dictate the actions of the individual for collective benefit, has always generated a variety of reactions; but historical comparison shows changes in our relationship with authority, changes which, to a degree, have altered our understanding of the relationship between law and justice.

In pre-modern Europe (i.e. prior to the seventeenth century) understanding of authority was tied to religious or divine authority. Church and state could claim direct authorisation from God, and authority could be construed as a strict, hierarchical, dissemination of authority downwards from God. Even where the authority of the Church or state was challenged (as during the Reformation) this was a challenge on the basis of another divine source, God revealed through religious texts (Copleston, 2003). There was no doubt that absolute authority existed, authority that legitimately dictated the actions of the individual and the collective. In such a context, law – whether its source was divine will alone, or divine will made real in the laws of the state – could be equated with justice. Any inadequacies in law and its remedies were attributable to the human corruption in the administration of justice rather than in justice itself (Cicero, 1998: 126; Aquinas, 2002: 65).

The modern world saw a shift in the understanding of authority. Scepticism of divine and human authority became acceptable; more optimism about the value of individual conscience and rationality meant more authority was invested in the individual. This shift towards the individual means that while collective authority – the authority of the state and of the law – remains our core understanding of authority, such power that the collective possesses is in part attributable to the authority that has been invested in the state or the law by individuals themselves. While explored more fully in later chapters (see Chapters 5 and 6), this can be considered in terms of the justice provided by stable constitutional arrangements.

The theorist Robert Alexy invites us to see the contradiction in an imaginary constitutional statement: 'X is a sovereign, federal, and unjust republic' (Alexy, 2004: 164). This sounds wrong because the constitution of the state, as a structure organising and distributing authority, simply *is* just. A constitution – the organisation of authority within a state – has claim to justice in its own right. The granting of authority within a state could be held to be an important, though in some respects narrow, issue of the value of constitutional law. However, all legal activities could be construed as depending upon the correct attribution of *the power to make a decision*, whether it is attributed to a judge or other official. The authority of law is therefore the law of authority: law structures the activity of decision-making. In other words, while the existence of laws may depend upon the *power* to make laws, the *authority* to make laws remains, as it was in the pre-modern period, something other than pure power.

EXAMPLE

JGE v The English Province of Our Lady of Charity / the Trustees of the Portsmouth Roman Catholic Diocesan Trust [2011] EWHC 2871 (QB)

Authority, and the legal responsibilities which flow from authority, can be construed in many ways in law. To exercise authority is not only to be a person or body capable of making decisions, but often to exercise powers delegated from a greater authority. The limits of that delegated authority may be unclear, as is the case here, where a priest exercised authority, in a general sense, as a religious practitioner. Is such delegated authority parallel to that of someone who is employed? If so, their employer would have to take some responsibility for their actions, in this case tortious and criminal actions.

I am satisfied, as I have already noted, that the relationship between Father Baldwin and the Defendants was significantly different from a contract of employment; no real element of control or supervision, no wages, no formal contract and so on. But are those differences such that the Defendants should not be made responsible for the tortious acts of the priest acting within the course of his ministry? There are, it seems to me, crucial features which should be recognised. Father Baldwin was appointed by and on behalf of the Defendants. He was so appointed in order to do their work; to undertake the ministry on behalf of the Defendants for the benefit of the church. He was given the full authority of the Defendants to fulfil that role. He was provided with the premises, the pulpit and the clerical robes. He was directed into the community with that full authority and was given free rein to act as representative of the church. He had been trained and ordained for that purpose. He had immense power handed to him by the Defendants. It was they who appointed him to the position of trust which (if the allegations be proved) he so abused.

5 Philosophy and justice

Introduction

The foregoing candidates for law's relationship with justice each indicate an important way in which law and justice could be said to be related. Some seem more complete or defensible than others, but no one candidate appears to capture their relationship completely. Furthermore, some seem more dependent upon perspective than others, i.e. our historical perspective and our perspective inside or outside legal institutions. The intention of this final section of the chapter is to consider how generalisations about justice are possible given this range of candidates, and given the possibility that everything we say about justice may well depend upon our perspective. Two initial questions can be given sharper outline: *are* generalisations about justice possible, and, if so, does justice have a distinctive, special or unique relationship with law?

The Ancient world offers some of the most fruitful perspectives on these questions, and Aristotle's work in particular focuses on disagreements surrounding justice. Aristotle's discussion of justice (in Book V of his *Nicomachean Ethics*) seeks to dissect ideas of justice, giving first a general definition (justice is related to 'excellence' (1987: 410)), giving specific definitions related to law and politics, and finally giving examples of its use. Foremost is the virtue of justice, a disposition to act in a just way towards others. Justice is 'that kind of state which makes people disposed to do what is just and makes them act justly and wish for what is just' (1987: 407). Justice is the best of the virtues because it is the most 'complete', i.e. it encompasses all other desirable actions.

He notes that we also apply justice to the state, in judging whether actions contribute to the common good. In this wider context, politics offers *distributive* justice, distributing wealth and power 'among those who have a share in the constitution' (1987: 411). This political justice demands that we understand *natural* justice, i.e. that certain things are always right, wrong or necessary in personal and social conduct. However, both political and distributive justice require laws made by 'human enactment' (1987: 412). Legal practices provide a *remedial, corrective* or *rectifying* justice to ensure that political and natural justice are realised; principally, to determine what is owed or what is deserved. Thus, politics decides what people need or are entitled to on the basis of their social status, but such things 'are not just by nature but by human enactment [and] are not everywhere the same, since constitutions are not everywhere the same' (1987: 412). It is legal justice that remedies errors and problems arising from different kinds of political distribution, thus the means and ends of legal justice may well differ depending upon the political context.

This analysis is useful and enduring. It reflects the fact that many of our candidates for legal justice concern solving problems rather than guiding the individual or collective to a single goal or objective. It also indicates that while law can be associated with things that seem timeless or necessary (natural justice), legal institutions have their own distinctive job supporting and correcting the social and political realisation of political and natural justice. However, is 'legal justice' *different but equivalent to* 'political justice', or should we see law, in its corrective role, as a 'handmaiden' to politics? Also, does this provide sufficient clarity on where and how we should use the term 'justice'?

In answering these questions we have to note that Aristotle assumes there is a division that can be drawn between law and politics; it is this that allows him to identify different kinds of justice. From our perspective, in the modern world, are we able to make the same assumption? Two, almost contradictory, assessments of Aristotle's division can be made. First, the relationship between law and politics is surely an intimate one. This is, negatively, because both law and politics are characterised by rhetoric and persuasion, but is also because both have a close relationship with the common good. The common good may be thought to require good governance; good governance can only be achieved under constitutions safeguarded by legal institutions. Power without authority is characteristic of the failed state or the mafia clan. If a state is constituted in a just way it employs, and is organised under, laws.

Conversely, while intimately related, we usually have no difficulty identifying something as legal rather than political. This may be because we already inhabit a state that is constituted in a justifiable way, i.e. where political authority is exercised under, and constrained by, rules of law. This means we are able to *see* where law is separated from politics – where law governs, or is in tension with politics – and we have, therefore, no problem using the word 'legal' to denote something other than 'politics'. Admittedly, to identify something as legal rather than political is not to say that it is just or to be preferred. However, we can at least draw a meaningful distinction between law and politics, and it may be that, from our modern perspective, it is the very possibility of distinguishing the two that gives us our most basic understanding of justice.

Clarification of justice could therefore take three routes. First, like Aristotle, defining or stipulating what 'justice' means. Second, through closer attention to the ways in which 'justice' depends upon, or is necessary for, distinguishing law and politics. Or, third, attending to the ways of *seeing and describing* social activities that allows law and politics to be distinguished. These will be considered in terms of 'meta-theory', 'scepticism' and 'pragmatism'.

5a Meta-theory

A decisive philosophical move would be to find a single over-arching theory that determined precisely what justice is, and then use this to distinguish the proper division of labour between law and politics. Such a theory would overarch other theories and draw together all the lines of enquiry that have been followed so far. This would be a 'meta-theory', a theory about theories, which decisively answers conceptual questions about all the uncertainties and conflicts within its province. Such a theory would be ambitious – identifying clearly when the word justice should or should not be used *or* saying definitively what the demands of justice are – but, if successful, would provide a theoretical framework that accounts for all relevant ideas, questions and anomalies. Three kinds of meta-theoretical perspectives are offered here: the first is related to equality, the second to fairness and the third to freedom.

Equality is a good candidate for an overall theory of justice because it points to common denominators between means, ends, collectives and individuals. Aristotle offers an argument concerning the *basis* of equality, namely that things equivalent to one another should be treated alike, and those unlike should be treated as unlike (1987: 415–16). What this stresses is that in order to decide how to treat people equally, or find the most equal distribution of a resource, there must be a prior decision of what counts as equivalent to another thing. Apples and bread cannot be treated equally as instances of fruit, but we could treat them equally as food. Men and women cannot be treated as biologically identical, but we can treat them equally as persons with rights. Husserl unpacks the importance of this prior decision:

> The concept 'equality' involves a relation. We must have at least two things – *a* and *b* – before we can speak of equality. The statement that *a* and *b* are equal presupposes a comparison. In comparing *a* and *b* we must refer to a something which is neither *a* nor *b*. In order to establish the existence of equality between *a* and *b* we need *c*, which serves as the *tertium comparationis* [the third part of a comparison]. (Husserl, 1937: 274)

This recalls discussion of law as a means: while law does not always provide the best outcomes it is the best instrument for deciding when and how competing claims should be *compared*; it provides the extra 'relations' needed for equality. The idea of the person is one such term; it assures a set of basic rights for each individual (see Chapter 2). This should also recall discussion of ends and means: in determining desert, law does not decide on what it would be best for people to have, but rather what they deserve when treated as equal members of a society equally entitled to certain basic rights.

Ronald Dworkin's work is the fullest exploration of an equality-based perspective on law and justice (1998). In essence, the function of law is to ensure, through the recognition of legal rights, that equality takes priority over political decision-making; law is the means by which we ensure that the state is neutral about what or who we are as persons and are given equal concern when decisions are made or disputes arise.

Fairness might serve as an overarching principle of justice, though it is more clearly a means rather than an end and therefore less ambitious in its scope than equality. Being treated fairly may be a necessary (indispensible) though not sufficient (complete) condition for a good life. We do not expect our legal system to provide us with everything that we need, but we do expect it to acknowledge our rights and respect our interests when we have disputes with others. The political theorist John Rawls (1921-2002) was concerned less with the procedural aspects of rights and more concerned with how a social system could be granted the status of *fair* from its foundations upwards. The best way to ensure this, says Rawls, is to make the rule of law primary in the structure of the state, and thereby ensure that politics *behaves* like law in its political and economic relationship with the individual. That is, the relationship between state and individual is *contractual*, and the role of the state is to ensure that whatever political or economic structures are in place, they appear reasonable (justified and rational) to individuals anywhere within its political and economic structures: '[t]he merit of the contract terminology is that it conveys the idea that principles of justice may be conceived as principles that would be chosen by rational persons' (1999: 14). For Rawls, justice flows from our accepting this initial account of fairness: a law-like, contractual and widely acceptable, relationship between individual and state. In addition, it is this that allows Rawls to say that 'justice is the first virtue of social institutions' (1999: 3). If justice is fairness, and we agree that fairness depends upon law-like neutrality and equality between parties, then all social institutions should exhibit the virtues of neutrality and equality we find in law (for further discussion of Rawls see Chapter 4).

There might be merit in reducing both political and legal ideas of justice to the expansion or maintenance of freedom. Freedom is a problematic term which encompasses positive freedoms *to act* and negative freedoms *from* certain constraints or impositions (see Chapter 2). The centralisation of freedom has no real precursors in the Ancient world because, arguably, a concern with the freedom of the individual is an eminently modern concern related to the status of the individual and the power of the state. In the work of Robert Nozick (1938-2002) the demand shared by political and legal justice is our entitlement not to have oppressive burdens placed upon us. Assuming that we must inhabit a state – and therefore do not possess untrammelled freedom – we nonetheless possess a range of rights which delimit the powers of the state. Rights do not provide us with an end-state or goal but act as 'side constraints' on the state ensuring our freedom: '[rights are] side constraints upon the actions to be done: don't violate constraints C. [. . .] The side-constraint view forbids you to violate [. . .] moral constraints in the pursuit of your goals' (Nozick, 1974: 29). In other words, Rawls cannot guarantee the justice of the state simply by making us accept his idea of fairness. Being born into a state is not a choice or contract, and for this reason the state is, above all, obliged to interfere as little as possible with the citizens that fall within its control.

> Treating us with respect by respecting our rights, [the minimal state] allows us, individually or with whom we choose, to choose our life and to realise our ends and our conception of ourselves, insofar as we can, aided by the voluntary cooperation of other individuals possessing the same dignity. How *dare* any state or group of individuals do more. (1974: 334)

The state should be a minimal 'night watchman' which ensures that freedom and property are protected. In this theory, law is important for justice only to the extent that it enshrines the negative liberties (the 'freedoms from') that are natural and just without the need for any further justification. This means that while legal rights are important, justice is not legal equality but the safeguarding of freedom in spite of the state.

EXAMPLE

'Treaty of Lisbon amending the Treaty on European Union and the Treaty establishing the European Community', signed 13 December 2007

Constitutions provide a kind of meta-theory for law: a justification of other legal rules, and final arbiter of tensions between rules and institutions. The Lisbon Treaty is a typical example of a modern constitutional document (albeit for a very atypical legal creation, the European Union). Equality and freedom are explicit, fairness implicit.

Drawing inspiration from the cultural, religious and humanist inheritance of Europe, from which have developed the universal values of the inviolable and inalienable rights of the human person, freedom, democracy, equality and the rule of law, [. . .] The Union is founded on the values of respect for human dignity, freedom, democracy, equality, the rule of law and respect for human rights, including the rights of persons belonging to minorities. These values are common to the Member States in a society in which pluralism, non-discrimination, tolerance, justice, solidarity and equality between women and men prevail. [. . .] The Union's aim is to promote peace, its values and the well-being of its peoples.

5b Scepticism

It is clear that 'legal justice' appears in a range of different forms – not only in different institutions and practices but also in both ends and means – which are not only different, but also potentially mutually incompatible. For instance, the common good might not be compatible with everyone having their day in court: legal processes are expensive and can slow social change. The rule of law might not be compatible with the status of particular individuals: rules should be impartially applied, but this does not guarantee that every individual has the status and recognition they deserve. These tensions may well lie in the ambiguity of 'justice' itself. The term is equivocal on at least four axes: in terms of values, virtues, means and ends. With that level of ambiguity at work, 'scepticism' – in the philosophical sense of deep and sometimes total doubt and suspicion about an idea – might be the best philosophical approach. Two kinds of scepticism are relevant here, linguistic and conceptual.

At the very least we can say that the word 'justice' is unclear. Justice is claimed by three spheres of activity (law, politics and individual virtue); 'justice' drifts between law, politics and ethics without being owned by any of them. Law not only fails to have a monopoly on the word justice but, paradoxically, legal invocation of justice frequently points to things outside legal systems (political principles or individual virtues). The word 'justice', then, is not only overlaid with various historical meanings, but may well depend upon those different contexts to have any meaning at all. This gives weight to a sceptical conclusion that 'legal justice' as a phrase might be treated as nothing more than a rhetorical flourish used to approve of certain kinds of activities, but which should be denied substantial theoretical, or moral, importance (Fuller, 1969: 12).

Conceptual scepticism is also warranted in relation to legal justice. It is at an unclear intersection between actions and outcomes. We want people to *be* just, and we want the *outcomes* of their actions to be just. This may be its strength. It is a useful way of criticising means, ends and motives. Indeed, the oft-quoted Latin phrase '*lex inusta non est lex*' – an unjust law is not a law – has been used, and interpreted, in a variety of ways in legal philosophy in order to criticism the means and ends of law (see Bix, 2004: 127). In broad terms it indicates that justice exists as a standard outside law by which to judge law. Nonetheless, this standard remains unclear: is it equivalent to divine will, to morality or to a standard unique to laws? In essence, justice has no stable 'referent'; it does not pick out, or refer to, any single thing in the world. Furthermore, a sceptical response could insist that justice is therefore indefinable or, differently, that questions about its definition are meaningless.

A radically sceptical approach to 'legal justice' would insist on the impossibility of law being justice. This position, associated with some scholarship in critical legal studies (CLS) (though not always, see Chapter 6), suggests that all attempts to judge human action and activity by stable standards are philosophical mistakes masking power. Any claim to justice on the part of law is an ideological smokescreen for decisions made on the basis of force, politics or vested interests. Such a position is dependent upon a particularly sceptical view of truth and of power. An especially sceptical philosophy has to be at work here because legal decisions rarely look as if they are merely the exercise of power: they have some claim, at least, to consistency (see Chapter 4). While this kind of radical criticism of law recalls the Ancient philosophers' suspicion about the relationship between law and power, the Ancient philosophers still felt able to appeal to truth and other meta-theories of justice (Morrison, 1997). In the most sceptical approaches to law, even these lines of escape are withdrawn.

EXAMPLE

Bradwell v *The State*, 83 U.S. 16 Wall. 130 (1872) (United States Supreme Court)

One reason to be sceptical of law's ability to deliver justice is that the legal profession, on whom so much depends, has long been populated by a limited and privileged segment of society that might not have any sensitivity to the pressures and needs of those petitioning a court. This goes too for the gender distribution of legal practitioners. In a predominantly male profession, the lives and experiences of women cannot be said to be perfectly represented or understood. In the present case, an application for a woman to practise law is rejected on the basis of notions which seem otherwise just (the divine, harmony and 'maxims of jurisprudence').

The natural and proper timidity and delicacy which belongs to the female sex evidently unfits it for many of the occupations of civil life. The Constitution of the family organization, which is founded in the divine ordinance as well as in the nature of things, indicates the domestic sphere as that which properly belongs to the domain and functions of womanhood. The harmony, not to say identity, of interest and views which belong, or should belong, to the family institution is repugnant to the idea of a woman adopting a distinct and independent career from that of her husband. So firmly fixed was this sentiment in the founders of the common law that it became a maxim of that system of jurisprudence that a woman had no legal existence separate from her husband, who was regarded as her head and representative in the social state, and, notwithstanding some recent modifications of this civil status, many of the special rules of law flowing from and dependent upon this cardinal principle still exist in full force in most states.

5c Pragmatism

Philosophical pragmatism insists that the true is the useful or efficacious. Pragmatists are sceptical of extravagant philosophical claims about truth, but they do accept that concepts and ideas can be shown to be real by virtue of their having a verifiable impact on reality: usefulness in practice, or the ability to make a distinction (see Patterson (ed.), 1996: 385f). We can therefore be pragmatic in two senses. Pragmatism in a 'loose sense' would look to salvage whatever is useful from the fact that we commonly *use* the idea of justice. One way or another, 'justice' is something we use in philosophy, in law, and beyond. A more fundamental philosophical pragmatism about knowledge would suggest that because 'justice' has some use, it also has some truth: our belief in the importance of justice changes us and the world.

In terms of pragmatism in the 'loose sense', it is tempting to concede our political or social order takes primacy over legal justice and that law contributes to a stable social order. We talk about law, we appeal to laws and we use social institutions, and without these things we would have a less harmonious society. Law is a useful means because it brings consistency to human affairs; how it does this does not really matter. This recalls appeal to 'the common good' because law works alongside politics to bring about a number of good collective ends.

Epistemological pragmatism – the association of truth and knowledge with verifiable usefulness – would indicate that we know legal justice by its social effects and by no other means. Only that which has some kind of impact on reality is real; only that which allows us to make a difference in the world can be classed as true or false. This is not a well-rounded theory of truth; we would wish to insist on the difference between a useful delusion that makes us happy and a useless fact which still 'holds good'. By this standard, however, justice has meaning as part of a two-way causal relationship between society and justice. Social activity generates different conceptions of justice over time (the Greeks associated justice with virtue, and we associate justice with the independence of the legal system as a means to a number of different ends). Justice in turn has some impact on how society views distribution and correction (justice as an ideal, even a complex and confused ideal, can be used to criticise social practices). In short, this idea, complex as it is, forms part of how we see the world and in that sense has meaning as a tool with which to discuss and analyse the world: '[t]ruth and justice are both partly a matter of experimentation, of finding out what works and trying out different forms of life' (Singer quoted in Patterson (ed.) 1996: 391).

Mindful of both the meta-theoretical and sceptical approaches to legal justice, it may be that a pragmatic middle ground is possible. It would be pragmatic, broadly speaking, to conclude that each meta-theory has some claim to plausibility and that there is merit in 'seeing what works' – what makes sense or what makes a difference – when we think about law and justice. This could be augmented by pragmatism in a philosophical sense: justice is a useful means of criticising social practices including law and to that extent it has some claim to meaning.

EXAMPLE

West Virginia State Board of Education v *Barnette* 319 U.S. 624 (1943) (US Supreme Court)

In this celebrated dissenting judgment, Justice Frankfurter defends the right of a minority, on grounds of conscience, to refuse to salute the national flag. Frankfurter is sceptical of justice being found exclusively in the words of a constitution: it has to be found in the convictions and habits of a people.

Our constant preoccupation with the constitutionality of legislation rather than with its wisdom tends to preoccupation of the American mind with a false value. The tendency of focusing attention on constitutionality is to make constitutionality synonymous with wisdom, to regard a law as all right if it is constitutional. Such an attitude is a great enemy of liberalism. Particularly in legislation affecting freedom of thought and freedom of speech much which should offend a free-spirited society is constitutional. Reliance for the most precious interests of civilization, therefore, must be found outside of their vindication in courts of law. Only a persistent positive translation of the faith of a free society into the convictions and habits and actions of a community is the ultimate reliance against unabated temptations to fetter the human spirit.

Questions

Section 1

- Does law aim to make people *happier*? Does it aim to make people *better*? Or does law aim to *control*? Does the answer to these questions depend upon whether we are inside or outside a legal system?

- Does making a legal judgment differ *as a mental process* from other kinds of judgment? For example a quick decision made while driving?

- Do legal processes provide certainty? If so, does this happen only after a decision is reviewed by a higher court? If not, on what basis, and by what standard, do they fall short of certainty?

Section 2

- Do the means used by law (e.g. impartiality or procedural fairness) require any further justification? Are they useful? Is their use obligatory?

- Should law be 'blind' to the identities of the parties to a conflict? Is this possible or desirable?

- Does 'treating people equally' make sense of what laws and courts do without reference to other goals such as allowing freedom, or allowing the truth to be heard?

Section 3

- Are *all* human activities, including law, intended to ultimately make individuals *happier*? Is there any human activity that cannot be explained by the pursuit of happiness?

- Can rights be equated with justice given that they are closely related to the interests of individuals, not the state?

- If humans have an important status – are deserving of special kinds of treatment and respect – could this status exist without law?

Section 4

- Does law help or hinder the common good? Are, for example, criminal law and financial law more helpful for the common good than human rights or constitutional law?

- Does the idea of the 'rule of law' make sense if laws are made by Parliaments who decide upon the rules and the exceptions to the rules?

- Are all ideas of authority ultimately explicable in terms of the power or force that people possess to impose their authority?

Section 5

- If all ideas of justice had to be summarised in one word, would 'equality', 'fairness' or 'freedom' come closest? Could we substitute all uses of the word 'justice' for equality, fairness or freedom?

- Is the word 'justice' hopelessly vague on the basis that it has a long history and is used in very different contexts?

- Do we need a theory about the meaning of the word 'justice' or is it sufficient to accept that people 'know what they mean' when they use it?

Concepts and methods: Theorising

Setting down the appearances

Collecting together intuitions or common ideas about something such as justice does not seem to be a systematic, or even philosophical, way to approach a question. We might assume that a properly philosophical approach requires abstractions and a technical vocabulary. Collecting together common ideas was, in fact, Aristotle's approach to philosophy – he termed it 'setting down the appearances' (1987: 431) – and he considered this the only way to approach an enquiry, be it enquiry in the natural sciences, theology or the social sciences. Some common ideas are found wanting: confused, inadequate or insufficiently general. However, sifting through common ideas and received wisdom also shows where ideas are resilient, attractive or indispensible: 'if we both resolve the difficulties and leave [. . .] reputable opinions undisturbed, we shall have proved the case sufficiently' (1987: 431). Comparing these common ideas is the best way to ensure that philosophical reflection is rooted in the world, not pure inventions of the human mind.

Theorising

The foregoing analysis of justice has been conducted as a theoretical enquiry. What exactly does this mean? The Greek word *theoria* means to 'contemplate' or 'survey'. It is, then, both to think in a sustained way about something and to get an overview of it. We have not simply been discussing the 'facts' of the matter as discovered, for example, in the workings of a Court. Rather, theorising involved interrogation of what particular words such as justice mean, how some accounts (of justice) are better than others, and how ideals (concerning justice) might be difficult to find in reality. Such reflections are theoretical by virtue of having no immediate practical importance (they would not necessarily change how a practitioner did their job), but they do involve evaluation and not simply description.

Analysis of language and evaluation of ideas are central to theorising. Analysis of meaning is important because meaning can change depending upon who is using certain words and in what context; without clarity on shared or agreed meanings, theoretical discussion would become senseless. This is an evaluative practice, demanding clarity on why some meanings are better than others. It is also a classificatory practice asking on what grounds we should compare things, people or ideas. For instance, should reality, or ideals, be our primary concern when we are analysing social institutions? It is always the case that the real diverges from the ideal. Many rules and procedures 'look good on paper' – are fair and reasonable – but have been unworkable in practice. In different manifestations, this tension between life as it is, and life as it should be or we how want it to be, is a recurrent feature of law, but should these two perspectives on reality be compared at all? The tension between facts and values is central to Chapter 2, and the relationship between the two is one of the most fundamental questions posed in legal philosophy.

Rationalism and empiricism

Clarification of concepts is always characterised by a philosophical struggle between the importance of ideas and the importance of facts. On the one hand, in order to decide whether a concept is clear and unambiguous, we can test it against our other ideas to see whether it 'makes sense' in our own minds. On the other hand, all of our ideas begin with factual experiences. However sophisticated our thinking – our analysis, our memory and our imagination – mental processes begin with the factual world and, if they are to be *useful*, must retain some kind of relationship with the facts of the world.

These competing approaches to concepts are, in a crude way, articulations of rationalism and empiricism. Rationalism insists that knowledge is possible simply through the interrogation of ideas and the working of our minds as rational beings. Empiricism argues that anything worthy of the name 'knowledge' must have a basis in the facts of the world. There is no need to 'side' with one position or the other in order to do philosophy, but any analysis of concepts sooner or later runs up against the question of whether concepts gain their validity from ideas or from facts (Patterson (ed.), 1996: 376).

Scepticism

Scepticism is on a spectrum from the mildly argumentative to 'global scepticism' about everything that exists. Scepticism can be a route to 'first principles', as in the work of the rationalist René Descartes (1596-1650), where Descartes used radical scepticism to clear away what he knew and begin knowledge afresh. This was a 'global scepticism' used to refound his knowledge on firmer foundations. Such radical scepticism is still used to draw knowledge claims, and ethical claims, into doubt.

Scepticism denotes a range of theoretical approaches which insist that knowledge (i.e. certainty or truth claims) must admit certain kinds of limits, or else run the risk of over-reaching the boundaries of knowledge. 'Fact scepticism' involves denying that our assertions about facts have a necessary relationship with states of affairs in the world. 'Rule scepticism' involves insisting that claims about rules are valid only to the extent that they describe certain regularities in the world, not that there is a special kind of 'force' in rules. These scepticisms will be returned to (Chapter 5). Suffice it to say, while philosophers do engage in radical scepticism (e.g. the 'Matrix' claim that everything we see is an illusion created by evil beings) other forms of scepticism are more relevant for legal concepts where they test the limits of what we can claim as certain or necessary.

Pragmatism

There is held to be a disjunction between theorising and practical activities; the former is 'merely' thinking, the latter doing. Pragmatism, as a theoretical position, breaks down this barrier and demands that every theoretical claim must have some practical correlate or consequence. This is not to say everything we think or believe has to be useful, but we would want everything we think or believe to denote something, draw a distinction, mark a difference or describe a state of affairs. If it fails to *do* these kinds of things then it ceases to be a useful idea and ceases to have any claim to knowledge of the world. Pragmatism is not a perfect theory of truth: we can imagine having ideas or parts of our vocabulary that were not useful in any obvious way and did not draw useful distinctions. Nonetheless, philosophical pragmatism is helpful in bringing theoretical debates back to the *use* of concepts. In addition, when engaged in conceptual enquiry about law, the pragmatists' stress on use is a corrective to extravagant claims about concepts, particularly those with as long, and complex, a history as justice or law.

Further reading

On the general topic of justice, Robert Alexy's article (2004) locates these debates within the 'discipline' of legal philosophy, Tom Campbell's book *Justice* (2001) provides an excellent overview of philosophical debate about justice, and Franz Wieacker's article (1990) covers similar ground in a way that is more centred on the history of law. Gerhart Husserl's 'Justice' (1937) grapples with some of the more difficult questions about equality and judgment. On the philosophy of justice, Spragens (1993) offers a comparable, but slightly different, scheme of approaches to the classification of (meta-theoretical, sceptical and pragmatic) philosophies of justice used here (he identifies 'hegemonic', 'sceptical' and 'pluralistic' accounts). Winthrop (1978) gives a clear analysis of Aristotle's position. Both Robin West's article (1998) and Del Mar's *New Waves in Philosophy of Law* (2011) place discussion of justice within the context of 'traditional' legal scholarship and the challenges which competing ideas of justice can present to such scholarship.

Visit **www.mylawchamber.co.uk/riley** to access tools to help you develop and test your knowledge of legal philosophy including Podcasts on leading thinkers and theories, discussion questions, diagrams showing interrelations between concepts, and weblinks

2 Person

Introduction

Each of the philosophies of justice considered in the last chapter depended upon an idea – equality, fairness or freedom – which itself relies upon a particular dimension of humanity: human rationality, human nature or the status of the person. Justice is achieved through making humans *equal persons* in the eyes of the law, by making social institutions fair because they are institutions *reasonable people* would consent to, or by exchanging the natural freedom of the human for the social *freedom of the citizen*. For arguments about justice to be settled we need a clearer understanding of the relationship between law and the person.

To the extent that the institution of law – a body of practices and procedures – has a basic idea of a person, it might be said that there are working assumptions in different spheres of law. For example, we are familial beings in family law, contracting beings in contract law. Law may need nothing other than these working assumptions because it is an institution which aims to govern human affairs or make human affairs predictable. Legal institutions are not created in order to dictate what humans are or should be, but to regulate their lives together. However, this is to refuse to acknowledge something that already takes place in law. To treat someone as a being capable of entering into a contract is to treat them as rational beings capable of free decisions. To treat someone as a member of a family is to make assumptions about biological links or about caring relationships. That humans are rational, or free or biologically 'linked' might be treated as obvious in some contexts, but these are not simple claims.

While we need clarity in the meaning of 'person' this demands entering into some of the most complex and vexed debates in philosophy. Philosophical analysis of the person not only encompasses ethical questions about character and obligation, it also triggers epistemological questions about knowledge. Is it possible for humans to have a perspective 'outside' humanity from which our nature and potential can be analysed? Or is humanity, as Protagoras said, 'the measure of all things' (see Plato, 1997: 169), in which case we alone can decide upon our nature and our potential? Our obligations depend upon what we are and what we can be. Is human self-reflection firm enough a foundation to answer such questions?

One way to demonstrate this complexity is to draw a difference between humans and persons. It might seem that nothing rests on this difference; the words denote the same categories of things, and confusion rarely flows from using one rather than the other in ordinary language. However, it is more accurate to say that while 'human' is a broad factual category, 'person' has a more specific meaning due to its close relationship with law. A person is a human recognised, protected and governed by law. In the language of 'humans' there is something natural or 'pre-legal' at work. In the language of 'persons' we find humans possessing legal status. When this status begins, and what this status entails, are questions that have reappeared throughout philosophical traditions. They demand that we know what is 'human' in a general sense, and what law contributes when it recognises humans as persons.

More specifically, it gives rise to the question of whether legal systems simply decide which rights accrue to the legal person, or whether there is a more complicated process here based on the demands, or the needs, of the person. We cannot assume that the values we attach to a human by recognising them as a person are universally agreed values. Indeed, Colin Dayan argues that law's relationship with personhood is precisely where illegitimate and dangerous ideas can enter into, and be made legitimate, by law: 'Law renders the meaning of persons shifting and tentative: whether in creating slaves as *persons in law* and criminal as *dead in law*' (2011: xii, emphasis in original).

To determine the meaning of human in a 'non-legal' sense is, arguably, impossible. Humans *are* beings capable of being subject to, or subjecting themselves to, laws. An adult human who has no sense of what is expected of them by other people is exceptional as a human. If, however, there is a necessary relationship between humans and law (we have always wanted or needed law), this relationship also appears highly variable and contingent (we change law and law changes us).

Moreover, 'human' is not an unchanging or unchallenged category; it can be understood in contradictory ways. A doctor's conception of a human as a biological machine is far removed from a religious idea of humans as images of God. The 'being' of human beings can be understood as static, changing or evolving. This is apparent if we consider the opposites (antonyms) of 'human'. Human has, variously, 'animal', 'inhuman' and 'natural' as opposites. Humans are distinct from other *animals*, though not clearly. While we are animals in zoological terms, we often treat our capacities – including complex communication, the capacity for self-reflection and sustained reflection on the past – as drawing a decisive dividing line. We are *inhuman* where we fail to exhibit basic levels or recognition, empathy or respect towards others. The idea of inhumanity is crucial to humanitarian law and is associated with the idea of degradation: inhuman acts degrade humans to a lower status than they deserve (the status of animals).

Furthermore, we are not the *natural* world; we are social beings and are not, arguably, part of the patterns of cause and effect that characterise nature. It is here that the idea of law returns. 'Law' and 'the social, rather than natural, existence of humans' may be synonymous terms. Human life has always been governed, or at least ideally governed, through the stable expectations that are associated with harmonious *social* life. In addition, to be a special, social, animal is less a matter of distinctive human *thought* and more related to our necessary relationship with *law and laws*.

Using 'nature' as a dividing line between human and non-human is made complicated by those philosophical traditions that treat humans as fundamentally divided between natural parts (the body) and non-natural (or perhaps supernatural) minds or souls. The natural is not only part of us but, in some currents of philosophical thought, something problematic to be tamed or denigrated if we are to be fully human (Plato, 1997: 1064; Kant, 1948: 66). We are natural beings, but we have a responsibility to become 'less natural'. This is not only a process of 'socialisation' that demands we dampen our natural or automatic behaviours and reflexes (see Chapter 6), but a more fundamental 'project' for humanity to shed its inheritance from nature. Our laws and our law-abiding behaviour are the most important manifestations of this progressive project.

In the light of these complexities, what generalisations can be made about humans and persons? The answer depends, crucially, on the difference between facts and values. A range of different approaches to our species are possible, all of which claim some authority to state what we as individual humans are. Some accounts of human beings stress the facts of biology, psychology or geography (Delaney, 2001). Some draw out the values and responsibilities that being human can be said to include (Glover, 2001). From these answers a range of different conclusions can be drawn about what law does for humans and what law should do. However, all of these different perspectives turn upon the division between *facts* and *values*. Facts concern what is the case, what has been the case, or what is potentially the case. Facts are the furniture of the world and the 'states of affairs' that these facts, together, constitute. Values are what should be the case, what we want to happen, and what states of affairs we should bring about. Values are not 'states of affairs', they are judgments about states of affairs.

These are, as will be discussed below, two different ways of thinking about the world and, arguably, two wholly incompatible ways of talking about the world. After all, if values do not *describe* the world then it is problematic to use them as ways of talking *about* the world. Suffice it to say, we concern ourselves with both facts and values (generally, and in law), and we have to be wary of blurring the difference, but it is difficult to disentangle them completely. Values have to be grounded in facts; claims about values are of no use to us if they are opinions without a sound basis. Conversely, facts always have to be judged in the light of values; that certain things are the case does not mean we have to accept or approve of them.

How does the fact/value division have an impact on our understanding of law? With respect to law-making it might be argued that our values should be at the fore of all our laws. Conversely, we can argue that the facts of law – the rules and obligations commanded by law-makers – are a clear and predictable set of facts. It is this very stability and predictability which, alone, makes law valuable. The *methodological* consequence of this is that whenever we choose values or facts to be our focus we choose an interpretive framework for understanding law. An emphasis on facts or values colours our entire understanding of laws and legal practices, and to try to see both perspectives at once is difficult.

1 Facts and values

Introduction

Consider a case where a Court has been asked to take a house away from a family because they have failed to keep up payments on a mortgage. Is it possible to keep the facts and values separate? The case could be summarised briefly: the family failed to fulfil a legal obligation to keep up payments; the Court has to follow a rule that obliges it to deny possession of houses to those who fail to repay loans. Where are the facts and values here? The Court has factual evidence to consider; the Court itself is constituted by a set of behavioural and institutional facts concerning authority, personnel and procedure. These facts would, of course, look different from the point of view of the family whose lives will be changed by the decision; they are concerned with the *values* of family, responsibility and their basic human needs. Moreover, there is the value we attach to legal decisions and the obligations that they help to maintain. Are these facts and values both strands of the same story or do they constitute two different stories?

The value we attach to certain states of affairs – individual happiness, access to basic goods such as housing and food, and predictability in how we are treated by others – is one way of bridging the gap between fact and value. Being human means we inevitably value certain things because we have biological needs, and we have expectations about what is due to us as members of a social world. These bridges between fact and value – physical need and social expectations – are important, but need further analysis. First, is there consensus on what needs we have over and above the biology of human survival? The answer, in part, is that 'ought implies can' (Kant, 1929: 473): our legal rights may well depend upon what it is practically *possible* for the state and others to fulfil. Second, are social expectations necessarily the same as legal obligations? The answer is that we can expect, because of law, the clear and predictable application of rules, but this is not the same as having all of our expectations met.

Law does not provide a simple bridge between fact and value. However, all law is a demonstration that we do not simply exist but *co-exist*. Moreover, the close relationship between law and 'persons' – the Greek *persona* is associated with the idea of a 'mask' – indicates two points of intersection between fact and value. The suppression or masking of the natural human animal in human societies, and the *need* for humans to inhabit social groups in order to be recognised as something more than an animal.

1a Humans and persons

Psychology, philosophy, law and science all claim to have a good, and useful, account of what it is to be human. Psychology starts with our capacities for perception and behaviour and finds regularity or predictability in these capacities for perception and behaviour. Science starts with biology and finds commonality between individual humans as biological beings.

Law and philosophy have rather more uncertain starting points. For both, the 'subject' is important. In philosophy we are first of all the subject *of* experience. That is, we are the recipients of 'data' about the world; we are subjects in a world of objects. In law we are, in the first instance, subject *to* law. That is, we cannot opt-out of being governed by laws, wherever or whoever we are. These are both general characteristics of being human but draw out rather different things. To be a subject of experience still leaves unanswered *what* does the experiencing. Are we essentially our minds or our bodies? In addition, to be subject to law still leaves unanswered *why* we are subject to law. Because we have to be, or because we have chosen to be, subject to law?

Psychology, philosophy, law and science overlap in many different ways. Law and science both see us as subject *to* laws: of society and of the physical world respectively. Law and psychology both depend upon a notion of self-conscious ability to choose our actions: we may be subject to laws but also retain the capacity for choice and self-determination. These four disciplines together locate us within physical and social worlds that govern us; but physical and social worlds from which we are distinguished as *individuals* because of our capacity for choice and independent willing.

Consequently, alongside 'humans' and 'subjects', third and fourth categories of 'individuals' and 'persons' should be distinguished. We can distinguish humans as a species from *individuals*, who are part of, but are not definitively characterised by, their membership of the human species. An individual exists whenever particular humans are *individuated* from the mass of the human species. The idea of a *person* is a more specific form of individuation which emphasises that individuals are embodied and self-conscious human beings. In an influential passage by John Locke (see Chapter 3), person is treated as a specialist ('forensic') term encompassing humans, their self-consciousness, and their capacity to act lawfully:

> [Person] is a forensic term appropriating actions and their merit; and so belongs only to intelligent agents capable of a law, and happiness and misery. This personality extends

it *self* [*sic*] beyond present existence to what is past, only by consciousness, whereby it becomes concerned and accountable, owns and imputes to it *self* [*sic*] past actions. (Locke, 1975: 346, emphasis and capitals removed)

Persons are not an interchangeable part of a species; they are distinctive beings having individuality and individual status. This individuation and granting of status is given in part through law, but also social and political processes more generally. It is questionable whether we could be a person if we were denied, or excluded from, relationships with other people. So, whereas talk about individuals can be another way of talking about humans in general, the language of person contains all that we think of as distinctive about humans: that we are self-reflective, conscious, and that certain duties and rights accrue to us. Persons are more than biological entities.

EXAMPLE

The Institutes of Justinian, Book I, Title VIII 'Of Persons' (533CE) (quoted in Lee (2007) pp. 79–80)

The word 'person' (persona) has Latin origins and it is in Roman law that we find the first codification of the nature and rights of persons. Free born adults are sui juris, *they have legal status in their own right. Slaves also had legal status within the Roman Republic (from around 510BCE), albeit a qualified status of* alieni juris; *this qualification means that their legal status is related to the interests of their master.*

> [S]ome persons are *sui juris*, others are *alieni juris*: and of these last some are in the power of parents, others in the power of masters. [T]oday no men subject to our rule are allowed to do violence to their slaves without lawful cause or beyond measure. [. . .] [I]t is in the interests of masters that relief against cruelty or starvation, or intolerable wrong, should not be denied to slaves who justly invoke it.

1b Science and facts

In developed societies science is held to give the most authoritative account of reality, of the 'hard facts' of the world. Science offers facts and theories that are reliable and trustworthy. Scientific ideas are persuasive because they offer a high degree of certainty. Depending upon the science, we can find the seemingly absolutely certain (e.g. that living creatures have a limited life-span) to the highly probable (that certain substances are bad for humans).

There are a range of scientific disciplines and approaches from the 'hard sciences' of physics and medicine to the 'human sciences' such as anthropology. The human sciences are less concerned with finding scientific *laws* and more concerned with *explanations* in terms of complex inter-relations of culture, perception and meaning.

Whatever the scientific discipline, science is a good route to determine what is certain about humans, what they need, and what they can be expected to do in different situations. Above all, science reminds us that we are biological entities, and that a number of common and predictable characteristics, tendencies and capacities flow from this (Monroe *et al.*, 2009).

However, science also seems to overstate what can be predicted about humans. We certainly share biological characteristics, but we are also characterised by a high degree of uncertainty. These uncertainties – even concerning what we ourselves will do in the future – seem to be part and parcel of being human. Moreover, even if science did promise to make us predictable, it could not necessarily tell us how we should organise society. Given that people will always have different needs and commitments, could there be a single, scientific, idea of a good society? For instance, does science dictate that society should become ordered such that the risk of personal harm is always minimised? This seems logical, and could, presumably, be measured and managed scientifically, but it takes no account of individuals' desire to have a private sphere where the state should not intervene, and it takes no account of the value of democratic decision-making. In short, can we *derive values from the facts* found in science? Together biology and anthropology tell us a great deal about what we are and where we have come from, but do not necessarily generate values to live by (Arendt, 1998).

EXAMPLE

Daubert v Merrell Dow Pharmaceuticals Inc., 509 U.S. 579 (1993) US Supreme Court

In the US Supreme Court case Daubert *the Court had to consider what judges should do if they are faced with conflicting scientific evidence, in this instance concerning pharmaceuticals and their possible side-effects. It was conceded that judges cannot be expected to be scientists, but that there are a number of tests that can be used to gauge whether something can be called 'scientific', principally by virtue of the methods used. This is important for a number of reasons, not least because it makes clear that science does not provide a single authoritative voice but has its own conflicts and controversies.*

Faced with a proffer of expert scientific testimony [. . .] the trial judge [. . .] must make a preliminary assessment of whether the testimony's underlying reasoning or methodology is scientifically valid and properly can be applied to the facts at issue. Many considerations will bear on the inquiry, including whether the theory or technique in question can be (and has been) tested, whether it has been subjected to peer review and publication, its known or potential error rate and the existence and maintenance of standards controlling its operation, and whether it has attracted widespread acceptance within a relevant scientific community. The inquiry is a flexible one, and its focus must be solely on principles and methodology, not on the conclusions that they generate.

⬛ 1c Humanity and human nature

Do humans form a single group? The scientific category of the human species, *Homo sapiens*, is a convenient classification, but does not tell us whether we really have anything (psychological or cultural) in common with all other humans, past, present or future. One alternative way of expressing the sense that all humans *do* have something in common is by using the term 'humanity'. All past and future humans might fall within this category. Humanity seems to capture more of what we mean by persons – humans with rights and responsibilities – rather than just biological humans. Furthermore, it seems to capture the significance of what persons share in terms of values and not just facts. The term humanity is a value as much as a category: the opposite of humanity is *in*humanity.

However, this generates two questions. What it is that gives us this common property of 'humanity'? If it is something biological, this does not account for what appears to be distinctive about *persons* (we value persons as something more than instances of a biological species). If it is a mental characteristic, we will encounter difficult cases of individuals whose thinking is not fully or distinctively human (e.g. young children) or those who do not seem to share whatever values are said to be characteristic of humanity (e.g. criminals who refuse to accept the binding obligations of law).

A middle ground between the facts of biology and the value of humanity would be 'human nature'. This suggests that we may have, by virtue of our embodiment (our vulnerability and our physical needs) or because of innate shared dispositions (to want to be with others, to want to act in certain self-interested ways), characteristics that are more or less consistent across time and culture. While this is often a useful way of talking about common traits and actions among humans it is frequently confused. Contradictory things are said to be human nature (to care for others and to be selfish; to be social and to be aggressive), and human nature is rarely a useful contribution to understanding law. 'Human nature' might be used to explain the drive to create laws regulating social conduct; it might also be used to suggest that humans are inevitably disposed to break the law for their own benefit.

It could be said that as soon as we cease to use the bare language of biology to describe humans we inevitably begin to talk about values. This is explicit when we talk of persons. Appeal to 'humanity' as the whole grouping of humans similarly straddles the fact/value divide. 'Human nature' can be used to introduce many different values into discussion. Each of these terms has a long philosophical pedigree, and certainly each plays a different role in our perceptions of what we are.

EXAMPLE

Crimes Against Humanity and War Crimes Act 2000 (Canada), s. 4

In international law it is relatively common to appeal to 'humanity'. International law aims to speak for all humanity, offering basic minimal standards that can be adhered to by all

➡

nations. *People and groups who attack vulnerable civilians are termed the 'enemies of all humanity' (hostis generis humanitas) and widespread crimes against innocent people are 'crimes against humanity'. The idea of crimes against humanity has long existed in order to describe acts such as piracy that are objected to, and policed, by all nations. Canada passed this Act, giving a definition of crimes against humanity, in order to become a Party to the Statute of the International Criminal Court, a permanent Court with jurisdiction over grave international crimes.*

'Crime against humanity' means murder, extermination, enslavement, deportation, imprisonment, torture, sexual violence, persecution or any other inhumane act or omission that is committed against any civilian population or any identifiable group and that, at the time and in the place of its commission, constitutes a crime against humanity according to customary international law or conventional international law or by virtue of its being criminal according to the general principles of law recognized by the community of nations, whether or not it constitutes a contravention of the law in force at the time and in the place of its commission.

2 Aristotle

Introduction

All of the humanities – the disciplines concerned with the nature and improvement of humanity – involve collection of facts about humans and the derivation of values from those facts. These facts (psychological or biological facts) are used to determine what is necessarily valuable to humans, thereby bridging fact and value. The Western philosophical tradition in particular emphasises what is *good* for humans, the subject of Chapter 3. While an attractive starting point for legal, political and ethical discussion, attention to the good does not provide a simple relationship between human needs and social structures. We might agree with Thomas Hobbes (1588–1679) that human life is 'nasty, brutish, and short' (1996: 84; see Chapter 4) and this may generate some radical conclusions about what humans should do. We might decide that humans are, above all, vulnerable biological beings and use this to legitimise paternalistic or authoritarian government with no concern for human freedom. We might, conversely, want to prioritise human freedom and therefore call for the minimisation of the power of the state. Nonetheless, starting with facts – any facts – seems to be a sound, concrete way of deciding which laws are the best for humans to live under.

Aristotle premises his influential political and ethical philosophies on the claim that we are a distinct biological species characterised by a unique kind of sociability. Both of these elements are important for understanding Aristotle's position: humans form a natural biological group, and like other biological groups we are sociable, albeit in a way that is distinctively ours. There are different explanations of why humans form societies. Aristotle asserts that nature itself is the origin of human groups; it is natural for family groups to form and for these groups to join others (1987: 507–10). The accumulation of large human groupings through the joining together of families is appealing as a starting assumption; it suggests that humans have been constant in their needs and behaviour, and it justifies the existence of larger groups (such as states) on the basis that they have natural origins in natural groups.

> The final association, formed of several villages, is the state. [S]elf-sufficiency has been reached, and while the state came about as a means of securing life itself, it continues in being to secure the *good* life. Therefore every state exists by nature, as the earlier associations too were natural. (1987: 509, emphasis in original)

This story of natural sociability is still prevalent in philosophical, political, biological and sociological thought. It is, nevertheless, challenged (see Chapter 4).

Not only has nature equipped us to live in groups but, like any natural species, we have the potential to flourish in good conditions and struggle in poor conditions. This idea of our flourishing, as biological entities, underpins Aristotle's argument that there is, by objective standards, a 'good human life'. It is this idea of a good human life that has given Aristotle's thought its longevity and attractiveness to legal and other philosophers. It makes sense of human lives and human institutions – they are necessary conditions for realising our natural goals – and such institutions can be judged by the objective standard of their contribution to human happiness. This is clearly a strong basis for analysing, and criticising, law.

2a The human species

Humans can be classified as biological entities. However, while we now expect evolution over time to be a characteristic of biology, Aristotle, like his contemporaries, assumed that biological species and types have, and will remain, unchanged. This static biological core is an 'essence'; and for Aristotle we are *essentially* creatures who live together in groups, cooperate and share. Aristotle's analysis of this essence is clearly and recognisably biological. We flourish and thrive as human beings where we are in a social situation which allows us to live without want, fulfil ourselves as persons and pursue our goals. We fail to flourish when we are denied the ability to live in a good culture where we are free to act as we should.

We are therefore, in essence, communal and communicating animals for whom the absence of other people to live and communicate with is unnatural. '[M]an is a political animal in a sense in which a bee is not, or any other gregarious animal. Nature, as we say, does nothing without some purpose; and she has endowed man alone among the animals with the power of speech' (1987: 509). We are not alone in being social animals, but we are creatures for whom social interaction, characterised by speech, is central to our being.

We therefore need others around us to fulfil our function as members of the human species. 'Fulfilling a function' as humans sounds artificial to modern ears. We are used to thinking of ourselves as persons, with the right to determine our activities in life rather than as biological entities with functions. Nonetheless, Aristotle insisted that all living beings have a goal (*telos*) of becoming what nature intended us to be. Our goal is to live a flourishing life, which is necessarily an active life. Like any biological entity we have to grow and change; a human life is never simply the passive possession of certain essential characteristics. Furthermore, we grow and change in the company of others with whom we learn to live harmoniously while pursing our own goals and objectives. Nature's *telos* provides us with a relatively modest goal – to live, as far as possible, harmoniously with other people – but it demands that we work to cultivate that harmony.

EXAMPLE

European Convention on Human Rights (1950) Article 8

The importance of drawing a line between our private, familial, lives and the wider needs of the state and society can be found clearly in the European Convention on Human Rights. Article 8 provides a clear insistence that people be allowed to pursue their lives without unnecessary interference. The second section of Article 8, however, accepts that this right is qualified substantially by the demands of society. Aristotle would agree with such qualifications.

1. Everyone has the right to respect for his private and family life, his home and his correspondence.
2. There shall be no interference by a public authority with the exercise of this right except such as is in accordance with the law and is necessary in a democratic society in the interests of national security, public safety or the economic well-being of the country, for the prevention of disorder or crime, for the protection of health or morals, or for the protection of the rights and freedoms of others.

2b Political animals

This is what Aristotle means when he insists that we are 'political animals'. We naturally spend time with other people, and this is essential for us, but human sociability also requires political decisions (in the widest sense) about how to deal with competing interests and arguments. In other words, we live best within a social system that allows us to pursue personal goals and ends, even though this may well involve some difficult (pragmatic and practical) decisions about how to live with other people pursuing different ends (see Finnis, 2011: 164–5). Consequently, Aristotle's view of social and political activity has two dimensions: an insistence that sociability is natural for humans, and sensitivity to the day-to-day complexities that this entails. This view of human life is not unlike the view of human coexistence we find implicitly within law. We can expect, even demand, a certain level of sociability from individuals, and many of these expectations are realised in laws from freedom of assembly to road traffic rules. We also expect people's lives to be complicated and sometimes antagonistic. Such antagonisms are the stuff of tort and criminal law.

The political animal is, therefore, neither political nor animal in the modern senses of the words. We are political because we have to cooperate with others and make compromises, whether or not we are involved in the running of the state. We are also animals for whom such political activity is part of our growth into maturity. While we are naturally social, we have to practise, and grow into, being good social actors. We are not *human* in any normal sense without this social dimension to our lives: 'man is by nature a political animal. Anyone who by nature and not simply by ill luck has no state is either [. . .] subhuman or superhuman' (1987: 509).

The political animal learns to, and has to, control itself through the exercise of virtue. While we are naturally social, we nonetheless have to work to cultivate good ways of dealing with others and avoid anti-social excesses in our activities. So, virtue for Aristotle is not a purely personal characteristic but encompasses civic, political, social and personal virtues. We need to cultivate moderate needs, tastes and wants and avoid excesses (vices). Not only is this moderation necessary for human coexistence, it is necessary to be fully human. In other words, if all truly human living is social, and sociality requires the exercise of virtues, then virtues are necessary to be fully human. Vice or excess is, conversely, contrary to a flourishing social life and, to that extent, inhuman. In sum, Aristotle's view of 'virtue' is not of repressive social mores (as the term virtue connotes in English), rather, it is a way of living which seeks moderation while pursuing the kind of life that is right for us.

Law helps us to lead virtuous lives. While law alone does not make us virtuous, it certainly guides us towards the public practices and personal dispositions that allow each individual to flourish in society. Good law is not, however, a single unchanging set of commands but the product of participatory politics where a range of views and voices contest, debate over and create laws suitable for their particular community. Accordingly, Aristotle is not a utopian with a model of a perfect state, but a (pre-modern) democrat with a dynamic view of good politics and good law. Indeed, Aristotle conceded that a flourishing life could be achieved in different communities, albeit that some communities are better than others; he has a preference for communities small enough for individuals to participate directly in politics (Barnes (ed.), 1995: 248–9). Nonetheless, he accepts that different communities have different merits and that social conditions can and do change over time, and he strongly criticises majoritarian systems where the many dictate to the few. A community which defended the needs of the poor, or the rich, or any class exclusively, is poorly governed. A balance of interests has to be represented.

EXAMPLE

Mabo v *Queensland* [No. 2] (1992), 175 C.L.R. 1 (Australian High Court)

The pursuit of a flourishing life for individuals in one group may well run into conflict with a country's laws as a whole. This is accentuated where an external power has taken control of land and disrupted the rights and freedoms of a pre-existing community. This is central to the major Australian land-rights case, Mabo. It concerned the right of the Meriam people to possession of land, the Murray Islands, which, it was contended, had passed to the British Crown on taking possession of Australasia. A number of things are at issue, including, implicitly, the question of whether pre-existing native practices consti-tuted law. It begins with a description from an eighteenth-century observer. A simple, but questionable, conclusion is drawn from this description.

It seems that before European contact social cohesion [among the Meriam people] was sought by the combined operation of a number of factors. Children were inculcated from a very early age with knowledge of their relationships in terms of social groupings and what was expected of them by a constant pattern of example, imitation and repetition with reinforcing behaviour. It was part of their environment – the way in which they lived. [. . .] Initiation and other group activities reinforced these patterns. A sense of shame was the out-come of a failure to observe. It could be reinforced by group pressures leading to retribution. Ultimately force might be resorted to by those who had access to the means of exerting it. Sorcery, magic and taboo were obviously important cohesive factors and a source of sanc-tion. [. . .] The findings show that Meriam society was regulated more by custom than by law.

2c The situated person

Aristotle's philosophy is coldly biological in some respects: we flourish or deteriorate according to whether we can put down roots in a good society. However, Aristotle was also sensitive to the irreducible differences between persons, and the difficulties and tragedies that can befall them. We are not merely instances of the human species, but have unique personalities and capacities. In the modern world we understand this uniqueness in a particular way. That is, that we are free human beings who are at lib-erty to choose our path in life, our roles, our commitments and our values. Aristotle, and the Ancient world, would not recognise this radically individualistic conception of identity. Rather, we are born into communities and social structures that define who we are and what our responsibilities are. We are always 'situated' in a historical and cultural context (the term is not Aristotle's but used by contemporary philosophers influenced by Aristotle (see Taylor, 1992)). We naturally have familial and social ties that determine who we are dependent upon and to whom we have obligations. This means that a strict division between fact and value is not meaningful: who you are, as a fact, determines what you should be, or are obliged to do. Values are not chosen, they are given. Some obligations fall upon us, whether we choose them or not.

Social life is therefore a mixture of obligations to others, and the obligation to fulfil one's own potential. Being human is not about the pursuit of a perfect life, it is about finding a balance between different obligations, social pressures and our own natural capacities and instincts. In this picture of social life some people will be denied, through luck and chance, the opportunity to live in a healthy flourishing society that supports them. In these instances, even the effort to live a good life can be frustrated, and people forced into tragic situations where nothing they can do will be good or right despite their best efforts (Nussbaum, 1986).

The possibility of tragic choices between equally undesirable outcomes preoccupied the Ancient Greeks. Greek tragedy, particularly in Sophocles' *Antigone* (1984), had dramatised the tensions between obeying the 'law of the land' and 'natural law', bonds and obligations among family members. Antigone is obliged to do both, but obeying either law would lead to unhappiness. At a more personal level for Aristotle, the first great Athenian philosopher, Socrates (c.470–399BCE), had been put to death by the state for seeking to question received assumptions and prejudices held by his fellow Athenians. In both cases, Antigone and Socrates, we find an assertion that we are obliged to obey the laws of the land. At the same time, both, ultimately, maintain that pursuing what we think is right can be a greater or higher obligation. Though such tensions are not always tragic, Aristotle's position is valuable in insisting that even where we want to do good, life and law often make this difficult for us. The tension between individual fulfilment and the law of the land is, says Wieacker, still in evidence today:

> All human law, being the work of humans, is condemned to reflect the misery as well as the greatness of human endeavour. The misery of human law reveals itself as soon as we realize the need to resort to compulsion, sanction, and punishment, in other words the very elements of positive law that stand accused today as 'repressive.' It also shows up in the insufficient fulfilment of personal expectations and needs, as well as in [. . .] the merely formal justice of general norms. (1990: 2)

EXAMPLE

Apology (Plato, 1997: 28)

The trial and execution of Socrates is the most important event in the long relationship between law and philosophy. The law of the land demanded Socrates' execution despite the charges against him (irreligion and corruption) being unfair; at the same time Socrates insisted on respecting the decision of a Court of law. The problem of a binding but nonetheless unjust law remains a central one for legal philosophy, as does the wider question of whether law (social rules) and philosophy (the pursuit of truth) are necessarily antagonistic. Plato's account of this trial is not an 'apology' in the sense of accepting blame. Rather it is a description of Socrates' evidence in Court and of his self-justification on the basis that he had obligations that his fellow countrymen could not understand.

[Socrates]: Indeed, men of Athens, I am far from making a defense now on my own behalf, as might be thought, but on yours, to prevent you from wrongdoing by mistreating the god's gift to you by condemning me; for if you kill me you will not easily find another like me. I was attached to this city by the god – though it seems a ridiculous thing to say – as upon a great and noble horse which was somewhat sluggish because of its size and needed to be stirred up by a kind of gadfly. It is to fulfil some such function that I believe the god has placed me in the city. I never cease to rouse each and every one of you, to persuade and reproach you all day long [. . .].

3 Humanism

Introduction

Humanism translates 'human' directly into a set of values. There are a range of ideas and positions that claim to be humanistic, meaning, roughly, that they consider individuals and their welfare to be central to their view of the world. Specifically, human*ism* (the '-ism' suffix denoting a system of ideas) suggests that humans, and the values connected with humans, can be said to provide a complete, or at least a powerful, system of ideas for politics, law and society.

Humanism as a term can be traced to the Renaissance, that period of European history (the fourteenth to the sixteenth century) driven by a rediscovery and re-vitalisation of Ancient philosophy, including Aristotle and Roman philosophers. The Renaissance put these ideas into action primarily in the area of education, stressing the cultivation of rhetoric, logic and other practical skills necessary for an active, flourishing, social life. However, education in these 'humanities' formed part of a wider movement re-evaluating humans' place in the universe. While medieval Europe had seen humans largely as part of a hierarchy of Creation (with humans little more than animals in need of salvation from the suffering of life on earth) the Renaissance placed humans much closer to God. Humans are *imago dei*, made in the image of God. As such, Renaissance Humanism represented a radical re-evaluation of what humans are, and therefore what is owed to them (Copleston, 2003: 207–30).

Humanism has come to have a number of confusingly different ideas associated with it, but they tend to share with Renaissance Humanism a strong view about how all humans should be treated. They should be treated as valuable in them-selves, and their lives and welfare should not be sacrificed as a means to achieve collective goals. It is these ideas that in turn fuelled the revolutionary period of the eighteenth century with its revolutionary tricolour of liberty, fraternity and equality. These were held to be universal values and standards applying to humans by virtue of their being humans. Humanism locates the origins of *law* in humans themselves, and implies that the content of law should be driven by the universal moral status of persons: law is found in, and should seek to sustain, human liberty, equality and fraternity. However, as we shall see, for all the immediate appeal of these principles they do not always easily translate into law and may well be, especially in the case of liberty, antagonistic to it.

3a Humanity and persons

The common thread between humanisms is a concern with what is owed to all humans, or, in other words, a centralisation of what is, and should be, universal in human conduct towards and between humans. This enriched idea of the person derived from Roman law, i.e. a person is a free-born human or a slave made subject to law and given status by law. Roman universality, however, was in many respects a pragmatic universality, enclosing conquered peoples within the scope of Imperial law. Humanism stresses that all persons are deserving of equal recognition by law, because each person – regardless of local laws – shares the elevated status as *imago dei* (Copleston, 2003: 421). Among some philosophers this shared status was said to form the basis of 'cosmopolitanism': the idea that our rights and duties transcend individual states, and that law was something shared by all peoples. In practice, Renaissance Humanism did not eradicate inequalities and injustices, nor was the rhetoric of equality and cosmopolitanism matched by a successful politics of social equality. Nonetheless, it set in train a philosophical reappraisal of what was owed to humans as humans.

The Renaissance changed the cosmological rank of humans, elevating them from near the bottom (close to the physical world of Creation, but above animals) to near the top (in God's image and a fingertip away from God). This reappraisal of humans as a collectivity can be seen as the birth of 'Humanity' as a concept. While we take it for granted that there is such a thing as humanity – humans in general – and while there have always been perceptions of commonalities between humans, the Renaissance created Humanity as the distillation of all that is best in humans. Humanity became an entity in its own right, possessing agency (Humanity 'acts' and 'wills') and possessing a moral and historical destiny (Humanity makes demands on each of us in its progress towards greater self-consciousness and harmony). This Humanity is not the class of all humans: it is our ideal selves constituting our ideal ruler.

The 'person' of the Renaissance – aspiring to and judged by the standards of humanity – in time became the 'citizen' of the Enlightenment. The notion of the citizen signals a political and philosophical augmentation of the category of the person. First (and philosophically), personhood was universalised, i.e. *everyone*, regardless of social station, has an elevated status due to intrinsic natural reason and freedom. Second (and politically), this demanded a real democratisation of social practices and institutions. The idea of a person becomes an irreducibly democratic concept involving a rejection of cosmological *and* social hierarchies. The destiny of Humanity could now be equated with the emancipation of all individuals into the status of rights-holding citizen.

The *person* of the Renaissance, with their intrinsically elevated status, is still a recognisable part of the modern era alongside the *citizen* of the Enlightenment (with inalienable rights and duties). The notion of the citizen is nonetheless problematic. It seeks to combine the particular (a citizen of this state) with the universal (citizens are all, and any, law-abiding individuals) and accordingly finds different expression in different legal cultures. For example, the citizen of the United States is predominantly characterised by rights, the French citizen is predominantly characterised by duties (Quinton (ed.) 1967: 153–9).

EXAMPLE

The Execution of Charles I, 27 January 1648 (quoted in Laughland, 2008: 29)

The trial of Charles I has significance as the legal rejection, by common people, of the natural elevation of sovereigns. However, the English Revolution was too early to allow truly democratic and revolutionary ideas to bear political fruit. Consequently, the English remain subjects, not citizens. The following is from the speech made by Charles on the day of his execution. Liberty, he argues, lies in the strong government of a monarch; by deposing the monarch the people themselves have been harmed.

> I desire their [the people's] liberty and freedom as much as anybody whomsoever; but I must tell you that their liberty and freedom consist in having of government, those laws by which their life and their goods may be most their own. It is not for having share in government, sirs; that is nothing pertaining to them; a subject and a sovereign are clear different things. And therefore until they do that, I mean that you do put the people in that liberty, as I say, certainly they will never enjoy themselves. Sirs, it was for this that now I am come here. If I would have given way to an arbitrary way, for to have all laws changed according to the power of the sword, I needed not to have come here; and therefore I tell you (and I pray God it be not laid to your charge) that I am the martyr of the people.

3b Liberty

The first element of the revolutionary tricolour is liberty, being both a specific defence of the physical liberty of the individual against arbitrary treatment by the state and a general defence of persons' need to choose their own destiny. The Enlightenment and the revolutionary era emphasised freedom and self-creation, i.e. humans taking it upon themselves to become something new. This commitment to change, growth and progress is only partially captured in the language of liberty. In fact, the idea of *autonomy* is more appropriate. To be *auto-nomos* – in a literal translation from the Greek, to be 'self-legislating' – is to take upon oneself the power and status of law-giver and being able to exercise and create laws.

There is clearly a close relationship between freedom or autonomy and humanistic ideals. As Raz asserts:

> [H]umanism calls for respecting the autonomy of persons, that is, their right and ability to develop their talents and tastes and be able to lead the kind of life they are committed to. The areas of a person's life and plans which have to be respected by others are those which are central to his own image of the kind of person he is and which form the foundation of his self-respect. (2009: 280)

This emphasis on the individual person's choice and self-determination is related to that fact that, in the revolutionary era, 'we the people' had taken over the powers of the sovereign in order to become, *en masse*, the sovereign. This foreshadows the iconoclastic trajectory of modernity wherein humanity took it upon itself to become *the* law-giver, ultimately challenging God himself as ultimate source of law (Chapter 7). The revolutionaries in France and America would not have seen their actions in these terms and would have rejected any radically irreligious conclusion to their political project. Nonetheless, this is in some respects the logical conclusion of the liberty pursued from the Enlightenment onwards.

One group of humanists, Existentialists, took this libertarian project to its logical (and potentially absurd) conclusion. These were twentieth-century humanists who saw liberty and autonomy as the most important dimension of the 'modern condition', but who stressed the burdens that this entailed and not just the benefits. Insisting that existence precedes essence – the fact *that we are* precedes *what* we are – the Existentialists argued that we are thrown into the world without any natural or essential way to be. We cannot appeal to the facts of nature to determine how to act because nature does not provide an essence, a proper way to be, for humans (see Moran, 2000: 238–40). Nor can we appeal to any distinctively human values because these will always be temporary by virtue of the fact that humanity is never a single thing, only the sum of people here and now. For the Existentialists, 'People are not essentially anything whatever, except that they are essentially free. They are free to choose what they will be, and collectively they are free to choose what humanity will be' (Solomon, 1988: 178). Some Existentialists insisted that this nonetheless represented a kind of humanism in that, as free humans, we have a duty to act freely, and never to masquerade as 'un-free' creatures at the mercy of others or of nature (Sartre, 2007). However, it also represents an ethic of liberty that runs close to the nihilistic, in so far as its injunction is to be free at any cost, but never to determine or insist upon any particular course of action.

EXAMPLE

Frasik v Poland ECHR (Application number 22933/02) 2010

Such is the political, legal and ideological significance of liberty that most states accept (through signing international treaties) that liberty should be taken from people as rarely

➡

as possible, including that of prisoners. While convicted criminals usually lose their liberty of movement and choice, this should not be amplified (it is held by the European Court of Human Rights) through additional losses of freedom and choice.

Personal liberty is not a necessary pre-condition for the exercise of the right to marry. Imprisonment deprives a person of his liberty and also – unavoidably or by implication – of some civil rights and privileges. This does not, however, mean that persons in detention cannot, or only very exceptionally can, exercise their right to marry. As the Court has repeatedly held, a prisoner continues to enjoy fundamental human rights and freedoms that are not contrary to the sense of deprivation of liberty, and every additional limitation should be justified by the authorities [. . .]. [There is] a non-exhaustive list of rights that a detained person may exercise.

3c Fraternity and equality

The two remaining revolutionary principles are fraternity and equality. Together these point to the importance of 'levelling' the social structure such that all people are not only equal in an abstract sense, but recognised and respected as rights-holding citizens.

Equality has a long philosophical history and found its first and most influential expression in Aristotle's work. In his dictum that 'like cases should be treated alike, and unlike cases treated as unlike', Aristotle offered a deceptively simple structure for understanding what we mean by equality (see Chapter 1). Part of what he is arguing for is captured in the simple notion of mathematical equality, that something is quantitatively equal to another thing. This cannot be all that is meant, however, because judging human actions and human needs is rarely a question of mathematical measurement, not least because we have to decide when two things should be compared and thereby considered capable of being equal. Consequently, equality in human affairs is often a question of *ignoring irrelevant differences*, most frequently differences such as colour, race or sex which are grounds on which two people should rarely, in legal contexts, be compared. This can also be expressed in terms of desert: two persons equally deserve something if they have an equal claim to it when all other legally and morally irrelevant circumstances and personal characteristics are excluded. 'If a law provides for the relief of poverty then the requirement of the principle that "Like cases be treated alike" would surely involve attention to the *need* of different claimants of relief' (Hart, 1994: 163). In these terms, we can make sense of the otherwise false assertion that all people are equal. In *prescriptive* terms, persons should be judged, participate and be considered on the basis of relevant characteristics (merit, need, entitlement) not on the basis of irrelevant characteristics. Failure to do this would entail that real but irrelevant *differences* can become morally objectionable *inequalities of treatment*.

Fraternity, 'brotherhood', is a more opaque, but also potentially richer, concept than equality. That is to say, fraternity is a term without clear meaning or scope, but captures much of what humanists understand as their moral and legal commitments. Over and above the much thinner commitment to equal treatment, fraternity is an essentially modern concept denoting ethical commitments beyond family and community. Although Aristotle would have accepted that we have responsibilities to our state as well as to our families, fraternity indicates a far broader moral and ethical attachment to all persons around us, an attachment demanding recognition of others' value and solidarity in the face of others' needs. The problem with such a demand is its positing an underlying link, a brotherhood, which transcends particularity, which generates a natural solidarity with others, and which renders personal and cultural difference irrelevant. Like other theories positing an underlying uniformity or solidarity between humans, fraternity leaves those who are, one way or another, 'different' excluded or ignored.

EXAMPLE

Coleman v *Attridge Law* **European Court of Justice (Case C-303/06) [2008] 3 C.M.L.R. 27**

Considering equality and non-discrimination, the European Court of Justice argues (drawing on the legal philosophy of Ronald Dworkin) that both are reducible to the idea of human dignity. This idea is said to transcend any political disagreements within and between states.

At its bare minimum, human dignity entails the recognition of the equal worth of every individual. One's life is valuable by virtue of the mere fact that one is human, and no life is more or less valuable than another. As Ronald Dworkin has recently reminded us, even when we disagree deeply about issues of political morality, the structure of political institutions and the functioning of our democratic states we nevertheless continue to share a commitment to this fundamental principle. Therefore, individuals and political institutions must not act in a way that denies the intrinsic importance of every human life. [. . .] The most obvious way in which such a person's dignity and autonomy may be affected is when one is directly targeted because one has a suspect characteristic. Treating someone less well on the basis of reasons such as religious belief, age, disability and sexual orientation undermines this special and unique value that people have by virtue of being human.

---

4 Feminism

Introduction

Feminism has a range of meanings, but it has always involved drawing attention to the differences in treatment, differences in opportunity and differences in lives experienced by men and women. It also stresses that what has been treated as 'human' often includes assumptions and value judgments about what is 'normal' for men and for women, namely inequality. In other words, while humanists, among others, have propounded liberating ideas about what humans are capable of and entitled to, such positions also betray blindness to those outside the public sphere and outside the traditional class of philosophical, political and social actors. What is tellingly described as 'Man' or 'Mankind' has systematically, and in the guise of what is 'natural' or 'rational', excluded women.

Recalling the revolutionary era and its trio of values, equality and liberty were demanded by and for a relatively small class of wealthy men. Note also that appeal to fraternity not only used a language of 'brotherhood' but, more fundamentally, presupposed uniformity within humanity, ignoring differences between the sexes. This was a defence of revolutionary cosmopolitanism, but in practice was characterised by the narrow concerns of one, male, political class.

Some pre-twentieth-century philosophy can be identified as 'feminist' in that it sought to place women at the centre of enquiry. Mary Wollstonecraft's (1759–97) work *Vindication of the Rights of Woman* is the most important of these. This text, a rhetorical addition to Wollstonecraft's more general defence of the French Revolution, unpicked the contradictions and hypocrisies of the Revolutions' conservative critics, not least their horror at the Revolution throwing the 'natural' division between the sexes into disarray (Wollstonecraft, 1997: 226f).

Despite some radical political and philosophical differences (Humm, 1992), feminist philosophies share a critical perspective on law: law has been a tool of inequality, oppression and injustice. Wollstonecraft's position and contemporary thought share the assumption that women have been both unconsciously and deliberately excluded from fundamental social struggles and ideological changes, and that law must be made to recognise the status, value and contribution of women to 'mankind'. From this starting assumption at least two further lines of enquiry and analysis are important:

> The first stresses women's differences from men and posits that women have a particular contribution to make to the practice of law which will mean greater fairness and justice for all parties in dispute. The second approach maintains that gender differences result from male domination which the law both reflects and perpetuates. Legal reform cannot change basic social inequalities because law reproduces them. (Roach Anleu, 1992: 423–4)

4a The second sex

Although not a universally agreed upon basis for criticism and analysis (see Kruks, 2005), Simone De Beauvoir's (1908–86) *The Second Sex* (1988) engages with a spectrum of issues crucial to feminism. The idea of a second, or secondary sex, refers to a way of thinking (with theological origins, but still prevalent) that womanhood and femininity are *derived* from men and masculinity. Rather than these two sexes being qualitatively different (in itself a contentious assumption), there is an implicit assumption that these qualitatively different sexes possess a natural order of priority with masculinity first and femininity second. 'Thus humanity is male and man defines woman not in herself but as relative to him; she is not regarded as an autonomous being' (De Beauvoir, 1988: 16). The reasons for this may well be partly historical and theological, involving acceptance of biblical idea that woman (Eve) was created after man (Adam) as a *means* of keeping Adam company and allowing Adam to produce offspring. This idea is however more complex, and insidious, than the acceptance of biblical stories. It is found throughout Western thought in the implicit assumption that women are men *minus* certain characteristics. For example, for Aristotle women are men without rationality; for Sigmund Freud (1856-1939) women are conceptualised as men lacking a penis (see Chapter 6): '[Freud] assumes that woman feels she is a mutilated man' (De Beauvoir, 1963: 63). Such discourses of female absence and inadequacy continue to flavour Western cultural assumptions about women and, for De Beauvoir, are the main barriers, in male and female thinking, to social change and justice.

De Beauvoir was working within the Existentialist tradition and she shares with other thinkers in this tradition an interest in 'the other'. The 'other' is the opposite to 'us' – those people and groups who are perceived by us to be different, alien, foreign or inferior – who, through their difference, allow us to understand ourselves better. De Beauvoir's analysis identifies women as humanity's 'other'. In other words, our cultural self-consciousness has been implicitly informed by the idea that '*we*' (men) derive our identity in comparison with '*them*' (women). This is not hard to discover when we consider the literature of the last two millennia and discover themes to the effect that we should value and applaud 'masculine values' (strength, courage, hardness) and denigrate and reject 'female values' (care, modesty and sensitivity) (e.g. Cicero, 2000: 44). Moreover, this orientation between 'us' and our 'other' informs our relationship with different, new and unfamiliar cultures. It is common to find appeal to 'our' 'masculine' culture, contrasted with the 'weaker' 'female' cultures. This was particularly true of European understandings of the 'orient', the Asian, Arab and Islamic world of the European imagination that was understood not in its own terms but as weak, fundamentally 'feminised' cultures addicted to luxury and vice (Said, 1978). Such is the potency and ubiquity of the ideology of 'the second sex'.

EXAMPLE

Hathaway's Case (1706) 12 Modern 556, 1516

Women's physical and economic vulnerability, their supposed 'proximity to nature', and various biblical passages, have meant that accusations of witchcraft are more commonly levelled at women. The motivation behind witchcraft accusations vary, but are generally reducible to the manipulation of popular fears. At some points law has been complicit with this manipulation; here judges were rather more suspicious.

One Hathaway, a most notorious rogue, feigned himself bewitched and deprived of his sight, and pretended to have fasted nine weeks together; and continuing, as he pretended, under this evil influence, he was advised, in order to discover the person supposed to have bewitched him, to boil his own water in a glass bottle till the bottle should break, and the first that came into the house after should be the witch; and that if he scratched the body of that person till he fetched blood, it would cure him; which being done, and a poor old woman coming by chance into the house, she was seized on as the witch, and obliged to submit to be scratched till the blood came; whereupon the fellow pretended to find present ease. The poor woman hereupon was indicted for witchcraft, and tried and acquitted at Surrey Assizes before Holt, Chief Justice, a man of no great faith in these things; and the fellow persisting in his [. . .] wicked contrivance, pretended still to be ill, and the poor woman, notwithstanding the acquittal, forced by the mob to suffer herself to be scratched by him. And this being discovered to be all imposition, an information was filed against him.

4b Nature as ideology

One way in which these myths about a hierarchy of the sexes have been sustained is their shrouding in arguments concerning what is 'natural'. These are arguments insisting that it is 'natural' for women to have a certain kind of status and certain kinds of roles, and that it would therefore be somehow 'artificial' if their role in society were to change. In fact, such appeals to 'natural' behaviours, roles and instincts, disguise oppression. Facts, states of affairs, do not translate directly into values concerning, for instance, a division of labour between the sexes. Nonetheless, various crude arguments concerning 'natural roles' in society are reproduced across the political and philosophical spectrum. One important variation of this kind of argument consists in locating women 'closer to nature' than men. Because of childbirth and because of the physical make-up of women necessary for childbirth, women are thereby located 'closer' to nature, as opposed to men located closer to the rational and therefore God. Women are 'naturally' equipped for nurturing and caring roles in the family, less rational and, importantly, more bound by the 'necessity' that characterises nature. Men are more capable of being free through the exercise of reason; women are enslaved by the structures and necessities of nature and are, therefore, less able to exercise freedom (see Aristotle, 1987: 508).

Nature and the natural also become tools of oppression when social expectations have met with modern notions of 'public health'. A relatively recent idea (emerging over the last few centuries) addressing the general conditions and health of the mass of (working) people, public health has been concerned with the threats posed by poverty and industrial and environmental pollution. These threats included a number of putative 'mental health problems', although such problems do not reflect the clinical criteria used today but rather concern a whole range of 'deviant' behaviours contrary to dominant social values. Promiscuity and prostitution were forms of deviance from norms that fell within the scope of public health, and the eighteenth and nineteenth centuries generated ideas of public health that justified the incarceration of women for such deviance (Luker, 1998). For example, the incarceration of prostitutes was a public health measure made on the basis of protecting the population from sexually transmitted diseases, the assumption being that it was prostitutes who were responsible for the spread of such diseases, not their customers (Bridgeman and Millns, 1998). At worst, sterilisation of women was justified on the basis of the public health benefits of 'deviant' women being prevented from reproducing. With complicity between society and law, women were identified as public health risks and robbed of reproductive autonomy, a step ultimately premised on what is thought to be 'natural'.

There are a number ways in which these appeals to the natural can be criticised and resisted, the main route being a distinction between sex (concerning physical reproductive characteristics) and gender (being structures of personality, associated with, but not determined by, sex). Sex may give individuals certain physical characteristics, but these do not entail that their gender is predetermined. Indeed, gender may be a far more flexible and variable thing than we are lead to believe. Using such a distinction allows resistance to simplistic appeals to nature and the natural and allows a more sophisticated psychology of identity.

EXAMPLE

Re D. (A Minor) [1976] 2 W.L.R. 279

The case concerned whether a young girl, with a severe but treatable mental condition, should be sterilised, and whether this decision could be made on the basis of agreement between the mother and a paediatrician. Here we see the Courts take a strong line against scientific wisdom and in favour of reproductive autonomy, at least to the extent that the girl's parent should wait until her daughter reaches eighteen to decide whether she has the capacity to make a decision about parenthood.

I cannot believe, and the evidence does not warrant the view, that a decision to carry out an operation of this nature performed for non-therapeutic purposes on a minor can be held to be within the doctor's sole clinical judgment. [. . .] A review of the whole of the evidence leads me to the conclusion that in a case of a child of 11 years of age, where the evidence shows that her mental and physical condition and attainments have already improved, and where her future prospects are as yet unpredictable, where the evidence also shows that she is unable as yet to understand and appreciate the implications of this operation and could not give a valid or informed consent, but the likelihood is that in later years she will be able to make her own choice, where, I believe, the frustration and resentment of realising (as she would one day) what had happened could be devastating, an operation of this nature is, in my view, contra-indicated. [. . .] For these, and for the other reasons to which I have adverted, I have come to the conclusion that this operation is neither medically indicated nor necessary, and that it would not be in D's best interest for it to be performed.

4c Identity politics

If the category 'women' has been determined by a group benefitting from structures of domination, should this very category be treated with suspicion? Allied to the separation of sex and gender, interrogation of this notion of 'woman' and 'women' yields fruitful ways of unpacking and understanding systems of domination. It is through these kinds of questions that we can chart the development of feminism as it is presently understood. This historical development is roughly divided into three 'waves' of feminism.

The first wave is a predominantly political grouping of the turn of the twentieth century driven by the Suffrage movement. This well organised, politically incendiary, and sometimes militant demand for voting rights was politically clear in its objectives, if philosophically limited. This was an inspirational movement with narrowly focussed goals, but it awaited the arrival of other social and economic changes following the First World War for the realisation of full enfranchisement. Voting had clear symbolic value as the final realisation of the Enlightenment and revolutionary goals of equal status and universal acknowledgement. The Suffrage movement did not, conversely, have a comprehensive view of how structures of inequality and oppressive thought were fundamentally enmeshed in culture and society, including within the idea of the natural.

The second wave emerged roughly in the 1960s and continues to have relevance today. This position sought to reclaim womanhood as a distinctive form of being entailing distinctive rights, rights not being met by the prevailing social and economic structures. Philosophically, this can be seen as a combination of biology and essentialism: there is a distinctive female sex with a distinctive essence and with distinctive needs. These translated into political demands for social equity and cultural liberty, and have supported a militant feminism encouraging women to seek self-determined forms of life. This was a radical position demanding concrete political change. It also involved fruitful use of the sex/gender division: 'The distinction between "sex" and "gender" was a key analytic of early Second Wave feminist theory; and many of the readings of Beauvoir [. . .] criticized her for inconsistency [in the use of these terms]' (Kruks, 2005: 295). However, even this distinction could not capture the subtleties of individual personality, individual need or individual situations within existing cultural and familial ties (Humm, 1992).

71

Out of these philosophical limitations a third wave of anti-essentialist feminism emerged seeking a more sophisticated understanding of female identity and the ways in which identity, commitment and social bonds are created and maintained. This is a philosophically clear position seeking a flexible account of how femininity and womanhood can be understood without the reduction of identity to antagonistic binary categories.

> During the 1990s, with the poststructuralist tide in feminist theorizing running high, the sex/gender distinction itself came to be put into question: biology was not a factual science but itself a highly politicized discursive practice; 'sex' was as much a social/discursive construct as 'gender'. (Kruks, 2005: 295)

Flowing from this is also an attendant loss of political focus. While this contemporary form of feminism reflects more accurately differences in identity and situation – i.e. the dangers of rigid classifications of identity – its political focus is less clear.

EXAMPLE

'UN Convention on the Elimination of All Forms of Discrimination against Women' (1979) Article 5

This international treaty outlines a range of rights (including reproductive rights and choice of nationality) and imposes a number of duties on states (including the revocation of all and any discriminatory law). In Article 5 it demands positive steps by the state to shape cultural perceptions of women, and cultivate acknowledgment that childrearing is not a solely, or naturally, female activity.

> States Parties shall take all appropriate measures: (a) To modify the social and cultural patterns of conduct of men and women, with a view to achieving the elimination of prejudices and customary and all other practices which are based on the idea of the inferiority or the superiority of either of the sexes or on stereotyped roles for men and women; (b) To ensure that family education includes a proper understanding of maternity as a social function and the recognition of the common responsibility of men and women in the upbringing and development of their children, it being understood that the interest of the children is the primordial consideration in all cases.

---

5 Freedom

Introduction

In this chapter we have not only described humans and patterns of human behaviour, we have also been concerned with what humans *should* do. That we have any responsibilities at all – individually and collectively – does depend upon at least one prior assumption, namely that we are free. Having obligations must presuppose the possibility of fulfilling those obligations. The most basic condition of fulfilling any obligation is being *free* to fulfil it. Any discussion of obligations and responsibilities, be they moral or legal, requires that we have some understanding of human freedom.

We live and act as humans assuming that, without evidence to the contrary, everything we do is freely chosen, that we are the 'author' of all our actions. Moreover, we hold other people *responsible* for their actions through judging and punishing them. Attribution of *responsibilities* varies on the basis of individuals and contexts; it is common to attribute social responsibilities from the moment an individual becomes an adult (though criminal responsibility begins earlier) and some responsibilities depend upon adults choosing to voluntarily enter into a legal relationship. However, it makes no sense to talk of responsibility if the individual is not the 'author' of their actions: there must be some kind of *causal* relationship between what we *intend* to do and what we *actually* do.

That humans are the causes of events in the world is clear. However, it is crucial in law to determine the extent to which individuals are responsible for the *outcomes* of their actions. Furthermore, law recognises degrees of culpability, degrees of causation and degrees of rationality among individuals and therefore degrees of responsibility. Yet areas of law attribute responsibility without evidence of freely chosen decisions; tort, the area law of most concerned with accidents, attributes causal responsibility without conscious responsibility. It also makes no sense to try to make human life predictable through laws if people's actions are not chosen and are therefore unpredictable both for ourselves and others. Nonetheless, social life and individual psychology are characterised by the uncertain and unpredictable.

Therefore, arguably the most important, and most vexed, point at which the idea of the person and law meet is in law's basic assumption that we are free and responsible, and in philosophy's insistence that human freedom is neither assured nor always coherent. Both law and philosophy are concerned with humans as subject to causal forces, but philosophy in particular has a wider concern with the causal compulsion arising from nature and the natural world, and the possibility that this might make ideas of freedom illusory or illegitimate.

5a Freedom as liberty

The competing facts and values of personhood inevitably meet at the idea of freedom. In Aristotle's work we are said to have an inheritance from nature, our sociability, which shapes our lives as humans but does not mean that we are slaves, robots or animals. We are more than the sum of our biological inheritance and our social context because we make choices, act, change ourselves and our environments, and can be – to a degree – the author of our own destiny. Aristotle, along with other thinkers, demonstrates a tendency to supplement the biological facts of the human species with the claim that we are freer than other parts of the natural world; physically and psychologically freer.

Philosophies that centralise the value of humans and persons have to give some account of how the capacity for free action can be reconciled with the mechanistic forces of nature. The special status of humans as part of, but in crucial respects different from, nature is assumed but not proven. Humanism takes this exceptional status as a core value, as do the Existentialists, who treat it as the meeting-point of human facts and values. Feminism (and in some respects humanism) aims to liberate individuals from ideas and social structures that limit the freedom of the individual to understand themselves in a way free from illegitimate assumptions.

These philosophies can, therefore, be linked together by way of the idea of freedom, but this does not mean that we are pursuing a single idea or concept. 'Freedom to choose actions', 'freedom from certain ways of thinking' and the 'freedom found in our collective lives together' can be seen as radically different kinds of ideas that do not cohere into any single idea of 'freedom'. The main connotation of freedom is that of the person living, acting and choosing with as few external social forces, as few constraints, as possible. So, living in a natural, wild, environment, while no doubt a hard life, would be free from social constraints and pressures. This can be opposed to living in a large, complex, social environment where laws, rules, expectations and demands are ubiquitous (see discussion of Max Weber, Chapter 6). For Aristotle, neither of these lives would be 'natural': we are political animals requiring fully social lives and also participating in the running of the state. There is then a middle-ground implicit in Aristotle (as in other legal and political philosophies). To the extent that we have to live socially we have no untrammelled freedom. However, social life does not have to be characterised purely by regulation, it is also characterised by participation.

It is law itself that makes this middle-ground possible. It provides the structure of our social lives together, but it also polices the boundaries between the public realm of collective action and the private realm of choice and self-creation. Law controls and oppresses, but it also makes space for freedom. How these lines are drawn and policed depends upon changing ideas within and beyond law (Alldridge and Brants (eds), 2001), but law remains a crucial means of balancing the relinquishing of certain kinds of freedom (complete natural freedom) with the creation of other kinds of freedom (a private sphere of choices and self-realisation).

This might encourage us to abandon the problematic term freedom in favour of 'liberty'. 'Freedom' is closely associated with the untrammelled freedom of the natural world, whereas liberty is much more naturally associated with the *freedoms* that are found in, or granted by, the state. Liberty encompasses the humanist and revolutionary idea of the constitutional state as the synthesis of natural freedoms and social expectations; the liberties granted by a constitutional state are arguably the closest that humans (as citizens) will now come to freedom in the modern world. The merit of this division also allows us a critical perspective on law. The liberties granted by the state may still fall short of what we consider to be our natural freedoms. After all, the state may offer or create liberties incompletely, it may draw the line between public and private badly; and liberty is still not freedom in the fullest sense. Anarchism, the political position that always places freedoms above legal liberties, reminds us that there is more to freedom than what we are granted by the state. Furthermore, while anarchy might appear unattractive from the perspective of well-regulated states, it is a competing claim about freedom to place alongside the complex, and perhaps repressive, liberties of the modern state.

EXAMPLE

'EU Council Framework Decision of 13 June 2002 on Combating Terrorism' (2002/475/JHA)

Terrorism has become a central preoccupation of states since the terrorist attacks of 2001 on New York. While it is often said that 'one man's terrorist is another man's freedom fighter', the freedom fought for in these attacks was unclear. In fact, the goals of terrorists are complex and often unclear, and accordingly, definitions of 'terrorism' have to separate the (wide and unclear) goals of terrorists from their (more narrowly defined) immediate aims. The European Union offers a definition of terrorist aims and specific acts linked to those aims.

'Article 1 Terrorist offences [are offences with the aim of]: seriously intimidating a population, or / unduly compelling a Government or international organisation to perform or abstain from performing any act, or / seriously destabilising or destroying the fundamental political, constitutional, economic or social structures of a country or an international organisation [. . .].

[Terrorist offences can encompass]: (a) attacks upon a person's life which may cause death; (b) attacks upon the physical integrity of a person; (c) kidnapping or hostage taking; (d) causing extensive destruction to a Government or public facility, a transport system, an infrastructure facility, including an information system, a fixed platform located on the continental shelf, a public place or private property likely to endanger human life or result in major economic loss [. . .].

◼ 5b Freedom as rationality

To identify freedom and rationality is one of the most important threads of the Western philosophical tradition. In essence, because of a capacity for certain kinds of thinking, it can be claimed that we are or can be separated from the natural world. If the natural world is bound by inexorable causal links (that effect always follows cause), human thinking, in contrast, is not bound by such links. This makes us not only capable of unique achievements but also divides us decisively from the rest of the natural world and the universe.

There are two ways to understand this equating of rationality and freedom. The first is a purely philosophical argument: free will, possessed exclusively by humans, is the one crucial exception to the otherwise purely mechanistic structures of the cosmos. The second is an ethical and political argument: that we as humans have a responsibility not only to realise the distinct potential given to us by reason, we must also pursue social structures and collective ways of living that are rational, because there is a responsibility to create social environments where as many people as possible have the opportunity to cultivate and exercise their reason.

The philosophical argument is by no means a compelling position at first glance. There are pragmatic reasons to want to exempt humans from the physical world: to attribute rationality and freedom to them because this allows us to respond to human action on the basis that it is chosen action. Without this assumption, persuasion and justification would be meaningless. Conversely, there is no way to prove that humans exist, physically or mentally, outside the causal chains of nature. One worldview assumes a mechanistic universe; the other assumes a universe with a special exception contained within it. There are no other means by which these two claims could be adjudicated. We have to assume the existence of one or the other, but could never disprove the other position without relying on the assumption that we began with: that *everything* is caused *or* mechanistic causes do not apply to human rationality. The 'compatibilist' position, which argues that the two positions are reconcilable (see Flew (ed.), 1979: 125–6), does not resolve these tensions; it says that everything is 'caused' (in one sense), but some things (many human actions) are not 'caused' (in another sense), because they flow from the choice of the individual. This position is defensible to the extent that it says that we should treat the word 'choice' as meaningful – some acts can be categorised as 'chosen' others not – while allowing strict causal determinism to hold more generally.

Law is equally equivocal because it does not draw a dividing line between caused and free actions but rather maintains – in some limited contexts – that what is experienced as a choice is sometimes a compulsion. The problems generated by this pragmatism are most obvious in criminal law, where we hold individuals to be responsible for their acts and are therefore candidates for rehabilitative (reformative) and retributive (desert-based) punishment. There is no opportunity in criminal law to argue that the defendant was acting out the consequences of causal forces outside their control. There is, for example, no defence of genetic predisposition to act in a certain way and limited chances of a successful defence of mental illness. Of course, even if law accepted a purely causal, involuntary, account of all and every crime, this would not wholly invalidate criminal law and punishment: legal processes are causal interventions that bring about a different set of effects that may be socially desirable (i.e. the incarceration of dangerous individuals or the deterrence of others). In fact, as a set of causes and effects in its own right we are no doubt better with criminal law than without it. Nonetheless, this pragmatic assumption of freedom does not square with some of the more benign therapeutic ideas of punishment (that punishment allows re-form and fundamental change in an individual), nor do they make sense of retribution (proportionate punishment) where the state is thought to have a duty to punish in order to communicate its disapproval of certain kinds of acts. Punishment is senseless if disapproval will make no difference to the actions that people will take in the future.

EXAMPLE

United States v *Dusky* (1960) 362 US 402 (Quoted in Arrigo, 2003: 57)

Whether someone is able to be prosecuted for a crime depends upon certain minimum assumptions about the rationality and freedom of the individual. Articulated in the United States in terms of 'competency to stand trial', the test of competency is derived from the Dusky *case and its demand that the defendant have a sense of what is a stake in the case (even if they do not fully understand it) and have enough cognitive capacity to participate in a trial (even if they have no wish to participate). It is a short, and potentially contradictory, test.*

It is not enough for the district judge to find that the defendant [is] oriented to time and place and [has] some recollection of events. [T]he test must be whether [one] has sufficient present ability to consult with [one's] lawyer with a reasonable degree of rational understanding and whether [one] has a rational as well as factual understanding of the charges against [oneself].

5c Freedom as autonomy

If we conceive of ourselves as free in the sense of 'the freedom of nature' or 'freedom from causal determinism', we are likely to run up against limitations, barriers and incoherence. Everywhere there are limits on what we can do; at some time or another we realise that, in the past, we felt we could choose otherwise in our actions but were mistaken. Aspiring to freedom in these senses is to ask for a different world where we are not social beings and not natural beings but gods choosing everything, including what we choose. This pride in humanity is understandable – we are rational and want to feel as though we are not slaves – but not philosophically defensible. What philosophers have tried to defend, in a less ambitious line of enquiry, is the idea we that we are each autonomous: sources of law. We can impose rules upon ourselves (when we act legally or morally), and can make decisions about what would be right for everyone.

This hints at excessive pride or hubris. It suggests that we are each law-makers and law-givers, and it threatens a paradox. We are free because we are each able make laws; if laws *constrain* action then, if we are law-makers, we are sources of constraints, not freedom. However, separating freedom as *liberty* and freedom as *rationality* at this point makes the claims about autonomy more intelligible. If we are rational we should be able to make our actions coherent (as opposed to impulsive patterns of behaviour), choosing desirable objectives and recognising limits to our objectives. To make laws that we apply to ourselves is to choose a coherent, and therefore desirable, life rather than one that is at the mercy of whim and accident. If we have exchanged absolute freedom for the liberties of the state, then there must be limits placed upon our actions, and it is better that those limits arise from our own freely chosen constraints rather than wholly external ('heteronomous') impositions of law. So, the ideal of autonomy is partly negative: we have to reject the twin tyrannies of an incoherent life at the mercy of fate, and a life at the mercy of laws chosen by other people. The ideal is also positive: with the use of reason we become the author of our actions, we use laws to liberate and not constrain ourselves, and we thereby become *sovereign* individuals both free and law-giving.

These ideas of autonomy, given their fullest realisation in the work of Immanuel Kant (1724-1804), provide foundations for understanding law and the state as a whole. First, and broadly, the state and law-givers should work on the assumption that individuals have the capacity to be autonomous; to assume otherwise is to treat individuals as slaves or automatons. Second, and more specifically, if the laws that individuals are imposing on themselves are rational, then they are not only coherent for that individual but should exhibit coherence with the laws that every other individual discovers through rational deliberation. In other words, rational laws are the same whosoever lights upon them in their own thinking and deliberating. On this basis, the state can make laws that have universality (everyone would choose them) and absolutely binding force (because they are founded on rational principles that every rational being can or does subscribe to). Here we have a potential solution to the problems created by freedom as liberty and rationality. Laws are not contrary to what is *natural* because they can be said to arise from capacities arising naturally within us: the capacity for rationality. In addition, rationality does not lead to freedom because it immediately exempts us from cause and effect: it leads to freedom because, through law-making, we choose something other than a life of chance, accident and obedience to others.

Does this provide a final meeting point of fact and value? Freedom as autonomy suggests that we *are* rational beings and what we *should* do is act as rational beings by imposing coherent laws upon ourselves. The role of the state is to create laws that coherently combine liberty and rationality. Such an idea, in different guises, has informed much thinking about law and society in the modern era (see Chapter 4); and as a starting-point for both the facts of law (what it should contain) and the value of law (why we have law at all) it is one that has an attractive, if thin, conception of humans, their freedom, and their potential, at its heart. It is a starting-point, however, that can be reread and reconsidered by all of the currents of thought addressed in this chapter. Does it make sense of our biology and our psychology? It is far removed from our natural instincts and our potential for irrationality, but it also accords with ideas of a social and political animal demanding a well ordered state. Also, does it fully encompass the value-driven ideas of the human found in humanism and feminism? The drive for autonomy, on the face of it, should not generate the blindspots and inequalities to which humanism and feminism draw attention. However, it certainly involves ambitious claims about reason – the universality of certain ideas and the capacity for the mind to understand its own workings – that are difficult to maintain if we take a more historical perspective on what has counted as 'rational' in human society (Chapter 6). In sum, autonomy gives rise to a foundation for law, but at the expense of a problematic idea of the person and their rationality.

EXAMPLE

First National Bank of Boston v Bellotti, 435 U.S. 765 (1978) United States Supreme Court

'Legal persons' are groups of individuals treated as a single individual for the purposes of gaining collective legal powers and legal duties. The idea of the personhood of a corporation was first used in Roman law (Lee, 2007: 103). The 'legal person' is interesting because it is a person but not a biological human; we can ascribe agency and interests to it, but not needs and vulnerabilities. This appears to be the logical conclusion of taking autonomy as the most important dimension of law: the capacity to make decisions and choices is given priority over biology. The US's Fourteenth Amendment ensures equal applicability of constitutional rights to all persons. In the present case, it was held that constitutional protections should be granted, though not without limits, to corporations.

[T]he Massachusetts Supreme Judicial Court held that the First Amendment rights of a corporation are limited to issues that materially affect its business, property, or assets. The court rejected appellants' claim that the statute abridges freedom of speech in violation of the First and Fourteenth Amendments. The court found its answer in the contours of a corporation's constitutional right, as a 'person' under the Fourteenth Amendment, not to be deprived of property without due process of law. Distinguishing the First Amendment rights of a natural person from the more limited rights of a corporation, the court concluded that 'whether its rights are designated "liberty" rights or "property" rights, a corporation's property and business interests are entitled to Fourteenth Amendment protection. [. . .] [A]s an incident of such protection, corporations also possess certain rights of speech and expression under the First Amendment.'

Questions

Section 1

● The word person stems from *persona* meaning 'mask'. Are we, to the extent that we are social beings, masking or hiding our natural human selves?

● To what extent should we distinguish ourselves from animals? Is it plausible to see ourselves as distinct from animals when we share the same kinds of biological needs?

- If our most basic, survival, needs are biological ones such as food and shelter, is there a moral and/or legal obligation to provide these for all humans?
- 'Humanity as a classification is useful, but humanity as a *value* is incoherent because it presumes that we can distinguish our behaviour from that of all other animals.' Consider this in relation to the prohibition of crimes against humanity.

Section 2

- If humans are 'political animals' in Aristotle's sense of the term, does this entail that everyone has the right, the need or the duty to engage in political and legal decision-making? Are we also 'legal animals'?
- Consider the meaning of 'virtue'. To what extent does this seem something to aspire to or cultivate, or conversely, something repressive?
- Consider whether your values are dependent upon on your background or upon your own freely chosen decisions about how to live. Are these separable?

Section 3

- Does humanity's history – including both great achievements and great inhumanity – provide any guide to our obligations as individuals? Does humanity's history offer any evidence of (moral or psychological) progress?
- Which of the two revolutionary maxims is most coherent or defensible? 'Liberty, fraternity and equality' or 'life, liberty and the pursuit of happiness'?
- Do we have obligations to those on other continents? If not, where do the limits of obligation end? If so, are those obligations premised on fraternity, i.e. a fundamental bond between humans?

Section 4

- Does our culture characterise people as generally 'lacking fulfilment'? How is this lack understood – spiritual, material or physical? – and does it take different forms for men and women?
- Has our culture made feminism redundant (e.g. through equal opportunity laws) or has our culture, rather, discredited feminism by implying that it demands too much or the wrong things?
- Are we born with gender qualities? Does *gender* on the one hand, and *sex* on the other, have legal consequences not possessed by the opposing term? Consider reproductive rights and freedom of expression.

Section 5

- Is the 'liberty' found in citizenship superior or inferior to 'natural freedom'?
- Does rationality make us free? If so, can freedom be understood in a wholly 'internal' or 'mental' way without reference to human *action*?
- Is there a difference in degree, or in kind, between the capacity for responsibility found in children and in adults?

Concepts and methods: Ideas and ideology

Ideas and ideology

Our main objective in this chapter, and book, is to clarify certain ideas. Ideas are both our starting-point and end-point. We have a common language in which we find and express ideas; and we face a philosophical challenge to clarify those ideas for accurate understanding of law. In this sense we need to keep at the forefront of our thinking that, while 'setting down the appearances' is a good basis for philosophy (see Chapter 1) it is a preliminary task in the pursuit of clear discussion and analysis.

Note that we have used the terms 'ideas' and 'concepts' interchangeably. For the purposes of this chapter no difference needed to be drawn. However, there is a philosophical distinction to be drawn between ideas – meaning anything mentally, and privately, owned by thinking beings – and concepts which are *categories* shared, publically, by language users. Accordingly, emphasis is placed in this book on concepts: shared categories used for thinking and debating.

Ideas can be more than something we possess or share. They can be treated as entire systems of thought and action. The various 'isms', from conservatism, to communism, to environmentalism, represent political positions, *ideologies*, as much as philosophical ideas or systems. They are 'ideologies' in a neutral sense of being systems of ideas or structures of discussion. They are also potentially ideologies in the pejorative sense: having a rigid hold on the way people think and deliberately resistant to critical interrogation.

Not all ideologies purport to be fully rounded, complete, philosophies. Nonetheless, ideologies offer a lens through which otherwise disparate and unconnected facts can be filtered and structured. Many ideologies create 'orthodoxies' that suggests that the truth can only be found in a particular way. Orthodoxy has benefits over 'epistemological pluralism' (the idea that there are 'many truths'). After all, 'the truth' is something we take to be a unitary thing, not something allowing contradiction or variation, but this kind of orthodoxy can also be unhelpful and reductive (it provides simple explanations where complex explanations are needed).

Analysis of law and laws is not always well served by ideological analysis. For example, to see law through a 'materialist' lens (i.e. that only the material form and consequences of law has reality) does not do justice to the ideas, concepts and perceptions that make up the non-material dimensions of law (see Chapter 6). Equally, to see law as the pale reflection of an ideal (i.e. justice) may neglect the value and everyday legal decisions and the normal, cultural and social, activities within which law is made *real*. The 'life of the law' has been described as experience, meaning, among other things, that it is not reducible to a single process or set of ideas: it is an evolving social practice.

Objective and subjective

This is a distinction with a long philosophical heritage and which also features frequently in legal philosophy. Roughly we, as conscious humans, are subjects: we are *subjects of* experience and we are *subject to* forces and influences outside ourselves. The non-conscious world consists of *objects* of various kinds: i.e. the physical objects which are the objects of our experience. The division is important but nonetheless unstable: other subjects (people) may appear to us as objects; objects may be subject to forces outside themselves. In fact, some philosophers have rejected the existence of one or other of the side of the classification. Idealists, for example, argue that objects only exist as ideas for subjects (see Kant, 1929: 345); behaviourists encourage us to replace discussion of subjective mental states with descriptions of behaviour (see Winch, 1958: 80f).

Dividing objective from subjective is important for revealing humans' distinctive relationship with the world. Whatever the status and power of the human mind, it certainly means that we cannot be adequately understood using the vocabulary of the physical sciences alone; but the meaning of the division between objective and subjective in law is often context-specific: the division as it is used in contract law may vary from that found in criminal law. In addition, law often involves *deciding* what someone's subjective state of mind is, rather than taking their word for it. Making a decision as to what was going on in someone's mind is clearly difficult, but law contains processes for attributing certain types of thought (e.g. that of a reasonable person). This stems from the need to achieve certainty in law, and because individuals may not be a reliable guide to their own motives, intentions and beliefs.

Uses of 'nature'

'Nature' is not only a component of some natural law theories (see Chapter 3), but has been a perennial component of legal and political debate. Appeal to nature allows us to overcome the fact/value division or reconfigure it into something less rigid; it also allows criticism of law as 'unnatural'. Here 'nature' is more than simply the sum of knowledge we have about the natural world, it is a key concept used to distinguish the goods determined by nature from goods determined by human convention. The basic good of survival may have a greater claim on us than political rights; conversely, if we are, by nature, political animals, both basic survival needs and civil and political rights should have equal legitimacy.

As with appeal to *human* nature, we should be cautious of the use of nature to bolster arguments concerning what form law should take and the use of nature to overcome the fact/value distinction. Nature is a way of bringing human goods and/or a good life into legal and political discourse. It is also a way of insisting that all law and politics should take a particular shape. This is a far more problematic claim. The natural is often contrasted with the *rational*. However, in the natural law school this contrast is denied (Finnis, 2011: 29-33). The natural is said to be rational: the fundamental structure of humans is such that it generates incontrovertible, rational and reasonable, value claims.

Associating nature with God, other than in that strand of natural law associated with monotheistic religion, is not a necessary component on natural law theory. Natural law is unified in its concern with the necessary and the rational, not in identifying obligation with God's will. Nevertheless, it is common to hear echoes of theology in natural law and, to a degree, positivism. Law, like God, demands obedience, even where the justification for its rules may be unclear to us (Austin, 1995). This points to a paradox shared by theology and some legal philosophy. God's rules must be followed. However, are God's rules good *because they are willed by God*, or are they willed by God *because they are good*? Accepting the first argument places authority over and above goodness; the second makes goodness something higher than God's authority. Neither conclusion is satisfactory. One makes obedience, rather than morality, central to religion and theology, the other makes God subservient to other, higher, moral principles. Equally, law demands and we obey, but is it the nature of *obedience itself*, or the *reasons for obedience*, that make law 'binding'? The resolution of this paradox demands attention to the nature of legal rules (Chapter 5) and the 'normativity' of law (Chapter 6).

Reflection and self-reflection

Underlying many of the ideas discussed so far is the simple fact that humans reflect on themselves. We as a species have always been of interest to ourselves, and we each have a unique perspective on humanity. Such self-reflection and self-consciousness are at the root of humans' claim to knowledge and truth. Be it the work of the human sciences or personal self-reflection, reflection is central to philosophy in the sense that knowledge (truths about the world) seem to be possible by *thinking* about the world. This is not equivalent to day-dreaming: it is looking for knowledge in what we perceive and how we perceive. For example, we sometimes come to realise or understand something fully, not through an additional piece of information, but because over time we 'see' something that we didn't see before. Equally, reflecting on the gap between our expectations and reality is an important precursor to understanding. If something seems strange, confused, anomalous, then in all likelihood this same 'dissonance' will have been experienced by other people. These dissonances are the route to further, deeper, reflection.

These kinds of self-reflection depend upon the fact that we seem to have privileged access to our own thoughts. What we think about is distinctly ours and not immediately accessible to other people. Self-reflection encompasses being aware of what we perceive (e.g. shapes, colours and movement around us), it is also consideration of what made us do certain things or behave in a certain way. Self-reflection is a way of clarifying our perceptions, which for various reasons may be unclear or deceptive. There is no 'right way' to reflect, other than carefully and in a sustained way: perceiving ourselves and the world is something which takes time (not least because the world is characterised by time and change). Note that what we anticipate often has an impact on what we see; we always use assumptions and expectations when we reflect, even upon our own thinking. While we cannot escape from many of our fundamental assumptions and prejudices, we can try to be aware of them.

The idea of a 'reflective equilibrium' is simply that we should compare the outcome of our theories with our intuitions about what the right answer to a problem should look like. This methodological tool is an attempt to balance our theorising and our intuitions in order to avoid reaching counterintuitive or unobtainable conclusions about our political or moral questions. It is a way of avoiding the grip of ideology on our thinking.

Reflective equilibrium is a way of adhering to the maxim 'ought implies can'. If we are to make decisions about what is obligatory, such obligations must, at the very least, be obtainable. More specifically, seeking reflective equilibrium is a way of ensuring that ideas that look universal or unconditionally obligatory do not neglect the particular and the local. Certain ideas about moral obligations (particularly those associated with utilitarianism, see Chapter 3) aspire to a 'scientific' account of morality using a measurable index of what is valuable (namely happiness). However, the calculations that it employs to gauge happiness, and the very idea of happiness itself, cannot be claimed as 'universal' without ignoring or at least downplaying different cultures' ideas of happiness and the means of achieving happiness.

The idea of reflective equilibrium was used by John Rawls as a dimension of his theorising about justice and fairness (Rawls, 1999: 18). Rawls held that while it is possible to propose theories about justice and the state which appear persuasive, these have to be tested against other moral principles that we hold. Where there is tension or contradiction (either in the moral principles or the theory), one will have to be amended or compromised in order to '[yield] principles which match our considered judgments duly pruned and adjusted' (1999: 18). Such a process ensures that neither our theories, nor our cherished moral principles, escape scrutiny when we are attempting to determine substantial moral or political commitments.

Further reading

Aristotle's *Politics* (various editions) is both readily intelligible and essential to understanding Western legal and political thought. Jonathan Glover's *Humanity* (2001) along with Tony Davies' *Humanism* (1997) are useful, and wide-ranging, introductions to the significance of humanity. For an analysis of personhood in legal contexts see Ohlin (2002); Robert C. Solomon's *Continental Philosophy Since 1750* (1988) remains unparalleled as a clear introduction to the significance of selves and selfhood in twentieth-century continental philosophy. For a wider ranging historical account of personhood, combining the legal and philosophical, see Donald Kelley's *The Human Measure* (1990).

Martha Nussbaum's *The Fragility of Goodness* (1986) is a comprehensive account of how the Ancient Greeks combined questions of personhood and ethics. Bridgeman and Millns' *Feminist Perspectives on Law* (1998) is an excellent compendium of debates and materials on law and feminism. On the methodological issues raised in this chapter, short, clear, descriptions can be found in Baggini and Fosl's *The Philosopher's Toolkit: A compendium of philosophical concepts and methods* (2010).

Visit **www.mylawchamber.co.uk/riley** to access tools to help you develop and test your knowledge of legal philosophy including Podcasts on leading thinkers and theories, discussion questions, diagrams showing interrelations between concepts, and weblinks

3　Good

Introduction

This chapter builds upon ideas of the human, the person and the relationship between facts and values. The idea of goodness bridges the *facts* of human life and the *values* we associate with law and does this through a range of ideas, principles and properties. These are familiar ideas: that 'it is always good for humans to do *x*'; 'it is always good for humans to possess *x*'; 'a good human life demands *x*'. They nonetheless require careful analysis and closer attention to the values associated with law and with persons.

A number of different philosophical ideas invoke the language of goodness. Ideas of 'a good life', the 'instrumentally good' and the 'intrinsically good' – once distinguished – help to make sense of what law is and what law aims to achieve. These ideas point, respectively, to law creating a world where a good life is possible, law being an instrument for bringing about human happiness, and law being a point at which facts and obligations meet.

A 'good human life' is something that law might assist us in maintaining or achieving. This in itself is a complex claim, but the relationship between 'good' and 'law' also shifts between ideas of 'what is good *about legality*' and 'what *goods* law should provide'. These are different kinds of questions, and they each touch arguments about the person, encountered in the last chapter. Legality itself is instrumentally good (i.e. useful) because it creates a world where other human goods are possible. Agreeing what these *further* goods are depends upon our view of humans and persons. The essentially social animal of Aristotle's philosophy needs both a good society and personal virtue; the autonomous person of the Enlightenment needs to be free from the slavery of other people's will.

We may also want to argue that law as a whole is intrinsically good: law is not just useful, it is inherently valuable. Such inherent value might be said to arise from the value we attach to the person. Persons could not exist without legal recognition, and to that extent alone, law might be intrinsically justified. If, conversely, our view of the human centres on the free, natural, individual then law might be considered, at best, a 'necessary evil' providing basic securities rather than being inherently valuable.

These different uses of the word good are divided – philosophically and in ordinary language – between the objective and the subjective. Many legal and political disputes could be resolved if there were a single good way for all humans to be, or for there to be a shared, comprehensive, list of things that it would be good for all humans to have. An *objective* standard of what is good for us as humans would undoubtedly make legal and political decision-making easier: there would be unassailable demands made by us as individuals, and clear aspirations for us as a society. While philosophically desirable, it is also difficult, and perhaps morally questionable, to insist upon an objective good for humans. If freedom (understood as liberty or as autonomy) is a crucial dimension of individual and social being, then any claim about the, objectively necessary, ingredients of a good life is unattractive. It may, by the same token, be good for individuals to determine, subjectively, their own interests, objectives and ideals, however much prevailing ideas of 'a good life' may run contrary to them. Moreover, human lives are always more complex – more historically and culturally 'situated' – then a template for a good life would seem to allow. What people desire or demand varies between cultures and has changed over time. In the face of this variability, a template for human fulfilment seems artificial and subjective preferences much more central.

Related to, but distinct from, this division between objective and subjective is the philosophical division between the 'intrinsically good' and the 'instrumentally good'. This distinction is subtle but important. Colloquially, we are more likely to talk of 'good' in instrumental terms (e.g. that 'vegetables are good *for* health', or a particular job is 'good *for* realising professional fulfilment'). In these terms vegetables and jobs are instrumentally good, but they are related to intrinsic goods: health and fulfilment. For something to be intrinsically good means that no further justification is needed in terms of what they are good *for*: they are desirable *states* that are to be valued regardless of any further consequences that flow from them. The distinction is not always easy to draw. For instance, 'unassailably good things for humans to have', for example friends or knowledge, could be valuable in instrumental terms (they *allow* humans to be fulfilled or happy), or something good in themselves (their desirability requires no further justification).

Along with the intrinsically and instrumentally good, philosophy has long been concerned with 'a good life'. Philosophical discussion of a good life often begins with Aristotle's view of the human, and the conditions of human flourishing. For that reason it should be understood in a 'holistic' sense of 'a life worth living' or 'successfully lived'; it is less directly a matter of living a *morally good* life, although this is important for Aristotle, Plato and others (below). A good life is the meeting point of a number of ethical, political and legal discussions, and to make sense of this idea would clarify a range of difference debates in law and beyond. Both of the previous distinctions should be applied to this idea. Of those philosophers who think the idea of 'a good life' meaningful, it is taken to be a life that is *intrinsically* desirable by an *objective* standard. On this account, while there are sound reasons to associate the evaluation of a life as a whole with the fulfilment of one's subjective ideas and perceptions, it is maintained that 'a good life' is a holistic assessment of human flourishing based on objective standards. Our fleeting experiences of happiness or pleasure are inadequate to evaluate whether living a particular kind of life is intrinsically good.

A 'good life' is the most obvious example of an intrinsic good: we do not hope for a flourishing life because it brings other benefits, it is the *realisation* of everything we might want to pursue. Thus, together 'a good life' and the 'intrinsically good' provide a bridge between fact and value. The claim that 'all humans desire a good life' does not require further justification for it to justify our seeking a good life: the goal is intrinsically valuable. Put in more abstract terms, discovering what is intrinsically good would be to discover what is *obligatory*. If anything provides humans with their values, it is their need and desire to live a good life, and this can be held to be 'self-evident' or 'axiomatic' when we discuss values. It would be senseless to state that we know what is intrinsically good and, simultaneously, say that there is no reason to act upon it, that there is still some further justification needed to bring about or maintain this good state of affairs. Put strongly, to identify something as 'intrinsically good' is to identify it as 'obligatory' if 'obligation' is to mean anything at all.

We will encounter a number of claims with this kind of form. Kant (Chapter 4) treats having a 'good will' as intrinsically good, and a person has a good will if, and only if, they act on their obligations rather than their interests. John Finnis treats our rational and practical pursuit of a good life – one reconciling a network of intrinsic goods – as an irreducible, axiomatic, *fact* of human existence and sees this as an incontestable component of any possible discussion of obligations. This is, nonetheless, a *network* of intrinsic goods, not a single idea of 'the good': 'no determinate meaning can be found for the term "good" that would allow any commensurating and calculus of good to be made in order to settle those basic questions of practical reason which we call "moral" questions' (2011: 115).

However, we will also encounter as many theorists defending the crucial importance of instrumental goods. Instrumental, subjective or 'context dependent' conceptions of what is good are much more flexible ways to determine our obligations. Personal safety is good, and payment of a ransom to a kidnapper is a means to that end. Paying ransoms is neither good in itself nor obligatory, but there are *good reasons* for paying ransoms, because they are means or instruments for maintaining personal safety. Thus, those philosophies that equate 'good' and 'obligatory' are challenged by utilitarian philosophies that prioritise 'good' in terms of the pursuit of human happiness. They would wish to say that obligations arise from discerning what is useful for bringing about happiness. This position has been attractive to lawmakers and judges because of its consequentialism (its interest in bringing about good ends) and its equal reluctance to commit to ideas of the intrinsically good.

Consequentialism is a useful tool for legal reasoning. While law is not, in any direct way, engineered to manufacture happiness, it seeks the best possible outcomes without committing to a single conception of what 'best possible' would mean in all and every circumstance. Substituting 'happiness' with 'welfare', we are closer to the kinds of outcomes law aspires to. We want law to contribute towards people's general welfare, not against it; we want law to contribute to people's flourishing not crush it. Furthermore, by substituting 'best possible' with 'least oppressive' we are closer to the kind of *instrument* law seeks to be. Law, as an instrument, compares well with other styles of 'social management' and 'social control'. Forms of militarism or tyranny are routes to social order, but legally regulated states are the least oppressive means to this end given law's balancing of individual and collective interests. For utilitarians, and consequentialists more generally, lives lived under law are not just stable, predictable and ordered. They are lives where welfare is maintained and oppression is minimised.

This chapter is an introduction to some philosophies using goodness in competing ways. We should note however that these approaches will be confronted, or indeed undermined, by those philosophies discussed in Chapter 4, which aim to make 'right' more important than 'good' in discussion of law.

1 The good

Introduction

Different uses of 'good' are in evidence in ordinary language. For instance, it makes a significant difference whether we are seeking to understand the word that is opposite to *bad* or opposite to *evil*. 'Good *versus* bad' is our basic evaluative opposition; it allows us to express evaluations in a limitless range of different contexts. 'Good *versus* evil' has theological origins, and while it can be used as part of moral evaluations (especially moral condemnation), its most common philosophical use is in contexts where the will of God is at issue ('evil' is where the will of God is contravened in a radical way). Moreover, ordinary English language provides us with good as a predicate (a property) and as a predicate modifier (an evaluation of a property). I can say that a particular person is a good person (they have the property of moral goodness) and that they are a good swimmer (they not only have the property of being able to swim, but swim in a good way). Some of these complexities are cut away by the philosophical idea of '*the* good'.

'The good' can be described as that end-point or objective of human actions which is intrinsically desirable and can be gauged objectively. This end-point is the summation of what all humans seek in their activities, so in that sense it has *some* subjective elements (we seek it individually when we act), but is ultimately objective. The good is an external standard of what I should need, desire or strive to achieve in my actions. This proposition finds its most important articulation at the beginning of Aristotle's main work on ethics, the *Nicomachean Ethics*: 'Every art and every inquiry, and similarly every action and choice, is thought to aim at some good; and for this reason the good has rightly been declared to be that at which all things aim' (1987: 363). This proposition recurs in various forms in different philosophies, and is given various foundations. It takes the form of all humans seeking success in their actions or, ultimately, all humans seeking happiness in their actions. It can be said to be founded on our 'rational nature', on God's plan for the universe or on the distillation of all of our political and moral ideas. For Aristotle, the proposition 'all things aiming for the good' represents the basic, logical, point that everything we do aims at success or completion, and this is true of every activity from the simplest tasks to living a human life (Barnes (ed.), 1995).

To begin to unravel the potential contained in this idea of 'the good', we can consider it in the light of previous discussions of the intrinsic versus the instrumental and the objective versus the subjective. Use of the good suggests that all uses of the word 'good' point to a single common denominator of goodness. For example, that everything we call 'good' contributes in some way to human happiness; all *instrumental* goods are said to contribute to a single *intrinsic* good. Or, more contentiously, the fact that we attribute 'goodness' to people, things and activities could be used to suggest that every thing, and not just every person, has an *ideal* which they can fulfil or fail to fulfil, a standard by which they can be judged. This way, all *subjective* ideas of what is good are subservient to a single *objective* good. In both cases, a single goal – human happiness or a universal standard of fulfilment – is posited.

If it makes sense to talk about the good as a single goal or standard it is undoubtedly a *value*. We use good in an instrumental sense to make factual claims about what will be *best* to achieve certain ends. However, when we judge an act as intrinsically, or objectively or morally good we give it an unequivocally positive evaluation. This kind of unequivocal evaluation is a powerful contribution to moral and legal debate. Identifying the unequivocally desirable is to identify what all social institutions and activities – 'every art and every inquiry' in Aristotle's terms – should aspire to. If we were assured that something was intrinsically good, we would have every reason to believe it desirable and obligatory at all times.

At the same time 'the good' is a concept which can be described as 'thin'. It is thin because it is applicable to all and any moral debate and in a range of situations, but is also extremely general. This could be distinguished from 'thicker' moral concepts such as courage or courtesy which, while clearly terms of approval, have a much closer relationship with the environment in which they are used. One culture's courage is another's aggression; one culture's courtesy is another's repression. No such variability should attach to 'the good'. It remains good whoever and wherever it is discovered.

On this basis, a further philosophical distinction can be added: whether our use of good is 'context dependent'. The instrumentally good may be context dependent:

theft is a good way to gain money quickly, but *in many contexts* it is a dangerous and uncertain route to gain money. The intrinsically good should not be context dependent. For example, it has always and everywhere been good to have health and friends. Those theories which reject context dependency can be described as 'monistic': the good is indivisible, timeless and unchanging. As a philosophical manoeuvre, monism is closely associated with Plato and his argument that there is a single ideal for all things, including humans. The merit of this appeal to a single good is that there is no problem whatsoever overcoming division between fact and value; value will always predominate in so far as there is always, on this view, a (good or ideal) form that things should take. This can be contrasted with pluralistic positions wherein the good is context-dependent (dependent upon who and where we are) and divisible (there is a hierarchy of goods). John Stuart Mill (see below) might be considered a defender of the 'divisibility' position, arguing that there are qualitatively 'higher goods' *versus* 'lower goods', roughly divided such that the higher goods are those that are distinctive to humans and the lower goods those that we share with animals.

1a The human good

Appealing to the good allows legal philosophers to put humans at the centre of legal theorising. Consideration of rules or rights certainly concerns legal persons and their legal status, but appealing to the good ties the functioning of law closely to the needs, interests and capacities of humans. Appealing to the good also bridges the fact/value distinction suggesting that because humans always need or desire certain things law should, *therefore*, provide them. Whether this argument truly overcomes the division (or whether law is better characterised as a rule-based *practice*) is a question at the heart of debate between natural lawyers (defending the good) and positivists (defending strict observation of the fact/value distinction).

The assumption that there is a single good for humans is realised in its most undiluted form by theocratic states where a picture of a good life, for the individual as part of the state, is given religiously sanctioned reality. Conversely, Aristotle, who had a settled view of flourishing as the good of every individual, also at times had re-course to context-dependent ideas of goodness (the possibilities open to us depend upon the state and culture we inhabit) and more specifically role-dependent ideas of goodness (being a good citizen and being a good person are different things (1987: 521)). Indeed, Aristotle's idea of the good is informed by a whole range of things that are instrumentally and intrinsically good and which together form part and parcel of *the* good. Friendship, a stable state, family life and civic life are all essential components in a general assessment of the individual's good. Following Aristotle, philosophers therefore talk of 'goods' in the sense of intrinsically or objectively good *properties, states or possessions* that form part of an overall assessment of the good.

'Basic goods' are those possessions and states which are universally (or at least generally) desirable. Basic goods are various and contested, but would certainly be thought to include life itself, certain social activities (e.g. expression or religion), or claims to self-realisation as an individual (Finnis, 2011). Depending upon our cultural background, these goods will seem self-evident human goods, or at the very least recurrent features of human civilisation. They are basic goods for individuals because they are the foundation of the good (a flourishing life) or, and this may amount to the same thing, because they fulfil distinctively human needs (social activities, expression or religion). They have a strong claim to be at the origin of legal systems, or to justify legal institutions, because these goods depend upon a well ordered social milieu. Put in opposite, but also plausible, terms it could be claimed that a 'well ordered state' is well ordered only to the extent that it allows individuals to pursue or achieve these goods.

In considering the human good we should recall the tension between objective accounts of goodness and those positions rejecting objective accounts. A purely subjective determination of the good would acknowledge our own individual perceptions of what is valuable, and argue against anyone (philosophers or law-makers) seeking to set up a standard of success or failure for others. John Rawls and others inhabit this position (Chapter 4). This emphasises an individual's right to determine their own 'conception of the good' and is closely linked to political liberalism with its emphasis on freedom and the limits of the state, but it is not a complete rejection of the idea of the human good. A *conception* is our own considered view on an 'essentially contested *concept*', in this case 'the good'. '[T]here is nothing necessarily right, or morally correct, about the point of view from which things are to be judged good or bad. One may say of a man that he is a good spy, or a good assassin, without approving of his skills' (Rawls, 1999: 354). In acknowledging different conceptions Rawls is not rejecting the good as unintelligible or illegitimate. He is suggesting that there will always be reasonable disagreement about it, and as a consequence of this, the conception of the good that each individual reaches should be respected to the extent that it is reasonable.

EXAMPLE

European Social Charter 1961 (revised 1996), Article 13

A later supplement to the European Convention on Human Rights, the European Social Charter codifies fundamental goods that have a social dimension. Aspiration towards these goods is a broad commitment on the part of the signatory state, though not one enforceable in Court. Health is among our fundamental goods and the provision of health services is a fundamental, though not unqualified, responsibility of the state.

Article 13 'The Right to Social and Medical Assistance':

With a view to ensuring the effective exercise of the right to social and medical assistance, the Parties undertake: 1/ to ensure that any person who is without adequate
resources and who is unable to secure such resources either by his own efforts or from
other sources, in particular by benefits under a social security scheme, be granted adequate assistance, and, in the case of sickness, the care necessitated by his condition;
2/ to ensure that persons receiving such assistance shall not, for that reason, suffer from
a diminution of their political or social rights.

1b A good life and justice

Are we entitled to all basic goods? If basic goods are 'axiomatic' – they require no
further argument to be treated as intrinsically desirable – then each of us has a
reasonable claim upon them. This does not necessarily entail that we are *entitled* to
them, if we treat entitlement as a more complex notion of desert within a particular
social and political context. All states, even the most egalitarian, must make difficult
decisions about how opportunities, and resources, can be distributed fairly.

The *opportunity* to pursue or realise basic goods is implicit or explicit in the constitution of any well regulated democratic state. A constitution provides order, and
order is necessary for any purposive human activity, but this does not mean that
all inequality in a state is illegitimate, only that opportunities such as educational
self-development or economic investment be open to all. The *resources* necessary to
pursue or realise these goods may be either minimal (friendship does not necessarily require financial investment) or substantial (knowledge requires access to information, and health may require some claim to medical resources). All states have
finite resources, and in conditions of scarcity the state has to treat some basic goods
as more basic than others. States therefore require an implicit hierarchy of goods.
In philosophical terms, this means that states rarely have monistic or indivisible
accounts of the good. States are not committed to a single idea of the good or to
realising all those basic goods that we have a claim to. Even if a state were to assert
the moral authority to decide on a conception of the good for its citizens, existing
conditions of inequality and scarcity would make this impossible to realise. This
still leaves open the possibility that *law* has a close relationship with basic goods
even where the state as a whole is subject to conditions of scarcity and inequality.

Whether we take our theory of justice from Rawls, Dworkin or Nozick, justice
requires that the interests of individuals not be sacrificed to the interests of the state.
Good law-making and good legal decision-making are the primary means by which
a society maintains this protection. A well regulated society is not one that simply
provides order, but it provides the individuals with the possibility of pursuing other
goods of their choosing. Among the Ancient philosophers, ideas of law, justice and
the good were much more closely linked. Law was a means of making people good,

and justice was an individual virtue central to living a good human life (Morrison, 1997). Few would now accept this close relationship between justice, the state and the good. Humans are more diverse in their interests and much more concerned with freedom; the modern democratic state is more impersonal, and more heavily regulated, than the states of the Ancient world. Nonetheless, the natural law school continues to place basic goods at the heart of what law should provide, and a number of natural law theorists propound ideals of what a legal system *should be* in the light of the basic good of individuals (Finnis, 2011). In sum, while modern thought eschews excessive monism in its discussion of the good, and there is no longer an explicit commitment to 'making people good', any discussion of justice tends to invoke two things: the distinctive contribution of legal institutions to our state and our lives, and law's protection of individuals' basic goods in the face of the pragmatism of politics.

EXAMPLE

Preamble of the Constitution of the International Labour Organisation (1919)

The only institution related to the League of Nations that remains in existence, the International Labour Organisation, works for social justice and raising the general living standard. Its focus is primarily upon work and working conditions. Work is a crucial 'instrumental' good: it creates personal and public wealth. However, good working conditions are arguably more than an instrumental good for maximising wealth, they are intrinsically desirable.

Whereas universal and lasting peace can be established only if it is based upon social justice; and whereas conditions of labour exist involving such injustice hardship and privation to large numbers of people as to produce unrest so great that the peace and harmony of the world are imperilled; and an improvement of those conditions is urgently required; as, for example, by the regulation of the hours of work including the establishment of a maximum working day and week, the regulation of the labour supply, the prevention of unemployment, the provision of an adequate living wage, the protection of the worker against sickness, disease and injury arising out of his employment, the protection of children, young persons and women, provision for old age and injury, protection of the interests of workers when employed in countries other than their own, recognition of the principle of equal remuneration for work of equal value, recognition of the principle of freedom of association, the organization of vocational and technical education and other measures [. . .].

1c Happiness and harmony

Two terms are closely related to the idea of the good. The first is that a good life can be thought of as one where individuals possess *happiness*. It is a commonplace that a life with material goods but without some kind of fundamental happiness would not be desirable. It is also true that many types of candidates for good(s) could perhaps be ultimately analysed as things which produce happiness in their possessor.

The other recurrent term, one with a more Ancient philosophical pedigree, is *harmony*, suggesting agreement or complementarity. This can be made compatible with happiness if we take happiness to be a kind of harmony within ourselves (e.g. between what we need and what we desire) or between our will, our social needs and our context. Harmony also indicates a more fundamental, sustainable, harmonisation between individuals and social reality. This captures the idea that humans are naturally social creatures who need good social relationships, and it may presuppose that there is a single true, authentic way for humans to live together. This can be a hard-headed defence of the idea that humans are co-dependent and have to work with others in order to achieve individual goods; it can also be a utopian concern with an ideal state where individuals live a sustainable, authentic and fruitful life together. In the work of Plato it is both.

Put in political terms, the notion of harmony proposes a single good for individuals, a single good for society, and the harmonious reconciliation of both individual and society. This lends itself to 'collective' positions: e.g. environmentalism or theocracies which make claims about social goods, individual goods and the necessary overlap between the two. Furthermore, such collective positions generally lead to substantial demands made upon law to structure – or 'engineer' – society in order to realise the good in individual and social terms. An appeal to happiness does not have to involve a single good for individuals or a single good for society, but rather suggests that there is benefit in seeing certain minimal principles at the heart of law and politics, principles that can be partially reduced to the notion of happiness. This lends itself to 'liberal' positions, e.g. libertarianism and utilitarianism, which do not dictate the content of a good life or state, but do insist upon analysing lives and states on the basis of their contributing to individual happiness. Such liberal positions deflate claims about 'the good', rendering it a *limit* to what law can do on the basis that every individual has the right to choose what will allow them to realise happiness (West, 1998).

EXAMPLE

Federalist Paper No. 78 [1788] (Hamilton, 2012)

In this passage, which has some claim to constitutional status in the United States, Alexander Hamilton insists on the importance of judicial review on the grounds of its ability to limit the action of those in power. In other terms, law and politics may sometimes conflict, but this does not preclude their having a complementary, harmonious, relationship in the governance of a state.

> By a limited Constitution, I understand one which contains certain specified exceptions to the legislative authority; such, for instance, as that it shall pass no bills of attainder, no ex-post-facto laws, and the like. Limitations of this kind can be preserved in practice no other way than through the medium of the courts of justice, whose duty it must be to declare all acts contrary to the manifest tenor of the Constitution void. Without this, all the reservations of particular rights or privileges would amount to nothing.

2 Plato

Introduction

The influence of Plato within the Western philosophical tradition is inescapable, and there is some sense in Whitehead's claim that 'all Western philosophy is a foot-note to Plato' (1997: 39), but Plato is not as central to the philosophy of law as his pupil, Aristotle. Plato's view of law is 'of its time' with an emphasis on strong rule, limited freedom and Spartan austerity. Nonetheless, echoes of Platonic thought can be found in any philosophy which asserts any one of the following propositions: doing good is synonymous with abiding by the law; there is a natural harmony of interests among individuals; the happiness of individuals depends upon their doing good and not evil; or, the commands of tyrants are not law because law 'proper' must bring about the good of all individuals in the state.

Crucial to Plato's mature philosophy, of which *The Republic* is the most important work, is monism. Plato insists that everything is the same in at least one respect. Everything is, represents or is an instance of, an *ideal*. Everything has an ideal form that it should take, and the ideal form of all ideal forms is the good (1997: 1128–9). As such, both knowledge and morality are aspirations to discern or achieve what is good, the best way for things or people to be. This can also be expressed in the language of 'teleology' meaning the pursuit of ends or goals. Everything has an end or goal, a proper way to be, namely its good. Teleology does not treat 'ends' as the fleeting outcomes of individual preferences or passing judgments: there is a single form that *everything* strives to and should take.

Plato's monism creates a complete philosophical system which is able to reduce explanation to a single term and idea. We must discover what the good is – for everything – and seek its realisation. It is also an invitation to mysticism. Translated into terms of 'one truth' hidden behind the multiplicity of appearances, Plato's system is not just a way to explain the world, but the creation of another world behind our own of which we see only pale and illusory imitations. It is this element of his system that had a profound influence on Islamic and Christian thought (Blackburn, 2006). Both were influenced by Neoplatonism (at its height in the third century, CE), a fully mystical version of Plato's thought, stressing the underlying unity of the world and the ability of thought (rather than the senses) to penetrate the underlying reality of the universe. However, Plato's significance for law lies in his view of psychology, and the relationship between psychology and justice.

2a The good and the individual

It has been suggested that Platonic thought can be discovered in contemporary thinking when we assert that unjust individuals cannot be happy. The idea seems both appealing and untrue because people who do wrong should not be happy, but nonetheless are. One of the main goals of Plato's work was to demonstrate the truth of the idea that the evil cannot be happy. The essence of Plato's argument is that harmony is the precondition of happiness. We must be harmonious within ourselves in order to avoid internal strife and tension; evil-doing is caused by, and causes further, internal conflict.

> [In a person's soul] there is a better part and a worse one and [. . .] whenever the naturally better part is in control of the worse, this is expressed as saying that the person is self-controlled or master of himself. [. . .] [When] the smaller and better part is overwhelmed by the larger, because of bad upbringing or bad company, this is called being self-defeated or licentious and is a reproach. (1997: 1063)

Where there is, conversely, good order within us there is both happiness and no inclination to wrong-doing. This conclusion requires a particular view of the self, divided and potentially in conflict, but also a necessary correlation between harmonious selves and happy selves.

Plato's tripartite (three-part) division of the self subdivides all humans into rational, spirited, and appetitive parts. Each is distinct, each is necessary, and each must be harnessed together to ensure that none is in overall control. The rational must make decisions for the whole, the appetitive part keeps the body alive and functioning, and the spirited part ensures that neither the basic animal appetites nor the rational mind are left to fight for supremacy (it provides both a strong will and a sense of self-worth). This view of the self is too simple; the categories are too neat, and the body made more or less irrelevant to selfhood. In many respects, however, it is a powerful descriptive account of the competing tensions within the individual. It is a persuasive insistence that individuals must struggle to harmonise, not eradicate, competing internal impulses.

Why is the harmony of the self decisive for Platonic ethics? If one part of the self gains control then familiar human failings arise. A criminal is a person who has allowed their appetites to gain control over their whole being. The overly ambitious are those for whom the courageous part has excessive influence. Those who think, but who fail to act or have too little self-respect, have not given sufficient rein to the spirited parts of the self. In each case there is a lack of internal equilibrium, and for Plato such a person simply cannot be happy because their self is not harmonious. Plato's conclusion, therefore, is that 'virtue is its own reward'. When we act virtuously we are maintaining a healthy soul; when we fail to act virtuously we are in a position where our soul has been hijacked (1997: 1074). We cannot be happy in these circumstances.

It is doubtful whether with these arguments alone Plato proved what he set out to prove – that only the just person is happy – but his argument is supplemented by two further arguments. First, Plato states that philosophers, who have special insight into truth and goodness, *know* that this is the case even if we, non-philosophers, cannot see it (1997: 1108–11). Such an argument based on the special, privileged, insight of philosophers is unpersuasive unless supported by further rational arguments. Second, he undertakes a substantial discussion of the state – as a kind of human writ large – and its contribution to human harmony.

EXAMPLE

Prosecutor v Erdemovic (ICTY) IT-96-22-T bis, para. 21

Holding individuals to account for their actions through punishment is important as a way of allowing that individual to repay a debt to society and reform their personalities. Where they plead guilty to a charge, such an admission is seen as evidence of willingness to change and can lead to a lesser punishment. Here such a reduction in punishment seems to be in tension with the need for wider social harmony and reconciliation pursued through harsh sentencing.

Discovering the truth is a cornerstone of the rule of law and a fundamental step on the way to reconciliation: for it is the truth that cleanses the ethnic and religious hatreds and begins the healing process. The International Tribunal must demonstrate that those who have the honesty to confess are treated fairly as part of a process underpinned by principles of justice, fair trial and protection of the fundamental rights of the individual. On the other hand, the International Tribunal is a vehicle through which the international community expresses its outrage at the atrocities committed in the former Yugoslavia. Upholding values of international human rights means that while protecting the rights of the accused, the International Tribunal must not lose sight of the tragedy of the victims and the sufferings of their families.

2b The good and the state

Plato initially argues that the state should be treated as analogous to the soul in order that the state should serve as a means of exploring the soul (1997: 1008). In other words, Plato makes no claim (at first) that the state, let alone all states, should themselves have a tripartite division mirroring the self. Rather, the roots of harmony and disharmony in the state are a good illustration of similar phenomena in the soul. Nonetheless, there is little doubt that Plato intended his model state, The Republic, to become a reality. The Republic would have rational rulers, a courageous military class and a labouring class. With this strict unchangeable division (enforced through eugenics, censorship and 'noble' lies about the divine necessity of the caste system) Plato insists that a harmonious, and therefore just, state would be realised. The labouring class maintains the basic biological needs of the state; the courageous military class protects it from external threat; the rational rulers maintain the order of the whole. Justice, it is argued, is precisely that order, or harmony, between the parts.

> [Justice] is concerned with what is inside him, with what is truly his own. One who is just does not allow any part of himself to do the work of another part or allow the various classes within him to meddle with each other. [. . .] He puts himself in order, is his own friend, and harmonises the three parts of himself [. . .]. [This is true of] the just man, the just city, and [what] justice is. (1997: 1075)

The rulers, 'Philosopher Kings' with complete knowledge of the good, would make any decisions necessary for the running and overall administration of the state. This technocracy (rule by philosophical experts), along with the censorship and generally illiberal nature of Plato's system, mean there is much that cannot be salvaged from Plato's thought. However, these considerable flaws aside, there is some enduring appeal in the idea that there could be a best, good, way for the state to be, that this ideal is in some way reducible to 'harmony', and that behind the state and 'harmony' are ultimately the good, i.e. the full realisation of human potential.

Plato's later political and legal thought takes a more authoritarian turn, and appeal to the good is superseded by a more pragmatic defence of strong government. The idea of a utopia was, of course, pursued in many different directions, and still has some appeal (not least because, when we criticise a state and its laws, we always implicitly make reference to some not-yet achieved ideal). Conversely, the dystopian aspects of Plato's thought also remain important, cautionary, points of reference in legal theory. A state without rights, with censorship, and with lies about how things 'should be', is more hell rather than heaven. Plato offers a cautionary tale of how over-emphasis on the good can lead to a dangerous under-emphasis on *law*.

EXAMPLE

'Sichuan Activist Sentenced to Five Years for 'Inciting Subversion of State Power'' 9 February 2010 (Human Rights in China, 2010)

A strong state requires harmony but should also be able to tolerate some dissent. Here a Chinese activist falls foul of a state where harmony is understood in non-democratic terms.

> In a brief hearing on February 9, 2010, in the Chengdu Municipal Intermediate People's Court, Sichuan-based writer and environmental activist Tan Zuoren was found guilty of 'inciting subversion of state power' and sentenced to a five-year prison term and three

years' deprivation of political rights. According to an informed source, when police led him away after the court hearing, Tan shouted, 'It is my honor to go to prison for the people of my hometown'. [. . .] Tan was first detained on March 28, 2009, just three days after online publication of the findings of an investigation that he conducted with a colleague, Xie Yihue, into the causes of the widespread collapse of school buildings during the May 2008 earthquake. The indictment, however, did not mention Tan's earthquake investigation or its findings as constituting 'incitement to subvert state power.' Instead, it listed as evidence a 2007 article that Tan wrote about the 1989 Democracy Movement [. . .] and interviews that Tan gave to foreign media about the 2008 earthquake. During the trial, the judge repeatedly interrupted the defense lawyer, Pu Zhiqiang, and Tan was not allowed to make his final statement.

2c Contemporary Platonism

Platonism continues to exercise an influence in legal philosophy, and not only in the natural law tradition. The suggestion that law not only changes and adapts but aspires towards an ultimate *ideal* has Platonic overtones, but does not necessarily have to involve utopianism. Nigel Simmonds argues that laws and lawyers do have or invoke some kind of ideal, namely 'the rule of law' (Simmonds, 2007). The rule of law provides that ideal by which actual legal systems can be judged, both in its instrumental role (as contributing to the good of individuals) and as something intrinsically good. The rule of law may never be fully realised – after all, many things that are neither legal nor necessarily good feature in legal decisions, such as politics and self-interest – but nonetheless the ideal allows us to say 'these are not really part of law, law *proper*'. It is the ideal that allows us to distinguish what is truly part of law and what is contingently associated with it. Because many things are associated with law,

> the most coherent solution to this problem is provided by an abstract archetype, [and] no problematic metaphysical commitments are involved: our practices themselves *create* the archetype in so far as they are structured by ideas that are best understood as pointing to the archetype. The thought that our concept of law may be structured by an archetype requires no commitment to a strange or luxuriant ontology [i.e. theory of what exists]. Yet it would nevertheless be a mistake to underestimate the substantial connections that obtain between this thought and the Platonic [. . .] tradition of idealism. (2007: 58)

Has Simmonds, or any other contemporary theorist, an answer to the questions that Plato sets himself, namely that individuals ought to do what is good, and that it is good to abide by law? There is some sense in which contemporary theory has moved to the opposite end of the spectrum from Plato in placing 'the good' outside the scope of legal philosophy, and centralising what is right – what is necessary or universal – rather than an ultimate good. Nonetheless, it seems that Platonism is at work in those contexts where an ideal is posited and where law, while imperfect, represents an *ideal* denoting something with intrinsic value and not simply instrumental value.

EXAMPLE

Dred Scott v *Sandford*, 60 U.S. 393 (1856) (at 426) United States Supreme Court

There is an intuition, reflected by Plato, that 'real law' should be construed as unchanging; that changing law is closer to politics than law proper. Dred Scott concerned the status of a slave both as a citizen of the United States and as, conversely, property. The majority of the Supreme Court found that Dred Scott was a slave and therefore property for the purposes of the constitution. The decision indicates why discussion of rights should be distinguished from discussion of goods; rights are here equated with property rights, certainly not the good of the individual slave. In a Platonic vein, the decision insisted that the law of the constitution was unchanging and should be without reference to common opinion or feeling.

The Government of the United States had no right to interfere for any other purpose but that of protecting the rights of the owner, leaving it altogether with the several States to deal with this race, whether emancipated or not, as each State may think justice, humanity, and the interests and safety of society, require. The States evidently intended to reserve this power exclusively to themselves. [. . .] No one, we presume, supposes that any change in public opinion or feeling, in relation to this unfortunate race, in the civilized nations of Europe or in this country, should induce the court to give to the words of the Constitution a more liberal construction in their favor than they were intended to bear when the instrument was framed and adopted. Such an argument would be altogether inadmissible in any tribunal called on to interpret it. If any of its provisions are deemed unjust, there is a mode prescribed in the instrument itself by which it may be amended; but while it remains unaltered, it must be construed now as it was understood at the time of its adoption.

---

3 Natural law

Introduction

The term 'natural law' has already been mentioned and identified as a philosophical school insisting on a necessary relationship between law and the good. This position, with origins in Ancient thought, has endured and continues to be a major contributor to philosophical debate. However, there are a number of natural law traditions, so no single position could be said to be 'the' natural law position.

In Ancient discussions of law and justice, metaphysics is important, i.e. the structures behind the natural and social worlds. Law – 'true', 'real' law – is found written into the fabric of the physical and social worlds. This explains the invocation of 'natural'. Law is discovered among more general laws of nature; law is as unchanging and dispassionate as the natural world. However, in order to prevent such a position simply demanding a return to nature – i.e. the 'survival of the fittest', or 'might makes right' – a narrower conception of nature is employed in natural law theorising. Natural law concerns the obligations that arise naturally. Those 'naturally arising obligations' stem from the social situation that we find ourselves in – the social hierarchy, or the legal and political system – not directly from nature itself. Nonetheless, in pre-modern contexts, where strict social hierarchy seemed natural, it was immediately intelligible to say that such social organisations possessed unchanging, pre-determined, forms and foundations and thereby generated 'natural' obligations (Cicero, 2000).

Modern natural law does not subscribe to a fundamental, metaphysical, identification of the natural and the obligatory. It argues, on one account, that there is a duty to govern human affairs through law. Such a duty is not simply an assertion of law's usefulness but of an essentially moral obligation to employ law and legal means in social affairs (Fuller, 1969). On another account, law necessarily has moral *content* (Chloros, 1958). These are two points that need to be kept apart. The first point is recognisable in the foregoing discussions of the good and of Plato, i.e. that law aspires to realise social or individual goods *or* legality is justified by supporting us in realising these goods. The second point is that law must have moral *content* or its content must overlap substantially with morality. If social mores dictate that certain behaviours are prohibited, or that certain actions are morally praiseworthy, then law should, respectively, prohibit or enforce them. Law has justification only in so far as its content reflects these goods. The two positions are separable (although it would be rare to support the second proposition but not the first) because one concerns the *initial justification* of law (law's inherent value) and the other the grounds of the *continuing justification* of law and laws (law's contribution to morality).

The origins of both positions can be traced to Ancient Greece, and it is tempting to suggest that they arise from a more primitive form of thought that had not yet discovered a conceptually clear way of distinguishing law and morality. In fact, from the earliest Greek thought, law was analysed within a complex and shifting analytical framework, setting *nomos* (human laws and conventions) in contrast to *phusis* (nature). The value of this opposition between convention and nature is its potential to throw easily blurred oppositions into a profitable conflict with one another (Barnes, 1987). For instance, do human conventions (*nomos*) have a natural (*phusis*) basis? Or, do human conventions (*nomos*) *free* us from nature (*phusis*)? We could answer no to the first question but yes to the second, suggesting that nature is something that we must be emancipated from through law. We could also answer no to both questions and thereby conclude that human conventions are repressive and that nature somehow encourages us to reject them. The opposition of 'nature' versus 'human laws' underlies debates in the philosophy of law still alive today.

3a Early natural law

While Plato formulated many of the questions that the natural law tradition seeks to answer, it is Sophism that laid the groundwork for a philosophy of natural law. Sophism – a movement active around 400BCE – did this on the basis of an underlying opposition to human institutions (Dillon and Gergel, 2003). As a 'movement' Sophism did not aim to create a philosophical school but to provide practical guidance to the rich, teaching them how to maintain status and self-respect as aristocrats and resist social and personal threats (particularly legal action in the Courts where individuals were required to represent themselves). Sophists saw in the development of institutions such as marriage, civic responsibility and general social expectations the growth of repressive strictures that unnecessarily constrained the individual. These institutions were criticised as *unnatural*: they are not found in, located in or created by nature. This leads to the assumption that we *should* be doing what is natural and that nature is a source of values and grounds of activity (Plato, 1997: 235f).

This is arguably so. Nature insists that humans eat, reproduce and have their basic needs met in order to survive as a species. To oppose such needs is not only unnatural but repressive. With this as their premise, the Sophists famously propounded the idea that 'might is right': those best equipped by nature to fulfil their needs and interests *should* do so. The Greek Sophist Antiphon is characteristic in this respect:

> [a person should] regard the laws as important when witnesses are present, but, when on his own without witnesses, the demands of nature. [. . .] [I]f a man transgresses the demands of law and is not found out by those who are parties to the agreement, he escapes without either shame or penalty; but if he is found out, he does not. (quoted in Dillon and Gergel, 2003: 150–1)

It is this kind of argument that Plato sets out to criticise in his works. His argument for the psychological and moral importance of internal harmony is a direct assault on the Sophist's endorsement of pure self-interest (1997: 992f); and it is these arguments in praise of the strong that have given 'sophistry' its pejorative sense of dressing up poor arguments as good ones simply in order to win at all costs. Philosophically, the Sophist position can be summarised as the idea that *nomos* should be challenged by *phusis*. Human conventions are socially convenient but repressive; *phusis*, nature, gives grounds to oppose them.

Plato and Aristotle used this opposition between human law and nature, but explored their potential harmonisation rather than their antagonism. In both philosophers there is a teleological conception of nature. If the natural world (the 'natural order') is characterised by progress towards an end (*telos*), then *phusis* itself is the guide to real or true law, and human conventions can be judged by the extent to which they harmonise with those natural ends. Those natural ends will be construed in terms of *the good*: the objective standard by which human lives are judged, and by which the value of a political system is gauged. It is good that human affairs are regulated by law; laws are, ideally, attuned to the real nature of things and should therefore be accepted as binding. Plato's criticism of the Sophists, and Aristotle's re-action to Plato, represents one of the most interesting strands of Ancient ethics (see Nussbaum, 1986). Suffice it to say, Plato and Aristotle's political and legal thinking offered much more than the Sophists' critique of law, but retained the Sophists' preoccupation with nature as a guide to necessity in the human world.

Stoicism had Greek origins but became the predominant philosophy of the Romans. The Stoics – of which Seneca and Marcus Aurelius are the most charac-teristic and Cicero the most famous (although his relationship with Stoicism is complex) – argued that the universe itself had a *nomos*, its own structuring laws, and accordingly there was no opposition, indeed a harmony, between *nomos* and *phusis* (Cicero 1998; 2000). The Roman Stoics, unlike the Sophists, valued human institu-tions, not least the Roman Empire. In this context, Stoicism became an individual ethic of self-control which demanded virtuous action, law-abiding activity and our detachment from the body (as a distraction from virtue and law). Stoicism was an all-encompassing ethic that demanded a harmony between humans, human law and the universal laws of the universe. This 'cosmic reason' is the summation of the view that law is written into the fabric of reality, not something created but discovered. In these conditions natural law became more than the unification of human laws and nature's laws, but a complete metaphysics. The Cosmos has law at its centre.

EXAMPLE

The Art of War, Sun Tzu (1994) (c. sixth century BCE)

The idea of a natural or moral law features in Western and Eastern philosophical tradi-tions. Whether such law arises from the natural world or something beyond the natural world, it serves as guide for human conduct. Here it is said to form part of the necessary preconditions of military success.

The art of war, then, is governed by five constant factors, to be taken into account in one's deliberations, when seeking to determine the conditions obtaining in the field. These are: (1) The Moral Law; (2) Heaven; (3) Earth; (4) The Commander; (5) Method and discipline. / The Moral Law causes the people to be in complete accord with their ruler, so that they will follow him regardless of their lives, undismayed by any danger. [. . .] Heaven signifies night and day, cold and heat, times and seasons. [. . .] Earth comprises distances, great and small; danger and security; open ground and narrow passes; the chances of life and death. / The Commander stands for the virtues of wisdom, sincerity, benevolence, courage and strictness. [. . .] By method and discipline are to be understood the marshalling of the army in its proper subdivisions, the graduations of rank among the officers, the maintenance of roads by which supplies may reach the army, and the control of military expenditure.

3b Natural law and religion

The first millennium of the Common Era did not change humanity's preoccupation with the good, either the pursuit of a good life or a good state. However, the spread of monotheism demanded a reconsideration of Ancient ideas on two grounds. First, and generally, religious scholars sought a synthesis of Greek and Roman thought with revealed religion (scripture and religious practices). Second, and specifically, Christianity demanded a clear demarcation between the powers of the Church and the state. Both required a clarification of where and how a hierarchy of law and authority was possible.

The Ancient philosophers' reflections on natural law were appealing to medieval scholars as ideas through which philosophy and religion could be mutually reinforced. Religion insists on certain and unequivocal moral precepts; philosophy seeks to explain how divine rules are written into the fabric of reality. 'Law' usefully serves to encompass ideas of morality *and* regularities in the natural world. God created a world exhibiting order and regularity, thus good order must be sought in the human world too.

Augustine (345–430CE) synthesised the Platonic notion of the good with Christian revelation concerning God. The good is our ultimate goal, and, echoing Plato's understanding of justice, the well ordered state and self-regulated individual are both necessary for harmonious existence.

> The peace of the body is the orderly proportion of its members. The peace of the animal soul is the orderly repose of its appetites. The peace of the reasonable soul is the orderly concord of thought and action. The peace of body and soul together is the orderly life and security of the living person. The peace of man and God is the orderly obedience in faith to the eternal law. The peace of men is orderly harmony. (Augustine, 1963: 343)

At the same time Augustine combined elements of Sophism and Stoicism. Human institutions and laws are rational, but a prelude to divine justice:

> [For Augustine] the secular commonwealth (*civitas terrena*) was a reflection of the divine common-wealth (*civitas Dei*) to the extent that human law and conduct were in unison with God's will. It was antithetical to the *civitas Dei* insofar as human law and conduct were not in consonance with the *lex aeterna* (eternal law). (Wieacker, 1990: 12, n. 14)

The Christian 'Golden Rule' of treating others as we would wish to be treated is an adequate basis for pursuing virtue. Human laws are a supplement to, but cannot replace, this rule. Nonetheless, human knowledge and the laws of the universe can be brought into a rational harmonious whole.

> The peace of the city is the orderly harmony of command and obedience on the part of the citizens. The peace of the heavenly city is orderly and harmonious fellowship in the enjoyment of God and of each other in God. The peace of the universe is the serenity of order. Order is the adjustment of like and unlike each to its own place. (Augustine, 1963: 343)

In the perfect state – The City of God – individuals follow the laws of God, and their own wills become harmonious with God's will. In these terms, the legacy of Plato's thought remains clear, albeit with a strong Christian flavour.

Averroës (1126–1198CE) also saw the possibility of a synthesis of philosophical and religious thought, in his case Aristotelianism and Islam. The most important elements of his thought are, first, that there is a harmony between religion and philosophy and that a synthesis of the two is always possible (Averroës, 1998). Second, that there is a teleology shared by humans and the natural world, a harmonious movement towards God:

> The heavenly bodies are endowed with life and reason, and their motions are a result of conception and desire. They conceive the good, which is their perfection, and desire to become like unto it. Inasmuch as motion is better than rest, since motion is life, they are constantly in motion. The movers not only move the heavenly bodies, but they give them their forms in virtue of which they are what they are, and hence they are thus agents, in a sense. (Husik, 1909: 425–6)

This is a development of Aristotle's biological approach and his teleology, arguing for an underlying unity among humans and the natural world in desire for a good established by God.

St Thomas Aquinas' work (1225–1274CE) is, in European thought, the most influential attempt to both combine philosophy and revealed religion. It seeks to make sense of the relationship between 'law' as a property of God's will, the Created order, and of human governance. His ideas synthesise aspects of Aristotelianism (its teleology and conception of the individual), with the Old and New Testaments, and encompasses the work of Augustine and Cicero. From Aristotle, Aquinas takes ideas of the universe working towards some end, and the individual pursuing the good; both the individual and the created world have an end or *telos* established by God. From revealed religion he takes the rules, established by God, for human governance and a conception of humans as rational creatures able to discern God's will in the world. From these roots Aquinas is able to draw out different, but complementary ideas of law.

Aquinas needs to show that there are different, but nonetheless complementary, ideas of law in order to establish the proper relationship between God, religious authority and secular authority. He produces a four-fold account of law. Eternal law, established by God, provides a *telos* for the universe as a whole (2002: 30). The eternal law directs the unfolding of the universe and is only known in its entirety by God. Divine law is the law revealed directly to humanity through scripture and prophets (2002: 20–2). This law provides a clear distinction between the good and the evil (i.e. what is, or is not, God's will). Natural law is that portion of the eternal law that humans can know through the exercise of reason (2002: 40). Reason provides us with knowledge of the good, what it is intrinsically good to pursue and what our duties are as social beings; and human law is the application of natural law to the general governance of human affairs (2002: 51). Human law is always for the good of a community, but flows from those with political or law-making power.

> And so every human law has much of the nature of the nature of law as it is derived from the natural law. And a human law diverging in any way from natural law will be a perversion of law and no longer a law. (Aquinas, 2002: 54)

Within this four-fold division, natural law and human law share the same rational foundations: in 'human affairs [. . .] things are just because they are right according to the rule of reason. But the primary rule of reason is the natural law' (2002: 54). Reason rather than nature becomes, through the work of Aquinas, the central motif of natural law thinking. This in turn provides resources for solving the problem of reconciling the demands made by religious and secular sources of law. While the importance of reason is evident in Augustine's discussions of human governance, and the importance of the will of God is given a richer analysis in Averroës, it is Aquinas who synthesises these strands of theorising into an idea of *law* which is recognisably human, and an idea of *reason* which is both practical and ideal.

EXAMPLE

Bruker v Marcovitz [2007] 3 S.C.R. 607, 2007 Canadian Supreme Court

The close relationship between religion and the natural law school is complex. Natural law is used to justify the rule of law and the pursuit of the common good. It can also, as discussed here, be used as a means to justify actions contrary to the state and its traditions. Should a Jewish divorce process (get) be recognised in the Canadian Courts? Here, in the final appeal, there is a twin discussion of the basis of obedience to the law, and whether the Courts should hear 'religious' disputes. The Court decided such matters did fall within its remit (though not a related question of damages).

> The underlying problem in any open and democratic society based on human dignity, equality and freedom in which conscientious and religious freedom has to be regarded with appropriate seriousness, is how far such democracy can and must go in allowing members of religious communities to define for themselves which laws they will obey and which not. Such a society can cohere only if all its participants accept that certain basic norms and standards are binding. Accordingly, believers cannot claim an automatic right to be exempted by their beliefs from the laws of the land. At the same time, the state should, wherever reasonably possible, seek to avoid putting believers to extremely painful and intensely burdensome choices of either being true to their faith or else respectful of the law.

3c Modern natural law

The problem of reconciling revealed, divine, laws governing the cosmos on the one hand, and the demands made on the individual by secular, mundane, authorities on the other awaited a solution concerning the sources of law and the limits of power

Aquinas' taxonomy of laws presented law in a hierarchy determined by *source*, but did not provide a guide for governing the multitude of tensions generated by new forms of *power*. In the pre-modern era both the state and the Church exercised significant political and economic power. The emergence of the modern era (i.e. from the sixteenth and seventeenth centuries onwards) amplified that problem. The co-existence between Catholic Church and state was disrupted by the establishment of strong Protestant powers in Europe (Tuck, 1999). This had significant political and legal consequences. Protestantism, which was more congenial to a division of Church and state than Catholicism, hastened the development of a 'private sphere' where individual religion and morality could be different from public religion and morality, and hastened a more general decline of religious influence on political thought (Kelley, 1990). Wars between Catholic and Protestant Europe also gave rise to the international legal system with the secular state as the prime legal entity (Steinberg, 1966). For these reasons Aquinas' hierarchy of sources of law was, to an extent, inverted with human law claiming predominance in human affairs and divine law relegated to personal ethics in the private sphere.

In addition to this, Western Europe was increasingly assuming power over territories, and therefore indigenous peoples, in the New World. This colonial 'encounter' encouraged rethinking the basis of legal rule and the nature of sovereignty. The sovereignty of indigenous peoples was called into question in order to justify European domination (Tuck, 1999: 89–108), but this begged the question of what quality – beyond effective control over a territory through custom and force – was absent in the political and legal ordering of non-European people. European sovereignty (i.e. 'true' political and legal sovereignty) had to be construed as something more than control, custom and the threat of force. Two distinctively modern ideas emerge from such reflection. The first is the emergence of positivism as an attempt to identify law with one source only – the secular sovereign – and deny the status of law to more opaque moral or religious principles (see Chapter 5). The second is a reformed conception of natural law which placed a moral duty on the sovereign to provide particular kinds of social ordering.

Combining a concern with the burgeoning commercial activity of Europe with the colonial encounters that were part of that commercial activity, Hugo Grotius (1583–1645) sought to put natural law on a footing that did not depend upon appeal to the Divine. Grotius did not entirely sever the relationship between law and God, but did assert that there was a normative and natural order independent of God's (eternal or divine) laws. It is in the exploration of these *independent* orders that modern natural law takes shape. Grotius' approach is to picture a global state of nature where all states contract with one another – i.e. create international law – in

ᵈ mutual destruction, enmity and warfare. This ties legal order to a rational
ᵢ is both religiously sanctioned and 'natural':

107

hich adjudicates between different peoples, or between the rulers of different,
ₛ, whether proceeding from nature itself, or established by divine laws, . . .

[is 'natural law' and] it stems by necessity from internal principles of man [and] God. (Grotius, quoted in Tuck, 1999: 100–1)

Although different states and peoples have competing views of the divine law, they can agree on basic rational principles that bring good ordering to human affairs. A social ordering within which respect for property rights is primary. Emphasis on basic, shared, principles like self-preservation and property rights is characteristic of modern legal and political thought, in particular the 'social contract' model of authority (Chapter 4). And while such basic principles are held to be *natural*, note a changing relationship with the notion of the *good*. The nature or legitimacy of law is no longer premised upon a fulsome account of human need, a good life, or a good state. Rather there is a minimal conception of human needs; the state is legitimised by the provision of minimal goods (e.g. survival, freedom from fear) rather than any substantial (Aristotelean or religious) vision of the good.

Two important theorists of the twentieth century have revitalised the natural law tradition in contemporary philosophy. Both Lon Fuller (see Chapter 6) and John Finnis identify law with *moral* commitments and a *purpose* or function for law related to the human good. Fuller's work reflects Grotius' minimal reading of natural law with an emphasis on the basic principles needed for human sociability. Finnis, conversely, represents a revival of Aquinas' position. Finnis insists that law, and only law, can provide certain basic goods for the individual (Finnis, 2011). These basic goods have their origins in human rationality, they are intrinsically good and require no further justification; they are not deduced from an assessment of what is (instrumentally) good for people to have, but are presumed in any assessment of practical reasoning, i.e. judgments concerned how to act. These self-evident goods – life, knowledge, play, aesthetic experience, friendship, practical reasonableness and religion – are axiomatic, intrinsically good, characteristics or capacities that it is reasonable (rational) for all individuals to pursue.

> A theory of natural law [. . .] may be undertaken, as this book is, primarily to assist the practical reflections of those concerned to act, whether as judges, or as statesmen, or as citizens. [This] undertaking cannot proceed securely without a knowledge of the whole range of human possibilities and opportunities, inclinations and capacities. (2011: 18)

Law must work with an idea of the individual seeking these goods – they are precisely what the 'reasonable person' would pursue – and make demands on law-makers and judges to have this conception of the rational individual at the heart of law and legal decisions. (Authority and the imposition of order is a necessary dimension of social life, but by centralising basic goods law makes an indispensible contribution to the 'common good'.)

Accordingly, Finnis' position is practical, deontological and perfectionist. It is practical because it aims to assist us in deciding how to act rationally. It is 'deontological' being concerned with duties on the part of law-makers and legal institutions; such duties are not law's own particular morality (as they would be in the case of Fuller) but rather intersect with moral duties more generally. It could also be described as 'perfectionist': the state cannot remain agnostic about different conceptions of the good, rather it has the duty to encourage the maintenance or cultivation of the basic goods. (At the same time it is not teleological, it does not presuppose an end-point or goal for the state or the individual.)

Given that Finnis sees the pursuit and protection of these goods as premised ultimately on rational principles, he subsumes this 'moral' dimension of his account into one basic good, practical reasonableness:

> the term 'moral' is of somewhat uncertain connotation. So it is preferable to frame our conclusion in terms of practical reasonableness [. . .]. [Practical reasonableness] is the view point which should be used as the standard of reference by the theorist describing the features of legal order. (2011: 15)

Self-evident goods offer *good reasons* for action; as such they can form the basis of practical reasoning about the world and what we should do in the world. Only by acknowledging the pursuit of basic goods as the foundation of sound reasoning about how to act in the world can we expect to judge our own and others' actions. Put another way, the idea of 'good reasons' intersects with the idea of reasonableness more generally. Reasonableness – the characteristic of being rational or justified – is not simply a principle that is, from time to time, imported into legal discussion. It is a moral principle associated with everyone's interest in pursuing or maintaining basic goods. Such a principle provides a standard by which individual actions, including the actions of individuals within legal institutions, can be judged.

EXAMPLE

Rylands v Fletcher [1866] LR 1 Exch 265

Still a decisive case in common law jurisdictions concerning the torts of nuisance and negligence, Rylands hinges upon natural and unnatural use of land and our liability when 'unnatural' uses of land have an impact on our neighbours. That we should take reasonable care or due diligence where there is a risk of causing harm to our neighbours remains a pillar of legal approaches to wrongs. The appeal to the reasonable here might be thought to intersect with Finnis' basic goods of life, friendship and perhaps aesthetic experience.

> The person whose grass or corn is eaten down by the escaping cattle of his neighbour, or whose mine is flooded by the water from his neighbour's reservoir, or whose cellar is invaded by the filth of his neighbour's privy, or whose habitation is made unhealthy by the fumes and noisome vapours of his neighbour's alkali works, is damnified without any fault of his own; and it seems reasonable and just that the neighbour, who has brought something on his own property which was not naturally there, harmless to others so long as it is confined to his own property, but which he knows to be mischievous if it gets on his neighbour's, should be obliged to make good the damage which ensues if he does not succeed in confining it to his own property.

4 Utilitarianism

Introduction

There is an appealing simplicity in the conclusion that everything 'good' is good by virtue of its giving us pleasure or happiness. From the simplest instrumental claim that 'x is a good tool for the job' to the basic good of life itself, the reason why something is good is that it will bring benefit – pleasure, happiness, well-being or welfare – to people. More fully, a useful tool gets a job done to a person's *satisfaction*; that is, where an individual's *preference* is satisfied, or where their *interests* are realised. In the ideas of satisfaction, preferences or interests a common standard can be posited: their contribution to the pleasure or the happiness of an individual or individuals. Positing a common standard is 'reductive' because it unifies at the expense of variations in what we mean by preference, satisfaction or interest. Nonetheless, this reductive move does have two immediate advantages. First, it may chime with a view of human psychology as pleasure or happiness seeking. Second, it has the advantage of simplicity. Why complicate our view of life with competing ideas of motivation, obligation, duties and values? 'Pleasure seeking' captures both what humans do and, within reason, what we should do. That qualification – 'within reason' – intimates moral constraints on our actions to be further discussed. We need to decide to what extent this argument holds water, particularly whether 'pleasure' does do the work we want it to, including whether it is always synonymous with happiness, and whether we can make sense of limitations on pleasure, i.e. seeking pleasure 'within reason'.

4a Hedonism

A neat reduction of 'good' to 'pleasure giving' can be both plausible and conceptually tidy. Why call something good unless it gives someone pleasure? Why act in a way that fails to bring you, or others, happiness? There is also a negative justification for identifying good with pleasure. The alternative is to argue that our actions should be guided by rules and duties, and rules and duties often make us, and others, unhappy. Duty-based systems of ethics might prohibit us from lying even though our lie will never be found out (*and* such lying might make many people much happier). To forbid it in this context seems to lose any justification. Again, if we demand that every criminal be punished, even if there is no victim to demand that punishment (*and* the criminal would themselves be made to suffer) this punishment seems to lose any sense or justice.

In the foregoing reduction of good to 'pleasurable' or 'pleasure giving' we have had recourse to the word *happiness*. The commingling of ideas of pleasure and happiness is in line with ordinary language, but it is conceptually untidy. In the English language, pleasure and happiness carry different connotations: the former a physical state, the latter an enduring state. Sharper differences can be drawn between purely physical pleasure and a state of happiness. Pleasure may be more intense, and we can never really doubt an experience of pleasure; happiness may be more fleeting or insubstantial, and it seems possible to doubt one's own, and others', happiness. We can be sceptical concerning a time in the past where we thought we were happy and we can be suspicious of others' claims to being happy in circumstances where we ourselves would not be. Nonetheless, cultural and philosophical traditions have tended to denigrate pleasure in favour of happiness (recall Plato's association of happiness and inner harmony). 'Merely' physical pleasure is seen as a transient and purely subjective experience, while happiness is treated a more desirable holistic state that can be objectively gauged. Pleasure may be a *necessary condition* for happiness (it is a precondition), but it is not the *sufficient condition* of happiness (the only, or complete, cause).

Indeed, simple thought experiments try to make that point. Would we choose a life of physical pleasure induced by artificial means, e.g. by being attached to a computer program? If we would, we are consistent, pure, hedonists treating pleasure as a sufficient condition of happiness. If, on the other hand, we argue that this life would be lacking something essential (something 'real') we may still be hedonists of sorts, but happiness pursuing, not pleasure pursuing, hedonists (Flew (ed.), 1979). This latter position, while possibly more appealing, creates a further philosophical problem. To say that happiness must be real, and not dependent on (potentially deceptive) mental states, requires an objective standard: what a happy life *really* demands or what, from an objective perspective, a good life should possess. Aristotle and Plato are able to claim justification for such positions. Those with a more subjective conception of a good life will not.

The relationship between happiness and law could be stated as a simple instrumental one. That all legal systems are a means of making as many people as possible happy. With some clarification of *happy* this could be made plausible. Legal systems do not produce unalloyed pleasure at every moment, but they do satisfy the interests and needs of many people. A more subtle description of the relationship could be framed in terms of expectations: what do we expect of people, and what *should* we expect of them? We expect people to want to do what will make them happy and a legal system that systematically frustrated that pursuit of happiness would be not only unpopular but perverse; but in law this is tempered by what *should* be expected of people. This might be the simple claim that the pursuit of happiness must be curtailed for the safety of other individuals (Mill, 1991). It might be a more substantial claim that the pursuit of happiness must be curtailed by the safety of other individuals and the interests of the state (Finnis, 2011). Even more substantially, some states might expect their citizens to identify their own happiness with the success of the state as a whole, in which case the systematic frustration of individual desires might be justified (Cicero, 1998). In each of these narrowings of the relationship between law and unadulterated human happiness there is, nonetheless, an acceptance that everything that is allowed or constrained by the state is allowed or constrained in the expectation that everyone pursues happiness. Accordingly, to posit a relationship between law and happiness requires expressing it in a way that is richer than a bare proposition stating 'law aims to make people happy'. Legal systems always involve a complicated relationship between happiness and coexistence: we expect people to seek the pursuit of happiness with *constraints* on that pursuit.

If legal systems involve expectations about constraints on the pursuit of happiness, they do not expect everyone to be saints. No legal system demands that we entirely sacrifice what gives us happiness for the interests of others, and even highly 'collectivist' states are seeking to construe individual happiness in a particular way *as a better or fuller conception of human happiness*. More generally, any view of human life or ethics that demanded total self-abnegation *or* total pursuit of happiness without constraint would be unattractive. The first is inhuman (even self-sacrifice has to bring some benefits), the second unreasonable (even happiness has limits placed on it by our physical needs and by our living in the world with others). So, a philosophy, a politics or a personal ethics of happiness, while having a common sense foundation ('the good is happiness or pleasure'), has constraints placed upon it on the basis of *reasonable* expectations. The demands of such reasonableness are central to Finnis' critique of utilitarianism (Finnis, 2011: 116). Demanding that we be saints would be perverse if we all pursue happiness; conversely, demanding that we be allowed to be happy does not mean that we are all pure pleasure seekers.

EXAMPLE

Regina Respondent v Brown (Anthony) Appellant [1994] 1 A.C. 212, at 273

The notorious case of consensual sado-masochistic sex among a group of men required the Court to consider the extent to which criminal legislation prohibiting harm could be used where the harm is self-inflicted and invited. This required consideration of the variation in individuals' preferences ('special interests'), and the responsibilities of a state committed to maximising freedom.

The [. . .] state should interfere with the rights of an individual to live his or her life as he or she may choose no more than is necessary to ensure a proper balance between the special interests of the individual and the general interests of the individuals who together comprise the populace at large. Thus, while acknowledging that very many people, if asked whether the appellants' conduct was wrong, would reply 'Yes, repulsively wrong,' I would at the same time assert that this does not in itself mean that the prosecution of the appellants under sections 20 and 47 of the Offences against the Person Act 1861 is well founded.

4b Utilitarianism

Utilitarianism is the most philosophically resilient form of hedonism. It involves three commitments: consequentialism (outcomes, exclusively, are subject to moral evaluation), a hedonistic reduction of the good to pleasure (or happiness, or welfare) and a democratic commitment to equality. If we take the 'utility' aspect of utilitarianism as primary we can analyse utilitarianism as a philosophy where intrinsic and instrumental ideas of goodness are combined. Anything *useful* can be described as good (i.e. 'good for achieving *x*'); any state of affairs where the sum of happiness outweighs the sum of unhappiness (disutility) is good intrinsically (i.e. without reference to any further goal). Thus J.S. Mill (see below) collapses the intrinsic and instrumental together: 'Whatever can be proved to be good, must be so by being shown to be a means to something admitted to be good without proof' (Mill, 1991: 4).

Jeremy Bentham (1748–1832), who coined the term 'utilitarianism', combined the instrumental good with other intrinsic and objective uses of good on the basis that everything useful and everything we approve of has one of two consequences: an increase of pleasure or an increase of pain.

> By utility is meant that property in any object, whereby it tends to produce benefit, advantage, pleasure, good or happiness, (all this in the present case comes to the same thing) [. . .] to the party whose interest is considered: if that party be the community in general, then the happiness of the community: if a particular individual, then the happiness of that individual. (Bentham, 2007: 2)

A good can-opener opens cans more quickly, leading to a marginal increase in pleasure; a good moral action may save lives leading to a substantial increase in pleasure. Conversely, bad can-openers *and* the loss of life are on a spectrum of things increasing pain in the world. A lot of work has to be done here by the terms pleasure and pain to encompass everything from life-defining activities to trivial inconveniences. Nonetheless, the reduction to this single standard – identifying what is good with what is useful for bringing about pleasure rather than pain – is held to provide a complete system governing individual action and collective legislation.

Bentham's utilitarianism is intended to be both scientific and democratic. His reduction of all decision-making to an *evaluation* of outcomes, and the reduction of everything we might plausibly hold as beneficial (pleasure, happiness or well-being) to the *value* of utility, produces an empirical view of action and value. Everything relevant to ethics – value and evaluation – is located in the empirical world of actions and probable consequences:

> . . . sum up all the values of all the pleasures on the one side, and those of all the pains on the other. The balance, if it be on the side of pleasure, will give the good tendency of the act [. . .]; if on the side of pain, the bad tendency of the act. (2007: 31, emphasis removed)

Interior mental processes or mysterious moral properties have no place in this system. To be sure, Bentham asks us to *evaluate* what may happen; he offers a number of rules for assisting in calculation of what is likely to produce the greatest quantity of happiness (2007: 30), but the place of ethical action and evaluation is the world and the consequences of our actions. What we should do, and what we should value, are on a single unitary scale of utility, and that scale is purely empirical and calculable. We can *calculate* how much pleasure or pain our actions may cause and thereby evaluate empirically what the best course of action is. With a monistic account of what is good, and with that good being something entirely empirical (rather than spiritual or mental), morality can be reconciled with science. We do not decide what is good, we calculate it.

The theory is not only scientific but also democratic on two grounds. First, in utilitarian calculations each person is to count as one, and only one. Individuals are not to be given greater weighting in calculation over one another. Second, Bentham makes no distinction between different kinds of pleasures. He famously argued that pub games and poetry should be judged on an equal footing; devoting time to either can be pleasurable (see Smart and Williams, 1973: 15). Admittedly, Bentham went to some pains to consider how the *quantity* of pleasure could be gauged scientifically (the 'hedonistic calculus') and in such a calculation poetry might come out better as producing enduring, and not just intense, pleasure. Nonetheless, our choice of activities and interests should not be dictated by a hierarchy of desirable goals, only by their capacity to produce pleasure.

A critical question to ask of Bentham's position is whether it is suitable to talk predominantly about pleasure where happiness is a better term for the type of reduction he wants to achieve. Bentham allows 'utility' to stand for the ultimate value of any activity. Nonetheless, if utility stands for both pleasure and happiness we could be presented with difficult problems when trying to choose between the maximisation of physical pleasures and the overall happiness of human lives. Without a hierarchy of goals there can be no distinction drawn between the pleasure of individual, self-seeking, individuals and the happiness of the whole. As Finnis puts it, the utilitarian's position 'affords them no principle by reference to which they could criticise as unreasonable or immoral any persons who set out to maximise their own happiness regardless of the welfare of others' (2011: 116).

Mill sought to enrich utilitarianism with a more sophisticated analysis of this unitary value. Mill agrees with Bentham that pleasure is a necessary condition of goodness: we do not treat things as useful or valuable if they lack the capacity to give pleasure. Nonetheless, pleasure is not always the *sufficient* condition of happiness. In some cases we will know that our happiness is incomplete, despite our lives containing much pleasure. We will know this, says Mill, if we have experienced 'higher pleasures' such as the pleasures of intellectual activity which leave us dissatisfied with 'lower pleasures', i.e. pure physical pleasure. (In this respect Mill's argument is not unlike Plato's, where his analysis of justice and knowledge is supported by the 'special insight' of philosophers. To the extent that such an argument is reasonable it depends upon the idea that, without having another point of comparison, we cannot make a definitive decision on the truth or value of something.) Accordingly, Mill is able to say that it is better to be Socrates dissatisfied than a fool, or a pig, satisfied (1991: 140). Here Mill has not sought to introduce two entirely different kinds of pleasure – if he did, his argument would cease to be monistic, would have failed in its reduction of value to a single term – he has simply observed that in some circumstances we have a greater awareness of what will give us fuller, rich or more sustainable pleasure. At the same time it seems that Mill is not only suggesting that we can become *aware* of 'higher' pleasure but that these are *essentially superior* to 'lower' pleasures, hinting at a pluralistic conception of the good that sits uneasily with Bentham's strict monism. Either way, we have no choice, as utilitarian decision-makers, but to seek to maximise those pleasures that have the most 'felicity' (endurance, intensity, potency etc.).

EXAMPLE

Ghaidan v Godin-Mendoza [2004] UKHL 30

This case concerned the status of same-sex partners in matters of succession to rented homes, i.e. whether they can retain the tenancy under legislation referring to 'his or her wife or husband'. Not surprisingly, the UK House of Lords ruled that this was a matter of equality, of happiness, and of rationality, and the right should therefore be granted. Note, however, that the justification for individual rights is linked to democracy, but not necessarily the desires of the majority. Neither the common good, nor democracy, are equivalent to majoritarianism (i.e. pursuing whatever happens to be the will of the majority). Can utilitarianism reconcile 'equal weighting' with the complexity of democracy in practice?

> Treating some as automatically having less value than others not only causes pain and distress to that person but also violates his or her dignity as a human being. The essence of the [European Convention on Human Rights], as has often been said, is respect for human dignity and human freedom [. . .]. [S]uch treatment is damaging to society as a whole. Wrongly to assume that some people have talent and others do not is a huge waste of human resources. It also damages social cohesion, creating not only an underclass, but an under-class with a rational grievance. Third, it is the reverse of the rational behaviour we now expect of government and the state. Power must not be exercised arbitrarily. If distinctions are to be drawn, particularly upon a group basis, it is an important discipline to look for a rational basis for those distinctions. Finally, it is a purpose of all human rights instruments to secure the protection of the essential rights of members of minority groups, even when they are unpopular with the majority. Democracy values everyone equally even if the majority does not.

4c Variants of utilitarianism

For utilitarian decision-makers (including ourselves as individuals and our law-makers) the most challenging responsibility is to identify that course of action which maximises utility for the greatest number of people. This has three specific dimensions. First, equality: each and every person, including ourselves, is to count as one, i.e. of equal importance. Second, a consequentialist dimension: we are only interested in the predicted outcomes, not the motives, of actions. Third, an evaluative dimension: we are acting in a way that is likely to bring pleasure on the basis of a calculation of the quality and quantity of that pleasure. Together these form the basis of deciding how to act, and expressed in this form constitute 'act utilitarianism'. Act utilitarianism asks us 'what are the possible outcomes in these circumstances' and 'which, among the possible actions in circumstances, will produce most pleasure or happiness? (Raz (ed.), 1978: 46f)'. The probabilistic dimension of this process is challenging We cannot control the outcomes of our actions; we as individuals may be poor at predicting outcomes; and we may be concerned about the long-term, and not just immediate, consequences of our actions. In short, people are often bad predictors of what will make themselves and others happy and no-one can foresee the wider consequences of their actions. To a point, the act utilitarian simply has to work within the normal limits of human agency and imagination: guessing that being nice to certain people will make them happier, or assuming that money given to a group of poor people will create more pleasure than its being spent by someone already extremely rich. But these examples do not capture the complex possibilities that any action, let alone a 'moral quandary' or legislative act, would have to envisage. The act utilitarian is asked to be both imaginative and pragmatic: consider all of the consequences of the act but not those too remote from it causally or temporally.

These problems have generated a variation of utilitarianism, rule utilitarianism, which is less reliant on multiple probabilistic calculations. The initial assumptions are the same: the reduction of morality to utility, consequentialism and equality among persons. Nonetheless, this asks us to formulate rules which will serve as a *generalisation* to simplify decision-making and as a more formalised or regularised approach to morality and legislation. 'Rule-utilitarianism is the view that the rightness or wrongness of an action is to be judged by the goodness or badness of the consequences of a rule that everyone should perform the action in like circumstances' (Smart and Williams, 1973: 9). This is a generalised or legislative approach because we are put in the situation of a legislator rather than an individual actor and asked to consider what rules would be best to maximise utility. This resembles more familiar approaches to morality formulated as universal principles of 'do not steal', 'do pay your bills' etc. However, it is still underpinned by, first, the equivalence of good, happiness and utility, and second, by a consequentialism which looks to outcomes and does not accept that there are absolute duties which stand in the way of calculating the best outcome.

Rule utilitarianism is structured but not inflexible. Given that rules are justified by their maximising utility, all utilitarian rules can admit exceptions: a utilitarian could happily construct a rule saying 'do not steal unless it would bring a great benefit such as saving a life'. Arguably this therefore collapses back into act utilitarianism: i.e. 'follow rules unless actions contrary to the rule would bring greater utility'. At the very least, the two positions are consistent with one another, with act utilitarianism guiding our actions as individuals, and rule utilitarianism able to guide a society needing general rules and expectations.

In this context it is also worth noting political and economic 'neoliberalism' as a distinctive variant on utilitarianism. This is the idea that the free market maximises the common and good and the state must support the market. Monistic (centred on wealth creation) and consequentialist, this is perhaps the most common form utilitarianism takes today. As such, the lasting legacy of utilitarianism might be said to be a defence of liberties (namely economic liberties) combined with a desire for quantifiable and calculable outcomes (namely increase of wealth). This does not look like an unquestionably good guide to legal and political action for everyone (see discussion of Sen below), but following the basic tenets of utilitarianism it does prevent the pursuit of wealth being viewed simply as a crude form of hedonism.

EXAMPLE

'Agreement on Trade-Related Aspects of Intellectual Property Rights' (TRIPS) World Trade Organisation, 1994

Flowing from the General Agreement on Trade and Tariffs, this international agreement deals with intellectual property and international trade. The function of such an international agreement is 'recognition' of a number of basic principles. This is an attempt to preserve both international trade and the protection of creativity (intellectual property) in the belief that both are necessary for wealth and happiness.

Desiring to reduce distortions and impediments to international trade, and taking into account the need to promote effective and adequate protection of intellectual property rights, and to ensure that measures and procedures to enforce intellectual property rights do not themselves become barriers to legitimate trade; / Recognizing the need for a multilateral framework of principles, rules and disciplines dealing with international trade in counterfeit goods; / Recognizing that intellectual property rights are private rights; / Recognizing the underlying public policy objectives of national systems for the protection of intellectual property, including developmental and technological objectives; / Recognizing also the special needs of the least-developed country Members in respect of maximum flexibility in the domestic implementation of laws and regulations in order to enable them to create a sound and viable technological base; [. . .].

5 Place and property

Introduction

Discussion of basic goods often revolves around relationships with others and certain kinds of personal fulfilment. Law protects relationships and, by taking reasonableness as its standard, allows personal fulfilment to take place without prescribing what form a fulfilled life should take. However, this seems to neglect the fact that, famously, 'property is nine-tenths of the law'. The fabric of law seems to consist, in large measure, of the relationships and problems generated by property. This is partly for historical reasons concerning the identity of law-makers and those with access to the Courts; law was made by, and for, a 'propertied' class (Thompson, 1975).

It also reflects the fact that ownership and property rights are not just one, among many, classes of rights, but among our most fundamental. The right to own or exchange property is rarely articulated as a human right because it is so frequently taken for granted as part of the constitutional rights of any citizen of a state (Locke, 1960: 327f; Hobbes, 1996: 164). This too is for historical reasons. The emergence of the modern state coincides with common land being parcelled or 'enclosed' into private property. It also coincides with sovereignty over new lands where indigenous claims to sovereignty and property were rejected as falling short of European understandings of ownership (Tuck, 1999).

If the modern state has such a close relationship with private property, we take for granted that constitutions, if nothing else, must protect ownership and property *rights*. But such rights can only be understood as fundamental because they meet basic human needs for place and property: to live somewhere, and to be recognised as having a claim to their belongings. Our legal relationship with property – its constitutional importance and its giving rise to rights – must relate to our valuing of it, rather than historical accident. Some basic ideas of property and ownership are discussed in relation to John Locke; some contemporary ideas concerning economic development are also considered.

The idea of 'place' also falls outside many discussions of the good. Those philosophies taking their lead from Aristotle will certainly be sensitised to the needs of the situated individual who depends upon their social milieu for structures of material support (and indeed depends upon it for their identities and responsibilities as individuals and citizens) (Taylor, 1992), but this picture is incomplete. Our relationship with the world as a whole – our environment and the material resources of the world – has complex legal manifestations. The environment has been treated by law as property from which property rights flow. Property rights are, again, crucial to personhood, but they are insufficient to understand our reliance on, and obligations concerning, the natural world. Given that the environment, and the resources that it generates, are central to our physical well-being, these must be considered in their own terms, and we must, arguably, resist the temptation to treat the world purely as territory, i.e. property in the hands of an individual or state.

5a Property

John Locke (1632–1704) is a key contributor to early modern conceptions of law and his work on government remains influential in common law traditions. It is his approach to property that is our central concern here and it can be summarised in a single assumption: because the natural can become property, property is natural. Locke sought to site the origins of legal and political legitimacy in the movement from a situation where there is no property and no legal rights, to one where individuals, and their property, are afforded legal protections. From a situation where the world was 'common' – open to anyone for appropriation and cultivation – individuals gained ownership by using our labour and work and thereby adding value to common natural resources. By gaining ownership through 'mixing labour' with the raw materials of the world, individuals could be rightly considered 'property owners' and therefore deserving of protection through law (Locke, 1960: 328). Individual labour, mixed with the resources of nature, is the essential basis of ownership. Ownership, therefore, is the most fundamental 'natural right', predating civil and political rights.

This assumes a fundamental equality between persons in so far as we are, from a 'natural perspective', equally free to take possession of nature and establish ownership, but there are also natural limits to individual ownership. Labour alone cannot provide us with much more than is necessary for survival and comfort:

> The measure of property, nature has well set, by the extent of men's labour, and conveniency of life: No man's labour could subdue, or appropriate all: nor could his enjoyment consume more than a small part; so that it was impossible for any man, this way, to intrench upon the right of another, or acquire, to himself, a property, to the prejudice of his neighbour. (1960: 334, capitalisation removed)

Locke's position is an appealing one to the extent that we do now take property rights as so fundamental that they are implicit, but rarely mentioned, in philosophical discussion of the good. Furthermore from this treatment of property rights as fundamental, a more substantial philosophy of state and government is possible: one dedicated to, but also limited by, the preservation of private property legitimately gained through work and labour. However, this view of rights arising from property has been justifiably criticised as ignoring inequalities of ownership stemming, in part, from the seizure of common land by already powerful landowners (Cole, 2001). Indeed, on a larger scale, it is the Lockean account of the origins of property and rights that was most frequently used to justify the seizure of colonial territory. The indigenous peoples of the New World did not cultivate land in a way that was recognised (or recognisable) to Europeans. Accordingly this 'failure' to use natural resources profitably meant the New World had the status of *terra nullis* – unowned, lawless, space – which was being civilised, rather than conquered (Coyle and Morrow, 2004). Moreover, treating the natural world purely as a basis of property has also (directly and indirectly) led to a view of the natural world as 'potentially-owned-material', a view which has been challenged by environmentalists.

EXAMPLE

Status of Aliens Act 1914, s. 17

We can lose sight of the fact that whatever good the law may do for people, such benefits conferred by law are determined by jurisdiction: the power to make law within a particular, geographically confined, territory. For those who move to another state but do not adopt a new nationality, their rights are limited to a greater or lesser extent by specific laws governing their legal status and legal relationships. Section 17 of the Status of Aliens Act 1914 (still in force) demonstrates that property may well be a basic good, but it is one closely related to place.

Section 17 'Capacity of alien as to property':

Real and personal property of every description may be taken, acquired, held and disposed of by an alien in the same manner in all respects as by a [. . .] British subject; and a title to real and personal property of every description may be derived through, from or in succession to an alien in the same manner in all respects as through, from or in succession to a [. . .] British subject: Provided that this section shall not operate so as to – (1) confer any right on an alien to hold real property situate out of the United Kingdom; or (2) qualify an alien for any office or for any municipal, parliamentary, or other franchise; or (3) qualify an alien to be the owner of a British ship; or (4) entitle an alien to any right or privilege as a British subject, except such rights and privileges in respect of property as are hereby expressly given to him [. . .].

5b Environment

Environmental law is a challenging area of law because it seems to contradict two basic tenets of domestic and international law: that the natural world can be treated as a property and that the scope of legal regulation is always confined within jurisdictions. The idea of the environment as property has its origins in a conception of humanity as having *dominion* over nature. Derived in part from Judaeo-Christian ideas, 'dominion' is the power, delegated from a sovereign, that a feudal lord has over a territory. A sovereign has unlimited power, but cedes some power to lords and barons over a sphere in which they hold power, power limited by the sovereign himself:

> The origin of this notion is to be found in the feudal system of the middle ages, when lands were granted to vassals to 'hold' of the lord on condition of performing certain services or paying sums of money. The theory implies, of course, that the King is in a sense the landlord as well as the ruler of the country, and is simply a survival from the times when a conquering chieftain did actually have the right to dispose of all the land as well as govern his dominions. (Hogg, 1908: 65)

Dominion of the Earth shares the same assumptions. We, like lords, have absolute power within our jurisdiction (the Earth) to rule as we see fit (conditional only on the will of God). On the Earth no authority higher than mankind exists, so dominion authorises a rule that is unconditional.

On a dominion model of nature, nature was a common set of resources that could be made the possession of any individual who used their own labour to harvest or take ownership. Locke makes this point directly:

> As much Land as a Man Tills, Plants, Improves, Cultivates and can use the product of, so much is his Property [. . .] God, when he gave the World in common to all Mankind, commanded Man also to labour, and the penury of his Condition required it of him. God and his Reason commanded him to subdue the Earth, i.e. improve it for the benefit of Life, and therein lay out something that was his own, his labour. (Locke, 1960: 332–3, italics removed)

This relationship between subjection, property and dominion means that *shared* environmental problems and concerns are difficult to manage. Individual ownership does not lead to a concern with the value of the whole (Coyle and Morrow, 2004). The objective of environmental law is therefore to reassert a harmony of interests in the maintenance of natural resources, which may, or may not, be articulated through the language of rights. More simply, it asks us to exchange the idea of dominion for that of stewardship: the *duty* to maintain a resource over which we have *temporary* control.

If environmental law involves rejecting a view of the Earth as property, it also has to be multi-jurisdictional. The environment cannot be easily conceptualised within law's territorial understanding of space (see Chapter 7). Much contemporary thinking on the philosophy of environmentalism is informed by Hannah Arendt's work in *The Human Condition* (1998). The negative implication of Arendt's work is that we, as a consequence of the pervasive influence of science, still inhabit a mind-set informed by notions of dominion and domination, and we have not yet fully accepted a stewardship view of the environment. The positive implication is that we share a human condition – i.e. we share the Earth, and the Earth limits our possibilities as humans – and this is the foundation of a whole philosophy of life and politics premised not on domination but on a shared relationship with the Earth.

Written in 1950, when use of nuclear power was in its infancy, Arendt saw in nuclear experimentation a novel relationship with the Earth (Arendt, 1998). Because nuclear experiments and their consequences cannot be contained within a laboratory, *the entire Earth* has become the site of an open-ended experiment. This dangerous state of affairs is the consequence of giving science untrammelled power and authority in our societies. Science, the *instrument* of human endeavour, has become an end in itself.

> If it should turn out to be true that knowledge (in the modern sense of know-how) and thought have parted company for good, then we would indeed become the helpless slaves, not so much of our machines as of our know-how, thoughtless creatures at the mercy of every gadget which is technically possible. (1998: 3)

Science has come to dictate our goals, namely greater and greater 'efficiency', rather than an instrument of our goals. When we treat the Earth as something that can be experimented upon without limits, it is symptomatic of the fact that the human condition itself has changed: science now dominates humanity's purposive activity, not the human good.

More positively, we as humans are all co-dependent upon the Earth and processing its materials. This co-dependence, and the temporal and material conditions that this places upon us – i.e. the fact that we cannot change the past nor can we draw upon materials beyond the Earth – entails that we all share a *condition*: common boundaries, and common limits to what is possible. In terms of the environment and society more generally, this condition is our common dependence upon *labour* (gaining control of natural materials), *work* (processing of natural materials) and *action* (social and political decisions concerning labour and work). This does not translate directly into a political and legal position in the sense of an environmental politics. Rather, this is a more fundamental call to see politics as based in a shared condition, and a rethinking of politics as more than the pursuit of efficiency in the management of human affairs. Politics should be a process of looking for new beginnings and new possibilities on a global scale. In short, the world is materially inter-related not in a metaphysical or physical sense, but because we have the power to damage the environment outside our own state, perhaps irreversibly.

EXAMPLE

United Nations Framework Convention on Climate Change (1992) Article 3

The UN defends a principle of sustainable development in environmental law, namely that law should seek to integrate economic growth and minimal impact on the environment. It also defends the 'precautionary principle' which encourages caution and constraint, even in the absence of strong scientific evidence of harm or risk. Science can never make us certain – we can never know what we will know in the future – accordingly, precaution and international cooperation are the best policies.

The Parties should take precautionary measures to anticipate, prevent or minimize the causes of climate change and mitigate its adverse effects. Where there are threats of serious or irreversible damage, lack of full scientific certainty should not be used as a reason for postponing such measures, taking into account that policies and measures to deal with climate change should be cost-effective so as to ensure global benefits at the lowest possible cost. To achieve this, such policies and measures should take into account different socio-economic contexts, be comprehensive, cover all relevant sources, sinks and reservoirs of greenhouse gases and adaptation, and comprise all economic sectors. Efforts to address climate change may be carried out cooperatively by interested Parties.

5c Capability

Development theory, at the intersection of politics, economics and law, has become an important feature of inter-governmental activity. The underlying assumption is that it is good for the international community to aid economic and social development in less developed parts of the world and that there should be legal structures supporting this. Whether this is instrumental (the economic enhancement of less developed states as a means to regional stability), or an intrinsic good (obligatory given its relationship with human flourishing), international development has powerful ideological force in international relations and is driven by both states and non-governmental organisations.

Organisations such as the World Bank and International Monetary Fund have powers, granted to them by the international community, to administer grants and loans to states in order to support economic growth conditional on internal economic and political restructuring. They work on the – economic and philosophical – assumptions that global economic development is both a question of increasing wealth and increasing capabilities (Twining, 2009: 219–24). Increasing material wealth is one way of increasing the good within a state and ultimately the good of its citizens. However, material wealth is not a sufficient condition of sustaining good lives for people. It is necessary to ensure that 'capability' is built within countries to ensure that wealth creation is sustainable. It is also important that individuals are given the resources – the education, the opportunities and the freedom – to determine their own lives and pursue their own conceptions of what a good life consists of. Accordingly, a 'capabilities approach' is now considered to be the guiding principle of UN organs, arguing that individual capacities and capabilities are at least as important as general wealth creation within a state (Twining, 2009: 221–2).

This capabilities approach is based on the work of Amartya Sen, who developed a theory of international economics built on Rawls' theory of justice (Sen, 1999). The capabilities approach argues that material wealth is an incomplete goal, and that giving people the capability – through education and infrastructure – to pursue their own goals and individual development should be the underpinning of international economics. 'Instead of asking about people's satisfactions, or how much in the way of resources they are able to command, we ask, instead, about what they are actually able to do or to be' (Nussbaum, 2000: 12). This approach can be characterised as 'liberal' in so far as the goods of self-realisation and empowerment are treated as limits on the power of the state. The capabilities approach is also more fulsome in its conception of the good than often found in liberalism, in that it includes an (Aristotelian) view of the importance of flourishing, and not simply preference fulfilment and equality of opportunity. Ultimately, liberal positions tend to be concerned with what is right rather than what is good (see Chapter 4), but in capabilities approaches we see some attempt to use both of these ideas to drive the direction of the global 'community'.

EXAMPLE

'Declaration on the Right to Development' United Nations General Assembly Resolution 41/28 (1986)

Consolidating ideas already found in international treaties, the UN's Declaration on the Right to Development grounds a set of state of responsibilities in both individual needs and capabilities (Art. 1(1)) and the needs and rights of peoples (Art. 1(2)).

Article 3(3):

States have the duty to co-operate with each other in ensuring development and eliminating obstacles to development. States should realize their rights and fulfil their obligations in such a manner as to promote a new international economic order based on sovereign equality, interdependence, mutual interest and co-operation among all States, as well as to encourage the observance and realization of human rights.

Questions

Section 1

- Is goodness a characteristic of natural processes? Could something be evaluated as good without any reference to humans?
- Can a person lead a *desirable* life without wealth, or friendship or knowledge? On what basis – subjective or objective – could this be decided?
- Can *legal* rights and duties be decided on the basis of a 'thin' – i.e. flexible – concept such as the good? Can *moral* rights and duties be decided on the basis of a thin notion such as the good? Why might the answer to the two be different?

Section 2

- Is what is 'valuable' ultimately monistic, i.e. reducible to a single value? Or are values pluralistic, i.e. there are many values?
- Does Plato give a plausible account of human psychology? Is a good psychological state the precondition of acting morally?
- Does there have to be a harmony between the individual and their state – a harmony of interests, values and expectations – for that individual to be happy?

Section 3

- Is nature something that is a source of law, or antagonistic to law?
- Why does the natural law school associate values with some facts (e.g. rationality in humans) but not others (e.g. the survival of the fittest in nature)?
- Is human *reasoning* a good guide to what is treated as *reasonable* in law?

Section 4

- Classical utilitarianism suggests that morality can become a science on the model of the 'hard sciences'. Is this desirable? Does utilitarianism offer a plausible account of how we *decide* how to act?

- Should law-makers always to achieve the greatest happiness for the greatest number? Should judges?

- Does utilitarianism provide justification for granting human rights? Would act and rule utilitarianism differ in their relationship with rights?

Section 5

- What kind of relationship do we have with the Earth? Does this depend upon whether or not it was created? Does this depend upon current scientific knowledge? How might such knowledge be limited?

- Environmentalism suggests that science sometimes offers an impoverished view of the world and of our responsibilities: we are more concerned with power and rights than with harmony and duties. Is this a fair account of the impact of science on our thinking about values?

- Can we reconcile property rights and duties to future generations?

- Does a 'capabilities approach' provide a useful combination of intrinsic and instrumental ideas of the good?

Concepts and methods: Values

Value and values

The language of 'values', 'what we value' and 'value judgments' are common to discussion in law, philosophy and beyond. Philosophy has a long tradition of analysing and clarifying our discussion of values in the form of political, ethical and legal philosophy. General study of values is termed 'axiology':

> Axiology can be thought of as primarily concerned with classifying what things are good, and how good they are. For instance, a traditional question of axiology concerns whether the objects of value are subjective psychological states, or objective states of the world. (*Stanford Encyclopaedia of Philosophy*, 2011)

Entertaining the possibility that value can be found, 'objective states of the world' axiology does not presume a division between facts and values but explores the nature of value and the preconditions of intelligible discussion of value.

The language of value is one where, characteristically, philosophical discussion can appear to stray far from common language and discussion. Nonetheless, our intuitions concerning value remain good starting-points. It should be immediately intelligible that there are things that we *value*: health, friendship, wealth etc. This sometimes does, and sometimes does not, equate with what we consider to be *values*. Values are more often articulated as positive generalisations (everyone is entitled to wealth), and sometimes negative generalisations (no-one should be forced into intolerable situations).

In making such generalisations it is important to distinguish exchange value (i.e. the market price of something) from the intrinsic worth of something (see Moore, 1959: 173). We can also distinguish exchange value from *labour* value, namely the value of the work that goes into a commodity or service (see Marx, Chapter 5). We should also distinguish needs from preferences (see Twining, 2009). A sub-division of 'interests' and 'preferences' is useful for this purpose. Humans' basic interests (e.g. survival) are relatively stable and predictable; human preferences vary considerably between and within cultures. 'Value as preference' could be reducible to *evaluation* (we, individually or socially, decide on the value of everything). 'Value as preference' can be described as a 'cognitivist' position: value is nothing more, or less, than the evaluation that takes place in our minds. Conversely, needs and interests are more likely to be *mind-independent*: valuable regardless of our subjective evaluations and therefore 'non-cognitivist' (see Baggini and Fosl, 2007: 112–13).

Analysing values

The most important approach to questions concerning what humans are, and what they should do, is to observe the division between facts and values. While 'what humans are' is related to 'what humans should do', they are nonetheless distinguishable. Be aware, and draw distinctions, where facts are easily blurred with values. For example, where something is said to be a 'natural' human instinct, behaviour or tendency this does not necessarily entail anything about what humans *should* do. Equally, exercise caution where values are said to be 'natural'. Many things have been said to have been natural (e.g. slavery) which are clearly not. Other things look quite natural (e.g. taking care of children), but may well vary radically from culture to culture. Also, exercise caution when presented with arguments concerning 'human nature'. Human nature can be used to generate opposing, even contradictory characterisations: greedy and benign, selfish and selfless, perfect and imperfect. Appeal to human nature should generally be avoided; common human traits, behaviours, dispositions and instincts are generally clearer.

There are powerful currents of thought, generally categorised as 'virtue ethics', where fact, value and human nature meet. This position, associated with Aristotle, suggests that ethics and morality are largely reducible to the cultivation of virtue (the disposition to do good or healthy actions) and avoidance of vices (the disposition to engage in bad or unhealthy actions). This does, of course, generate important questions about what virtues, in general, people should cultivate; it also demands clarity on what kind of social relationships are conducive to virtue (Moore, 1959: 172–3). Virtue ethics can therefore be associated with more familiar discussions of rights and duties, but it can also be allied with certain forms of scepticism about moral universality. While this does not seem to encompass all that we mean by ethics and morality, it certainly gets to the heart of the combination at the heart of the concept 'human': facts (what we are) and values (what we should be).

Practical reasoning

The subjective processes of thinking and judging, while 'private', can be evaluated by the standard of whether they are reasonable. Rational thinking may be characterised as relating ends and means in a sensible way (e.g. staying in bed is not a rational means to achieving success), or it may involve having a 'rational' view on what is good for yourself or for others (it is not rational to eat mud or encourage others to do so). Where there is a failure to match ends to means, or see one's own basic interests clearly, this can be characterised as unreasonable.

This has wider significance for law and morality. The ends of a legal system (social stability, order, fairness) are different from the means to those ends (laws and procedures). It is generally accepted – in international law and beyond – that it is unreasonable to use others *purely* as a means to one's own ends (i.e. slaves of one kind or another). This is one of the main ends of human rights law: this asserts that everyone is entitled to certain levels of freedom and respect. There are, however, some grey areas here, from the person who works hard but is taxed heavily (through taxation they become a means to general social ends) to those working in the sex industry whose bodies become commodities.

The work of Finnis encourages us to think carefully about the relationship between practical reasoning and law in such contexts. Practical reasoning is deliberation about action (as opposed to theoretical, speculative or pure reason). Deciding how to act is different from purely theoretical reasoning. We are not speculating about the world or deducing propositions from first principles, but deciding what we should do as rational individuals with a set of complex interests. When we deliberate about what to do we draw together a mixture of beliefs – about the world, about what is possible for us, what is desirable for us, how we can justify our actions to ourselves and others – and derive from these beliefs judgments about what we should do. This generates hypothetical imperatives or descriptive norms: 'having to do x to achieve y'. It also encompasses some categorical imperatives and prescriptive norms: 'I have obligations regardless of my preferences.' Reasons for action may not have a strict 'logic' but beliefs can be assessed as justified or unjustified, and some means can be judged better than other means as reasonable for the chosen ends (Raz (ed.), 1978: 33–45).

However, good practical reasoning must involve more than justifying our beliefs and fitting our means to our ends. It has to involve choices between ends: our objectives or designs for life. Accordingly, those engaged in practical reasoning – whether private individuals or judges – may have, ultimately, to make an assessment of basic goods in Finnis' terms (2011: 100–26). That is, determine what it is that is self-evidently or unassailably good to achieve.

Categorical and hypothetical imperatives

This is an old philosophical categorisation investigated most fully by Kant (see Chapter 4). Imperatives are things that should be done. Hypothetical imperatives are those things that should be done as a means to ends. Categorical imperatives are those things that *must* be done, regardless of the consequences they produce or the cost for the person doing them. Kant sought to demonstrate that truly moral actions are those pursuing categorical, not hypothetical, imperatives (Kant, 1948). His position makes sense of at least some of our intuitions about morality, not least the idea that we have duties and that these make demands upon us which do not always lead to pleasurable outcomes.

Identifying categorical imperatives is not easy for the same reasons it is difficult to identify *necessary* truths. To make a certain class of acts obligatory or necessary in all possible circumstances is likely to run up against the complexity of the world and yield demands for exceptions. Note that governments and legal systems rarely function on the basis of categorical imperatives, rather hypothetical ones about the welfare of the majority of people. Categorical statements of value more generally are rarely found within legal reasoning, however, this is sometimes a feature of human rights discussions (see Chapter 5).

Further reading

For broad philosophical accounts of the good, Nussbaum's (1986) work combines analysis of both Plato and Aristotle. G.E. Moore's *Principia Ethica* (1959) is central to modern, analytical, approaches to the use (and misuse) of the good in philosophy. Iris Murdoch's *Sovereignty of the Good* (1970) is rather more complicated, and presumes knowledge of Kant on the part of the reader, but is still a powerful defence of the good as 'axiomatic' in our thinking. Among the voluminous literature on natural law Finnis (2011) and Fuller (1969) are both crucial. Simmonds' (2007) work has a more Platonic slant; D'Entreves (1957) is more Thomist (i.e. informed by Aquinas). Smart and Williams (1973) is not only a good introduction to utilitarianism but also a good example of philosophical debate in practice. Coyle and Morrow provide a valuable philosophical introduction to environmental law. Nussbaum (2000) and Sen (1999) provide different renderings of the capabilities approach.

Visit **www.mylawchamber.co.uk/riley** to access tools to help you develop and test your knowledge of legal philosophy including Podcasts on leading thinkers and theories, discussion questions, diagrams showing interrelations between concepts, and weblinks

4   Right

Introduction

The good provides an appealing interpretive perspective on law. Law has a number of ends – those ends associated with justice such as the common good, judgment, desert and others – and it aims to achieve these ends by the best means that it can: through the use of general and public rules, and through maintaining the basic goods of the individual. Through this interpretive lens we see law as making a distinctive contribution to social life and as something valuable in itself. However, this picture of law is a partial one. While it offers us a way to understand how law, as part of the governance of social affairs, can be assessed or justified, it does not capture two distinctive aspects of what we see at work within legal systems and legal institutions.

First, while legislators may see their law-making actions in terms of aspiring to the common good, legal officials (judges and lawyers) have a much closer relationship with the means that are distinctive to law: adjudication, impartiality and the enforcement of rules. These means are, in legal practice, separable from any ends they may serve; lawyers and judges construe their professional responsibilities in terms of upholding those means (i.e. 'professional integrity') rather than explicitly serving more substantial social or moral ends. Put simply, legal officials seek the *right answer* to legal questions.

Second, to the extent that the functioning of law serves the basic goods of individuals, this is more often discovered in the granting and protecting of rights. While basic goods may make unassailable moral claims on us as individuals and as a society, law generates and preserves a complex system of rights which grant both more, and less, than basic goods demand. They grant more because law gives rise to a complex system of rights: civil, political, social, contractual, constitutional, economic, familial, welfare and other rights. They grant less because such rights are conditional on the political and economic conditions within which law is created and are not, conversely, unassailable *moral* demands which hold unquestionably and unconditionally.

This does not lead to the conclusion that goodness and rightness are wholly incompatible ways of approaching law. If it is *good* for humans to live in groups, it is therefore *right* that social institutions should be preserved through the rule of law. Nonetheless, 'good' is used widely to denote social and personal ideals, while 'right' seems far closer to the privileges and protections at work *within* law.

These two features of the 'internal perspective' on law (i.e. the perspective of those working within and for a legal system) point towards two important aspects of law that are contained within the language of 'right'. Legal practitioners strive to find the right answer to legal problems, and that is the right *legal* answer, not necessarily a right answer in the sense of morally or socially right. Second, law is characterised by *rights*. The language of rights (rather than goods) seems appropriate for discussing the kinds of claims that legal practitioners routinely deal with. These two ideas – the right legal answer and law's relationship with rights – are the focus of this chapter. The remainder of this introduction outlines these two ideas.

What is it to find the right answer to a legal question? If we consider a Court case in a common law jurisdiction, finding an answer to a legal question is the responsibility of a judge (or in the case of criminal responsibility, a jury) and the right answer is a match between general rules (usually legislation) and a specific case at hand. This is not always simple. A Court may be aware of a number of rules which seem to apply with equal force, and a jury may have to make a judgment beyond reasonable doubt in circumstances where the boundaries between doubt and certainty have been blurred. Nonetheless, the right answer can emerge in these cases: we would say 'the evidence is strong and no other decision is possible' or 'over time it has become clear that this particular decision was the right one for the parties and for society as a whole'.

These are slightly different kinds of 'rightness'. On the one hand, we are saying that the decision follows logically from the rules and the evidence. On the other hand, we are saying that this was the right decision from a wider social, policy or historical perspective. It might be tempting to say that the second of these kinds of rightness is actually closer to the realisation of the good, that is, that the law is here making a better contribution to the common good. However, decisions that are good 'from a wider social or policy perspective' still have to be *right* answers for the parties whose case is being decided; and they have to be the *right* answer in the sense of emerging from the legal principles contained within a legal system. Legal decisions, even when serving the good, must first pass the threshold of being right in the specific circumstances of a dispute.

Drawing these species of 'right answer' together – the logically right and the circumstantially right – we can begin to treat 'legally right answers' as possessing a distinctive *coherence* or *correspondence*. To make the right logical decision is to draw a conclusion that *coheres* with (is drawn or derived from) its premises; in parallel, the right legal decision is the one that moves coherently from general rules, to specific facts, to a judgment. To be circumstantially right is to make a judgment on the basis of all relevant factors: the decision must *correspond* to relevant facts and legal categories. In sum, coherence associates 'the right answer to a legal question' with logical rigour, correspondence denotes the idea that the right legal answer must be one which corresponds to a pre-existing set of facts.

The language of *rights* is one of the most important contributions that law makes to our lives. When we claim that we have the right to something – from the trivial (the right to park here) to the profound (to be free from inhuman treatment) – we are making claims that have power and potency because they are supported by, and enforceable with, laws. Rights are immediately intelligible from a perspective external to legal institutions. Everyone should feel empowered to claim their rights, i.e. what is rightfully theirs or their right to certain basic forms of treatment.

In fact, while widespread, such claims are context-dependent and can be legally incorrect. We may not, for example, inhabit a legal system that protects our right to self-expression, or we may articulate our aspirations for social and economic justice in terms of rights, but find that no enforceable legal rules correlate with our aspirations. We often articulate (social, political and moral) claims in the language of rights, but this can mismatch the legal rights that are enforceable in law. Therefore, one of the most important responsibilities for analytical legal philosophy (see below and Chapter 5) is to distinguish between different kinds of legal rights, in order to prevent the language of rights becoming an undifferentiated mass of radically different rules and powers including those 'rights claims' which have no enforceable legal basis. It is also a responsibility of 'normative' legal philosophy (see Chapter 6) to consider what rights law should grant to people. This is a much more wide-ranging task drawing upon moral and political philosophy.

This chapter looks first at 'rightness' in law, moving from general analytical distinctions to more substantial questions of how philosophy, particularly political philosophy, underpins our ideas of what it is for there to be rightness in law. It then turns to rights, looking at ways to differentiate rights and looking at the philosophical challenges presented by 'human rights'.

1 Right

Introduction

The idea that the right is merely a variation on the theme of the good is partly persuasive. If a decision is the right one it must be good for someone. If something is right for us it must be good for us. However, the converse does not hold. What is good for us may not be right. A good outcome might be achieved at someone else's expense. An increase in overall happiness could be at the expense of *wronging* a minority. In sum, a good decision may be good in an instrumental sense (i.e. useful) but not *right* in a more fundamental sense that it is *justifiable*. Thus the good and the right are closely related notions, but sufficiently different to generate different conclusions about values and obligations.

There is an argument, common to a range of theorists, that both the right and the good are united in the justification of freedom or liberty. This emphasis on the defence and expansion of liberty is found in Hegel (below) and is also defended by Hobbes:

> It is not against reason that a man doth all he can to preserve his own body and limbs, both from death and pain. And that which is not against reason, men call RIGHT, or *jus*, or blameless liberty of using our own natural power and ability. (quoted in Tuck, 1999: 132)

This 'natural right' to not have our natural liberties curtailed without justification will recur within discussion of the right, and is, for those theorists who prioritise the right, the most important good defended by law (Sadurski, 1988). Law can be said to provide and defend a number of good things, but the right legal answer is always one which corresponds with fundamental liberties and freedoms.

It may also be the case that appeal to the right can overcome some of the practical and philosophical problems related to philosophies of the good. If the goal of human activity, including law, is the pursuit of the good, this still requires us to identify a social structure or legislative programme which prioritises goods and allows individuals to pursue their own good. In order for this not to become a prescriptive and potentially oppressive project, this must be limited in its application. One way to do this is to argue that the state must allow individuals to pursue their *own* conception of the good and ensure that the conditions of individual basic goods and the common good are protected. Prioritising the right – right legal answers, and rights – ensures that individual freedom is protected and collective goals can be pursued. Different accounts of this reconciliation of the good and the right are offered by Hegel and Mill (below).

1a Right and truth

The word 'right' in English is both a noun ('a right') and an adjective ('to be right'). One way of keeping these ideas separate is to concentrate on their antonym. Right as an adjective has its opposite in *wrong*. Right as a noun has various opposites among the most important of which is *duty*. The *Oxford English Dictionary* has the noun right denoting 'that which is consonant with justice, goodness, or reason; that which is morally or socially correct'. More simply, it describes right as a synonym of 'justice'. The adjectival form has 'right' denoting the property of 'agreeing with some standard or principle; correct, proper' or 'rightful, legitimate, lawful'. This connection between right, law and justice is even clearer in Latin where *ius* is translatable as either law or right, and in other European languages where the equivalent of the

English 'right' – *Recht* in German, *droit* in French – encompasses everything that we mean by 'right' *and* by 'law'. Putting these definitions together, it can be said that the English word 'right', like its European synonyms, is intimately related to justice, and to law, and that there is some overlap between noun and adjective.

The noun and the adjective overlap around the ideas of 'agreement' and 'correctness'. Together these words point towards the importance of correspondence and coherence in our understanding of 'right': to be in agreement with something is to cohere with it; to be correct is to correspond with a standard. Why are 'correspondence' and 'coherence' related to law? The 'rightness of law' lies in its capacity to give us *certainty*, and in the *authority* with which law and legal decisions are invested. Rightness – understood as certainty, authority or coherence – has a relationship with logic and necessity in a way that goodness does not. A 'right answer' is one that is not only desirable, but one that has the force of a *truth*. At this point the nature of 'rightness' draws us into ideas of certainty and truth.

There are two ways of construing 'truth', both of which have a relationship with rightness and with law. First, a right answer in law may share something with a right answer in mathematics: it has a force that rational persons cannot reject. Admittedly, any analogy between mathematics and law will be strained. Mathematics deals with ideal objects, law deals with the – less than ideal – social world. However, it may be that the conception of truth which we find in mathematics has at least one important similarity with that we find in law. Not all mathematics exhibits correspondence with the world as we perceive it; mathematics does not need *correspondence* with anything in the perceptible world to be true, it requires *coherence*. Mathematical proof is internal agreement between different mathematical assumptions; it does not need to be verified by our senses. On this basis we can analyse the idea of 'rightness' in law at a fundamental epistemological level (i.e. concerning the foundations of knowledge). The idea of the right is not about corresponding to a truth or set of facts outside law, it is about finding what is coherent within the system itself. As such 'legal rightness' is specific to law; a correct legal decision has its own distinctive claim to truth.

In distinction to this coherence account of truth, we could construe truth on the model of the empirical sciences, saying any claim that is made, and has the possibility of being true or false, must have a correspondence with a state of affairs in the world. The inner coherence of a system is irrelevant unless it has some link with a factual state of affairs in the world. On that basis, legal reasoning must correspond with a set of facts – rules, evidence, precedent – to be correct, and rightness is in that sense *correspondence*. Precisely what law is required to correspond *to* is contested: it may be previous legal decisions, rational principles, the underlying commitments of a community or a correspondence between law and human need. In each case, however, a right legal answer has force and necessity because it is in harmony with an external standard of truth.

> **EXAMPLE**
>
> ### *Šilth* v *Slovenia* ECHR (Application number 71463/01) 2009
>
> *The applicant brought a case to the ECHR claiming that they had been denied a fair trial. The Court here (as it has elsewhere) refuses to decide on the merits of particular cases (i.e. who should have won given the facts) and stresses instead its commitment to find general principles for fair trials. It thereby ensures certainty for the Parties to the Convention, and ensures coherence in its jurisprudence.*
>
> > The Court will be forced to carry out complex and questionable assessments on a case-by-case basis that will be difficult to dissociate from the merits of the case. The impact this is likely to have on 'legal certainty' (which the Court has rightly referred to) is, I would venture, both obvious and harmful. [. . .] For these reasons, we are in favour of following the case-law set by the decision in the *Moldovan* case, which appears to us to be more faithful to the principles governing the liability of States for acts or omissions occurring before the entry into force of the Convention, to ensure greater coherence in the Court's case-law and to be more compatible with the important principle of legal certainty.

1b Right answers

When we use 'right' to describe a correct answer or moral obligation, we are describing the special force of the answer or obligation. Understanding how use of 'right' is a distinctive way of describing something, particularly in the context of law, requires us to consider force and the related idea of necessity. For something to be right requires more than it benefit someone, it must have a *force* that is derived from something other than fleeting goals and needs. Put in sharper terms, the right, unlike the good, deals in what is *necessary*, rather than what is instrumentally useful or desirable. The nature of this necessity is difficult to capture. Partly it is *logical necessity*: some conclusions are inescapable if you accept a line of argumentation. Partly it is *factual necessity*: decisions and judgments must conform to the facts of reality. Unlike good things that we aspire to or desire, rightness is conformity with a pre-existing legal or factual standard of correctness.

Logical necessity concerns being compelled to accept the conclusion of a line of argumentation. Logic itself concerns the structure of argument and specifically the structure of deduction: the derivation of conclusions from premises (parts of or steps in an argument) in a *structurally* acceptable way. A common syllogism (a short logical argument), and a structurally defensible one, runs: 'Socrates is human, all humans are mortal, therefore Socrates is mortal.' The conclusion – the part after 'therefore' – is validly derived from the premises, indeed it is already contained in the premises. A rational person accepting the premises must – is forced to – accept the conclusion. Note that logic concerns structure, and an argument can be structurally *valid* without necessarily being *sound* (i.e. true). The following argument, having the same form as the Socrates argument, is valid but not sound: 'The Queen is human, all humans are invertebrates, therefore the Queen is an invertebrate.' That argument is valid – it is a structurally valid deduction of a conclusion from its premises – but the conclusion is false. A sound argument is both structurally defensible and has true premises. Ultimately, we should accept the logical force of an argument if we accept the premises, and the conclusion is validly derived from those premises.

Legal arguments are not always this simple. We have first to ask whether we are sure the premises are true. In a legal context this encompasses questions about whether evidence is reliable, and whether the right rules are being applied to the case. Moreover, we have to be sure that a conclusion really does follow from its premises. Has a sound legal judgment been deduced from a combination of general rules, evidence and facts?

Consider the following description of a legal process. A witness sees a crime and picks the defendant out of a line-up; on questioning, the defendant has no alibi; the jury concludes the defendant is guilty. Even this simple legal question has contested premises and a potentially contested conclusion. Was the witness reliable? Are there other reasons why the defendant has no alibi? Can guilt follow from the testimony of a single witness? Such questions about facts and conclusions make legal reasoning much more complex than the use of simple logical syllogisms. Nonetheless, the goal of legal judgment remains a sound conclusion: i.e. a factually *and* structurally correct conclusion.

The alternative idea, that rightness is *conformity with facts* rather than logically binding, represents a different understanding of truth. If to be right requires that our statements and our actions conform to reality, to how things really are, we are not saying '*right* equals *logical*' we are saying '*right* equals *true*'. This is related to the 'correspondence theory' of truth, i.e. that theory of knowledge where, for our statements to be true, they must correspond to a state of affairs in the world. As a theory of truth this is problematic. For example, consider statements about long dead or historical figures; are they necessarily *false* because they do not correspond with reality as it is *now*? But as a way of specifying the function of 'right' – i.e. has a correspondence with, or is grounded in, reality – this seems like a strong approach capturing, along with logical necessity, where rightness diverges from goodness.

EXAMPLE

Chester v Afshar [2004] UKHL 41

We demand clear answers from law, but it also has to confront uncertainty and unpredictability. Here a doctor is held responsible for not mentioning a small (one to two per cent) risk routine back surgery (a procedure of which he was an expert) could have serious and debilitating side effects, side effects that Miss Chester suffered after the surgery. If legal judgment depends on probability and 'counter-factual' arguments about what might have happened, can it ever be said to correspond to reality, or is a right legal answer – at best – a coherent one?

It is now, I think, generally accepted that the 'but for' test does not provide a comprehensive or exclusive test of causation in the law of tort. Sometimes, if rarely, it yields too restrictive an answer [. . .]. More often, applied simply and mechanically, it gives too expansive an answer: 'But for your negligent misdelivery of my luggage, I should not have had to defer my passage to New York and embark on SS *Titanic*.' But, in the ordinary run of cases, satisfying the 'but for' test is a necessary if not a sufficient condition of establishing causation. Here, in my opinion, it is not satisfied. Miss Chester has not established that but for the failure to warn she would not have undergone surgery. She has shown that but for the failure to warn she would not have consented to surgery on Monday 21 November 1994. But the timing of the operation is irrelevant to the injury she suffered, for which she claims to be compensated. That injury would have been as liable to occur whenever the surgery was performed and whoever performed it.

1c Right as justice

The noun 'right' (as in 'human rights') is in some languages associated with law and justice as a whole.

> The usual definition of a legal right [...] more or less consciously presupposes that law and right are two different phenomena which are not to be subsumed under a common general term. The English language countenances this dualism by the very fact that it has two entirely different words: 'law' and 'right' [...]. (Kelsen, 2006: 78)

A strict separation between the meanings of 'law', 'right' and 'justice' is denied by Kelsen and others. But the idea that 'right' is somehow related to *justice* seems too grand a claim. While the good seems to lend itself to substantial notions of social and individual well-being, rights, while important, are a contribution to justice but not in any obvious way the 'essence' of justice. However, some theorists have made rights central to their understanding of law and the state. Among others, Hegel claims the development of a notion of 'right' and its diffusion into law and politics represents a considerable development in the structure of human thinking. The basis for such a claim will be considered below, but we can partially distil this into the notion of *universality*. If something is logically necessary or logically binding it is not just right here and now, but potentially everywhere at all times. The good may be local and contingent, but basic (constitutional or human) rights have to be universal and necessary.

Thus, one way in which universality, necessity and justice meet is in defence of basic liberties for individuals. The reason being that, as already considered, appeal to the good may prove oppressive when we claim knowledge of the objectively good for others. Conversely, if we make minimal but binding claims about what is owed to every individual (universally) then we are claiming something is right in the sense of coherent with, or corresponding to, our other commitments. Consequently, basic liberties, either on their own, or treated as the entire basis of a political and legal project (see Dworkin, 1998), have been defended in terms of what is right, i.e. what is logically consistent with our other commitments.

EXAMPLE

Snyder v *Phelps*, 131 S. Ct. 1207 (2011) United States Supreme Court

Rights sometimes produce unsatisfactory outcomes. Here the right to freedom of speech in the United States allows the public picketing of funerals by homophobic radicals. Nonetheless, legal defence of their speech flows from a right which has unassailable importance within that culture. Defending the universality of free speech is held to be more important than the good – the desires and welfare – of the individuals involved.

Westboro [Church] believes that America is morally flawed; many Americans might feel the same about Westboro. Westboro's funeral picketing is certainly hurtful and its contribution to public discourse may be negligible. But Westboro addressed matters of public import on public property, in a peaceful manner, in full compliance with the guidance of local officials. [. . .] Speech is powerful. It can stir people to action, move them to tears of both joy and sorrow, and – as it did here – inflict great pain. On the facts before us, we cannot react to that pain by punishing the speaker. As a Nation we have chosen a different course – to protect even hurtful speech on public issues to ensure that we do not stifle public debate. That choice requires that we shield Westboro from tort liability for its picketing in this case.

2 Right as correspondence

Introduction

The idea of truth was first considered in Chapter 1, where it was suggested that both law and philosophy had crucial, but complicated, relationships with truth. Here we consider the possibility – highlighted by the concept of right – that law has its own relationship with truth. First through the idea of correspondence, then through the idea of coherence.

The relationship between truth and correspondence is this: that any claim we make, or anything we claim to know as true, must correspond to reality. Sometimes put in terms of 'justified true belief', for our ideas to count as knowledge they must be justified by corresponding to a real state of affairs (Dawson, 1981). This is an appealing account of truth because it makes sense of the basic intuition that only by making our (internal) ideas correspond with (external) reality can we say anything true, meaningful or justified. This basic commitment to truth-as-correspondence is found throughout philosophical thought (Sartwell, 1992). Here we consider three different, but related, philosophers who not only have diverging views on how we should construe this idea of correspondence, but also have diverging ideas about the social world, ideas that have consequences for how we should understand law.

This trio of philosophers – Kant, Hegel and Marx – are only paralleled by Socrates, Plato and Aristotle in their importance for the history of ideas. While not influential on one another through personal contact as were the Ancient thinkers, they each took ideas from the previous philosopher and radically reworked them. Each has complete, or at least extensive, accounts of how ideas and reality can be said to correspond. Of equal importance, each has ideas about the basis of right and its relationship with law. Note that, as German speakers and philosophers, 'right' for them is (for the most part) synonymous with 'law', and their work is characterised by a rich analysis of how rightness is also the most important dimension of law as a whole. The territory on which the debate was conducted is sketched here.

Immanuel Kant's (1724–1804) notion of right is closely tied to the idea of rationality. Human rationality shows us what is necessary, and not just desirable in our actions and choices. It is also correspondence with the rational that constitutes the basis of law. As universal and necessary, rational decisions by one individual should coincide with the rational decisions of other individuals, and rational decisions can be said to, together, form a 'kingdom of ends' where everyone's decisions can be said to be rational and therefore compatible (Kant, 1948). In short, good laws should allow the exercise of rationality; and right (as an adjective, i.e. rightness in action) is conformity – correspondence – between laws and human rationality.

G.W.F. Hegel (1770–1831) in his *Philosophy of Right* accepts the *form* of right that Kant identified – the meeting of law and rationality – but insisted this correspondence had to be contextualised within concrete social situations. Rather than treating the foundation of law as the individual's pursuit of their self-generated choices, Hegel insisted on beginning his analysis of law with the structures of *social life and state institutions* that are the necessary condition of freedom to choose. The state has to provide the conditions for individual freedoms, and the rightness of an action does not begin with the autonomous individual but with the state, understood as the embodiment of freedom and rationality. Social institutions have come, through long historical evolution, to embody rationality – evolved human thinking has been made concrete in modern social and legal practices – and right actions are those where institutions and rational actions correspond. Hegel's philosophy of right is a philosophy seeking an ultimate synthesis of the right action of the individual, our right to exercise our liberties and the state as the provider of freedom through law and governance.

Karl Marx (1818–83) took Hegel's criticisms of Kant much further. Rightness is not only related to rational actions within a just social context. That social context has to be one where law and legal rights – fictions used to diffuse social conflicts – are replaced with a social system that corresponds with the needs of individuals. In making 'rightness' concrete in the state, Hegel treated the state as a necessary condition of right. Marx, conversely, sees the modern state, and the inequalities on which it is founded, as a barrier to right and the *dissolution* of the state the necessary condition of right. Making a social system without antagonism or contradictory class interests would dissolve a temporary and incomplete correspondence between interests and laws and replace it with a true correspondence between the material conditions of existence and social life.

This, then, is the trajectory of 'rightness' through the three theorists. From law's correspondence with reason, to correspondence between the state and rationality, to correspondence between material and social reality.

2a Kant: right as duty

The essence of Kant's philosophy is opposition to 'dogmatism', that is, the unreflective and uncritical acceptance of received ideas and opinions. His philosophy denies authority to anything external to the individual and makes our faculty of reason the final determinant of what is true and right (Kant, 1929). Ideas of individual freedom and rationality suffuse his writings on law, and Kant's account of law, his 'doctrine of right' (Kant, 1996), is closely related to his general moral theory.

Kant's moral theory begins with the premise that the only unconditionally good thing is a good will. While the consequences of our actions can be judged good or bad, the will to do good can be separated from the outcomes of our actions and is an unconditionally good thing. Second, a good will seeks to perform duties, rather than pursue good ends or outcomes. Good outcomes or states of affairs can become bad outcomes or states of affairs; to will or pursue our duty is always a good thing. Finally, our duties are identified as those actions that everyone should, and can, perform. We should think of ourselves as legislators who have to make rules for everyone, universally. If we can make such a rule it is a duty, a 'categorical imperative'. If we cannot make such a rule it is merely a hypothetical imperative, something that may, hypothetically, bring about a good state of affairs (Kant, 1948: 56–7). When we identify our duty we are identifying a categorical imperative: something that must be done regardless of possible states of affairs.

This rational basis for determining the basic principles of ethical action has echoes of a religious principle, the 'golden rule', of doing to others only what we want them to do to us. The value of Kant's articulation of this as the categorical imperative is two-fold. It is logical because it demands that we avoid contradiction in our actions. Second, it is focussed on individual freedom. We are not free when we have our actions dictated by people and things external to us (including the moral dictates of God or the physical dictates of nature). By choosing action on the basis of duty alone we are acting from a pure will uninfluenced by authority, dogmatism and the forces found in the natural world. This also allows Kant in his mature work on morality, *The Metaphysics of Morals*, to divide his concerns into doctrines of right (concerning law) and doctrine of virtue (concerning action), but insist that both ultimately concern freedom (Kant 1996: 165). Doctrines of virtue concern 'inner' freedom, the conditions by which we freely determine our duties. Doctrines of *right* concern our 'outer' freedom; they concern the legal and political conditions that allow us to act rationally and pursue our duties.

Kant's doctrine of right is, accordingly, an explanation of how laws should correspond to individual freedom and rationality. The kinds of laws that Kant favours do not diverge from the kinds of civil and criminal laws that are common to European legal systems. His concept of constitutional law favours a constitutional monarchy where public codes provide for freedom and well-ordered social coexistence (Kant, 1996). While his legislative programme is not radical, Kant's philosophical rethinking of legal systems looks to achieve correspondence between reason and external law. Without such correspondence individuals cannot be free, and law becomes an external, oppressive, imposition on the individual.

While criticism of Kant's position will be taken up by Hegel and Marx it is worth considering the merits of this position. First, in a fundamentally uncertain world where we can never have control over the consequences of our actions, we can understand why Kant applauds those who identify and pursue their duties and do not allow circumstances to dictate their actions. This could be expressed in terms of the virtue of integrity: pursuing the right course of action despite pressures to the contrary. Second, his work stresses the intrinsic or inalienable value of the individual. The reason we have categorical duties is because without such duties we would treat others, and ourselves, as merely having a 'market value' to be calculated. On the contrary, we have a 'dignity', an irreducible status. Third, while not radical from our own contemporary perspective, Kant argued for a limited government and limited state intervention into the lives of individuals, associating his ideas with democracy.

EXAMPLE

'Peep Show Case', German Constitutional Court, BVerwGE 64, 274 (1981)

In this case the German Constitutional Court had to consider whether a live 'peep show' (an enclosed space containing naked dancers who could be viewed at a price) was degrading and caused a loss of dignity to the performer. In an eminently Kantian decision stressing the importance of valuing individuals' dignity through upholding their status as free and rational individuals, the Court decided that certain forms of sex work were incompatible with constitutional protection of the individual.

[In contrast to other instances of nudity] in the peep-show the woman appearing is assigned to a degraded, objectified role, to which end several circumstances of the event cooperate: those owing to the kind of payment which establishes an atmosphere of a mechanical and automatized event, by which the spectacle of the naked woman is bought and sold like a commodity through the slot of a machine. [. . .] This justifies the decision that the woman displayed in the show is degraded through this manner of performance – the peep-show – characterized (in its own peculiar way) as 'professional public performance' [. . .] and thereby received a dignitarian injury.

2b Hegel: right made social

If Kant's philosophy is an attack on submission to dogmatism and an insistence on the authority of reason, Hegel's position is, among other things, an assault on certain kinds of natural law ideas. Far from rationality being discovered in a world beyond the human, Hegel relocated necessity in the human being: we ourselves are the determinants of what is rational and what is necessary. Moreover, the natural law tradition's interest in the good is held by Hegel to be symptomatic of an earlier, less evolved, conception of rationality (Hegel, 2008: 47). Humanity is on a path of mental and cultural evolution from the 'priority of the good' to the 'priority of the right' (Sadurski, 1988). This is more than a terminological shift: it is humanity's reorientation towards something more rational and universal.

Hegel is in agreement with Kant that freedom must be central to any philosophy of human life and action and that this must include an account both of the individual and of the laws that govern them. Hegel's philosophical system, however, aims to demonstrate that the *evolution* of human ideas and human civilisation are much more important than Kant's (much less historically sensitive) theories would concede. The unfolding of human history has been driven by the expansion of self-consciousness, both of the individual and of humanity itself. This 'coming to self-consciousness' is a complex process of overcoming inadequate understandings of reality, but can be summarised in Hegel's assertion that 'what is rational is actual and what is actual is rational' (2008: 14): the world mirrors the structure of our mind and *vice versa*. Within this view of the world, 'right' has a central role because it is a notion that has emerged as a consequence of humanity gaining a fuller conception of itself and its rational responsibilities. As we move to a greater understanding of our place in the world, we also come to possess a more sophisticated understanding of social and individual responsibilities, namely the centrality of the right as a combination of what is true and what is obligatory (2008: 70–1).

Note that Hegel is not entirely removed from natural law. The identification of rational and real resembles the underlying motif of natural law thinking, but Hegel is not arguing for a correspondence between the facts of nature and values. He is arguing for a correspondence between evolved human thinking and evolved human structures: a full understanding of our rationality and the *modern, rational, state.*

Hegel therefore seeks to offer us a 'science of right'. This is not only a description of the uses of 'right' as they have emerged over time, but a more ambitious account of how the concepts of right and legal rights have developed together. At the heart of this abstract philosophical account of the right is the nature, function and evolution of the state. It is the state that has driven our awareness of right; the existence of the modern state has shown us that certain goods can be delivered universally or fairly without intruding on the freedom of the individual, and without establishing a prescriptive account of what it is to be human. Also, it is the state that has made right concrete; the state not only maintains legal rights and legal relationships but also sustains the conditions of fuller, more substantial, ethical bonds. As such, right is the correspondence between the state and the freedom and rationality of the individual. Without the state we would not see what is rational let alone be able to pursue what is rational, and without the state we cannot have laws that correspond with our emerging and evolving idea of the – universally and necessarily – right.

Modern institutions, particularly the state, mean that when we now think of 'right' we are thinking not of isolated individuals making self-interested claims, but of the individual and collective joined in a mutually supporting bond. Put in different terms, right is not just 'my rights' but the essence of individual and social existence. Note that Hegel's account of right does not seem to be an accurate historical account of the evolution of a word, rather he is trying to chart the evolution of a concept. This provides an explanation of how certain ideas seem to 'make sense' at certain times and not at others. We now cannot talk of 'right' without thinking of ourselves as members of a state that makes demands on us and upon which we make claims. With this firmly in mind we can understand why it is that the language of right is so potent and says much more in political and legal terms than claims about what is good for any single individual. It is a modern way of thinking which arises from a complex relationship with others and with the state.

EXAMPLE

Korematsu v United States, 323 U. S. 214 (1944) United States Supreme Court

Hegel grants considerable power to the state to maintain the concrete bases of right, including criminal justice powers and other administrative powers. Emergency powers are not always easy to square with the rule of law: they can be discriminatory and arbitrary. Korematsu, an 'American citizen of Japanese descent' challenged war-time constraints placed on him for national security reasons. The US Supreme Court held that these were acceptable measures (though a later Court held the decision to have been illegitimate as it was based on fabricated evidence.) For Hegel, such excessive use of sovereign powers would be unacceptable; our rights cannot be suspended by sovereign will.

[. . .] We are unable to conclude that it was beyond the war power of Congress and the Executive to exclude those of Japanese ancestry from the West Coast war area at the time they did. True, exclusion from the area in which one's home is located is a far greater deprivation than constant confinement to the home from 8 p.m. to 6 a.m. Nothing short of apprehension by the proper military authorities of the gravest imminent danger to the public safety can constitutionally justify either. But exclusion from a threatened area, no less than curfew, has a definite and close relationship to the prevention of espionage and sabotage. The military authorities, charged with the primary responsibility of defending our shores, concluded that curfew provided inadequate protection and ordered exclusion. They did so [. . .] in accordance with Congressional authority to the military to say who should, and who should not, remain in the threatened areas.

2c Marx: right made material

Marx's relationship with law can be understood as rejection of a form of legal positivism. In opposition to Hegel and others, he opposes the idea that the laws commanded by the state are the basis of 'rightness'. Justice does concern the protection of the rights, interests, freedom and rationality of the individual, but these have to be understood at a more basic level of correspondence between social organisation and the *material* world.

Marx criticises Hegel for his Idealism, i.e. his assumption that ideas are the driving force of history. The real is not rational but, according to Marx, *material*. This turning Hegel 'on his head', making the material dominant, has consequences for how we understand rightness. First, it means criticism of the idea of *rights* as fundamentally positive and progressive contributions to legal and political thought. Rights arise from social structures characterised by inequality; rights reflect, but cannot remedy, this inequality. Second, Marx criticises Hegel's defence of the modern state. In Marx's view, the state generates antagonisms which a conservative rule of law helps to support. In contrast, Marx sought a more fundamental, less 'statist', correspondence between social life and human needs.

First, abstract rights cannot give universal respect and protection to individuals. To reduce all of our moral and political interests, demands and needs to rights is a harmful approach to ourselves and others. When we assert our rights we are assuming that the state can fulfil these demands universally and fairly and that our particular interests as individuals and as members of groups will be met by the state. In fact, the things that unite us, the people we know, the culture we share and the commitments we have made are either poorly protected or not protected at all by rights. Even where rights are protected by law, this is predominantly in the domain of private property where the law is concerned to maintain the rights of existing property owners rather than ensure that there is a just distribution of property (Hunt, 1986). There is, in other words, a close relationship between legal right and property which clearly and systematically disadvantages the class with less property and less influence. Furthermore, we have the strongest bonds with people around us with whom we do not have rights relationships, but rather stronger bonds of mutual need (as in our commercial and working relationships) and affection (our personal relationships). These are relationships that cannot be understood in terms of rights, but are stronger *material* relationships established through shared human experiences. As such, they would exist in the absence of legal rights and should not be understood as maintained by rights (Easton, 1961).

This suspicion concerning the basis and function of rights is part of a wider critique by Marx of our relationship with the state. Recall that for Hegel the ultimate trajectory of talk of 'right' is the state. The state is the ultimate defender of fair treatment, objectivity and fairness. While he agrees that the priority of the right is important, Marx rejects Hegel's belief that right has found its fullest realisation in the modern state. 'Right can never be higher than the economic structure of society and its cultural development' (Marx, 2000: 615). The state is not the ultimate defender of right, it is not the logical realisation of the state as defender of the interests of both individual and collective, but is, rather, a reflection of existing inequality and exploitation. We are afforded a number of rights, but these are ultimately defending private property and, by extension, property owners. The state is the scene of 'alienation': our relationships with others are not construed in terms of our needs but in terms of efficient production and wealth creation (Easton, 1961). 'Right' is an ideology, a structure of thought imposed upon us, that gives the impression that the state and legal rights are the only true bonds between individuals; right and the state are, in actual fact, ways of justifying exploitation.

In the light of this we can make sense of Marx's claim that the state will 'wither away' and be replaced with material relations of production which are non-exploitive and not premised on possession of private property (Easton, 1961: 196). Hegel (and Kant's) optimistic views about the rationality and universality of the right are too ideal; they miss the correspondence between individual status and our collective reliance on the material world of production and consumption. In sum, Marx's view of 'the law of the state' is clearly critical and radical, but the idea of making the social and material correspond – fairly, and without exploitation or antagonism – is a way of arguing for just social architecture without establishing a prescriptive vision of the good.

EXAMPLE

Committee On Economic, Social, and Cultural Rights: 'General Comment No. 15 (2002)' [on ICESCR Articles 11 and 12]

Marxism has an ambivalent relationship with rights, and the 'right to water' is a good example of why. Clearly no-one would question the need, value or importance of access to water. However, is the correct orientation towards this fundamental human need the creation of a right? Here a United Nations body overseeing economic and social rights outlines where such a right would find its legal and moral basis.

The legal bases of the right to water:

[. . .] The human right to water entitles everyone to sufficient, safe, acceptable, physically accessible and affordable water for personal and domestic uses. An adequate amount of safe water is necessary to prevent death from dehydration, to reduce the risk of water-related disease and to provide for consumption, cooking, personal and domestic hygienic requirements. [The Covenant on Economic and Social Rights] specifies a number of rights emanating from, and indispensable for, the realization of the right to an adequate standard of living 'including adequate food, clothing and housing'. The use of the word 'including' indicates that this catalogue of rights was not intended to be exhaustive. The right to water clearly falls within the category of guarantees essential for securing an adequate standard of living, particularly since it is one of the most fundamental conditions for survival.

3 Right as coherence

Introduction

We do not have to work within a legal institution to know that law has its own way of doing things. We know that law can be used if we have a conflict with our neighbours and we know that the law will deal with that conflict by its own rules. Those inside the legal profession have been trained to work with a set of rules and procedures that are not found anywhere else in the social world. Law has its 'own rules' not only in the sense of being constituted or characterised by rules but because it has its own way of doing things and dealing with the world; distinctively *legal* decisions can be made and *legal* answers can be found. Law produces right answers in its own distinctive way on the basis of its rules and its unique means of adjudication.

The idea that law has its own internal way of generating right answers is related to the coherence view of truth: systems can produce right and wrong answers on the basis of their own internal assumptions without having to show correspondence with reality. Of course, we could treat rules as part of that reality and the division between coherence and correspondence would thereby become blurred. Nonetheless, the idea that law can generate its own standard of correctness, without appeal to anything beyond law itself, is a distinctive and widespread conception of what law is and does.

One famous way that this 'internal coherence' has been expressed is through law being seen as a 'seamless web' (the phrase is attributed to Frederic Maitland, see Berman, 1977; Bix, 2004). This suggests that understanding law is not about learning a number of discrete topics; rather to 'know law' we have to have synoptic view of an entire legal system. This is because law is a web of interconnected rules, principles, precedents and practices that do not respect neat boundaries. We have to know how use principles from one field (e.g. contract) to make sense of another field (e.g. tort). The reason this is the case will be historical (legal systems emerge over time in haphazard ways that do not respect boundaries), but also because legal systems have their 'own way of doing things' that are valid whatever the subject-matter. If this picture is correct, the web is 'seamless' because law can always draw upon its own resources to come to a decision in a particular case, and this may explain the fact that a 'right legal decision' is always possible. When a dispute is accepted by a legal institution (where a court accepts jurisdiction over it) it will always find some kind of answer. Laws can always be found to respond to a dispute, and law is always capable of generating a decision: a *legal* decision not just an *ad hoc* decision.

The following theories from Hobbes, Mill and Rawls represent different ways of making sense of how law's inner coherence – its self-generated rightness – can be explained. The common denominator among them is that legal rules and legal institutions are given a basis of justification in a particular political arrangement or by a political principle (contract, liberty and fairness respectively). These are not theories suggesting that law should be subservient to political goals; they each defend the independence of law and legal institutions. Nonetheless, for each there is a core principle of political legitimacy with which legal institutions and legal decisions must cohere in order to be valid. It is coherence with an underlying or justificatory principle (contract, liberty or fairness) which means *right* legal decisions can be made within a legal system even when the rules run out.

Put another way, these theorists can be understood as trying to cohere contradictions and tensions at work in any theory of law and state. Hobbes is attempting to reconcile or cohere political power with consent. Mill is reconciling utilitarian governance with the belief that the state should not dictate what is good for the individual. Rawls is reconciling the liberties of the individual with fair social practices. The 'rightness' of law and legal decisions, in each case, depends upon supporting the reconciliation of these competing principles.

3a Hobbes: right as contract

The importance of Hobbes' work for legal scholarship lies in his treatment of the origins of law as something *legal* – a contract – meaning that law never has to be justified by anything other than itself. Legal institutions possess rightness or correctness because they are already authorised as, or acknowledged to be, legal. Law is inherently justified, and does not have to correspond to any external standard.

In the middle of the seventeenth century, Hobbes found himself between two warring factions in the English civil war, Crown and Parliament, both claiming legal legitimacy for their cause. In this situation Hobbes sought (for both scholarly and personal reasons) a new theory of legal legitimacy (Tuck, 1999). He avoided appeal to divine support for the *status quo* (the predominant medieval approach to politics which had been adopted by the Monarchist cause); nor did he grant automatic authority to those with the *de facto* power, wealth and money (i.e. the wealthy gentry of the Parliamentary cause). The theory arising from this tension traces authority to the origins of human social life. Hobbes' story concerning the origin of social life does not paint a picture of either haphazard emergence of political power nor divine ordinance. Real legal authority arose from neither divine nor political sources: it arose from a purely legal event.

To imagine the origins of human social activity, Hobbes posited 'a state of nature'. This is a situation without the structures and boundaries of human society wherein individuals live in constant fear of each other because of natural predatory impulses and the absence of a legal authority to remedy or prevent predatory action between humans. In this situation human life is fragile and human endeavour is fruitless because human effort can never be supported nor human life respected. Without social protections and boundaries life is, famously, 'solitary, poor, nasty, brutish, and short' (1996: 84). In such a situation an ultimate power, a sovereign, would be like a God, able to ensure order and justice.

Contracting with one another to grant legal and political power to a sovereign means rescuing humans both from nature itself and from each other. Without this single, powerful, sovereign any kind of social ordering will founder on human weakness and fear:

> somewhat else must be done, that those who have once consented for the common good, to peace and mutual help, may by fear be restrained, lest afterwards they again dissent, when their private interest shall appear discrepant from the common good. (1996: xxxiv, emphasis removed)

The sovereign, as the conglomerate of many individual wills, is the ultimate power and authority, able to make decisions, support complex social ventures and mete out punishments. However, the sovereign is also, crucially, a *legitimate* power in so far as its power derives from the decision of the individual to cede their own power. Hobbes gives one of the first secularised accounts of how legality is legitimately founded and justified. It is founded in a contractual decision, and all subsequent legal commands are justified by virtue of flowing from this legal origin. Hobbes also supplies a plausible account of why we should, pragmatically, accept the authority of law: in essence, because any law is better than no law.

However, there are a number of questions that can be asked of Hobbes. If this truly is a contract, what responsibilities lie with the sovereign? Hobbes seems to demand unconditional obedience to all and any sovereign powers: '[anyone], if they do tolerate not their king, whatsoever law he maketh [. . .] do violate their faith, contrary to the divine law, both natural and positive' (1996: 387, emphasis removed). We as citizens have the clear responsibility to obey the law (we have made a contract to create laws enforced by the sovereign). Conversely, the sovereign is placed under no such strictures (although may be subject to divine vengeance) (1996: 422). The fabric of a legal system – its rules and traditions – seems, at best, secondary to the pure power of a sovereign to impose *order* on an otherwise warring populace. Hobbes may have given social *order* an inner coherence, but has he provided a good description of the particular coherence of *law*?

More specifically, consider the 'solitary' aspect of 'solitary, poor, nasty, brutish, and short'. To the extent that there has been any real state of nature (a 'pre-legal' state of instability) that environment would surely not have been solitary. For there to be people at all there have to be two parents; the survival of humans, as uniquely vulnerable animals, depends upon some kind of cooperation or nurturing. From this we could draw different conclusions about the natural. That the family is natural, as are groupings of families (as per Aristotle's account of the origins of the state). Or that some kind of *law* will always be natural in the form of kinship bonds (the rules within and between families) or patronage (rule by strong, paid, individuals). For these reasons, Hobbes' work is less useful as an account of how law 'came to exist' than as a model of law in a modern state where there is an identifiable sovereign consistently enforcing the law and little difficulty distinguishing *de facto* and *de jure* power. The degree to which Hobbes can also be used to demonstrate that law is justified from its inception (that it has an inner coherence based on contractual origins) should be similarly curtailed: he has not provided fundamental justification for all *legal practices,* but rather explained the coherence of talking about *legality* as something distinct from religion and class.

EXAMPLE

***Legality of the Threat or Use of Nuclear Weapons* (International Court of Justice Advisory Opinion, Dissenting Opinion of Judge Weeramantry) 1996 I.C.J. 226**

Grotius, whose ideas are similar to Hobbes', remains an influential source ('publicist') of international law. In this opinion by the International Court of Justice, Grotius' work is used to consider the origins and pedigree of jus in bello, the law which applies in warfare. Warfare remains a constant reminder of the possibility of a 'state of nature' returning and the Court here suggests that, to a degree, there is historical value in Hobbes' state of nature narrative.

Grotius' concern with the cruelties of war is reflected in his lament that: 'when arms were once taken up, all reverence for divine and human law was thrown away, just as if men were thenceforth authorized to commit all crimes without restraint' [. . .]. The foundations laid by Grotius were broad-based and emphasized the absolute binding nature of the restrictions on conduct in war. In building that foundation, Grotius drew upon the collective experience of humanity in a vast range of civilizations and cultures. [. . .] Humanitarian principles have long been part of the basic stock of concepts embedded in the corpus of international law. Modern international law is the inheritor of a more than hundred-year heritage of active humanitarian concern with the sufferings of war. This concern has aimed at placing checks upon the tendency, so often prevalent in war, to break every precept of human compassion. It has succeeded in doing so in several specific areas, but animating and underlying all those specific instances are general principles of prevention of human suffering that goes beyond the purposes and needs of war.

3b Mill: right as liberty

We have encountered the utilitarian dimension of J.S. Mill's thought (Chapter 3). The liberal aspect of his philosophy is considered here. The bridge between these two theoretical positions is Mill's acceptance that, while happiness is the good towards which individuals' actions work, the political and legal realisation of this utilitarianism demands a (politically liberal) acceptance that people should be able to – within limits – pursue their own ideas of the good and their own 'experiments in living'. He is, in other words, seeking to allow the right, understood as liberty, and the good, happiness, to coexist.

Mill's position possesses some similarity to Hegel's. Hegel argues that we have moved beyond the good as our prevailing social value to the right as the most developed, universalisable, basis of social life. Unlike Hegel, however, Mill has much more interest in deciding on the *limits* of law – and therefore right and rights – rather than showing how law and reason exhibit a necessary, logical, correspondence. With the freedom that law provides, repressive social mores can be exchanged for rights which give the individual the possibility of pursuing fully realised lives. For Mill this involves important limits to the state, namely respecting the private sphere and resisting undue influence on private choices (Mill, 1991).

This gives rise to Mill's 'harm principle' whereby the power of the state is limited to the prevention of harm, as opposed to cultivating the good: 'the only purpose for which power can be rightfully exercised over any member of a civilized community, against his will, is to prevent harm to others. His own good, either physical or moral, is not a sufficient warrant' (Mill, 1991: 14). The state should certainly seek to prevent individuals physically harming one another, but has a more fundamental responsibility to allow the fullest possible range of liberties. These liberties extend to a free press, wide voting rights and representative legislatures (Gray, 1996).

Mill's emphasis on the liberties of the individual does not point to a simple divide between public and private 'spheres'. Rather, Mill separates 'self-regarding' actions, that only concern our own actions and welfare, and 'other-regarding' actions, where the actions and welfare of others are affected. The state has no right to dictate self-regarding actions, but is authorised to regulate other-regarding actions where our actions have an impact on those who may not have consented, or be able to consent, to our influence on them.

> In the conduct of human beings towards one another, it is necessary that general rules should for the most part be observed, in order that people may know what they have to expect; but in each person's own concerns, his individual spontaneity is entitled to free exercise. (1991: 85)

Mill's position is therefore less a neat drawing of lines between the public and private spheres, more an attempt to cohere an act utilitarianism governing our actions in relation to others, and defence of (a necessarily more opaque) liberty of thought and action for us as individuals.

Problems arise with Mill's harm principle. Certain forms of self-inflicted harm in the private sphere (e.g. drug-taking) would seem to be protected from state intervention (and would seem to be compatible with 'experiments in living') but also entail 'social harms'. As soon as we concern ourselves with social harm, however, we subscribe to a more substantial 'social programme' than Mill's position is intended to support. Accordingly, the minimal definition of harm that Mill gives us generates a (perhaps undesirably) minimalistic political philosophy. Conversely, as a working assumption for legal systems this seems to have merit: it demands that the law and judges refrain from making substantial judgments about the good and serve a minimal 'watchdog' role. Mill's harm principle, and his more general commitment to allowing a plurality of conceptions of the good accords well with the impartiality and equality that legal institutions should support. Law is not intended to correspond to a pre-established political or rational order, but is intended to help cohere the different ideas of life that people can reasonably pursue.

EXAMPLE

Charter of the United Nations (1945)

The Preamble to the Charter of the United Nations contains a rousing assertion of the basic obligation of states to be 'good neighbours' in order to pursue 'better standards of life'. A harm principle (of sorts) is given prominence: force can only be used for the common interest.

We The Peoples Of The United Nations Determined to save succeeding generations from the scourge of war, which twice in our lifetime has brought untold sorrow to mankind, and to reaffirm faith in fundamental human rights, in the dignity and worth of the human person, in the equal rights of men and women and of nations large and small, and to establish conditions under which justice and respect for the obligations arising from treaties and other sources of international law can be maintained, and to promote social progress and better standards of life in larger freedom.

And For These Ends to practice tolerance and live together in peace with one another as good neighbours, and to unite our strength to maintain international peace and security, and to ensure, by the acceptance of principles and the institution of methods, that armed force shall not be used, save in the common interest, and to employ international machinery for the promotion of the economic and social advancement of all peoples [. . .].

3c Rawls: right as fairness

Social contract theories depend upon a conjectural situation where the protections of society have been stripped away and humans are shown to lack liberties – rights, duties, securities and freedoms – despite possessing natural freedoms. Two elements of this were revived in John Rawls' work. An attempt to find on what rational basis consent to law would be given; and a thought experiment involving individuals outside their normal social situation. The essence of both of these steps is Rawls' idea of 'justice as fairness' (see Chapter 1). Here we consider the policies that flow from this principle: social structures which create as many opportunities as possible without being radically redistributive, and the creation of laws which ensure equality without imposing a radical egalitarianism.

Rawls does not imagine a brutal state of nature but rather an 'original position'. This is a situation where individuals are required to make a decision about what would be the best social system in which to live (1999: 102f). They are to make their decision behind a 'veil of ignorance': they are stripped of any knowledge of where they will be located in the social system they are devising (1999: 119). They are, because of this, *rational* (not purely self-interested) decision-makers who are being asked to decide on the best overall shape of a social system for rational decision-makers such as themselves. Moreover, they know that the situation cannot be perfect, that there will be inequalities, scarcities, benefits to distribute and burdens to share. Consequently, they should, on these methodological assumptions, be inclined to choose a system that offers the best range of rights and opportunities for the widest range of individuals: 'each person is to have an equal right to the most extensive scheme of equal basic liberties compatible with a similar scheme of liberties for others' (1999: 53). After rejecting systems that allow substantial inequalities in benefits and burdens, these decision-makers would, says Rawls, choose an economic system avoiding excessive gaps between rich and poor: 'social and economic inequalities are to be arranged so that they are [. . .] to the greatest benefit of the least advantaged' (1999: 266). They would also choose a social structure suited to increasing the welfare of the widest group of people possible: 'an inequality of opportunity must enhance the opportunities of those with the lesser opportunity' (1999: 266).

What Rawls provides us with is a defence of many existing political practices and institutions, specifically the rule of law, being a 'basis of legitimate expectations. They constitute the grounds upon which persons can rely on one another and rightly object when their expectations are not fulfilled' (1999: 207). A wide, basic, set of liberties would be chosen by anyone who could not guarantee that they were part of a privileged caste for whom the basic protections of law were unimportant. It is also a criticism of social systems where civil rights are limited and where there are considerable disparities of wealth between richest and poorest.

These conclusions are defended on the basis that Rawls' liberal political system would provide individuals with the greatest possible range of opportunities and protections. To that extent it possesses elements of utilitarianism; welfare and overall happiness are important, though these will be the by-products of a fair system, not its goal. It also has elements of Kantianism to the extent that it is premised on what would be consented to by rational individuals. While Hobbes and Mill have their own views on the psychological underpinnings of legality and politics, Rawls is happy to assume that legality should be justified on the basis of the individual with rational self-interest. Whether this philosophical move is justified remains a topic of philosophical debate (Taylor, 1992).

This social contract argument generates demand for a *fair* social system, not just one that 'saves' us from nature, and that this fairness is the essence of good social institutions such as law. Justice and fairness can be equated because it is fairness that allows us to reconcile respect for individuals (as rational and autonomous) with the difficult choices concerning benefits and burdens which always accompany political activity. In other words, it is right and just that we should live under a rule of law, in a state which does not compromise basic liberties, and one that does not entail redistribution of wealth other than to benefit the poorest in society. Such values are fundamental, and can be written into the structure of the state, they do not have to be generated by utilitarian conjectures about good outcomes. This offers a thin view of what is good for us, namely to be treated fairly. However, it does offer us a substantial view of what is right: fairness, just social institutions and the rule of law. A rule of law that embodies this fairness has justification and legitimacy; law does not need to correspond to any more substantial programme of social and political reform.

EXAMPLE

Associated Provincial Picture Houses Ltd v Wednesbury Corporation [1947] 2 All ER 680

Rawls' assumptions about the choices of a reasonable person are among his most contentious. This is a vitally important common law case where the notion of 'reasonableness' received its general formulation. 'Rightness' in the actions of public officials can be considered through the lens of the reasonable: what is rational or justified in that context. It is therefore a variable standard. In this case the idea of unreasonableness looks similar to the idea of unfairness.

[Which actions by public authorities should concern the Courts?] Bad faith, dishonesty – those, of course, stand by themselves – unreasonableness, attention given to extraneous circumstances, disregard of public policy, and things like that have all been referred to as being matters which are relevant for consideration. In the present case we have heard a great deal about the meaning of the word 'unreasonable.' It is true the discretion must be exercised reasonably. What does that mean? Lawyers familiar with the phraseology commonly used in relation to the exercise of statutory discretions often use the word 'unreasonable' in a rather comprehensive sense. It is frequently used as a general description of the things that must not be done. For instance, a person entrusted with a discretion must direct himself properly in law. He must call his own attention to the matters which he is bound to consider. [. . .] He must exclude from his consideration matters which are irrelevant to the matter that he has to consider. If he does not obey those rules, he may truly be said, and often is said, to be acting 'unreasonably.' Similarly, you may have something so absurd that no sensible person could ever dream that it lay within the powers of the authority. Warrington LJ, I think it was, gave the example of the red-haired teacher, dismissed because she had red hair. [. . .]

---

4 Rights

Introduction

In Hegel's concern with rights as the defining mark of the modern state, and in Rawls' concern with the distribution of basic liberties, we have seen claims made about the power and importance of rights. Rights undoubtedly inhabit an important place in our general conception of what law is. Even when rights claims are not supported by clear law or legal remedies, claims about our rights still seem to have a powerful impact upon the user and the listener. When someone claims their right to do *x* they are asserting, in a forceful way, that they have the *power* or the *justification* to do something. The language of rights is ubiquitous, rhetorically powerful and inescapable.

Such ubiquity and potency requires philosophical caution. The fact that the word 'right' could be attached to a range of interests and preferences means that the lawyer will wish, at the very least, to distinguish what is legally enforceable from what is the expression of desire and aspirations. The philosopher of law will also want, over and above this, to clarify how it is that rights claims are meaningful at all. What are the conditions under which rights claims have acquired legal force, and do all rights claims possess equal force? For instance, how is it that our claim to our own private property can be construed as a right (is this based on other, contractual or constitutional, rights?) and does this right have a legal force equal to, say, the right to privacy in one's home? The latter right does not look like a species of contract, rather a more fundamental human right. Moreover, there is a need to consider whether rights claims always function in the same way. Whether they always act as an assertion of an *individual's* power to act, or whether some rights act in more sophisticated ways concerning the *relationship* between the rights claimant and those they make claims against whom.

For that reason we have to distinguish carefully the *forms* that rights take from their *functions* in law. Hohfeld offers a systematic analysis of the forms of rights in law. Dworkin and Nozick analyse rights' functions as peremptory 'trumps' which override certain kinds of argument in legal discussion (Dworkin) or as ways of mapping the proper limits of law and the state (Nozick).

4a Hohfeld: distinguishing rights

The American scholar Wesley Hohfeld's (1879–1918) most celebrated work was an attempt to analyse the nature of rights claims (Hohfeld, 1913). He notes that 'rights talk' is ambiguous: 'the word 'right' is used generically and indiscriminately to denote any sort of legal advantage, whether claim, privilege, power, or immunity' (1913: 17). A 'right' can refer to any number of kinds of legal assertion or legal relationship. Hohfeld's first move is to distinguish four different kinds of legal right. The first is a *claim-right* which denotes what we would normally consider to be a 'legal right', i.e. the product of legal relationship where *x* has a particular claim on others (to act or forbear from acting). Second are *liberties* (or privileges), assertions of the right to do something, either the general right to do anything that the law permits or something more specific related to a particular status (e.g. to alter one's own will). Third are *powers*, concerning what a person is authorised to do within a particular role, for example the powers that can be exercised by a government official; they also encompass the creation of legal roles and relationships (e.g. in a marriage or a will). Finally there are *immunities*, rights against others to insulate an individual against violations of their person and status, including having their legal status changed (e.g. to annul a marriage or change a will).

Put in such abstract terms, these subdivisions make right claims seem complex, and indeed they are, but each of these four basic terms cannot, in Hohfeld's view, be further reduced or analysed. They are 'what may be called "the lowest common denominators of the law"' (Hohfeld, 1913: 58). For example, an immunity such as the 'right to privacy' can be understood in different ways from the perspective of law, politics and public policy, but an immunity itself represents a kind of legal *relationship* – an ability to stop the actions of others – which is legally fundamental.

Indeed, each of these basic terms indicates some kind of *relationship*. Each of them (even when they resemble an assertion about *one's own* legal powers, capacities and capabilities) entails something about one's relationship with others. It is this way of conceptualising the four basic components of rights claims that leads to Hohfeld's next step, analysing the 'correlatives' of these kinds of rights for others. Each simple form of a right (claim, power etc.) imposes a correlative duty on another. The basic form of right, a claim-right, entails some kind of *duty* on another. A liberty (a general right claim) does not seem to imply any correlate relationship with another, however it could be also be expressed in terms of the denial of another's right, or in Hohfeld's terms that another party has *no-right*, no claim over me when I exercise the liberty. A power entails a *liability* on the part of another, i.e. they are liable to be subject to my actions when I exercise a power. Finally, my immunity entails a *disability* for another, another party is rendered unable to alter my legal position, and they are rendered unable to exercise particular kinds of power over me.

Given the breadth of rights-talk in law and culture, it could be said that Hohfeld's technical analysis of these terms diverges from ordinary usage. We neither colloquially nor legally recognise a consistent and authoritative set of terms and correlatives associated with our assertion of rights. Indeed, it might be argued that we simply know from the context what is being asserted (and demanded) when someone expresses 'their rights'. Nonetheless, Hohfeld does offer clear means of dissecting otherwise confused and even contradictory legal rights claims, and does so in a way which makes sense of the fact that my rights assertions rarely only concern my own powers and capacities, but also make explicit and implicit demands of others.

It is interesting to note that while it originated in the context of the US legal system, Hohfeld's analysis offers a powerful way of explaining the relationship between rights and the unusual structure of the UK constitution. The underlying assumption of this unwritten constitution is that every act is to be presumed legal and justified unless there is a legal rule indicating otherwise (Lester, 1976). There are certainly constitutional principles, institutions and conventions that give fuller shape to the state, but this principle of 'freedom except in the absence of positive prohibition' can be understood as premised on *liberties* in Hohfeld's sense. These liberties can be expressed in the language of rights, and indeed the constitution does provide specific rights (claims, immunities and powers). At its heart, however, is the liberty to act with the correlate responsibility for the state to refrain from interfering in our liberty. From our liberties, other claims, powers and immunities are secured.

EXAMPLE

Re KD (A Minor) (Ward: Termination of Access), House of Lords, [1988] A.C. 806

The case involved the question, within adoption proceedings, of the relative priorities of the 'welfare of the child' and the 'rights of the parents'. Here the Court is seeking to argue that there is no significant difference between these two principles and they can both be considered 'rights'. Echoes of Hohfeld's analysis are clear.

Such conflict as exists, is, I think, semantic only and lies only in differing ways of giving expression to the single common concept that the natural bond and relationship between parent and child gives rise to universally recognised norms which ought not to be gratuitously interfered with and which, if interfered with at all, ought to be so only if the welfare of the child dictates it. The word 'right' is used in a variety of different senses, both popular and jurisprudential. It may be used as importing a positive duty in some other individual for the non-performance of which the law will provide an appropriate remedy, as in the case of a right to the performance of a contract. It may signify merely a privilege conferring no corresponding duty on any one save that of non-interference, such as the right to walk on the public highway. It may signify no more than the hope of or aspiration to a social order which will permit the exercise of that which is perceived as an essential liberty, such as, for instance, the so-called 'right to work' or a 'right' of personal privacy.

4b Dworkin: rights as trumps

Dworkin's work in the philosophy of law is among the most influential of the twentieth century and further consideration of his work will be found in Chapter 7. At present we are concerned with how Dworkin understands rights as functioning in law. For Dworkin, law is always more than a system of rules, it has to include decision-making tools – policies and principles – that allow decisions in difficult cases. Policies (the political objectives of the state) and principles (axioms or values which determine permissible ways to resolve conflicts) are used to determine how legal rules should be interpreted.

Pre-eminent among these tools are rights. Rights for Dworkin function as 'trumps': they 'trump' claims made by the state (Dworkin, 1977). This functioning can be described as a peremptory function, automatically preventing the use of certain kinds of legal argument (see Simmonds, 2008: 291–3). Specifically, they prevent utilitarian claims, i.e. claims asserting the primacy of the general good and of good outcomes, in favour of the interests and will of the individual. The fact that we have rights, and that they have this powerful capacity to be deployed or relied upon at any time, is the most significant dimension of any liberal political and legal system. They prevent the individual and their interests being sacrificed for general gains or collective goods, and they help to ensure that a right decision can be made in difficult cases: a right decision coheres with the underlying commitments of a liberal state (Dworkin, 1975).

Dworkin's later work treats rights as part of law's distinctive *integrity*. If we are to make decisions which are fair, impartial and reflect the general moral commitments of our society, then we must demand of judges and law-makers that they prioritise and protect rights; only this can be said to represent the pursuit of integrity. For a decision to exhibit integrity in a social system with a *history* of protecting the rights of the individual, such a decision must demonstrate concern for rights or fail to integrate legal decision-making with the collective values of the society.

> Law as integrity denies that statements of law are either the backward-looking factual reports of conventionalism or the forward-looking instrumental programs of legal pragmatism. It insists that legal claims are interpretive judgments and therefore combine backward- and forward-looking elements; they interpret contemporary legal practice seen as an unfolding legal narrative. (1998: 225)

Dworkin's functional analysis does not seek to explore the forms of rights. For the most part, Dworkin seems to identify rights with immunities. Nonetheless, he suggests that legal systems in liberal states will use two, broad, kinds of rights that protect individuals from being ignored or negated by utilitarian decision-makers (1975: 1063f). The first are *background* political rights which seek to protect the individual against the state as a whole. The second are *institutional* political rights protecting the individual within the context of a specific institution such as a Court. Consequently, Dworkin takes a different tack from Hohfeld, offering an account of how rights are presupposed by a particular (liberal) political milieu where they function predominantly as immunities. This allows a combination of positions: Hegel's and Mill's expansive view of the importance of rights combined with a nuanced account of how Courts actually apply and use rights. The subtleties of his position require sustained analysis, but even in broad sweep demonstrate how and why rights-talk is particularly important in liberal legal contexts.

EXAMPLE

Soobramoney v Minister of Health (Kwazulu-Natal) (CCT32/97) [1997] South African Constitutional Court

Basic rights, concerning life or health, seem to provide unassailable grounds for claims against the state. However, even prosperous states have to place limits upon what they grant in terms of social and economic rights. This is all the more acute where the state (here South Africa) is poor and recovering from systemic social inequality. In such a context rights, even constitutional rights to health, do not 'trump' the decision to limit access to resources. In the case, it was concluded that the denial of dialysis to a terminally ill patient was not unconstitutional; the Court confined itself to ensuring that procedures for deciding upon allocation of resources were respected.

[A]ccess to housing, health care, food, water and social security are dependent upon the resources available for such purposes, and [. . .] the corresponding rights themselves are limited by reason of the lack of resources. Given this lack of resources and the significant demands on them that have already been referred to, an unqualified obligation to meet these needs would not presently be capable of being fulfilled. This is the context within which section 27(3) must be construed. [. . .] In this case life is indeed potentially at stake and this Court is enjoined therefore not only to find a humane and morally justified solution to the problem at hand, but also to examine assiduously the process by which the solution is reached and the legal foundation on which it rests. The state undoubtedly has a strong interest in protecting and preserving the life and health of its citizens and to that end must do all in its power to protect and preserve life.

4c Nozick: rights as constraints

As a balance or corrective to the expansive functional claims made by Dworkin, Robert Nozick argues for a far more curtailed conception of rights within legal and political systems. Like Dworkin, Nozick identifies rights with a broadly liberal conception of law and politics. They are important because they act as a counter-weight to strictly utilitarian decision-making. But rather than being the key, direct, realisation of liberal commitments, rights for Nozick are *constraints* on action, prohibiting certain forms of action. Rights are a way of articulating the limits of the state and the most minimal *protections* for an individual in a liberal state. While there are echoes of Dworkin here, Nozick is not echoing the fulsome claims made by Dworkin. For Nozick, rights are part of a fundamental moral and political obligation on the part of the state to constrain itself from intrusion into our lives.

With rights claims we prohibit, absolutely, all forms of instrumentality in human affairs, i.e. slavery. Slavery, for Nozick, includes redistributive taxation under which we can be said to be working purely for others. The problem with both slavery and redistributive taxation is not that they have simply become (historically) undesirable. Rather, they are contrary to the very essence of a liberal, freedom-preserving, legal system. In contradistinction, rights function to constrain the actions of the state. Following Locke, Nozick believes that the essence of politics and law is the just creation of private property through free labour and the social protection of that justly held private property (1974: 26–7). Therefore, *contra* Rawls, Nozick does not support any redistributive measures whatsoever in politics, even to the point of decrying most forms of taxation.

More generally he defends a minimal state which does not interfere with our pursuit of entitlements. Without such a minimal state we have poor protection of the entitlements of individuals or indeed of groups (1974: 119). As such, rights are part and parcel of a general protection of minimal entitlements, entitlements that are minimal or negative – they prohibit state action against the individual – but which are not positive in demanding substantial commitments on the part of the state (for example healthcare or education). In short, Nozick's position is liberal to the extent that it values the freedom of the individual (and the market) to pursue their goals on the basis of their entitlements, but without their necessarily making 'excessive' rights-claims against the state.

EXAMPLE

Alvarez-Machain v *US* (2003) 331 F.3d 604, C.A.9 (Cal.)

A case concerning the US 'Alien Torts Claim Act'; this Act allows prosecution of torts and crimes committed by non-nationals, in other jurisdictions, in the US domestic Courts. Use of the Act requires engagement with the notion of universality as a basis for claiming jurisdiction. Here the rejection of the norm in part of the United States is treated, logically, as a lack of universality. In Nozick's view should any norms be treated as universal if they demand action from the state rather than limits its powers?

> Such analysis fits with our case law's incorporation of the requirement that an actionable norm of international law be 'universal.' The case at hand does not require us to delineate the bare minimum level of acceptance that would constitute 'universality'; instead, it invokes the simple proposition, stated explicitly in Martinez and implicitly in other cases, that in determining whether a norm is 'universal,' the United States is to be counted as a part of the universe. A norm to which the political branches of our government have refused to assent is not a universal norm. It is not the judiciary's place to enforce such a norm contrary to their will. [. . .] The final requirement under our law is that an actionable norm be 'obligatory.' Our cases have used this term to mean 'binding' [. . .]. Binding norms 'confer [. . .] fundamental rights upon all people vis-à-vis their own governments.' [And] the class of obligatory norms is further restricted to those that are obligatory in the literal sense, i.e., those that nation-states must obey.

---

5 Human rights

Introduction

The idea of legal rights has now become dominated by one group of rights which have become uniquely important elements, not only of law, but of our politics and our society. Human rights are that group of rights that can be seen as truly fundamental rights. Fundamental in the sense that they are legally, often constitutionally, fundamental to legal systems, and fundamental in the sense that they protect basic values and basic human interests. In essence, they are fundamental to recognising humans as persons, that is, recognising each individual as deserving of recognition and protection. Paradigm examples are the right to life, to be free from torture, to vote and participate in elections, and to have a fair trial. They reflect some of the basic protections that have been the target of historical struggles and popular demands for several centuries. They are rights which have been demanded by people of the state over many centuries, if not (in one form or another) since the earliest stirrings of democracy. They are also fundamental to what we are as humans – hence *human* rights – because they reflect the basic needs and demands of humans: to be free from arbitrary treatment, fear and oppression and to have our status as humans recognised by others.

All of the claims to fundamentality appealed to above are not without controversy. These rights are arguably dimensions of Western, liberal, history and by no means found uniformly across the world. Moreover, even the idea of the human and their needs (an apparently incontrovertible basis for rights claims) is not without its critics in the sense that many cultures may value order over individual rights, or, more philosophically, that the good (as determined by certain states and cultures) overrides claims to human rights on the part of individuals. These criticisms deserve answers, and this demands explanation of whether human rights can be severed from their cultural origins without losing their meaning.

5a From natural rights to human rights

There are different accounts of the origins or foundations of human rights. There is no doubt that there is an important resemblance (in form and function) between human rights and the ideas of natural rights that long predate modernity. Ancient cultures distinguished the free-born and the slave. So, while Ancient cultures were therefore democratic only in a limited sense, these cultures had a sense of equality – equal treatment and equal status – within the class of free-born individuals. Also, while many Ancient cultures endorsed slavery, they also demanded equal status within their groups: citizens should not be treated as instruments, as means to an end. 'Since, then, law is the bond which holds together a community of citizens, and the justice embodied in the law is the same for everyone, by what right can a community of citizens be held together when their status is unequal?' (Cicero, 1998: 22). These ways of articulating the status, value and basic demands of individuals, while far from today's representative democracy, are still a recognisable approach to the basic rights of humans.

Between the Ancient discussions of natural rights, and the human rights movement of the twentieth century, lie the revolutionary and Enlightenment movements. The Enlightenment pursued the notion of equality between humans, albeit a philosophical equality among persons. As we saw in Kant's defence of the bare characteristics of rationality and autonomy in our understanding of the human, this entails that all humans have the capacity to be rights-bearers but also, equally, to be held responsible for their acts. The individual is understood in terms of their autonomy: as able to govern themselves and, therefore, as creators of responsibilities as much as bearers of rights. However, it took the revolutionary period to turn this philosophical equality into *political* equality among humans. Among the French and American revolutionaries there was consciousness that nominal philosophical equality has to be translated into concrete civil and political recognition (Paine, 1969). The language of 'natural rights' here evolves from theoretical assumptions about what nature has provided humans with, to a radicalised demand for concrete civil and political safeguards for each and every individual. Anti-instrumentality remains important here – rights articulate that individuals have to be recognised as autonomous and not treated as means to an end – but philosophical assumptions about autonomy become less important than constitutionalised civil and political rights.

The twentieth century is the point at which the language of human rights becomes widespread. In the first half of the century, human rights became a way of articulating the blind-spots in the revolutionary conception of natural rights, namely a narrow understanding of the civil rights of men, and the retention, by the state, of the power to visit misery on their own populations through poor governance, and on other populations through war. Two deadly World Wars demanded a radical reconsideration of the adequacy of the state, alone, to protect individuals' welfare. The promulgation in 1948 of the Universal Declaration of Human Rights represented the International Community's agreement that mass murder and systematic dehumanisation should never again be shielded behind the sovereignty – the territorial integrity and legal superiority – of the state. The twentieth century also gave rise to a far more sophisticated understanding of economic and social inequality among humans, as well as the specific needs of women, the 'colonies' and the poor. In short, a more egalitarian understanding of society, and a more global outlook, demanded expansion of the scope of possible rights claims.

Most importantly, after the end of the Second World War there was a drive towards international constitutional values. Given impetus by the Holocaust and the inhumanities of World War, there was an acute awareness that the basic rights of the individual are not always protected by the state alone, and human rights must have international purchase (Glover, 2001). Out of these origins we now have 60 years' worth of international human rights law and jurisprudence seeking to protect the individual in the most basic ways, often from their own state. This century has inherited a substantial body of law, but also the fundamental tension that human rights often seek to protect the individual from the state that should be, legally and morally, their principal protector and provider of rights.

EXAMPLE

'Reservations to the Convention on the Prevention and Punishment of the Crime of Genocide' (1950–1951) International Court of Justice – Advisory Opinion of 28 May 1951 [1951] I.C.J. 15

It is difficult to be optimistic about the emergence of 'international values', but there is strong support for certain, minimal, legal principles. The Genocide Convention comes as close as any treaty comes to universal assent, but even this has its detractors. Here the universality of the Convention is considered: whether it is better to gain state signature with reservations than to have fewer overall parties to the treaty.

It is an undeniable fact that the tendency of all international activities in recent times has been towards the promotion of the common welfare of the international community with a corresponding restriction of the sovereign power of individual States. So, when a common effort is made to promote a great humanitarian object, as in the case of the Genocide Convention, every interested State naturally expects every other interested State not to seek any individual advantage or convenience, but to carry out the measures resolved upon by common accord. Hence, each party must be given the right to judge the acceptability of a reservation and to decide whether or not to exclude the reserving State from the Convention, and we are not aware of any case in which this right has been abused. It is therefore not universality at any price that forms the first consideration.

5b Particularity versus universality

While human rights are distinguishable from other rights by being in some way fundamental, they share with the general notion of right an aspiration towards universality and necessity. That is to say, they are not good as instruments for certain ends, but they can be treated as the right thing for us to be afforded at all times. These kinds of claims are much less likely to be made with respect to legal rights or Hohfeld's 'claim-rights' which seem to be embedded within, and arise from, particular legal and political systems. Rather, they are special because they are universal, transcending the state and the particularities of time, circumstance and other contingent elements in politics and society.

That human rights can be said to be 'universal' requires further analysis because on the face of it this is plainly false. It is not the case that everyone everywhere enjoys the exercise of these rights. In response to this, it can be argued that human rights discussion has always involved *aspiration* towards universality. The aspiration towards universality can be read in two ways. As a claim of *normative universality*, insisting that everyone should be afforded certain standards of treatment, contrasted with *factual* universality claiming that everyone actually possesses human rights. The first, normative, claim is familiar from natural rights discourse and from Enlightenment ideals: the abstract equality of persons. Human rights are in accord with the liberal principle of political equality, where people are treated with equal minimal respect and never as mere means to ends; no state is authorised to arbitrarily discriminate between rational and autonomous persons. The second, factual, claim is articulated by different theorists in different ways. They require grounding human rights in the 'human person'. Liberal theorists such as Kant and Rawls appeal to universal, factual claims concerning the equivalence of 'legal person' and 'rational person' in order to form a basis for normative claims (see Rawls, 1999: 221–2). Non-liberal theorists will appeal to thicker characteristics – i.e. needs and interests – in order to find factual bases for universality claims. In either sense, universality is central to what human rights are trying to do and articulate.

These defences of universality have met with a number of fierce attacks. What unites them is the value of particularity, the value of preserving and protecting what is particular in individuals and in cultures. This is the thrust of the 'cultural relativist' critique of universalism (see Ohlin, 2002). That is, human rights depend upon a liberal political milieu in order to have legal and moral significance. Liberalism is not factually universal, it depends upon *universalising* assumptions. In sum, other cultures have chosen other systems or accept other systems. Liberal politics and human rights have no meaning in these contexts; they are projects and agendas originating from, and limited to, specific historical and political circumstances.

This position can be augmented with other points of critique, not least the fact that humans are not factually equal: people vary radically in their capabilities and capacities, and equality is at best a convenient – but parochial – political assumption shared only by particular states with particular histories (Kelley, 1990). Another line of critique is that Enlightenment assumptions are too thin; they have too abstract a conception of the individual to identify universal qualities (Taylor, 1992).

These kinds of criticisms are made by critics of human rights from across the political spectrum but they are united by a sense that particularity – individuality, idiosyncrasy, difference or otherness – is something to be celebrated and not swept away in easy assertions about universality. Factual universality is a difficult claim to sustain when people and cultures are so different; normative universality is difficult to defend because it depends upon identifying what should be case everywhere, not itself an obviously liberal position to inhabit.

EXAMPLE

Gabcikovo-Nagymaros Project, (1994) 197 International Court of Justice 7

The International Court of Justice here considers which materials international law can draw upon, i.e. which disciplines and ideas. International law must draw upon more than rules: it must consider all civilisations and cultures. This might be thought of as a plea for 'epistemic plurality': that we should see all forms of knowledge as valuable, not only those originating in Western cultures.

[I]nternational law, [. . .] needs to be multi-disciplinary, drawing from other disciplines such as history, sociology, anthropology, and psychology such wisdom as may be relevant for its purpose. On the need for the international law of the future to be interdisciplinary, I refer to another recent extra-judicial observation of that distinguished former President of the Court that: 'there should be a much greater, and a practical, recognition by international lawyers that the rule of law in international affairs, and the establishment of international justice, are inter-disciplinary subjects' [. . .]. Article 9 of the Statute of the International Court of Justice [. . . .] requires the 'representation of the main forms of civilization and of the principal legal systems of the world' [. . .]. I see the Court as being charged with a duty to draw upon the wisdom of the world's several civilizations, where such a course can enrich its insights into the matter before it. The Court cannot afford to be monocultural, especially where it is entering newly developing areas of law.

5c Human rights and liberalism

Perhaps the most acute criticisms of human rights have come from those critics of liberalism, communitarians, who criticise the whole sweep of liberal *philosophical* commitments while offering their own defence of the gains made by modernity (Price, 1989). Communitarians attack both the philosophical foundations of human rights and liberalism itself by arguing that liberalism's conception of the individual is too abstract, and that liberalism says too little about the fact that individuals need to be embedded within a community. This is augmented with criticisms of the social realities of liberal states which are said to suffer from a breakdown in community and social bonds. This deterioration is held to be a consequence of liberalism, specifically the excessive individualism fostered by human rights claims in society (Tushnet, 1991).

If these criticisms are correct, would it still be possible to defend human rights? There are three ways in which it is possible to sever human rights from liberalism and salvage them from potentially fatal attacks from communitarians and from those defending cultural particularity. The first is to jettison liberal politics in large measure and defend human rights on another political basis. Ernst Bloch's (1885–1977) Marxist defence of human rights provides one possible picture of what this would look like. Bloch returns to the earlier natural law traditional and identifies – in its appeals to both natural rights and human rights – a shared, and perennial, opposition to degradation (Bloch, 1986). Bloch insists that opposition to degradation cannot be parochial and does not depend upon liberal (or any other political) assumptions, only individuals' realisation that they are not animals and should not be treated as such. Bloch encourages us to return to the core of human rights claims. The basic, and universal, assertion that humans can be distinguished from animals and should be protected from degradation to the status of animals (see also Douzinas and Gearey, 2005).

The second approach could be called an ideological approach, insisting that the force and value of human rights exists because of the language of the ideology that they generate. This approach can be used to account for the greater success of 'human rights talk' in some cultures. In Lynn Hunt's work, the origin of human rights is explained ideologically, but not politically. While human rights are clearly associated with Western liberal states, this is not because they are the corollary of a political programme, but because such states were in the process – driven by popular culture – of a growing consciousness of the suffering of others. 'Ultimately at stake in this conflict of views about the novel was nothing less than the valorization [increased value] of ordinary secular life as the foundation of morality' (2007: 57). The idea that 'human rights' provide a means of expressing our perceptions about the suffering and need of others does, admittedly, have liberal supporters such as Rawls and Habermas who both, in different ways, seek to show that human rights are principles that would be demanded by people if they were allowed to decide upon their political system and their commitments unencumbered by their social and cultural past (Sadurski, 1988). However, this is not confined to liberals, and the communitarian Charles Taylor makes a similar point, arguing that differences between cultures cannot be ignored but that certain values, and laws, can be agreed upon as common points of reference (Taylor, 1992). These positions often begin with the concession that human rights lack strong, unassailable, ethical foundations, but they do share the view that human rights claims are *meaningful* outside the constitutions of liberal states.

Third, an 'ordinary language' defence of human rights takes this one stage further and shows that human rights are meaningful in any number of contexts. Human rights language, like the Revolutionary language of natural rights, is a way of stirring others and empowering others to engage in social and political activity and to assert claims about what is rightfully theirs. These claims may change over time and have degrees of success over time, but there is no possible denial that this language has allowed people to see themselves differently and articulate strong claims about what they want and need. This may well also be another way of expressing what Bloch is saying about human and natural rights: the language may change and mutate, but the core of *empowerment* remains constant.

EXAMPLE

'African [Banjul] Charter on Human and Peoples' Rights' (adopted June 27, 1981) OAU Doc. CAB/LEG/67/3 rev. 5, 21 I.L.M. 58 (1982)

The creation of an 'African Charter' of rights was an opportunity to create new rights reflecting the values of non-Western states. In fact, there is substantial overlap with the dominant international (Western) instruments, and some clear ideological links with the Lockean/social contract approach to rights found in Western states. Whether this is grounds for applauding or criticising the Charter is another question.

Article 21:

1. All peoples shall freely dispose of their wealth and natural resources. This right shall be exercised in the exclusive interest of the people. In no case shall a people be deprived of it. / 2. In case of spoliation the dispossessed people shall have the right to the lawful recovery of its property as well as to an adequate compensation. / 3. The free disposal of wealth and natural resources shall be exercised without prejudice to the obligation of promoting international economic cooperation based on mutual respect, equitable exchange and the principles of international law. / 4. States parties to the present Charter shall individually and collectively exercise the right to free disposal of their wealth and natural resources with a view to strengthening African unity and solidarity. / 5. States parties to the present Charter shall undertake to eliminate all forms of foreign economic exploitation particularly that practiced by international monopolies so as to enable their peoples to fully benefit from the advantages derived from their national resources.

Questions

Section 1

- The right answer to a question is not always a good (useful/beneficial) answer: what then is the nature of 'rightness'? Could there be a right answer to a legal question that benefitted no-one?

- If some languages make no distinction between 'right' and 'law', does this suggest that 'right' is a more important concept for understanding legal systems and institutions than 'good'?

- For a legal decision to be 'the right legal decision', does that decision have to have some kind of necessity to it? What if the right legal decision is one based on reasons of public policy (or stability, or administrative convenience)? Could that be 'right under the circumstances', but not necessarily the only answer?

Section 2

- For something to be right or wrong does it have to correspond to a state of affairs in the world? Is the proposition 'the present King of France is bald' *false, nonsense* or neither?

- Is being in the right the same as having a right? Is the former a moral status and the latter a legal one, and could they overlap?

- Does law have to correspond with rational ideas, rational social structures or the economic basis of our social structures? Would a legal system survive if it were constantly at odds with prevailing social and economic conditions?

Section 3

- Does law have to cohere with political principles underlying our social systems? If so, what are the political commitments underlying our own social system and how does this have legal consequences?

- Is, or was, there a single point at which legality commenced, a contractual moment? Would this contractual relationship need renewing with every generation?
- Which is more important: liberty or fairness? How might the prioritisation of one or the other have legal consequences?

Section 4

- Could a legal system have legitimacy if it did not offer a wide range of rights?
- Is it useful to distinguish rights, duties, claims, powers and immunities? Are these all reducible to legal *rules*?
- Do rights always provide an answer to legal questions? Do all instances of rights have the property of being 'trumps' which counteract utilitarian arguments?

Section 5

- Why do human rights have particular force in legal contexts? What, if anything, is 'universal' about human rights?
- What is culturally specific about human rights? Could we imagine a culture where people did not appeal to their rights, but only what is good for them? Is it for the same or different reasons that some have challenged the cultural universality of human rights?
- If we did not have the language of human rights would it be more difficult to oppose immoral laws?

Concepts and methods: Logic

The universal

One distinguishing feature of appeal to 'a right answer' is that it implies that the right answer is true *everywhere*, not just useful or correct here and now. Universality is a concern of logicians, and 'universals' are abstract sets of things or properties that hold good everywhere at all times. These have a problematic ontological status (how could we know that such things exist?), and complex epistemological features (how can we distinguish things that were universal from their instantiation in actual, particular, objects?) The uses of universality in legal and moral theory are clearer, but there is still an important requirement in debate to distinguish *descriptive* and *prescriptive* universality. Descriptive universality (what *is* universal) might be thought to include certain properties, inclinations or capacities on the part of humans; prescriptive universality (what *should be* universal) would include familiar moral claims about things we should all do, e.g. observe the prohibition of murder.

The Kantian test of duty – whether something could be a universal law – has long been a useful guide for identifying overarching moral and legal principles. Note that Kant intended this as a means of generating general moral principles, not as a guide to all human action. It is a powerful way of identifying those kinds of actions, duties, which can be demanded universally and yet should be acceptable to any rational individual. However, it is often worth bearing in mind Hegel's criticism of this principle: it can be become an 'empty formalism' (Hegel, 2008: 46–7). 'Do unto others' provides a rule of thumb for avoiding contradiction and hypocrisy but does not yield a complete account of what we, as individuals or as a society, should do. For Hegel and Marx, discovering our basic, concrete, social and economic objectives as a society requires a far more complex understanding of how individual and society must, of necessity, interrelate.

Care needs to be taken to avoid conflating the prescriptively and descriptively universal. Concerning cultural assumptions, it is best not to point to the 'universal' too readily; it is generally possible to find contradictory evidence concerning any social practice. Equally, use of prescriptive universality requires caution: identifying what should be done in all circumstances is more difficult than it appears.

The necessary

Logical necessity concerns the correct derivation of conclusions from premises (steps in an argument). Logic is concerned with *valid* arguments that are structurally defensible, i.e. where the conclusion follows from the premises because it is contained within, or adds nothing to, the premises. Unlike the search for sound arguments (where the premises have to be true) logical validity should hold good in all possible worlds. A valid argument produces a necessarily, and not just temporarily, true conclusion.

'Necessity' is much more problematic if we move outside logic to facts. While the idea of necessity in the physical world appears to be a natural extension of our understandings of cause and effect, it is susceptible to scepticism (Hume, 1975). 'Causal necessity' (that something will be or must be, necessarily, the effect of a particular *cause*) should be distinguished from normative necessity (that something must, necessarily, be done). These are on two different sides of the fact/value distinction, and although sometimes linked (e.g. 'torture necessarily causes suffering therefore must necessarily be wrong') run the risk of blurring fact and value.

We can distinguish the *necessary* from the *contingent*: i.e. what will always be the case (necessarily) and what may only be temporarily the case (contingently). It is also common in philosophy to distinguish 'necessary conditions' from 'sufficient conditions'. This is a way of analysing both causes and properties. Some states of affairs (i.e. some conditions, causes and facts) will always, necessarily, bring about a particular effect. Where there are a number of conditions, causes and facts needed to bring about a particular effect, these are individual *necessary conditions*. When a single cause is enough to bring about a particular effect, this cause is a *sufficient condition*.

Unpacking and distinguishing causal and normative necessity is a good analytical approach to those claims about law which seem to equivocate on the fact/value division. The fact that something is necessary for certain ends does not make it morally necessary; equally, moral necessity does not mean that something will be useful or efficacious. Necessity frequently has rhetorical function, e.g. 'we/they must necessarily do *x*'.

The *a priori*

The logical thrust of claims about what is right, though partially captured in necessity and universality, can be distilled into the notion of the *a priori*, namely those things that are true necessarily and *without reference to the empirical world*. The term is a medieval one (with earlier philosophical roots) and is used in contradistinction to the *a posteriori*. What can be considered true without using our senses (*a priori*) is contrasted with what requires us to consult our senses (*a posteriori*). Claims about the right, unlike those about the good, can generally be classified on the *a priori* side of this distinction, that is, claims about the right aim to be true *come what may*.

Consider how something would be verified: it will either be by thinking, or by using your senses. Knowledge provided by the senses can be thought to include the whole panoply of possible evidence provided to us by other people's testimony. Knowledge gained through thinking is all the possible judgments that can be made about evidence from the senses. As such, these categories encompass anything we can possible know. However, there is much less that fits into the *a priori* category beyond simple truths of logic (and arguably mathematics). Thus, claims to be necessarily true should be treated with suspicion. The opposite of any empirical proposition is always possible (see Hume, 1975), so logical truths are preferable if we seek absolute certainty. However, logical truths do not tell us anything beyond what formal characteristics an argument should have: it should not be contradictory and should not entail conclusions that are not contained in the previous steps.

Conceptual parsimony

'Ockham's Razor' can be summarised as the idea that 'the simplest explanation is the best explanation'. This idea has had a long philosophical life (see Baggini and Fosl, 2010: 209–11) and features in the work of the realists and positivists. For example, one of the main attractions of legal realism (see Chapter 6) is its commitment to conceptual and explanative parsimony. Complex theoretical explanations are exchanged for description and prediction of the actions of judges and the virtues that they need to exhibit. Any discussion of the force of law is thereafter tied to the *rhetorical* strategies, national and interpersonal *politics*, and the *tendencies* exhibited by judges. As such, no complex value structure is needed and no further explanation of the obligatory force of the law. Such conceptual parsimony is attractive in its empiricism and its anti-metaphysical worldview.

Searching for the simplest explanation is not the same as denying the value of theoretical reflection altogether. It is, however, advisable to explain phenomena such as law with as little metaphysical scaffolding as possible. While we could discuss law's relationship with the 'laws of nature', other explanations using rules, practices and institutions are preferable on the basis that we are more likely to make sense of our initial institutions about what the word 'law' means. Ockham's razor also applies to values and obligations. Although we receive powerful explanations of the origins, structure and nature of our values from Kant, Hegel and Marx, a more minimal, but nonetheless powerful, account of values is offered by Hobbes and his focus on our fear of anarchy.

Further reading

The relationship between law, right and theories of truth is set out well by Fernandez (2009). Fine (2001) provides a careful introduction to the relationship between Hegel and Marx and the political dimension of 'right' more generally. Neither Kant's *Metaphysics of Morals* nor Hegel's *Philosophy of Right* are straightforward texts, but most modern editions contain useful and extensive introductions. Marx is perhaps the most difficult to read of the three philosophers (his texts were written for specific audiences rather than for philosophical exposition); his 'Economic and philosophical manuscripts', 'On the Jewish question' and 'Critique of Hegel's Philosophy of Right' encompass his criticisms of Hegel and wider philosophical position (all available in Marx, 2000). As ever, Solomon's text (1988) is an excellent introduction to the philosophical figures and movements of the last four centuries. Douzinas and Gearey's *Critical Jurisprudence* (2005) puts many of their arguments into the context of Western philosophy and law. Rawls' *Theory of Justice* (1999) remains a touchstone of later twentieth-century thought on law and politics.

Visit **www.mylawchamber.co.uk/riley** to access tools to help you develop and test your knowledge of legal philosophy including Podcasts on leading thinkers and theories, discussion questions, diagrams showing interrelations between concepts, and weblinks

5 Rule

Introduction

Rules are a crucial dimension of law. If we were asked to identify where law was to be found it would be above all in rules. Why is law intimately related to rules? Laws are promulgated – they are made, and are made publically – in the form of general rules. Law's rules are generalisations about actors, activities, practices, institutions and indeed the whole spectrum of human life and conduct.

If rules take the form of generalisations, their function is to guide our behaviour and tell us what should, and should not, be done. Surely one of the most basic tasks of a system of laws is to tell us, through rules, what to do and what will happen if we fail to act. The practice of law consists of the analysis of our conduct through the lens of these rules.

Both of these aspects of legal rules will be our concern in this chapter. Their form: what characteristics legal rules possess that other things (such as the rules of physics) do not possess, and their function: what legal rules *do* that other things (such as requests and threats) do not. The form and functioning of rules is related to our previous concerns with the right and the good. Rules function to support *basic goods* such as certainty in human affairs and predictable action by the powerful. Moreover, if we treat a 'rule' as any kind of generalisation that justifies a course of action, we are using rules whenever we act in a way that is rational or reasonable; in contrast, to act without reference to rules is to open ourselves to the arbitrary and unreasonable. The general form of rules, their being *generalisations*, recalls the necessity and universality which are associated with the priority of the right. By making expectations and standards public, clear and impartial, legal rules become a standard of rightness to which our actions should conform.

It is important from the outset to consider three characteristic properties of rules that not only help to distinguish them from other phenomena, but also draw out their relationship with the good and the right: *generality, justification* and *guidance of behaviour*.

First, we have noted (Chapter 1) that judgment is a relationship between *general* rules and particular cases. Legal rules (and indeed any rules) are generalisations, assertions about what should happen whenever actions or events fall within the scope of the rule. Because they assert what *ought* to happen, many rules (including legal rules) can be classed as prescriptive generalisations; they do not describe a generalisation, but demand or counsel a particular course of action. A legal case is the comparison between such prescriptive generalisations and a particular situation. If the facts of the case fall within the rules, the rules determine what should have happened and what should happen in the future.

Second, we have seen that law's relationship with justice involves ends (judgment) and means (adjudication) which seek to regulate human behaviour. Legal rules either regulate the actions of legal professionals or provide guidance to the public on what is expected of them. Explicit expectations provide the basis for judging our actions or determining what we deserve. Accordingly, rules *justify* certain kinds of behaviour and justify certain responses to behaviour. The rule 'walking faster gets you to your destination quicker' can be used to justify my walking fast. The rules of property law justify my taking and using these particular belongings (and justify a penalty if they are not my belongings).

Third is the capacity of rules to *guide* our action. Rules are instructions determining what actions should or should not be done. Our actions should conform to rules either in order to achieve a certain end ('for better coffee always add some cold water'), or because they are binding without reference to any further end ('always refrain from theft'). How it is that rules can 'bind' or obligate us will receive further attention. It is enough at present to note that while some rules offer us choices depending upon our preferences, and some take the form of an unconditional 'thou shalt', all rules provide a guide to action and therefore provide a degree of *certainty in action* that impulsive or arbitrary behaviour does not possess.

Despite these common functions, it is clear that rules can take many forms. From rules that we *may* wish to follow *if* we want better coffee, to moral rules that are universal in scope and without exception. Within the class of legal rules, rules can be written, unwritten, clear, unclear, implied, statutory, customary and so on. Are all of these equally rules? In the sense that they all share the function of rules – general prescriptions that serve to guide action and provide justifications – they are certainly rules despite their difference in form. It is certainly tempting to say that some are more rule-like than others, for example a statutory rule is 'more' of a rule than the rules governing etiquette in Court. (Perhaps because statutes are written down or are more likely to be associated with a specific penalty for their violation.) However, while one rule may well be more *important* than another, rules are no less rules for lacking a written form or not being supported by explicit threats.

The form and the function of legal rules will be our concern, but analysis of legal rules often turns on their foundation, that is, how they come into existence.

The foundation of rules must be either something real (in the world) or something ideal (among our ideas). Both of these possible sources have attractions. On the one hand, rules require having a *mental understanding* of why and how we should act:

> . . . a dog's acquisition of a habit does not involve it in any understanding of what is meant by 'doing the same thing on the same kind of occasion', this is precisely what a human being has to understand before he can be said to have acquired a rule. (Winch, 1958: 61)

On the other hand, whether written or unwritten, rules must be *publically* 'knowable'. For a rule to guide our actions it must be in some way public; we cannot follow a rule without knowing what the rule is. For this reason there are some problematic questions concerning whether the forceful or compulsory dimension of rules is something objective or subjective. A rule has to be publically known or knowable, but without subjective agreement over the meaning and significance of a rule, the rule cannot be said to guide action. This question is considered in the light of the work of Ludwig Wittgenstein (1889–1951), who stressed the public dimension of rules, and H.L.A. Hart (1907–92), who analysed both the 'internal' and 'external' aspects of legal rules.

This chapter considers the basic structure of rules and rule-following, but note that consideration of rules will take place, as far as possible, in isolation from discussion of 'norms'. 'Norms' and 'normativity' pinpoint the force or obligation separating rules from other facets of the world. While this is an important aspect of analysing rules (particularly legal rules) and is a useful way of considering the binding force of rules, it merits distinct concern. Normativity takes over much of the work that we attribute to rules in law as well as, additionally, making sense of why legal rules do not always have to be associated with a threat (or even a legal institution) to be legal rules. In short, while it is artificial to treat normativity in isolation from rules it is analytically defensible: the distinctive *form* that legal rules take can become lost in generalisations about norms.

1 Rules

Introduction

What is meant by the phrase 'rules are rules'? This tautology (a seemingly uninformative repetition) says a great deal about the role that rules play in our lives. Rules encompass the many things that we are obliged to do and 'rules are rules' is another way of saying 'this is obligatory'. Rules also concern what people are justified in doing, as opposed to what they *desire* to do. So, rules bind us, but often without them agreeing with our immediate interests or impulses. We accept that the rules of a game, or of a building site or of a club have justification even if we cannot see their justification; rules have control over our actions even if they do not agree with our immediate interests or have immediately intelligible functions. The evasive tautology 'rules are rules' is another way of saying that rules can retain their power over us even when their justification is unclear or unappealing.

For this reason, rules have a complex relationship with the good and the right. Rules can be said to ensure goods. They provide certainty and reliability in human affairs. This does not mean that a rule is always right, that it coheres with our other commitments or corresponds to our fundamental social principles. We might argue that in general it is good to use rules to govern human affairs but, in a particular case, it would be right to find an exception to the rule. Conversely, use of a rule could be said to be right but not good. Rules provide clarity and logic in decision-making. That is, they lend themselves to decision-making because rules are always public (the parties know on what basis a decision will be made) and logically deducible from other rules. At the same time, this may provide answers or outcomes that makes no party any happier. Rules yield clear answers, but there is no guarantee that they are desirable answers for all concerned.

It might be objected at this point that *legal* rules are different. There is always a distinctive justification of legal rules, namely that they are *legal* rules, and legal rules are binding on us regardless of any relationship with the good or the right. Legal positivism (see below) encourages us to see legal rules as a distinctive category of rules possessing the same characteristics as other rules (guiding, binding, generalisations) but which, *taken as a whole*, have special – obligation generating – properties. Before such analysis can take place, however, we have to be clear which rules *are* legal rules, and in the first instance 'legal rules' identifies a class of rules (and not an entirely clear one at that) rather than a qualitatively distinct *form* of rules. The class of legal rules could be said to be subsumed under all those categorical rules that compel us to act, rather than being those prudential or hypothetical rules that we follow out of convenience (see below). That legal rules are binding does not distinguish them from moral rules, and, moreover, does not distinguish them from the coercive commands of a criminal or tyrant. We do not follow such commands out of convenience, but because they leave us with no choice.

The phrase 'legal rules' does not even pick out a set of rules with a *single origin*. Legal rules are not always from a single source, i.e. a Parliament, or sovereign, or single law-maker. We inherit legal rules from previous generations through precedent; rules with the 'force of law' can be created by government ministers, local government and trading blocs; the rules of international law are created by the various, sometimes competing, practices of states. The task of understanding law's relationship with rules is initially, therefore, the task of understanding whether there is a distinctive class of 'legal rules' at all.

1a Rules as commands

Rules instruct us as to what we should do, and do not always need further justification in order to do that 'telling'. The 'thou shalt' rules of religion – that no-one is ever permitted to steal, lie or kill – are not supplemented with justifications. They

are categorical commands: unqualified and unequivocal. To the extent that such categorical commands are justified, it is on the implicit understanding that the origin
of the rule, God, *can command without further justification*. The question of whether
this provides a good analogy for the functioning of legal rules is an important
point of contention in legal philosophy. The 'command theory' of law (see below
and Weinreb, 1978: 926f) is an explanation of why we *should* see the rules of law
as much closer to religious injunctions than to the rules of cookery. Legal rules are
categorical instructions, not a menu of options serving our preferences.

Not all rules have this quality of commanding. Prudential or hypothetical rules
are 'rules of thumb' that guide us to a particular end should we want to achieve that
end. However, the rules associated with morality, and often with law, have a commanding quality that gives them a different complexion to prudential rules. Laws
assert that it is an 'offence', or 'illegal' or 'forbidden' to engage in a particular act.
Laws assert that a particular act is 'required', 'necessary' or 'should' happen. They
command or proscribe behaviour on the part of the actor(s) that they are directed
towards. For this reason, there is a long, and persuasive, tradition of associating
law not only with rules, but with rules as commands to act in particular ways. Such
theories focus on the form of rules (commands), the source of rules (a commanding
sovereign power) and on the function of rules (to compel us to act).

As suggested, law shares with morality a capacity to command, and many legal
rules look like the kind of categorical commandments that are found in religious
and non-religious moral systems. To the extent that rules are commands, not hy-
potheses about what a course of action will bring about, they are deontological
(duty-based) rather than consequential (outcome-based). But two important differences between law, and deontological *morality*, have to be observed for analytical
clarity. The first is that law's commands often have a distinctive source, namely the
state or sovereign. Morality's commands are not seen as conditional on the will,
actions or decisions of a single law-making power-holder. A central task of legal philosophy is to determine who is permitted to command, thereby securing a particular
set of commands as distinctively or authoritatively 'legal' commands.

Second, law's rules, while often seemingly unequivocal, are supplemented by
an array of exceptions. Moral theories can be supplemented with exceptions (e.g.
Nozick's 'side constraints'(1974: 28–33)), but exceptions are peripheral to the main
'compulsory thrust' of a moral theory. Exceptions are far more central to understanding the function of legal rules. Legal rules are rarely intended to bind *all* persons;
they are more often intended to apply universally and unequivocally to a *carefully
specified class* of persons and actions. (The fact that the laws we encounter most commonly in the media, criminal laws, do apply to a very wide class of persons should
not distract us from the fact that the majority of laws apply to a specific class of
persons with specific duties.) Laws apply when we adopt legal duties through form-
ing particular relationships. Furthermore, any set of rules will be accompanied by

exceptions that specify, much more carefully than the general rule, where the rule is not to apply and where alternative courses of action – by individuals and by law-enforcers – should be made available. Exceptions themselves come in the form of rules, but they are rules that narrow the scope of the most general legal rules.

EXAMPLE

***R v Immigration Officer at Prague Airport and another ex parte European Roma Rights Centre and others* [2004] UKHL 55**

The basic characteristic of a sovereign is their power to make rules for a territory; the rights of the persons on that territory are, in some respects, secondary to such commands. This case considers the origins and fundamental principles concerning the treatment of 'aliens' in England. It suggests that sovereign commands have been replaced by statutory rules.

The power to admit, exclude and expel aliens was among the earliest and most widely recognised powers of the sovereign state. In England, it was a prerogative power of the crown. Sir William Holdsworth [rightly stated]: 'I conceive the King had an absolute power to forbid foreigners, whether merchants or others, from coming within his dominions, both in times of war and in times of peace, according to his royal will and pleasure; and therefore gave safe-conducts to merchants strangers, to come in, at all ages, and at his pleasure commanded them out again.' But the crown's prerogative power over aliens was increasingly questioned, and since 1793 the power to exclude aliens has in this country been authorised by statute, whether temporary in effect [. . .] or permanent [. . .].

1b Forms and functions of rules

It should be clear from the range of legal materials encountered by anyone studying law that legal rules come in a variety of forms. Contemporary law is dominated by statutes where a carefully drafted set of rules regulate specific areas of activity. Some jurisdictions also possess a range of rules derived from the common law (rules that arise from particular legal decisions, decisions which then bind lower Courts). The contrast between the two is instructive. Legislation provides a sparse set of classifications, procedures, definitions and commands governing a specific field of activity. Common law rules are much less specific and can be much more difficult to articulate in a simple formula. The merit of legislation is the creation of rules with systematic attention to a single field of activity. The merit of common law is the generation of rules through a longer process of application, contest and trial and error.

Whether of statutory or common law origin, rules provide classifications as well as commands. They are not purely rules of the form '*x* is prohibited / required', but a complex web of classifications distinguishing actions, relationship, rights and duties. Moreover, the commands and classifications of statutory and common law are also supplemented with the rules governing legal institutions and legal practitioners: procedural rules in court, rules governing who is qualified to make legal decisions and rules governing the conflict of rules. With such variety in form of rules, the command theory, with its strong emphasis on the *source* of the rules, is not helpful in making sense of the many *forms* of legal rules. It is therefore necessary to distinguish, on grounds other than source, legal from non-legal rules, and, second, different types of legal rules.

One way to (provisionally) divide legal from non-legal rules is to recall the Kantian division between hypothetical and categorical imperatives. The distinction is intended to determine whether actions can be turned into moral duties, but the distinction has wider application to rules. If hypothetical imperatives are those courses of action which we pursue because they *might* or *could* lead to good outcomes, this can be found in many of our day-to-day activities. We might think it *generally useful* to be polite to people because this is likely (hypothetically) to make others happier than if we are not polite. This is certainly a *generalisation* that guides our *behaviour* and which can be used to *justify* our actions. As such it is rule-like, but such a rule is based on hypothetical outcomes. It can be contrasted with a categorical imperative which insists that 'no-one, under any circumstances, should tell a lie'. This too is a *generalisation* that guides our *behaviour* and which can be used to *justify* our actions. But this rule is intended to hold good regardless of any particular outcomes: it identifies a category of actions that should always be done. Legal rules are much closer to categorical than hypothetical imperatives. They are not rules that we follow just in case they have a good outcome. They are a category of rules that demand action (or omission) unconditionally. Legal philosophy is concerned with distinguishing the two, although this is not always easy. Those 'inside' law (i.e. legal practitioners) may see the rules they use as categorical (until they are changed by a higher legal authority). Those 'outside' law – for example Oliver Wendel Holmes' bad man – may see legal rules as a species of hypothetical rules: they do not bind our action unconditionally, but rather ask us to make an assessment of whether or not we are *likely* to meet with a penalty if we disobey them.

Another distinction, also attributable to Kant but taken up by John Searle (b.1932) and other philosophers, separates constitutive and regulative rules. This is especially useful in classifying legal rules and it centres on the *functions* of the rules. Regulative rules regulate conduct. They are what we would most commonly associate with legal rules: they tell us as individuals what to do, tell judges how to classify actions and provide society with an array of rules with which to conduct its affairs. Constitutive rules are those which create or constitute our social institutions and practices. They are the precondition of other rules being applicable. A constitution is predominantly a set of constitutive rules concerning how a state and its organs should function and interact. The institutions created by a constitution *themselves* make rules, regulative rules, which cannot be fully understood without recourse to the underlying constitutive rules. For example, we cannot make sense of how it is that criminal laws are binding on us without reference to the constitutive rules that empower the criminal justice system and the police in the first place. Without them, when a police officer enforces a rule, this would not be distinguishable from instructions from a member of the public who (for reasons of their own) wants us to act in a particular way. The regulative rule is justified by the existence of another, constitutive, rule.

Both constitutive and regulative rules are generalisations; they refer to 'any', 'all' or 'every'. However, legal rules are drafted such that they, despite being generalisations, *include* and *exclude* as carefully as possible. Whatever source a legal rule originates from, and whatever it is intended to do, the rule will encompass some actors and circumstances and exclude others. Even the most general (or 'global') rule of international law is directed at the actions of states rather than individuals; it is implicit in the rule that it is not enforceable between private persons. Rules governing contracts for services are intended to include every party who has entered into such a contract; they exclude everyone else who has not entered into precisely this kind of contract.

However, this is not to say that all rules look like rules in statute books with a carefully drafted set of criteria for inclusion or exclusion. Rules can be customary activities, general principles to be applied in particular cases, or a set of unspoken assumptions in a particular context. What a statutory law, a common law principle and many rules outside legal contexts have in common is something of the form: if conditions A and B are fulfilled, then C is relevant but everything else is irrelevant. For example: 'if you are in a Court, and you are a suspect in a criminal case, then your behaviour during the events at issue is relevant, but your conduct prior to those events is irrelevant'. A further rule could be added to make an exception to this, namely 'the foregoing rule is relevant *except* in those circumstances where your previous conduct may be relevant to evidencing a propensity to act in a particular way'. This common characteristic of legal rules is termed 'defeasibility'; legal rules have the capacity to be 'defeated' (Bix, 2004: 50). The characteristic of defeasibility indicates that, while generalisations, legal rules are always components of larger systems of inclusion and exclusion (or 'applicability' and 'non-applicability').

In other words, law's generalisations are conditional on certain explicit (and often implicit) assumptions about what is to be included within the scope of the rule; this sometimes has to be settled by other rules of interpretation that either draw attention to the context of the rule or look to the purpose for which it has been created. Such rules of interpretation are needed because laws have a tendency to both over-inclusive and over-exclusive generalisations. Frederick Schauer gives the example of the simple rule 'no dogs allowed' (1991: 32). In terms of the ends it is intended to serve (a quiet and safe place), it is over-inclusive (not all dogs are noisy or dangerous) and under-inclusive (it is not only dogs that are noisy or dangerous). Law generalises through rules, but even careful generalisations remain generalisations.

EXAMPLE

McTear v Imperial Tobacco Ltd No 1 [2005] CSOH 69

A range of rule-related issues are raised in this case about the liability of a tobacco company for the death by lung cancer of a smoker. The rule on the claimant's part was the rule set out in Donoghue v Stevenson *(1932): that a duty of care goes beyond parties to a contract. The defendants pleaded* volenti non fit injuria, *a rule concerning the illegitimacy of a claim when the claimant has brought injury upon themselves. The Court also considers it necessary to consider policy as a supplement to these rules.*

[T]he maxim *volenti non fit injuria* [applies when] the pursuer had taken a chance. [O]nce an individual was aware that there was a risk in what they were doing, then the consequences of the risk fell on him, because he could choose whether or not to take the risk. The cases on *volenti non fit injuria*, where the acceptance was of a future risk, where there had not yet been negligence, such as driving carelessly, could be contrasted with the type of circumstance found in Titchener, where the alleged fault had already taken place, in that case the state of the fence. These circumstances were important in determining as a matter of fact whether the pursuer had accepted a risk, waived a claim and so on. It was sometimes very difficult to get to *volenti non fit injuria*, because by the time one was looking at that one had already decided that there was no breach of a duty of care. Counsel submitted that Titchener afforded an insight into the general policy of the common law, which was founded on the notion of individual freedom, and the notion that the individual took responsibility for his own actions. The common law recognised that individuals were entitled to do things which involved risk to their health or well-being, but if they did so they must accept responsibility for the consequences of their actions.

1c Formalism and anti-formalism

If the common form of a legal rule is a generalisation, and the function of legal rules is to regulate and constitute, legal rules might be thought to be rigid rules not unlike those found in religion. However, the complex processes of inclusion and exclusion associated with law means that this picture of generalisation and rigidity is incomplete. Through inclusion and exclusion, legal rules determine, with a *high degree of specificity*, what must happen when an action or event falls within the scope of the rule. Whether we are concerned with statutory rules, common law principles or professional standards, we find generalisations concerning commitments or obligations. The way that rules determine obligations through generalisations reflects the analysis of law provided by the idea of 'right'. A coherence in law that allows the generation of right answers. Such 'inner coherence' of law comes from its relationship with logic (*right* answers can be logically deduced, they are not just good answers to a problem) and with universality (duties, on a Kantian model, can be discerned when an obligation can be made general or universal).

It is these kinds of assumptions that gave rise to a loose grouping of early twentieth-century legal scholars labelled 'formalists' (Bix, 2004: 69–70; Tamanaha, 2010). To the extent that they share a common position, it is that rules are the most important dimension of law because rules have the capacity to generate right legal answers. A right legal answer can be established because of the formal qualities of rules (they are generalisations) and by their functional qualities (they function in a 'binary' way to determine, unequivocally, whether something is right or wrong – i.e. coherent – within a legal system).

Formalism, a movement associated with analysing the common law system of the United States, insisted on rules creating right legal answers out of the 'completeness' of law. The combination of statutory and common law rules allowed the correct legal answer to any legal question to be determined through the logical application of existing legal rules. This echoes the 'seamless web' conception of law as a complete, inter-related set of rules (see Berman, 1977). The characteristic of legal rules – their categorisation of facts through inclusion and exclusion – has the capacity to encompass any possible state of affairs and any possible conflict.

This entails a strictly limited role for judges: enforcing and applying rules. Judges do not make legal rules. Rule *creation* is found in the evolution of the common law through judicial interpretation and in legislative activity; legal judgment is exclusively the application of those rules. The merit of formalism is that it accords with many of our ideas about what legal activity is concerned with (rules) and what legal activity rejects ('making up the rules as we go along'). It also supports a potentially radical view of legal judgment. If all human activity can be brought within the ambit of a rule or an exception, then there is infinite potential for the application of rules. Law therefore contains the possibility for replacing decision-making by judges with a wholly automated process. After all, if everything can be designated as falling within a rule or an exception to a rule, there is nothing logical to prevent every event being processed by a computer, i.e. a machine ultimately processing facts in a binary fashion as 0 or 1: included or excluded, applicable or inapplicable. This is arguably the 'coherence' conception of the right taken to its final conclusion.

There are strong currents of anti-formalism associated with 'legal realist' movement (Chapter 6; Tamanaha, 2010). This rejects the rigid straightjacket that formalism places on law and legality. The first ground of anti-formalism rests on a distinction between rules, principles and standards. There is an argument to suggest that while most elements of a legal system seem to take the *form* of rules, the *functioning* of standards and principles is different. Standards establish criteria by which actions can be judged; they substitute generalisations for a narrower set of expectations. Principles, as broad moral commitments, guide the ways in which judgments can be reached without including or excluding anything in advance: they are there to *prevent* the use rules in certain circumstances. This kind of distinction is useful for analysis of judicial decision-making and is crucial to Dworkin's analysis of law (1998) (although, given the generalisation, guidance and justification that they allow, the classification of principles and standards as something other than *rules* is problematic).

A second objection to formalism concerns logic and judgment. It is argued that a formal system cannot replace human judgment. While it may or may not be the case that every event can be captured by a rule, the application of a rule always requires *classification of facts*. It is only when we have classified something as a member of a class of facts that we can decide which rule is applicable to it. This classification is not a logical process but a process of human judgment, i.e. comparison, evaluation and also intuition. Without these subtle evaluative processes and the subjective judgments they require, the whole system of rules and rule application cannot commence. Put strongly, the 'autonomy of rules' is a mythology: some would like to think that objective rules can replace subjective judgment, but this is impossible because classification always contains something more than the application of a rule (Wilkins, 1990).

Finally, formalism does not reflect the dynamism required by law (see Chapter 7). To the extent that both individuals and social life are dynamic phenomena that change or emerge, the governance of rules is likely to become repressive if it does not follow or map those changes. This could be argued for in the language of the good in so far as the good of the individual and of the state change, and rules are there to reflect that good, not determine it. It might also be articulated in the language of the right to the extent that even our basic rights and duties are liable to change over time and depend upon the social situation we inhabit: i.e. the right is established through correspondence to our underlying political commitments. Existing legal rules are only temporary and contingent manifestations of those principles perceived to be basic or fundamental.

EXAMPLE

O'Reilly and Others Appellants v Mackman and Others Respondents [1982] 3 W.L.R. 1096

Are prison rules (here the UK Prison Rules of 1964) subject to judicial review? In other words, are rules governing the running of prisons (prison boards) part of the powers exercised by a member of the Executive or are they simply a set of regulations with an informal status? Even if they are informal, should basic rules of 'natural justice' apply? On the one hand, the legal formalist has no answer to these questions because they concern the applicability of rules, not the use of rules; on the other this could be settled by the constitutive rules of the constitution (as the formalist model would suggest).

Many of the men complained about the conduct of the board of visitors. They said that the board had failed to comply with the rules of natural justice. [. . .] [The appellant] has issued a writ against three gentlemen who were the board of visitors and heard his case [. . .] and has said: '. . . the board failed to give the plaintiff an opportunity to call alibi witnesses in his defence notwithstanding that he requested them to do so and that the evidence thereof was relevant and material to his said defence.' [. . .]. Rules of court can only affect procedure: whereas an Act of Parliament comes in like a lion. It can affect both procedure and substance alike. [. . .] In the absence of express provision to the contrary Parliament, whenever it provides for the creation of a statutory tribunal, must be presumed not to have intended that the tribunal should be authorised to act in contravention of one of the fundamental rules of natural justice or fairness: *audi alteram partem* [no-one should be condemned unheard].

2 Positivism

Introduction

The theory of law most closely associated with rules is legal positivism. We will consider some of the reasons rules are important to positivists and only then consider at length the most important rule-centred theory of law, Hart's *The Concept of Law*. What is significant about Hart's work for present purposes is that he reflects aspects of the 'scientific positivism' that was in the background of most academic and philosophical thinking in Anglophone countries during the twentieth century. While the relationship between legal positivism and scientific positivism is not a simple one, understanding the latter is a good basis for understanding the former (see Hutchinson, 1995).

What is 'positivism' in general terms? The 'posited' part of 'positivism' concerns what is posited or immediately found in reality by the senses, as opposed to what is 'hidden' and needing further explanation. Positivism is one of the least sceptical philosophical positions: the world, as we find it, provides certain and reliable knowledge. Positivism, in more specific terms, denotes the belief that science (systematic, observation-based enquiry) offers the best model of knowledge or the most authoritative account of reality. While positivists vary in their commitment to science as the only justified style of thinking or analysis, they are unified in what they reject. They reject metaphysics, that is, the founding of knowledge on assumptions insulated from empirical enquiry. This encompasses scepticism about the mental realm, and philosophical 'idealism': appeals to our minds, or our inner worlds, are not justifiable as explanations. This approach had considerable impact on how law was understood in the eighteenth and nineteenth centuries, with legal positivists pursuing this agenda through emphasis on how law is posited (made or created) rather than looking for any single kind of *content*, *justification* or *essence* of legality.

2a Origins of positivism

Scientific positivism owes much to empiricism, the view that all knowledge must ultimately come from the senses. Positivism's departure from (and arguably radicalisation of) empiricism arises from, first, its insistence that knowledge begins and ends with scientific enquiry and no further discussion of metaphysics or ideas is necessary or desirable (Skorupski, 1993: 119–20). This is a radical epistemology: all knowledge must come from, or be sought through the methods of, scientific research. A second departure from empiricism is the application of these principles directly to moral and ethical thought. Ethics is required to reconstitute itself on scientific lines or risk being branded metaphysics. 'Value' itself must become something intelligible in scientific terms (Ayer, 1970). We have, therefore, an assertion that the sole route to truth is through science, that all metaphysical speculation is misguided and that values should be reduced to facts.

The historical evolution of positivism in the nineteenth century – at which point what we now label 'legal positivism' had already begun to take on its own distinctive characteristics – betrayed difficulties and internal conflicts in this aspiration. Auguste Comte (1798–1857), one of the founders of the discipline of sociology, exhibited the merits and excesses of positivism. On the one hand, he applied scientific methods to the study of society (which at that point had changed little from the observations of Aristotle) and pursued an encyclopaedic, and historical, view of what it is to be human within human society. On the other hand, this was combined with a quasi-religious view of the progress of humanity through the pursuit and use of scientific rationality (Skrorupski, 1993: 119). By embracing ideas of humanity's progress Comte did not escape from or reject metaphysics, nor did he satisfactorily reduce value to fact. The facts of science have no such simple correlation with the values of society.

We have inherited some of these tensions to the extent that we as a society are prone to assume that science is authoritative in all domains, that positing the existence of anything outside the world constructed by scientific investigation is mere speculation, and that *therefore* scientific methods and analysis provide the only authoritative guide to the organisation of human affairs. The premises and conclusion of this argument are false and the deduction itself is invalid. Science is a source of debate, not certainty, and science's assumptions are not a direct guide to social values.

The positivist worldview is also generally interested in and well disposed towards rules. As with empiricism there is an assumption that all nature exhibits regularity, that nature is law-like (Hampson, 1968). This means explanations and predictions about nature are possible, and such explanations will take the form of rules. These could be general rules up to and including the rule that 'nature exhibits law-like regularity' (an important, though often implicit, assumption in scientific research). It also means that all scientific observation, and therefore all reality, is amenable to expression in the form of rules. This is distinguishable from other empiricist philosophies which concede that we cannot treat 'nature's law-like regularity' as a universal rule. (David Hume, despite being central to empiricism, was sceptical of such claims (Hume, 1975)). It is also distinguishable from those positions that seek to preserve a distinctive realm of value where public rules are not appropriate or are misguided (see Wittgenstein, below). Positivism is, in short, the philosophy that has (albeit indirectly in some instances) formed the basis of our modern understanding of the world and particularly of law as a set of public rules.

EXAMPLE

Regina v *Turner (Terence)* [1975] 2 W.L.R. 56

Powerful claims made in defence of science and scientific expertise are still a feature of our Courts. Expert testimony provides clarity for jurors in complex trials. But Courts are becoming suspicious of the quantity and quality of expert witnesses in Courts.

> We all know that both men and women who are deeply in love can, and sometimes do, have outbursts of blind rage when discovering unexpected wantonness on the part of their loved ones; the wife taken in adultery is the classical example of the application of the defence of 'provocation'; and when death or serious injury results, profound grief usually follows. Jurors do not need psychiatrists to tell them how ordinary folk who are not suffering from any mental illness are likely to react to the stresses and strains of life. It follows that the proposed evidence was not admissible to establish that the defendant was likely to have been provoked. The same reasoning applies to its suggested admissibility on the issue of credibility. The jury had to decide what reliance they could put upon the defendant's evidence. He had to be judged as someone who was not mentally disordered. This is what juries are empanelled to do. The law assumes they can perform their duties properly. The jury in this case did not need, and should not have been offered, the evidence of a psychiatrist to help them decide whether the defendant's evidence was truthful.

2b Logical positivism

The already radical agenda of positivism became intensified in the early twentieth century with the foundation of the 'Vienna Circle' of philosophers and physicists (Skorupski, 1993). This group, influenced by the early Wittgenstein and his work on sense and logic, sought to purify positivism of metaphysics and re-found enquiry on the basis of 'verificationism' (Ayer, 1970). In this form of positivism, propositions (i.e. statements about the world in the form of sentences) only have *sense* if they are true by definition (tautologies or mathematical statements) or empirically *verifiable*. Verification requires a set of statements or conditions whereby a proposition could be checked empirically by the senses; propositions that cannot be so verified are metaphysical, and therefore nonsense. For example, statements about objects in the universe are meaningful because there is, in theory, a set of processes by which they can be verified. Conversely, 'murder is always morally wrong' yields no means of verification – by what means could we verify the existence of 'wrongness'? – and is therefore nonsense.

Verificationism clearly leads to a problematic relationship with psychological and moral ideas, and indeed with any assertion based on cognitive rather than empirical judgment. It led to the 'behaviourist' movement in psychology where all talk of mental states is replaced with testable and verifiable behaviour (Winch, 1958). Furthermore, in the context of moral theory it gave rise to 'emotivism', the idea that all values claims are intended to *persuade* but are, strictly, nonsense (Baggini and Fosl, 2007). When someone insists that 'murder is wrong' this may well have some impact on how we think about life and how we should act, but this is not because the proposition is 'true'. In fact, the proposition is wholly meaningless but exerts a powerful, emotional, effect on people who hear it.

Importantly we can, however, distinguish the proposition 'murder is wrong' from the proposition 'murder is illegal'. This, on the contrary, indicates something that can be verified using laws in statute books or the practices of courts. Law fairs much better in the logical positivist's world as a set of empirically verifiable assertions about what law-makers have commanded and what generally happens when law is implemented in the Courts. Nonetheless, any necessary relationship with morality has to be rejected (see Skorupski, 1993: 28–9). If all moral propositions lack sense, this nonsense is likely to infect our understanding of law and legal systems. The challenge presented by the logical positivists would be to wholly expunge any appeal to unverifiable value claims from legal discussion. But such a position is not adopted by most *legal* positivists because while there may not be any necessary overlap between the content of law and content of morality, the language of morality still has some role to play in analysing law (see Hart, 1994: 172–3).

EXAMPLE

Vellore Citizens Welfare Forum v *Union of India* (1996) 5 SCC 647 Supreme Court of India

This judgment, the consequence of a claim brought against tanneries whose industry was poisoning drinking water in the State of Tamil Nadu, invokes two key principles of environmental law. First, the precautionary principle that demands action even in the absence of clear scientific evidence, and second the polluter pays principle which puts liability, after an event of environmental harm, on the polluter to serve as a deterrent to others. Is there a contradiction between normal scientific research into cause and effect and the legal assumption that risk exists without scientific evidence?

> The authority so constituted by the Central Government shall implement the 'precaution-ary principle' and the 'polluter pays' principle. The authority shall, with the help of expert opinion and after giving opportunity to the concerned polluters [to present evidence,] assess the loss to the ecology/environment in the affected areas and shall also identify the individuals/families who have suffered because of the pollution and shall assess the compensation to be paid to the said individuals/families. The authority shall further determine the compensation to be recovered from the polluters as cost of reversing the damaged environment. The authority shall lay down just and fair procedure for completing the exercise.

2c Legal positivism

The fact that a form of positivism has come to dominate debate about law should not surprise us. Both the general objectives of positivism (attention to posited real-ity and a rejection of metaphysical explanation) and its implicit agenda (to rid en-quiry of unverifiable dogmatic assumptions) offer to *demystify* law and at the same time to give it its proper – social, not metaphysical – place within the evolution of a culture and state. Legal positivism is, then, a bid to clarify and demystify an area of activity where there is a tendency towards categorical anarchy. All life is contained within law, and all means (political, psychological and emotive) seem to be at its disposal to reach judgments; adding to this mixture the contested idea of morality is a recipe for confused (or certainly 'unscientific') thinking.

In fact, legal positivists share the assumption that there are distinctive means available to legal systems that allow us to distinguish law from other social phe-nomenon, namely its *source* and its *form*. Law does not reach decisions by just any means, but by using legitimate means authorised by legitimate sources of authority. Moreover, positivism seeks to give law its 'proper place' in our lives and our thinking by distinguishing our social and political culture from our legal system. Our society gives rise to and requires a legal system, but that system must be, in many respects, independent of that society. Positivism allows us to separate out these closely re-lated ideas by showing that law does have a specific and distinctive origin and that it is distinguishable from the 'mores', the morality, of a society. Two core ideas are at work here. First, the positivist 'social thesis' that law is a social phenomenon; the source of law is social practices (see Bix, 2004: 203–4). Second, the 'separation the-sis' that law can be analytically separated from morality (Raz, 2009). We turn first to one form of 'social thesis': Austin's command theory.

In its 'classic' form as promulgated by John Austin (1790–1859), legal positiv-ism seeks to demonstrate that law is the 'command of a sovereign' supported by force. While this picture of the nature of law is much criticised (e.g. Tur, 1978) it has one clear merit: identifying exactly what should be labelled 'law' and exclud-ing that which is potentially *law-like* but only a social trend, ethical commitment

or religious injunction. There is some intuitive appeal in seeing law as ar
to a set of obligations taking the form 'do this or suffer the consequen
all, we may debate and discuss other areas of life – politics, morality an
commitments – but we *obey* the law.

By specifying exactly what the origin of law is, Austin gives us the means to
distinguish laws from all other rule-governed activities. That origin is the sovereign understood as that entity that commands within a given territory and is not
commanded by any higher authority: 'If a determinate human superior, not in a
habit of obedience to a like superior, receive habitual obedience from the bulk
of a given society, that determinate superior is sovereign in that society' (Austin
quoted in Freeman, 2001: 251). The sovereign is that body or person whose commands we habitually obey and who, conversely, is not in the habit of obeying any
other source of commands. At the root of any and all legal rules is a single person
or body who has the power to promulgate rules and whose rules are habitually
obeyed (see Bix, 2004: 10–14).

While we might find this command account of law too centred on power (law is
surely more than a variation of 'might is right'), legally inadequate (in marginalising customary and common law) or even morally suspect (there are, ostensibly, no
limits to what a sovereign can command), it has clear value in separating out the
territory of legal enquiry. It respects the distinction between facts and values, and
delineates what should be left to political or moral decision-making. A well defined
'province' is created for lawyers and legal philosophers – the commands of the sovereign – leaving moral and political philosophers to concern themselves with the
shape that action and society *might*, ideally, take. Moreover, the command theory
treats law as (exclusively) a set of facts with verifiable social origins. Whatever legal
rules we encounter are, either explicitly or implicitly, endorsed or commanded by the
sovereign; anything purporting to be a legal rule without such origins is mislabelled.

Due to some of the difficulties already indicated in Austin's account – the limitless power of the sovereign, and those legal rules that have not come directly from a
Parliament but from custom and practice – modern (twentieth-century) legal positivism has sought to find a way to maintain the distinctively 'posited' dimensions
of law without recourse to commands or to morality. One way of doing this is by
paying closer attention to how law is *effective* in society. In contrast to simple ideas
of obedience, appeal to social efficacy requires isolating those sources that give rise
to law and law-abiding behaviour including, but not exclusively, the sovereign. For
example, this could be the fact that legal rules are *understood* and *accepted* as creating obligations, and therefore legal rules do not have be associated with a threat.
Treating the rules of law as garnering or generating obedience does not thereby
commit us to the idea that law is another form of social *more* (an unconscious,
customary, pattern of behaviour) or, worse, as a variation of the threat of the armed
criminal. Law generates a sense of obligation (see discussion of Hart, below).

Another version of the social thesis is found in the work of Joseph Raz (b.1939). In his account – a stronger form of social thesis named the 'sources thesis' – legal rules give us a special and distinctive set of reasons for acting, reasons different from those found in morality or in prudential, instrumental, thinking. Those reasons lie in the proven authority of legal systems, as social institutions, to give decisions that are fair and justified (Raz, 2009: 12–16). This, for Raz, means that we only to need to look at legal institutions, their practices and our attitudes towards them in order to understand law. There is no need to turn to external or higher sources of authority and justification to treat law as an authorised and justified set of rules and practices. A certain set of rules are *authoritative* – they have a socially accredited sources – and this authority does not rely on any justification outside society. In Hart and Raz the emphasis is on *facts*: what is verifiably associated with law, but its rules, or the acceptance of rules by a society.

The more specific 'separation thesis' takes as its guiding principle that legal rules can be wholly separated from *moral rules*. This position accords with one key part of the positivist agenda, namely the rejection of the idea that law is in any way dependent on 'external' justification by morality. While it is clear that there is a contingent relationship between law and morality – the rules of one are often the rules the other – laws do not need justification on the basis of moral rules or principles (see Bix, 2004: 198–199). While this has been construed as a 'project' of insisting that judicial decision-making be free from moral content and moral judgments (Kelsen's work could be seen as an instance of such a project, see Chapter 6) few positivists would want to suggest that law-*making* should be isolated from wider moral concerns, nor would they deny that there is a recurrent overlap between law and morality. Rather – and this is where the separation thesis can be subsumed under the social thesis – legal rules of all kinds arise from social sources that do not need validation by anything 'outside' society, its practices and its institutions.

EXAMPLE

Parliament Act 1911

With a bicameral legislature (e.g. the two Houses of Parliament or the two Houses of the US Congress) are one or both Houses sovereign? In the 1911 Parliament Act, the UK House of Commons specifies circumstances when – with popular support and in anticipation of wider reform – it would excise power without the Lords' consent. Does this make the Commons the ultimate source of law? A command theory would say, in these circumstances, make the Commons alone the source of law; a wider view of law's sources could encompass the Lords, Commons and common law.

> Whereas it is expedient that provision should be made for regulating the relations between the two Houses of Parliament / And whereas it is intended to substitute for the House of Lords as it at present exists a Second Chamber constituted on a popular instead of hereditary basis, but such substitution cannot be immediately brought into operation / And whereas provision will require hereafter to be made by Parliament in a measure effecting such substitution for limiting and defining the powers of the new Second Chamber, but it is expedient to make such provision as in this Act appears for restricting the existing powers of the House of Lords: [. . .] (1) If a Money Bill, having been passed by the House of Commons, and sent up to the House of Lords at least one month before the end of the session, is not passed by the House of Lords without amendment within one month after it is so sent up to that House, the Bill shall, unless the House of Commons direct to the contrary, be presented to His Majesty and become an Act of Parliament on the Royal Assent being signified, notwithstanding that the House of Lords have not consented to the Bill.

3 Hart

Introduction

The work of H.L.A. Hart (1907–92) is, in Anglo-American philosophy, the most influential work of the twentieth century and in many quarters remains the starting point for discussion in analytical jurisprudence, i.e. philosophy concerned with analysing legal concepts and the distinctive characteristics of law. This means that his work is a shared reference point for engaging in contemporary debate on the philosophy of law. It is also significant for the centrality of rules within its vision of law. Hart's analysis of rules is powerful and nuanced. It provides the analytical clarity sought by legal positivism, but also contains an element of conceptual scepticism that runs counter to aspects of scientific, logical and earlier legal positivism.

The debt owed to the earlier legal positivist tradition is explicit in Hart's work. He is a legal positivist taking as his starting-point law as a set of facts. Facts *partially* characterised by being rules promulgated by a sovereign *sometimes* backed with the threat of force and possessing *what resembles* habitual obedience. The fact that this is a hesitant characterisation of law is central to Hart's project. Command theories fail to capture, *inter alia*: the functioning of legal institutions and legal practices lacking any obvious coercive element; the fact that law is not created and administered by a single body but by complex institutional arrangements; and the fact that our 'habitual obedience' is actually conscious acceptance of a system of governance, not unthinking obedience to any single sovereign.

In constructing his criticism of command theories, Hart commences with Wittgenstein's sceptical analysis of concepts (see below). Concepts such as just, good, state, rule and so on, are not neatly defined things with single, univocal, meanings or functions. They are used in different ways in different contexts, with no single common thread running through their uses. That 'common thread' is what we are searching for if we are determined to find *the* meaning of a word, but no such thread can be found (Hart, 1994: 280). Accordingly, legal philosophers should not seek to find hidden uniformity in the uses of 'law' or 'rule'; rather we should accept that important terms have a 'core' meaning and a 'penumbra' (a halo) of other uses. The central challenge of Hart's work is to do this with the concept of 'law'.

3a The concept of law

Hart's pursuit of a concept of law is not, therefore, an empirical enquiry concerned with precisely isolating what should, and should not, be called law. Rather he is concerned with what is meant by law among those most versed in, or qualified in, the use of law. The intention behind this is not to find out, empirically, what in- formed people say 'law' means, it is to isolate one particular set of practices within which the word 'law' is used – namely practices within legal systems – and analyse what is being meant by law in that context. Put in negative terms, Hart is resisting the temptation to stipulate a single authoritative meaning for 'law'. After all, 'law' connotes rules (from the rules of courtrooms, to the generalisations of the natural sciences), but it would be a distortion of language to say that only one class of uses is *the* legitimate or correct use: 'this book is offered as an elucidation of the *concept* of law, rather than a definition of 'law' which might naturally be expected to provide a rule or rules for the use of these expressions' (1994: 213).

From this foundation, Hart outlines the deficiencies in Austin's command theory. This is the 'classic' positivist argument that law is a set of facts characterised by use of rules, promulgated by a sovereign, which are then reinforced with the threat of coercion. Hart shows that this theory cannot make a distinction between the com- mand of a sovereign and that of a gangster making demands with menaces: both are commands supported with the threat of force. We would surely want to say that there is something rather more consensual (if also *potentially* coercive) about the laws of the land. Nor does this make sense of the function of common law and customary law, forms of law accreted over time and separable from the will of any particular sovereign. Further, a command theory cannot make sense of the transi- tions between sovereigns. In the absence of sovereign (during an 'interregnum' or dissolved Parliament) law would presumably cease to exist.

From this set of criticisms, Hart moves to enrich our understanding of legal rules and our obedience to them. Rules, for Hart, are not merely things external to us but have an *internal* force. We can see rules objectively ('in the world') when we see people engaged in behaviour that is law-like: when *everyone* stops at a red light, or *everyone* pays their taxes. However, to see this habitual obedience as law-like *behav- iour*, in the same way that a scientist sees law-like regularity in the orbit of the moon, is missing something crucial: that the people exhibiting this behaviour see and *perceive themselves* as being obliged to follow a rule. If we want to understand why it is that law exists in the absence of single sovereign individual, why common and customary laws are laws 'proper', and most importantly why it is that we distinguish the sovereign's rules from the gangster's rules, we look to our 'internal' relationship with those rules. This is not to say we constantly and persistently give our conscious consent to the rules that we abide by. Nor does it mean that everyone, without exception, is law-abiding. Rather, legal rules are rules that we appear to 'habitually obey' because we have *consciously acknowledged* the force of a rule, *not* because we are automatons who have learnt to fear the consequences of not obeying. '[I]f a social rule is to exist some at least must look upon the behaviour in question as a general standard to be followed by the group as a whole. A social rule has an 'internal' aspect [. . .]' (Hart, 1994: 56).

This internal aspect allows us to make an important distinction with respect to obedience. It was suggested that moral rules, legal rules and the commands of a criminal all have some claim to objectivity; these rules have an objective, public, element because they come from 'outside' ourselves and are reinforced by the practices – and sometimes the threats – of those around us. However, some of these are rules that we assent to (e.g. moral obligations to others), some are simply obligations that are placed upon us (coercive threats). Hart wants to, in a similar vein, distinguish 'being obliged to' and 'having an obligation'. We can be obliged, compelled, to do many kinds of things. But *'having an obligation'* means being bound by something that has justification and that we know has some kind of justification. We recognise and acknowledge certain things as binding rules (we 'have an obligation') and are simply coerced in other contexts (we are 'obliged'). To confuse the two is to confuse the internal and external aspect of rules. Externally, a criminal's instructions and a legislative rule may both look like coercive commands. Obedience to those commands shows that the subjects of the commands were obliged. Only in the case of following the legislative rule does the actor see themselves as *having an obligation*, and there is good reason to see this as the mark of – all and any – legal rule.

Hart's account separates a legal rule from a categorical imperative. A categorical imperative binds us in the absence of hypothetical judgments about the likely outcome of acting. Legal rules certainly share some kind of similarity in their creating obligations, but this is not, unlike a categorical imperative, independent of all internal perceptions, decisions and judgments. On the contrary, the imperative force of law is somewhere between the categorical (it represents obligation) and the hypothetical (it is a *decision* to abide by a legal rule, even if such rule-following is contrary to our immediate interests). Our relationship with legal rules is, in other words, distinguishable from moral rules that hold good independently of our decisions, and distinguishable from the merely prudent decision to act in such a way as the risk of bad consequences is avoided.

Hart thereby offers us the foundations of a more robust positivist view of law, although the picture is not yet complete because Hart has more to say about the relationship between rules and the concept of law. Note at this point, however, that Hart's conception of rules is both *objective* and *internal*. Rules are part of the world, because they are found in the practices and behaviour of persons. At the same time they are 'internal' because rule following cannot be understood without the *sense* of obligation. This is a persuasive combination of two quite different dimensions of legal rules, their public nature *and* their dependence on 'internal' rule-following.

EXAMPLE

French Civil Code (As Amended 2004), Title 3, Chapter 1

The law of contract naturally varies between countries, and the rules governing the creation of valid contracts show some difference between jurisdictions. The French Civil Code provides a set of rules for identifying where a contract exists and whether it is valid. Conscious adoption of an obligation is central, as it is in other jurisdictions. Do such rules make sense as the 'command' of a sovereign?

Art. 1101:

A contract is an agreement by which one or several persons bind themselves, towards one or several others, to transfer, to do or not to do something. / Art. 1102: A contract is synallagmatic [imposes mutual obligations] or bilateral where the contracting parties bind themselves mutually towards each other./ Art. 1103: It is unilateral where one or more persons are bound towards one or several others, without there being any obligation on the part of the latter. / Art. 1104: It is commutative where each party binds himself to transfer or do a thing which is considered as the equivalent of what is transferred to him or of what is done for him. [. . .] Where the equivalent consists in a chance of gain or of loss for each party, depending upon an uncertain event, a contract is aleatory. / Art. 1105: A contract of benevolence is one by which one of the parties procures a purely gratuitous advantage to the other. Art. 1106: A contract for value is one which obliges each party to transfer or do something.

● 3b Primary and secondary rules

Legal rules are, then, that group of rules which we habitually obey and which guide our actions. However, we do not immediately associate them with the threat of violent coercion by the sovereign, rather we obey them because they give rise to a sense of obligation. Within a stable democracy, people obey legal rules *because they are the law* and not because they fear for their safety, but these rules are not a single homogenous set of rules, and this is especially clear to those working within a legal system and administering its rules. Those who work within legal institutions also work with, and under, rules of a more complex nature. That is, rules about creating legal rules and using legal rules. In other words, legal systems possess another system of rules which underpin the action-governing generalisations we generally think of as legal rules: legal systems involve constitutive and not just regulatory rules.

Hart calls the main body of regulative rules 'primary rules'. These are the 'laws of the land' which guide our action whether we are closely involved in legal matters or just dimly aware that there are laws that constrain what we can do. The governing that takes place under primary rules is not coercion by force but the outcome of the creation and acceptance of obligations. Primary rules give us standards of behaviour not unlike, but nonetheless distinct from, the standards of behaviour offered by morality. The difference is that law always takes the form of rules, always arises from social decisions and social institutions, and moreover, contains rules which change and vary over time through the exercise of other rules.

> Under rules of one type, which may well be considered the basic or primary type, human beings are required to do or abstain from certain actions, whether they wish or not. Rules of the other type are in a sense parasitic upon or secondary to the first; for they provide that human beings may by doing or saying certain things introduce new rules of the primary type, extinguish or modify old ones, or in various ways determine their incidence or control their operations. (1994: 81)

These other rules are secondary rules. These are rules which allow for the legitimate change of, and adjudication between, primary legal rules. Without such rules of change and adjudication we would have to see all rules as sovereign commands: binding us unconditionally until such time as the sovereign chose to modify them. Law possesses rules for adjudication, i.e. rules for determining how conflicts between rules are decided. Also rules of modification: rules determining how and in what circumstances rules can be changed (1994: 92–4). This is what we would expect to find within a mature legal system: a complex web of rules wherein major decisions are rule-governed decisions not diktats from a sovereign or executive.

Perhaps most importantly, this group of rules contains the ultimate rule by which any rule, primary or secondary, is to be recognised as a legal rule: the rule of recognition. The rule is the means by which any rule can be judged to be a part of the legal system; it is the standard by which any other rules can be said to be included within the legal system: '[t]his will specify some feature or features possession of which by a suggested rule is taken as conclusive affirmative indication that it is a rule of the group to be supported by the social pressure it exerts' (1994: 94). Adjudication and modification cannot take place without a clear indication of whether a rule is truly a legal rule. However, the precise nature of the rule of recognition is difficult to pin-point. In the UK legal system it would be the *fact* that legitimate legislation is created by Parliament in accordance with the UK's constitutional arrangements. In the international legal system, Article 38 of the Statute of the International Court of Justice (which states the legitimate sources of international law) takes its authority, ultimately, from the Charter of the United Nations, which in turn takes its force from the ability of sovereign states to agree to the existence of international legal organisations. However, there is also a sense in which recognition relates to that dimension of legal rules – we see them as creating obligations – which means that they generate more than slavish obedience. In this sense the rule of recognition is less the *fact* of a constitutional origin for legal rules and more a state of mind whereby those administering primary and secondary rules *see* and *accept* certain kinds of rules as legal ones using 'criteria of validity which [. . .] refer not to the content of the law but to the manner and form in which the laws are created or adopted' (1994: 258).

The concept of law is, then, most adequately captured by this combination of primary and secondary rules. This is not only for the negative reason that command theories fail to capture the nuances of rules and of obedience. It is for the important conceptual reason that the use of the word 'law' by those most closely associated with legal systems always designates *two* sets of rules and denotes a definite group of rules that fall within the scope of the rule of recognition. This is not to say that 'law' only or authoritatively *means* the union of primary and secondary rules under a rule of recognition. It does entail that if we want to understand 'law' in a way meaningful to those within legal institutions then we must attend to the internal aspect of rules and the regulation of rules by rules.

EXAMPLE

Vienna Convention on the Law of Treaties (1969) Articles 31 and 32

This Convention contains the basic rules of interpretation in international law. Command theories of law could not grant international law full legal status because it lacks a single, commanding, sovereign. Nonetheless, international law clearly possesses secondary rules that govern its primary rules.

Article 31 General rule of interpretation:

1. A treaty shall be interpreted in good faith in accordance with the ordinary meaning to be given to the terms of the treaty in their context and in the light of its object and purpose. / 2. The context for the purpose of the interpretation of a treaty shall comprise, in addition to the text, including its preamble and annexes: (a) any agreement relating to the treaty which was made between all the parties in connection with the conclusion of the treaty; (b) any instrument which was made by one or more parties in connection with the conclusion of the treaty and accepted by the other parties as an instrument related to the treaty.

3c Hart and his critics

The influence of Hart's work has been considerable and much contemporary analytical jurisprudence takes Hart's work as its starting-point. Three areas where his work has been extended or criticised are considered: the role of legal institutions, responses by natural lawyers and direct attacks on Hart's picture of rules.

Neil MacCormick's (1941–2009) work places greater emphasis on the state and the institutions within which legal rules function. As suggested above, Hart's concept of law concerns the behaviour and perceptions of those *within* legal institutions. MacCormick stresses the centrality of this context and this point of view. Without legal institutions providing and administering secondary rules, the union of primary and secondary rules makes little sense. Thus MacCormick's account maintains the importance of primary and secondary rules but, significantly, shifts focus away from rules to institutional *norms*:

> Normative systems are systems that guide the judgements and actions of rational agents. A rational agent concerned to observe the norms of a particular system needs to have means of discovering which norms belong within it at any given time, hence needs to know what purport to be its norms, and which of the purported norms are genuinely valid and have not (yet) been terminated. (1988: 342)

The crucial importance of this shift of vocabulary to the language of norms is the subject of Chapter 6.

As we might expect, Hart elicited response from those that might be broadly categorised as natural lawyers. Patrick Devlin (1905–92) made the argument that rules alone could not explain the particular *content* that we demand from law (see Dworkin (ed.), 1977). Engaging with Devlin on the specific issue of content, Hart, amplifying the aspects of his work that accord with the separation thesis, denies that there is a necessary relationship between the content of morality and the content of law. This does not deny that there may be a close relationship between law and morality. On the contrary, morality is always a critical perspective on legal rules, and Hart himself insists that law should have a 'minimum content of natural law', i.e. certain commitments, reflecting humans' interest in survival, that are among the most important primary rules: 'without such a content laws and morals could not forward the minimum purpose of survival which men have in associating with one another' (1994: 193). This 'minimum content' seems to concede considerable ground to the natural law position. But note that these are primary rules that we would *expect* to see in a sustainable legal system given the problems perennially generated by human coexistence and the (pragmatic not moral) requirement of a legal system to acknowledge them. However, if they were essential to the *concept of law* they would have to have the status of secondary rules, i.e. they would have to be among those rules necessary for primary to rules to be administered, adjudicated or recognised. They are not a moral gauge or threshold by which a legal system and its primary rules are judged. They are elements of any normally functioning legal system.

Finally, while Hart divides primary and secondary rules, his account seems reductive in portraying all aspects of legal *procedure* as rules. This reduction is attacked by critics of 'formalism' where rules are seen as complete and exhaustive answers to any legal question (see Chapter 6). More specifically, for Dworkin, hard cases, where rules cannot provide a simple answer to a legal question, are the key to understanding a legal system (1975; 1998). In hard cases, where a judge has to use a combination of rules, principles and policies, we see the full potential of legal *adjudication*; adjudication is not a mechanistic response to a problem, it is the point where law, politics and morality meet in a harmonious way. This is not to say that rules are not important or that law is not conceptually distinct from politics and morality, but the combination of primary and secondary rules is not a guarantee that an answer can be found to a legal problem. The range of tools available to judges are wider than rules, and particularly in hard cases – where what is owed to the parties is unclear, or where the interests of public policy are clearly at odds with the strict application of rules – *principles* can be deployed that do not formally or mechanistically determine an outcome but allow judges to integrate the wider, political, commitments of a society with its legal activities. In essence, Dworkin, and other critics of formalism, point to the fact that Hart's account appears to describe *any* well regulated system of rules. A club or organisation may well have primary and secondary rules. The decisive characteristic of a legal system is that it can, and must, generate *just* answers where rules are incomplete, inconsistent or unfair.

EXAMPLE

Shaw v *DPP*, House of Lords [1961] 2 W.L.R. 897

In an obscenity trial concerning the distribution of material with the capacity to 'deprave and corrupt', this Court found itself considering the moral welfare of the state as a whole. Clearly something more than primary rules is at work in such considerations. Issues of public policy are often mentioned which, while generalisation, are not obviously rules. Nonetheless, Hart was perfectly aware that law 'follows' public policy and 'public morals'; he simply denied that law was conceptually dependent upon them.

In the sphere of criminal law I entertain no doubt that there remains in the courts of law a residual power to enforce the supreme and fundamental purpose of the law, to conserve not only the safety and order but also the moral welfare of the State, and that it is their duty to guard it against attacks which may be the more insidious because they are novel and unprepared for. That is the broad head (call it public policy if you wish) within which the present indictment falls. It matters little what label is given to the offending act. To one of your Lordships it may appear an affront to public decency, to another considering that it may succeed in its obvious intention of provoking libidinous desires it will seem a corruption of public morals. Yet others may deem it aptly described as the creation of a public mischief or the undermining of moral conduct. The same act will not in all ages be regarded in the same way. The law must be related to the changing standards of life, not yielding to every shifting impulse of the popular will but having regard to fundamental assessments of human values and the purposes of society.

4 Wittgenstein

Introduction

Ludwig Wittgenstein's (1889–1951) work is given close attention as a powerful analysis of rules, and because his work had a great impact on both logical positivism and on Hart's work. While his significance for legal theory as a whole is contested, understanding his work sheds light on positivism and on the analysis of rules more specifically.

Wittgenstein's work on rules and rule-following clarifies what it is we understand by rules and what we should expect from rules. Put bluntly, we expect certitude and guidance from rules. However, for Wittgenstein, that guidance comes from the whole world of our experiences and our social practices not from *rules themselves*. If we want to know how to follow a rule, or whether we have followed a rule correctly, we have to look to the actions of those around us and their judgments about successful and unsuccessful rule following (Wittgenstein, 2001: 68–77). Following a rule is a social activity, not a mental activity.

The early Wittgenstein shared with other philosophers of the early twentieth century an interest in the use and foundations of logic. He sought to show that the entirety of our world – to the extent that it is intelligible – is reducible to simple facts which can be placed in logical relationship with one another. Whenever language is used to assert facts, or assert relations between facts, it is able to perfectly 'picture' the facts: 'A picture presents a situation in logical space, the existence and non-existence of states of affairs. / A picture is a model of reality' (1974: 9). Every fact can be described in a proposition (a complete idea or sentence) designated true or false; every combination of facts can also be pictured as true or false in this way. 'What any picture, of whatever form, must have in common with reality, in order to be able to depict it – correctly or incorrectly – in any way at all, is logical form, i.e. the form of reality' (1974: 11). Thus, with the aid of logic, our world in its entirety can be pictured through language. 'It is a beautiful idea that logic expresses the essential structure of fact – the logical structure of the world – that is, of everything that is the case' (Skorupski, 1993: 174). The negative consequence of this 'picture theory' of language is that where assertions *cannot* form a picture of the world (i.e. where our assertions attempt to say something 'metaphysical' about the structure of the universe or make judgments concerning the value of a state of affairs), then they are strictly meaningless. This does not mean that other experiences of the world should be ignored (like experiences associated with religion, art, morality). But these cannot be expressed in language – they do not admit or truth or falsity – and they cannot, therefore, make sense: 'they are indeed, things that cannot be put into words. They *make themselves manifest*. They are what is mystical.' (Wittgenstein, 1974: 89, emphasis in original.)

The merit of this picture view of language is that it explains how language, logic and the world are inter-related: a perfect correspondence, through adherence to logical structures, between the world and the picturing of the world by language. Furthermore, it sets the standard of meaning high (logical correspondence with reality and verifiability) in a way that is attractive to the scientifically or empirically minded. However, unravelling of this philosophical position came with consideration of the very first move: that *language* is able to perfectly reflect *logical* standards. This presumption – that the logic we aspire to in our arguments is able to give rise to perfect pictures of reality – is far from obviously true. Language is far more complicated, and less logical, than this. In successful communication we depend upon localised practices ('forms of life') which give rise to public, shared, language practices (Wittgenstein, 2001: 75). These 'language-games' – 'games' only in the sense that the word 'language', like the word 'game', denotes a set of localised practices without a single common denominator – are the main characteristic of language (2001: 4). This means, in sum, that 'logic' and 'facts' are secondary. Human activities, human practices and the human 'form of life' are primary.

While this rejection of his earlier view leads to sceptical conclusions about the role of logic and the limits of language, there is some continuity between the two positions, not least the idea that much of what we attempt to express about our judgments (including in ethics, law and art) are not matters of logic and fact, but attempts to *say* what ultimately has to be *shown*. After all, it is perhaps impossible to say to someone, to *persuade* them, they should see the world differently (perhaps to 'act in a more responsible manner') unless and until they themselves *see* the world differently. In a similar way, understanding language through use and practices shifts our attention away from conceptual analysis towards what people actually do with language: we have to *see* how language works before we can picture it in language. Nonetheless, crucial to the shift in Wittgenstein's position is the idea that rules, including the rules governing how we should act, are not straightforwardly logical *things* which our language can describe, but rather a set of social and behavioural practices that our language helps us to *perform*.

4a Rules and sense

The early Wittgenstein, then, is preoccupied with language and language's capacity to make sense or to be nonsense. This distinction is more important than it seems, because once the limits between these two capacities of language are drawn, there is nothing further that can be said about 'truth'. If language makes sense, it successfully says something logical or empirical about the world. If it fails to say something logical or empirical it is nonsense. This covers all and every possible relationship between language and reality and as such nothing more needs to be said about truth.

Our knowledge of the world remains, of course, important, but this can either be expressed with logical clarity or cannot be expressed at all. What we perceive about the world around us involves facts and logic and can therefore be expressed. Conversely, if our experiences are so unique, subjective, or so fundamental to our knowledge of the world that they cannot be expressed (as in certain moral or religious experiences) then we must 'pass over it in silence'. They simply cannot be expressed and we should not try. The irony at the heart of this view of language and logic is that the basic relationship between language and reality that Wittgenstein is trying to explain *cannot be expressed in language*. It does not picture the world: it is trying to discuss how we picture the world. It is neither fact nor logic. Therefore the theory is, strictly, nonsense.

Those things and experiences that we have to 'pass over in silence' (1974: 89) are important for understanding both Wittgenstein's relationship with rules and the relationship between his early and his later work. Wittgenstein is not saying that the whole of human experience is reducible to the logical or the empirical (as the logical positivist tried to argue). Rather he is delineating in what ways language can be used and be said to possess sense. This approach – delineating what language is *used for* – is pursued to its logical, and perhaps absurd, conclusions in Wittgenstein's later work where a 'use theory' of meaning is developed. Here the meaning of a proposition is not a relationship between language, reality and logic but whatever constitutes successful use of words in practice. 'The King of France' says nothing about reality or logic (there is presently no king of France and no necessary relationship between 'king' and 'France') but this phrase *makes sense* when it is *used* in some contexts (e.g. in history books, or as an example in a book).

The idea of rules is an important aspect of this later work and requires attention to both sense and to use. We could describe a rule (be it a law or the rule of game) and this would make sense as a description of something in the world, but to understand why someone should obey that rule, we are identifying a compulsion that is neither logical nor empirical. As such, the *force* of the rule is something that has to be shown and cannot be said. We can make a similar but slightly different point in the language of the later Wittgenstein. 'Rule' means many different things when used in different circumstances. Some uses may or may not be successful: if I instruct someone to obey the rules of chess during a Court case or golf tournament my use of 'rule' fails to convey any meaning in that context. The rules belong to different contexts but both are rules. Again, using French rules of evidence in an English Court means no longer playing that game: both are rules *but the context is crucial*. The question then becomes not whether some aspect of rules 'cannot be said but only shown', but rather 'what social conditions make rules meaningful?' The answer to this is not a matter of degrees: it constitutes the meaning of the word 'rule'. 'The word 'agreement' and the word 'rule' are *related* to one another, they are cousins. If I teach anyone the use of one word, he learns the use of the other with it' (Wittgenstein, 2001: 73).

EXAMPLE

R v Ann Harris (1836) 173 E.R. 198

In the 1830s, the rules concerning 'wounding' and 'assault' looked similar. But they can be separated out by looking at the intention of the statute that created the rules, as in the present case. Looking at the intention behind the rules is not always a simple task. It may concern other parts of the same legislation; it may demand consideration of the debates that took place prior to passing the legislation. These yield very different results. In either case, the additional job of 'gauging intention' makes the functioning of rules look a lot less automatic, and a lot more interpretative, than they often appear to be.

The prisoner was indicted under the statute [. . .], for wounding a female by biting off the end of her nose. Patteson, J., told the jury that in *Rex* v. *Stevens*, which had occurred a short time ago, the prisoner had been indicted under the same section of the same statute for biting off the joint of a policeman's finger, and the case having been reserved for the opinion of the fifteen judges, they had determined that the offence of biting off [. . .] the joint of a finger did not come within the words 'stabbing, cutting, or wounding'; and the decision proceeded on the ground that it was evidently the intention of the legislature, according to the words of the statute, that the wounding should be inflicted with some instrument, and not by the hands or teeth; and therefore, in the present case, they must acquit the prisoner, who, however, would not escape punishment if she was guilty, as she would be indicted for an aggravated assault. Verdict: Not guilty.

4b Rule scepticism

The significance of this radical contextualisation of meaning that we find in the later Wittgenstein can be understood as a form of scepticism. Meaning is not a stable relationship between language and reality but something wholly context-specific. This analysis includes rules. Rules only have meaning in the course of human lives. Were this the extent of Wittgenstein's analysis, it would be limited to making the simple but important point that what is meant by 'rule' depends on who is saying it and where they are saying it. What is important and challenging about Wittgenstein's position is that he wants to discourage us from asking further questions such as 'what mental processes are involved in following a rule?' and 'what is *meant* by a rule?' Wittgenstein's project is to free us not only from the assumption that every word must pick out a group of 'things' with a common denominator, but from the more general temptation to talk about rule-following as an 'event', a 'process' or any other way using categories from the empirical world. Rather, as Landers puts it, the questions that we should be asking are: '"What rule did I purport to be using?" and "What result does the use of that rule yield?"' (1990: 203). This has an impact on our understanding of rules because of the temptation to perceive rules as having a force or meaning that we see or follow or grasp 'in our minds'. For Wittgenstein, rules and rule-following are not 'internal events' and we should not picture them as things 'followed in our heads' and then 'followed, in fact, in the world'. There is no *sense* in talking about the 'internal' meaning or internal force of rules: following rules is something we do, not something we think.

This can be thought to lead to sceptical conclusions about rules and, in particular, to hit home at Hart's 'internal perspective' on rules. Social practices make rules, not something internal to rules, and those practices have nothing to do with things 'going on in people's heads', but everything to do with successfully doing things in the world. Hart's analysis of obligation is misleading if it means translating the force of rules into *interior assent or interior recognition*. Rather the force, form and function of rules are always *objective and public*. Whatever force or authority underlies rules, they are ultimately to be located in social practices that *show* us when a rule has been fulfilled. The explanation of someone following a rule might be that they feel obliged by it, but we cannot know of what that obligation consists until we join others in following that rule in practice.

Wittgenstein is seeking to demystify rules, and avoid appeal to 'forces' by showing that we see *rule-following behaviour,* rather than *'interiorise the force of rules'* . However, this does not invalidate Hart's analysis. Hart, like Wittgenstein, is not interested in the 'internal perspective' on rules because he is claiming access to our interior mental processes. Rather he is saying that there is a group of social practices that we, quite legitimately, call 'following a legal rule out of a sense of obligation'. This does not require him to give account of mental processes. It only asserts that we are drawing an important distinction when we say that '*x* is following a legal rule' rather than '*x* has been compelled to act in a certain way'. 'What is necessary is that there should be a critical reflective attitude to certain patterns of behaviour as a common standard [. . .]' (Hart, 1994: 57).

A sceptical conclusion might be suggested by one further aspect of Wittgenstein's analysis: if rules are public practices and public behaviour then you cannot follow a rule on your own. Because the gauge of following or observing a rule is social practice and not the conjunction of an interior 'mental event' and an action, without social practices demonstrating that you have followed the rule, you could never be certain that you had followed it:

> 'obeying' a rule is a practice. And to *think* one is obeying a rule is not to obey a rule. Hence it is not possible to obey a rule 'privately': otherwise thinking one was obeying a rule would be the same thing as obeying it. (2001: 69)

If we set ourselves a rule (or a law), and attempt to abide by it we have no-one with whom to agree on what counts as 'the rules' and 'successfully following the rules'. Were the rule a public one there would be parameters set by the practices of individuals; without such practices the 'rules' become strictly meaningless because there is no 'agreement in judgment' underlying the rule.

EXAMPLE

'Identifying photocopy machine poses problem for Cuyahoga County official' (*Cleveland Metro*, 2011)

The newspaper report provides 10 pages of a Court transcript. The Court case, concerning office expenses, stalled on the word 'photocopier'. The witness had only ever used the word 'Xerox' and his counsel demands clarity concerning Xerox machines and photocopiers. In part this illustrates the fact that meaning has to be connected to use. In part it represents the strategic use of rules that is sometimes a feature of Court cases.

> Marburger: During your tenure in the computer department at the Recorder's office, has the Recorder's office had photocopying machines? / Cavanagh: Objection. / Marburger: Any photocopying machine? / Patterson: When you say 'photocopying machine,' what do you mean? / Marburger: Let me be . . . let me make sure I understand your question. You don't have an understanding of what a photocopying machine is? / Patterson: No. I want to make sure that I answer your question correctly. / [. . .] Patterson: When you say 'photocopying machine,' what do you mean? / Marburger: Let me be clear. The term 'photocopying machine' is so ambiguous that you can't picture in your mind what a photocopying machine is in an office setting? / Patterson: I just want to make sure I answer your question correctly.

4c Anti-scepticism

If we are to understand how rules work we cannot appeal to a mysterious prescriptive force that takes hold of our thinking. We are describing successful or unsuccessful behaviour, success being a gauge or standard found in social practice not in the 'rules themselves'. The sceptical conclusion to be drawn from this is that rules do not seem to have the 'force' we assume they possess, because they do not entail special mental events called 'following a rule'.

We do not have to treat this conclusion as a sceptical one, however. We need to recall the view of truth, knowledge and language that Wittgenstein applies in his work. In the first instance, Wittgenstein is concerned with showing, rather than saying. Certain things do not belong to the realm of facts and logic, but they are no less significant for that. Rule-following could be included here: the relationship between a rule and an act is not a logical one, nor is it one concerning mental and real facts. It is an agreement *in judgment* between humans. Applying the rules of evidence in Court is meaningful; applying the rules of evidence in a party game is meaningless. Thus, while rules might well be tied to social behaviours and practices, they are also intimately related to what we understand by meaningful or meaningless. Wittgenstein insists that we should not strive for a more substantial link between language, truth and reality.

As we return to ideas and positions more directly concerned with legal rules, we can consider the potential significance of Wittgenstein's work for understanding law. One important thing to note about the *form* of rules is that, for Wittgenstein, rules appear in many different contexts and rules do not always have something in common with one another. Rather, they have 'family resemblances' – overlapping characteristics – with one another. Rules of games are not just rules by analogy with 'proper' rules: all sorts of rules can be considered rules. This means we should not look for a single form or function for legal rules. This can make sense of why in some contexts, particularly international law, we talk about both 'hard' and 'soft' rules, with the latter closer to guidance or recommendations, but *still in some respects rules* (see Twining, 2009). There is no reason to deny the latter the status of rules: the important thing is the practices that surround them. Moreover, there is nothing fundamentally incompatible with Wittgenstein's analysis and our intuitive understanding of rules. We generally consider that legal rules are binding both because of from whom they come (Courts or the sovereign) and because they are *socially* considered binding. Such conclusions are entirely compatible with the idea that rules are dependent on human action and at the same time lack a 'mental component'. We only face conceptual trouble if we see ourselves as following a legal rule by 'having it in our mind'. We are on far safer ground if we assume from the outset a close relationship between rules and social practices, behaviour and expectations.

EXAMPLE

Babbitt, Secretary of Interior et al. v *Sweet Home Chapter of Communities for Great Oregon* et al. 515 U.S. 687 (1995) United States Supreme Court

From the headnote of the case, this is an application of the noscitur a sociis *rule to clarify responsibilities with respect to endangered species. Discussing the word 'take', the Court narrows its meaning to active intervention with a protected species, not change to its environment. However, even this seems to stretch the ordinary (and legal) use of 'take' beyond its normal use. This is intelligible as the application of one rule (* noscitur a sociis*) but not another ('the provisions of statutes should be interpreted as literally as possible').*

As relevant here, the Endangered Species Act of 1973 (ESA or Act) makes it unlawful for any person to 'take' endangered or threatened species [. . .], and defines 'take' to mean to 'harass, harm, pursue,' 'wound,' or 'kill,' [. . .]. [The] Secretary of the Interior further defines 'harm' to include 'significant habitat modification or degradation where it actually kills or injures wildlife.' Respondents, persons and entities dependent on the forest products industries and others, challenged this regulation on its face, claiming that Congress did not intend the word 'take' to include habitat modification. The District Court granted petitioners summary judgment, but the Court of Appeals ultimately reversed. Invoking the *noscitur a sociis* canon of statutory construction, which holds that a word is known by the company it keeps, the court concluded that 'harm,' like the other words in the definition of 'take,' should be read as applying only to the perpetrator's direct application of force against the animal taken.

5 Disobedience

Introduction

Positivism is a powerful means of isolating law from other kinds of obligations and other social institutions. It is, however, more difficult to use positivism to analyse the justification or authority of law. While positivism isolates, by virtue of its source, what can be correctly identified as law, positivism distinguishes this from the question of whether particular laws are justified. Justification, as Austin would have argued, is the province of morality not jurisprudence (Austin, 1995).

Nonetheless, even without external justification – i.e. moral validation – legal rules, and legal systems, can be said to have authority. This is highlighted in the disagreements between 'exclusive' and 'inclusive' legal positivists (see Bix, 2004: 123–4). Exclusive positivists adopt a strong version of the separation thesis, insisting that the authority of a legal rule can never depend upon morality. Law's origin and authority always flows, exclusively, from its social sources (see Chapter 7). Inclusive legal positivists concede that while there is no necessary relationship between law and morality, a legal system *may accept or encompass* moral criteria within its positive law. Such criteria are criteria for judgment authorised by a legal system.

Civil disobedience is a challenge to both. Acts of civil disobedience express the belief that something wholly external to law can negate the authority of a law (in opposition to exclusive positivism), or that law's own inner, moral, resources justify the rejection of some laws (pushing inclusive positivism to the point of absurdity). Our present concern, then, is the extent to which analysis of the *content*, but also the *sources*, of law can make sense of 'a right to disobey the law'.

'Civil disobedience' – breaking the law as a deliberate gesture of defiance – is an expressive act of protest. Civil disobedience involves refusal to obey a rule, or disruption of society, in order to communicate a principled point of view. It may or may not involve violence, and it may or may not involve a protester freely submitting to punishment, accepting that this is a necessary consequence of their actions. Whatever form it takes, and whatever consequences are expected to flow from it, civil disobedience expresses a belief that, while laws in general have authority, a particular rule or rules should be changed.

> Civil disobedience is not a matter of challenging the legality of a law or of ascertaining the meaning of a law. It is a matter of a man rejecting a moral demand of his society at the same time that he admits the legal right of his society over him. Men do require society, and society requires government. Government requires an ultimate sovereign power, a final legal authority such that once it has spoken there is no appeal beyond it except to heaven. (Rucker, 1966: 143)

This should be distinguished from a number of other positions.

First, civil disobedience should be distinguished from *lawful* protest; a lawful protest is a democratic right justified by legal rules. Civil disobedience involves deliberately illegal acts from the outset. Second, civil disobedience does not entail seeing all laws illegitimate as might, for example, criminals or anarchists. A criminal may treat all legal rules as hypothetical imperatives concerning the likelihood of being punished (legal rules present risks but not obligations). Some anarchists consider all legal rules to be illegitimate because they originate in the state, and the state has no moral authority, only *de facto* force at its disposal (Gerry, 2011). This is closer to civil disobedience – it claims a moral justification – but denies that any legal rules can possess moral authority because of their relationship with the state.

Distinct from lawful protesters, anarchists and criminals, there have always been individuals who feel compelled to break the law on grounds of principle but who otherwise accept the binding force of law. Principled disobedience or civil disobedience involves expressing opposition to rules through breaking rules – the specific rule being challenged – on one or many occasions. That is, directly violating a law that is disagreed with, for example refusing to pay a tax held to be unfair. This breaking of specific rules reflects commitment to certain over-riding duties, i.e. moral duties that are thought to supersede the obligation to follow a specific legal rule. Such positions compel us to look more closely at law's sources as validating or justifying a legal system, and at the possible ways of understanding law's own claim to *authority*.

5a The Socratic paradox

The most important philosophical engagement with disobedience is to be found in Plato's accounts of Socrates' trial and execution in the *Crito* and the *Apology*. Socrates argued – and died defending the idea – that we should respect the rules of the state, even unjust rules. This is paradoxical on a number of levels, not least because the most forceful expression of this position in the *Crito* seems at odds with his criticism of Athens and its laws in the *Apology*. First, in the *Apology*, Socrates places the authority of reason and conscience above the authority of the state: he refused to accept any law preventing him from engaging in philosophy (Plato, 1997: 27). Second, to argue, as he did in the *Crito*, that even unjust rules require obedience appears to put greater value on rules than on justice. On these assumptions, tyrants deserve obedience and their rules are held to supersede justice (Plato, 1997: 46). The fact that Socrates decried rule by tyrants, and identified justice as the primary virtue, gives rise then to one of Socrates' famous paradoxes. Such paradoxes are not just contradictions: they are challenges to the intelligibility of ideas such as rule, justice and obligation.

> Socrates did not consider himself as a destroyer of the laws when he said that he would not obey any order to desist from his philosophic activities. He openly stated that there were certain things that, as a man, he would not do; yet, as a citizen, he stood prepared to undergo execution if so ordered. Had he tried to evade his punishment once he was sentenced, he would have been a destroyer of the laws. (Rucker, 1966: 142)

Socrates' explanation of this paradox (or Plato's answer on behalf of Socrates) is complicated. Socrates felt that the Gods had ordained his death and that it would be impiety to disobey the Gods. Flowing from Plato's argument concerning equilibrium within the soul, Socrates is said to be demonstrating that action in accordance with law is analogous to justice ruling our souls; without justice in ascendency (and analogously, good order in the state) we can be neither good nor happy (1997: 1075). Socrates also defends a form of social contract argument. Legal rules secure collective goods and avoid the trauma of civil war. Moreover, on recognisably natural law grounds, Socrates intimates that there is something binding about law – its contribution to the common good – even if the governing regime is morally objectionable (1997: 28).

The most consistent, but nonetheless paradoxical, way to interpret Socrates' actions is that, in allowing himself to be executed, he demonstrates *both* that we cannot pick and choose which laws to obey *and* that we should follow our conscience. Obedience to the law is a good, both collectively and individually. At the same time we should not have to live in a way contrary to our conscience. It was Socrates' 'luck' that obedience and conscience coincided: he obeyed the law and believed in the fundamental value of lawfulness.

While this offers some grounds for dissolving the paradox – we have a general commitment to law but may wish to reject individual laws on moral grounds – Socrates' identification of 'law-abiding action' and 'moral action' leaves him in a paradoxical position. Without such a contentious commitment (and positivism is surely correct in seeking *some* division between law and morality) we can ask two further questions. If it is not purely moral authority, what, if any, *legitimate* authority does a legal system as a whole possess? And what legitimate authority do *individual laws* within a system possess and on what grounds can such authority be questioned?

EXAMPLE

Martin Luther King Jr, 'Letter from a Birmingham Jail' 16 April 1963

Not strictly a legal text but one that contributed to upheavals in the law. Martin Luther King's philosophy is a Christian one, but his message resonates throughout our culture.

There comes a time when the cup of endurance runs over, and men are no longer willing to be plunged into the abyss of despair. I hope, sirs, you can understand our legitimate and unavoidable impatience. You express a great deal of anxiety over our willingness to break laws. This is certainly a legitimate concern. Since we so diligently urge people to obey the Supreme Court's decision of 1954 outlawing segregation in the public schools, at first glance it may seem rather paradoxical for us consciously to break laws. One may well ask: 'How can you advocate breaking some laws and obeying others?' The answer lies in the fact that there are two types of laws: just and unjust. I would be the first to advocate obeying just laws. One has not only a legal but a moral responsibility to obey just laws. Conversely, one has a moral responsibility to disobey unjust laws. I would agree with St. Augustine that 'an unjust law is no law at all.' [. . .] Now, what is the difference between the two? How does one determine whether a law is just or unjust? A just law is a man made code that squares with the moral law or the law of God. An unjust law is a code that is out of harmony with the moral law. To put it in the terms of St. Thomas Aquinas: an unjust law is a human law that is not rooted in eternal law and natural law. Any law that uplifts human personality is just. Any law that degrades human personality is unjust.

5b The authority of legal systems

The idea of 'authority' will be distinguished below from other ideas (like validity and efficacy) with which it is easily conflated. For present purposes two approaches, associated with the main schools of jurisprudence, can be used to explain the relevance of authority to disobedience. The first will be a *moral* idea of authority, discussed in relation to Fuller's natural law theory. The second will be a *rational or reason-giving* idea of authority associated with positivism.

Natural law theorists are concerned with both the moral content of law and the overall authority of a legal system, but this need not mean that morality is something wholly external to law. Lon Fuller (1902–78) sees certain structures of law-making, and characteristics of legality, as necessary for law to be truly considered law. He identifies eight characteristics or 'desiderata' of law which, together, are the minimum characteristics necessary for law to be rational, fair, and a contribution to good human governance. He demands that laws be publicised, non-retroactive, stable, capable of being fulfilled, general, clear, compatible with one another and congruent between the letter of the law and its realisation in practice. These characteristics are what any legal system should aspire to (even if few or no systems perfectly fulfil them all) and are needed if law is to fulfil its purpose:

> The demands of the inner morality of the law [. . .] demand more than forbearances; they are, as we loosely say, affirmative in nature: make the law known, make it coherent and clear, see that your decisions as an official are guided by it, etc. (1969: 42)

This 'inner morality of the law' makes basic demands on law-makers: to make law using rules that are reasonable and capable of being followed. This is distinguished from a 'morality of aspiration' (our own individual pursuit of the good), and the 'external morality of law' (principles such as equality or justice which are used to evaluate law but are not *part* of law). As such, Fuller's position can be characterised as a form of 'procedural naturalism'. While law has its own morality concerning reasonableness in the use of rules, there is no relationship with the *good* such that we find in canonical natural law theories. It is procedural because law's status as a morally justified social practice is dependent upon the form in which law is created and which it takes, rather than particular substantive content.

To embark on the enterprise of subjecting human conduct to the governance of rules in- volves of necessity a commitment to the view that man is, or can become, a responsible agent, capable of understanding, following rules and answerable for his defaults. [. . .] Every departure from the law's inner morality is an affront to man's dignity as a responsible agent. To judge his actions by unpublished and retrospective laws, or to order him to do the impos- sible is to convey to him your indifference to his powers of self-determination. (1969: 162)

For Fuller, a legal system with moral authority observes certain *formal* require- ments in its law-making, and where there is a multiple or repeated violation of these formal requirements then our own 'morality of aspiration' would trump or super- sede the legal system's claim to authority (1969: 41). However, the idea of 'authority' can be further disassociated from what Fuller would recognise as 'morality'. Claims about the rationality of law (reaching their peak in Hegel's system) also point to another idea of authority: that law is, or should be, rational. In some ways this is making a similar point to that of Fuller – irrational laws are law's own form of im- morality – but it can also be a much wider idea that law provides a certain kind of rational authority, that it can give rational reasons for action that are different from the reasons that *individuals alone* have to act.

For the same reason Joseph Raz (b. 1939), a positivist, grants law an authority – authority to give *reasons* and to *justify* action – that morality does not have. A legal sys- tem observing liberal principles deserves obedience because of the freedoms it affords us (Raz, 2009). (As considered below, this still provides some grounds for opposing individual laws on the assumption that not all states provide equally compelling rea- sons for action given their constitutions and constitutive rules.) Raz warns us against the apparent 'paradoxes of authority' (2009: 3f). Such apparent paradoxes arise from the fact that law is treated as *externally* validated by its contribution to maintaining freedom. Ostensibly, freedom (in the Kantian sense of making our own, autonomous, decisions) is in tension with the authority (in the sense of anything, external to us, that has power over us). However, for Raz, law *is* authority, *social* authority. Asking whether it is an 'authorised authority' only makes sense if we are committed to the view that law is validated by something outside itself, an assumption that Raz rejects.

EXAMPLE

Director of Public Prosecutions Respondent v Jones (Margaret) and Another Appellants, House of Lords, 4 March 1999, [1999] 2 W.L.R. 625

Is there a right to protest? This is a paradoxical question if it is understood as asking whether there is a right to break the law: there could be no law justifying violation of law. Conversely, law-makers and Courts (as here) seek to legitimise peaceful protest within reasonable boundaries. Such legitimation is reasonable on the basis that the state must constrain itself from trying to prevent and police all and every instance of disorder.

I am of opinion that the holding of a public assembly on a highway can constitute a reasonable use of the highway and accordingly will not constitute a trespass and I would allow the appeal. But I desire to emphasise that my opinion that this appeal should be allowed is based on the finding of the Crown Court that the assembly in which the defendants took part on this particular highway, the A344, at this particular time, constituted a reasonable use of the highway. I would not hold that a peaceful and non-obstructive public assembly on a highway is always a reasonable use and is therefore not a trespass.

5c The authority of individual laws

In the main, we cannot pick and choose which laws to obey. Law's contribution to the common good lies in the generality (and therefore impartiality) that flows from governance by rules. This argument, on the face of it, denies any possibility that any particular law can be rejected for moral or principled reasons. The interests of individual and collective have already been reconciled by the use and maintenance of law, albeit not necessarily to everyone's satisfaction. Can any clear point be identified when individuals and groups are so disadvantaged by laws that breaking them becomes legitimate *despite* this overarching defence of the value of law?

Natural law provides a quick, albeit opaque, response to the legitimacy of individual laws: an unjust law is not a law. This can be derived easily from Sophist and Stoic currents in Ancient natural law. Law exists beyond human conventions, and some human conventions can or should be rejected. Aquinas' position provided some justification for resistance to tyrannical laws and wrongly constituted authorities (2002: 65, 101). In Finnis' modern natural law, pursuit of the common good provides law (as a whole) with an external justification while allowing that obedience to law should not be treated as an absolute duty: 'rulers have, very strictly speaking, no right to be obeyed [. . .]; but they have the authority to give directions and make laws that are morally obligatory and that they have the responsibility of enforcing' (2011: 359).

In the context of positivism, analysis of disobedience requires disentangling three, easily conflated, ideas. The first is a law's efficacy, the second is a law's validity and the third is a law's authority. These can become blurred because all three point to ideas of *justification* of a particular law. The command theory does not give easy grounds to assess the justification of laws: the efficacy or effectiveness of a law, associated with a sanction, is enough for it to be classified as law proper. Hart's positivism (along with Kelsen's positivism, see Chapter 6) are able to distinguish those rules that have *validity* from those rules that do not (they are recognised as valid legal rules). Again, however, this identifies what is truly or properly a legal rule – it is accepted as obligatory – but does not provide any additional criteria for deciding where a valid rule can lose validity on the basis of moral repugnancy.

Positivism, to the extent that it provides the means of justifying disobedience, points towards the importance of constitutive rules: rules that fail to govern the state and its legal system in a defensible way can have their authority called into question. An argument to this effect can be found in Raz's work (2009: 272f). Raz distinguishes states constituted on liberal principles which have the authority to limit our freedoms because of other, wider, constitutional commitments to freedom; illiberal states lack the constitutive rules necessary to make certain of their regulative rules on protest, expression and other obligations binding.

The events of the twentieth century, in Fascist Europe in particular, sharpened positivists' concern with disobedience and the authority of law. Gustav Radbruch (1878–1949) who, before the war, could be described as an orthodox positivist (and with this asserted the unequivocal duty to obey the law) came to the conclusion that individuals have the right to reject laws if they are contrary to conscience. For Radbruch a law may well be perfectly legitimate in its origin and characteristics as law (i.e. fulfilling all of Fuller's desiderata) and yet still be such that reasonable people simply cannot abide by it. Under such circumstances we must concede that the law loses its status as law:

> One thing [. . .] must be indelibly impressed on the consciousness of the people as well as of jurists: There can be laws that are so unjust and so socially harmful that validity, indeed legal character itself, must be denied them. (Radbruch, 2006: 14)

EXAMPLE

'Resolution of the Council of the International Bar Association of October 8, 2009, on the Commentary on Rule of Law Resolution' (2005)

The International Bar Association (IBA) represents lawyers across the international community. Because the first decade of the twenty-first century seemed to involve a great deal of compromise of the rule of law, the IBA both issued a resolution of the rule of law and reiterated in 2009. Particular attention is paid to the significance of states of emergency where rules are often suspended and where it is more likely that legally and morally objectionable rules might flow from a limitless sovereign power.

States of Emergency: The Rule of Law is most likely to come under threat, even in countries which claim to abide by it, in times of war or other emergency, when the Executive is most likely to seek and the people most likely to be willing to grant it exceptional powers. This is a time when the utmost care and calm, rational consideration is required and when it is least likely to be provided. In such cases, the absolute necessity for a rigorous separation of powers becomes all the more important, because it will be the Executive which calls for the exceptions and it will be for the Legislature to create and for the Judiciary to interpret and oversee them. A proper balance must be struck. Even in such cases, exceptions to the fundamental requirements of the Rule of Law should not be admitted, otherwise the society in question will risk self-destruction. In many countries, the threat of war, counterrevolution or other emergency is frequently used as an excuse for not introducing the Rule of Law in the first place.

Questions

Section 1

- What is it about rules that makes them relevant to *legality*? Could there be a system of public rules that were not a legal system? Could there be a legal system that did not use rules widely?

- Is there any foolproof way of distinguishing the rules of law from the rules of a game? Is the difference in their outcome or their form?

- Are some legal rules less binding than others? Compare criminal laws and civil procedure rules.

Section 2

- Does science provide a good model for understanding law? What, if anything, would be lost if we could only describe law using factual claims, not value claims?

- Is moral language best explained by emotivism (that all moral claims are an attempt to persuade)? Could emotivism be used to explain the role of morality in legal decision-making?

- Is the 'sources thesis' an improvement on Austin's 'command theory'? Could (social or political) coercion explain the reason why the social sources of law are important?

Section 3

- How do we recognise a rule as a legal rule? Is a legal rule 'legal' because of its pedigree or its context?

- Why is the *concept* of law different from the *history* of law? Does Hart's account of the *concept* of law mean that only legal systems with developed secondary rules are legal systems?

- Give examples of secondary rules. Are these easy to distinguish from primary rules? Are secondary rules closer to *procedural practices* than rules?

Section 4

- How do you know whether you have followed a signpost correctly? How could you be sure that you had not misread it but found your destination by accident?

- How do we know that a judge has followed the rules? For example, is there any necessary relationship between a prison sentence delivered in a *decision* and the *rules* of sentencing? Is this to be decided on a logical relationship between argument and conclusion, or by whether other judges would agree with the decision?

- Do lawyers follow rules, or follow practices established by rules?

Section 5

- Does 'the rule of law' have any moral significance? Is it good (justified by its outcomes) or right (justified by its coherence with, or correspondence to, our other commitments)?

- If law justifies the use of violence by the state, does this negate any moral obligation to obey the law?
- Is there a moral duty to disobey the law when it is morally wrong, dangerous or contradictory? Are there any other circumstances in which there is a moral duty to disobey the law?

Concepts and methods: Rules and exceptions

Finding and following legal rules

There is a tension between the idea of legal rules as commands (emphatic injunctions to do, or not do something) and the fact that legal rules frequently generate the question 'is this rule applicable?' We can find any number of contemporary and historical legal rules, but we are only required to follow those rules that are (amongst other things): the rules of our jurisdiction, in force, applicable to us as individuals with particular characteristics, applicable to us as individuals with particular roles and applicable provided that other rules do not have a greater claim to authority. Finding legal rules is one thing, deciding which to follow is another.

We cannot follow two contradictory rules, but developed legal systems frequently make demands on us that appear contradictory. Surgeons are obliged to do things to people that, in other circumstances, constitute criminal harm. Public bodies are required to protect personal data *and* release personal data if it is in the public interest. We can draw two conclusions from this. Either, there are never real contradictions in law (one rule will always supersede another, and what looks like a contradiction is merely an exception). Or, that law creates real contradictions that it is the responsibility of Courts to mediate or overcome. Which of these solutions we choose depends very much on whether we see rules as a 'seamless web' of self-governing, harmonious, rules (the formalist approach), a mass of commands which judges have to reconcile on the basis of principles found outside legal rules (the realist approach) or a combination of the two (Dworkin's interpretive approach, see Chapter 7).

Finding and using legal rules is a skill, one requiring training and patience. It requires training because legal materials (both legislation and case law) contain much that is very general and also much that is very specific. It requires patience because of the quantity of potentially relevant legal rules in any given circumstance. At the same time, the principle that 'ignorance of the law is no defence' *either* suggests that legal systems do not care about the complexity of finding legal rules or, more defensibly, that for the most part 'law-abiding' behaviour is behaviour that is unexceptional, common, intuitive or normal. The idea that our 'normal' behaviour maps onto legal rules (and *vice versa*) is considered in Chapter 6. At present we can conclude that law assumes that its rules are largely harmonious with our intuitive or common sense assumptions *except* where we have assumed special responsibilities (duties of care or explicit contractual relationships). In these instances there is a greater requirement for the public, and lawyers, to find out their specific legal responsibilities.

▌ Exceptions

Legal rules are always accompanied by exceptions. Here are three examples. General rules are always *supplemented* by more specific (but nonetheless also general) rules about when the main rule is not to be applied. Second, general rules of law always implicitly *exclude* a great number of things (e.g. the rules of this offence do not apply to other offences, or that the rules of this country do not apply in another). Third, the implementation or enforcement of rules in legal institutions includes *discretion* by which some rules can be set aside in favour of a decision about the most just remedy (e.g. 'equitable remedies').

There is a saying that 'there is an exception to every rule'. Putting to one side the problem of that saying *itself* taking the form of a rule and therefore requiring its own exception, it is the case that every legal rule could have some exception either to its applicability ('this rule does not apply, another rule applies') or to its scope ('this rule does not apply *here* or to *these* parties'). In the latter sense, exceptions help to *define a rule*, clarifying where it does and does not apply; exceptions form *part* of rules, the negative part identifying where they are to be disapplied. We also say that exceptions 'prove' a rule – which makes no sense in the normal sense of 'prove', i.e. 'demonstrate the truth of' – but indicates that exceptions *refine* a rule. An exception refines a rule by narrowing it down and limiting its application. These maxims point to two distinct ways of approaching legal rules. Exceptions *refining* legal rules, but also every legal rule being accompanied by an exception to its applicability or scope.

A legal rule that had no exception would be too general to be just. It would be over- or under-inclusive: regulating the behaviour of too many, or too few, people; it would justify too little, or too much. Of course, all legal rules could be thought to have implicit caveats attached to them insisting that 'the present rule holds good unless it is changed or suspended in accordance with the law' and that 'this rule holds good only within the jurisdiction within which it is promulgated'. Thus there are always exceptions to a rule's *applicability*, but there are also always exceptions to its *scope*. No legal rule is so fundamental that it does not have exceptions or qualifications. For example, the 'right to life' is qualified by only applying to the actions of states; it also admits of exception in times of war, or where resources are rationed. It is this close association between rules and their exceptions that is captured in the idea of defeasibility: we always expect, and find, exceptions that 'defeat' the rule.

213

Rules and ruling

To rule is to be in command of a given territory. There are *de facto* and *de jure* elements to this. To rule is, *de facto*, to have 'effective control' over a territory: to be able to command and have one's commands generally followed. To rule is, *de jure*, to have some legal claim to exercise that effective control. It certainly falls within the scope of legal philosophy to explain the meaning of *de jure* ruling: what is it to have a legal claim to exercise power (see Marmor, 2004; Kelsen, 2006). This can be answered, partly, by identifying the constitutional rules governing assumption of power (especially, but not exclusively, democratic procedures). However, it is also a question of in what ways *de facto* ruling can *become de jure* ruling. Fuller's work (1969) is a good example of this. It does not matter how a sovereign gained their capacity to rule; for their rules to be *de jure* they have to conform to the inner morality of law, the shape that any law worthy of the name must take.

Accordingly, the idea of ruling can be analysed through attention to those constitutional rules that grant the power to make law. But the direction of enquiry can also be reversed such that promulgated rules become the gauge by which their origin is judged (Fuller, 1969). Rules are not solely the by-product of power: they are the principal means by which we gauge the legitimacy of power. Legitimate rulers not only command but command consistently. They avoid uncertainty and confusion concerning how our actions are to be judged. They should certainly avoid promulgating laws that are either impossible to adhere to or are morally repugnant to the majority of people to whom they apply. This is partially, though not always clearly, captured in the language of the rule of law. The rule of law indicates that all are bound equally by the public rules of the state; it means that social disputes will be settled by general rules, not the will of the powerful. In these terms, a defensible state is one governed by a system of public rules without unjustified exceptions.

Nonetheless, a rule of law will contain exceptions. The language of the rule of law can obscure the fact that laws always involve exceptions; the *rules of law* are not categorical imperatives but systems of generalisation, inclusion and exclusion. Note also that sovereigns will often make themselves, through law, an exception to the rules. In the United Kingdom, freedom of information rules apply to public bodies, but not Parliament; defamation rules apply to all speakers, except those within Parliament. We have to approach the idea of the rule of law as a broad commitment to rules and to equality, but we should not see it as denoting the social and political dominance of categorical rules.

Liberalism and utilitarianism

The political commitments of a state can inform how rules are used and evaluated. In those authoritarian political systems where order is given priority over freedom, rules will certainly be used, but they will be considered less important than the capacity of the state to control the actions of its citizens, with or without rules. In liberal states, rules are used to ensure equality and maximise liberty. Rules will not be seen in instrumental terms (their contribution to good order) but as having intrinsic value: they provide a coherent system of expectations and justifications that have a rational foundation, or they, through their generality and impartiality, correspond with the underlying value of liberty.

Utilitarianism has a more ambiguous relationship with rules. Like liberal positions, utilitarianism is concerned with equality. Each person is given equal weight in utilitarian calculations, and this is realised in part through the generalisations that we find in laws. However, like more authoritarian political positions, it evaluates rules by their contribution to utility: a rule should provide the greatest happiness for the greatest number. This could be seen as an asset of utilitarianism; it provides a principle of equality for adjudication, and an idea of goodness to determine legislation. Thus it could also be seen as a weakness. Only rule utilitarianism gives sufficient weight to the fact that we have to make generalisations about what is needed and what is owed to people, and even this would appear to allow the sacrifice of minorities and their interests to the pursuit of the collective benefit.

Further reading

Twining and Miers' 'primer' *How to do Things with Rules* (2010) is a classic introduction to the nature of rules and the use of rules in legal contexts; Schauer's work (1991) is of a more technical nature but covers similar ground. Teichmann's 'Explaining the Rules' (2002) is an analysis of rules as 'reason-giving' with a Wittgensteinean slant. The origins and scope of positivism, along with analysis of different aspects of legal positivism, can be found in the *Stanford Encyclopedia of Philosophy* http://plato.stanford.edu/. For a better sense of the functions of legal positivism and the heated debate it can generate, compare Kramer (1999) with Simmonds (2008). Hart's *The Concept of Law* (1994) is both indispensable and accessible reading. Raz (1994) offers a refinement (or alternative) to Hart's position, as does MacCormick (2007). Hacker (1997) provides a short, clear introduction to Wittgenstein.

Visit **www.mylawchamber.co.uk/riley** to access tools to help you develop and test your knowledge of legal philosophy including Podcasts on leading thinkers and theories, discussion questions, diagrams showing interrelations between concepts, and weblinks

 mylawchamber

6 Norm

It is common to those inside and outside legal institutions to picture law as a collection of rules. This picture is both familiar and accurate, but a view of legal rules as sovereign commands is inadequate. Something else is needed, something both subjective (our assent to rules) and objective (the practices associated with legal rules).

The language of norms and normativity is rather more specialised than that of rules, but it enables us to isolate precisely that component of legal rules which is associated with both practices and assent. Normativity enables us to understand why law is more than a set of commands, and it enables us to understand the relationship between social expectations and legal rules.

'Norm' echoes the word 'normal'. The *normal* expectations found in society have a relationship with the obligations that are enforced by law; the fact that 'ignorance of the law is no defence' relies on that fact that in many instances law reflects what is considered to be normal in a society. Thus 'norms' are expectations or regularities in behaviour, and 'normative' is the quality of being, or creating, an expectation. 'Legal norms' and 'legal rules' are occasionally treated as synonymous but, more accurately, calling attention to a rule's normativity picks out the obligatory element of the rule. Legal rules are binding, not as coercive threats, but as expectations of behaviour, expectations that are perceived to be, or are accepted as having, a binding 'normative force'. Nonetheless, the precise relationship between rules, norms and law is not easy to identify:

> Unsurprisingly, no agreement exists about what the normativity of law comes to, let alone about what 'normativity' is. We can point to certain phenomena that law regulates; that legal claims, as H.L.A. Hart famously observed, standardly incorporate normative language, the language of rights, duties, obligations, and powers; that law is viewed, at least by those who accept the system, as providing a standard of criticism and reasons for action; that law claims authority and purports to give us obligations and reasons for action that we might not otherwise have. (Rosati, 2004: 297, footnotes removed)

We can say that for something to be normal it is generalisable: 'in normal situations a person is *likely* to do this' or 'it is normal here to do x, so *you should* do x'. Because of their relationship with normal expectations, rules and norms share the characteristic of being generalisations; generalisations about what is likely to happen (hypothetically) or what should happen (categorically). However, the generalisations found in legal rules are qualified: they include and exclude, and they are defeasible generalisations which hold good until another rule defeats them. We can understand norms without necessarily having to consider those formal characteristics associated with rules. 'Norms' – in the widest sense of both social and legal expectations – entail no such careful qualification. They are generalisations about what is likely to happen within social and legal practices and the obligations that these practices give rise to.

The fact that we can talk about what is 'normal' in terms of what is likely to happen *and* what should happen indicates that the language of norms and normativity can be both descriptive and prescriptive. Social and legal norms can take both forms. For instance, they can take the form 'in this culture you greet a person in this way' thereby describing what is normal – what behaviour is regularly found – in that culture. That norm can also be expressed in prescriptive terms: 'you should greet a person in this way – this is an obligation – and you will cause offence if you fail to observe this norm'. Similarly, a legal rule can be expressed as a descriptive norm: what we would expect a judge or lawyer to do under these circumstances. We could also express it in terms of a prescription: a legal rule provides us with the standard by which actions, including judicial decisions, can be judged right or wrong.

So, on the one hand, the language of normativity contains an ambiguity: it encompasses describing and prescribing, risking a blurring of the fact/value divide. Legal rules clearly prescribe, and we could argue, therefore, that analysis of rules is more important for understanding *law* than using the problematic language of norms. On the other hand, as Hart shows, the important element of legal rules is not their being pure prescriptions or commands, it is that they are rules which we have accepted as obligations and through which our own, and others', actions can be judged. This exhibits the same combination of elements we find in norms. In other words, Hart's 'internal point of view' centres on the normative aspect of rules, both in their capacity to say what is expected (legal rules involve insisting on a course of action and criticising deviation from it), and their internal, mental, aspect (we understand a course of action *as the norm*). The language of norms picks out precisely what is important and distinctive in Hart's account of legal rules: to will that something should happen (prescribe it) and to know that a rule (an observable, general, practice that can be described) is being followed.

The bivalence (the double meaning) of 'norm' as descriptive and prescriptive means that this is a useful, if broad, way of isolating generalities in behaviour and generalities in obligation. When we consider *social* norms we are largely concerned with norms in the descriptive sense, what regularities there are in society concerning expectations and obligations. *Moral* norms are prescriptive generalisations: what should happen in all or most instances. *Legal* norms can, importantly, be both. We have seen that normativity – as a prescriptive or obligatory power – is one of the most important dimension of legal rules, but it is also the case that we can describe a legal system in terms of what we would expect its officials to do. For instance, one way to describe the work of a lawyer is to say that they are skilled in anticipating what a judge is likely to say and on this basis either prepare a case or do their best to avoid a problem being taken to the Courts. Judges themselves will make decisions on the basis of what a higher Court would or might be expected to decide given the present case. Thus, even within a legal system, there is an important role played by descriptive norms: what behaviour we would expect from the judiciary.

Is there any distinction between the normativity of legal and moral prescriptions? Because of their shared normative language – the imperatives 'should', 'ought' and 'must' – it is not obvious that there is a clear dividing line. We can distinguish legal obligations from categorical imperatives on the basis that legal rules are far more specific as to whom they apply; they often involve the prior assumption of legal relationships and responsibilities; and legal obligations are defeasible involving exceptions and over-ruling. However, to the extent that they are both, nonetheless, obligatory means that they share the same 'normative force'. That force, that binding or obligatory quality, is presumably the same whether the rules are moral or legal: an obligation is an obligation.

However, the breadth and variety of norms allows us to make a more careful analysis at this point. Legal rules justify action. Social norms also justify actions, but in a different way: the fact that everyone does something does not mean that we automatically have an obligation to do it. This difference becomes sharper if we look closely at the point where descriptive social norms (for example, the fact that people often give up a seat on the bus to someone who is infirm) become prescriptive norms (there is a social obligation to give up a set on the bus to someone infirm). The point at which the regularity becomes an obligation on society at large is unclear, but it is certainly related to generality in practice (most people do this) and censure or social disapproval for not doing the act (most people disapprove of not doing this).

Under these circumstances a norm has emerged, but legal norms do not always have such a gestation period. They can be 'created out of nothing', and they bind and justify regardless of widespread social practice. Moreover, the morally prescriptive (everyone has an obligation to do this) can, but does not necessarily, become legally prescriptive (giving up one's seat could, theoretically, become a law). The fact that not all social norms do become legal norms could be for any number of reasons: a state's general political commitments, or the cost of enforcing the rule. Nonetheless, the existence of a social norm can give rise to the idea that it is a moral (prescriptive) norm and thereafter, potentially a legal norm. This process is discussed below with reference to social norms and realism. We have not shown that there are 'degrees' of obligation or 'binding force', but we have seen ways in which various prescriptive and descriptive norms can be mutually supportive and give rise to the *likelihood* of something becoming a legal obligation.

In essence, norms have the capacity to be both behavioural regularities and prescriptive rules because they are both *real* and *ideal*. That is to say, norms are real, observable practices among people, and they are also ideas, perceptions or intuitions in our mental realm. Either of these points of view yields interesting perspectives on law. Real, concrete, patterns of human behaviour have varied over time, and have, in turn given rise to different views of morality and legality. Posner defines social norms as:

> mere behavioural regularities with little independent explanatory power and exogenous [external and compulsory] power to influence behaviour. They are the labels that we attach to behavioural regularities that emerge and persist in the absence of organized, conscious direction by individuals. (2000: 8)

This real, behavioural, aspect of norms encourages us to consider the historical context (the situations and social practices) wherein social norms are generated, and consider whether this explains why law has the particular form it does at particular times.

Nevertheless, norms are also ideal. That is, they are mental, idea-based phenomena. We perceive certain things as 'the done thing' in certain contexts; we perceive certain rules in our society as legal rules and therefore as binding or as authoritative. In Korsgaard's definition, norms are ideal; they are those things 'that outstrip the world we experience and seem to call it into question, to render judgement on it, to say that it does not measure up, that it is not what it ought to be' (quoted in Del Mar, 2007: 355). Ultimately, the great merit of the concept of a 'norm' is to make us squarely engage with the fact that law – its rules, institutions and practices – have both a real and an ideal dimension, a dual characteristic that is sometimes lost in the empiricism of legal positivism.

The objectives of this chapter are as follows. First, to see how normativity can be used within a positivist framework. Second, to explain the relevance of social customs, practices and obligations to legal rules. Third, to consider the 'realist' conception of norms and normativity. Finally, to consider the extent to which law's normative 'force', despite its historical and institutional complexity, is ultimately a coercive force.

1 Norms and normativity

Introduction

The language of norms and normativity is a useful language, but also one apt to lead to confusion. It is useful because 'normative' picks out the common denominator hinted at in the words 'obligatory', 'binding', 'compelling' and 'mandatory'.

Different kinds of norms are found in different social practices. Some practices generate especially generalised, authoritative, norms, law being the obvious example. But other social situations seem to have their own norms – manners in society, rules in sport, ways of eating – that are the normal ways of acting or behaving but are much closer to 'expectations' or 'the done thing' than unequivocal obligations. One question that we have to ask is whether, given there are different normative 'spheres', there are also *degrees* of normativity. Or, on the contrary, whether there is a strict division between our general expectations concerning behaviour and the binding – 'true' – normativity of legal and moral rules.

It is, in the first instance, important to distinguish the classes of prescriptive and descriptive norms. Prescriptions are encountered in law and in ethics. Certain things are obligatory for us and, whether or not they take the form of rules, bind how we act. In this sense 'normative' can be treated as synonymous with 'obligatory'. The fact that legal norms are more narrow generalisations than moral norms does not detract from the fact that *if* applicable, a legal rule is unquestionably a species of prescription. In fact, by virtue of being much more focussed prescriptions, legal norms appear more prescriptive than the broad generalisations found in some moral discussion.

A descriptive norm is of a different order: it describes what happens with regularity, what we would expect to happen. It is a norm that, for example, people speak quietly in libraries and drink warm beer in English pubs. What is asserted here is what is generally expected, what is normal. It is not an unequivocal obligation to do these things, but note that doing the opposite of these things may be 'frowned upon'. There may be no obvious penalty for deviation from such norms, although it is significant that deviation from such norms is likely to involve penalties in terms of the extent to which people are *trusted* (see discussion of 'law and economics', below). Suffice it to say, although we are principally concerned with prescriptive norms (legal imperatives) we also have to consider descriptive norms because of the ways in which they can be translated (both socially and legally) into prescriptive norms.

1a Law as binding

The 'bindingness' of law has emerged as a common thread among our critical concepts. Law concerns obligations, and the word 'obligation' is derived from *'ligare'* meaning 'to bind'. We can analyse the binding nature of law in terms of its contribution to human needs (particularly good social order), its being intrinsically good, its being right or as a dimension of rules (good order arises out of clear public generalisations about conduct). However, we can approach this question rather more directly if we ask, not whether it *contributes* to certain ends that are binding, but whether law itself is binding, has normative justification or normative force.

The question of whether law does have a fundamental normative force – if law as a whole binds us – is different from the question of whether individual laws and rules can be justified by reference to their source or their moral defensibility. It is to ask whether a system has internal or external justification.

The idea of internal justification can be explained by appealing to the distinct 'rightness' of law, i.e. that it has an inner coherence which does not need any further justification outside the system itself. Conversely, the normative justification of law can be said to arise outside a legal system, either in its moral justification (its realisation of the good) or from a particular source (the sovereign, as in a command theory). Such questions demand consideration of the range of concepts discussed so far, but they benefit from conceptualisation in the language of normativity because this allows us to consider the *prescriptive* power of law without committing ourselves to an idea of prescription which is tied to the idea of a commanding sovereign. Normativity, something simultaneously real and ideal, allows us a more subtle picture of 'binding'.

The search for a normative foundation of law – a complete explanation of the bindingness or any rule within a legal system – would be to answer questions both about how we can distinguish law from other legal practices and how it is law can coerce us. We could argue that law has a basic justification in its having a certain authority (God, the state or the sovereign) or a certain utility (it contributes to the good or the right); any norm that we find embodied in legal rules can be said to find their ultimate normative force in that authority or utility. However, Kelsen (below) insists that there is a normativity behind law which arises from neither authority nor utility but which is wholly unique. The legal 'scientist' should be concerned with finding the patterns of obligation within legal practices themselves, not with any practice, justification or force external to a legal system. This, as we will we see, is difficult to defend. Law certainly seems to generate its own distinct system of obligations that are distinguishable from compulsions and from moral rules. But even legal norms have to have some correlate in our practices: a norm that was not recognised, observed or potentially enforced through sanctions, would have a questionable claim to be a legal norm. Put differently, Kelsen's distinctively *ideal* conception of norms has to be supplemented with a description of the *real* functioning of norms.

Normativity can also be used to analyse 'anti-foundationalism' in law. There is much to commend the argument that not only is there no need for external validation of legal rules, there is no ultimate justification of law *per se*. Starting with the pragmatic assumption that things are true only to the extent that they are useful, we could argue that there is no use, no function served, in appealing to the 'normative foundations of law' (see Ross, 2004). Law functions without having continual recourse to self-justification. If primary rules stand in need of justification there are secondary rules to do this. If we ask for justification of secondary rules we end up with the brute fact that law is perceived to be law: explanation must end somewhere.

More strongly, there is no need to explain the obligatory force of legal rules and legal systems at all, because this is missing the fact that we are governed by legal institutions and legal practices that exhibit norms – regularities in behaviour and conduct – which do not need explaining in prescriptive terms. This approach is shared by legal realists who would wish to see 'legal normativity' reduced as far as possible to descriptive norms about what people (the public and judges) generally do, what people expect to happen (Frank, 2009). Explanation of law and the nature of law need not, and should not, stray beyond these descriptive norms because they are sufficient to answer questions about why people do, and should, obey the law. The public follow the rules because they know there is a system of legal remedies in place to challenge deviation from the rules. Judges are *likely* to respond to disputes in a particular kind of way, but this predictability lies in the identity and training of judges (and therefore psychological propensities), not because legal rules have a special force. This kind of pragmatic anti-foundationlism discourages us from looking for dramatic, all-encompassing, ideas of justification and foundation when we consider law and normativity.

EXAMPLE

The Sunday Times v *The United Kingdom* ECHR (Application no. 6538/74) 1979

This case before the European Court of Human Rights concerns the right of a newspaper to publish stories concerning the company Distillers who manufactured the drug Thalidomide. The company had not tested the drug thoroughly before marketing it and it caused birth defects in hundreds of children in the 1960s. The UK government sought to suppress press comment on a Court case against the company. At issue then is a tension between Article 10 of the ECHR allowing freedom of expression, and Article 10(2) which qualifies this right 'The exercise of these freedoms, since it carries with it duties and responsibilities, may be subject to such formalities, conditions, restrictions or penalties as are prescribed by law.' Does 'prescribed' demand a single, clear, rule?

In the Court's opinion, the following are two of the requirements that flow from the expression 'prescribed by law'. Firstly, the law must be adequately accessible: the citizen must be able to have an indication that is adequate in the circumstances of the legal rules applicable to a given case. Secondly, a norm cannot be regarded as a 'law' unless it is formulated with sufficient precision to enable the citizen to regulate his conduct: he must be able – if need be with appropriate advice – to foresee, to a degree that is reasonable in the circumstances, the consequences which a given action may entail. Those consequences need not be foreseeable with absolute certainty: experience shows this to be unattainable. Again, while certainty is highly desirable, it may bring in its train excessive rigidity and the law must be able to keep pace with changing circumstances. Accordingly, many laws are inevitably couched in terms which, to a greater or lesser extent, are vague and whose interpretation and application are questions of practice.

1b Normativity and the jurisprudential schools

The differences between the different schools of legal thought encountered through-out this book are clearly highlighted when we consider their relationship with the idea of normativity. It demands that they pin-point 'where' law is, ultimately, to be found: in certain practices (such as the use of rules or social practices) or in certain ideas (such as rationality or moral principles).

Positivism strives to find the most defensible distinction between legal and other norms: for Austin it is their source, for Hart it is their source and their structure, and for Kelsen (below) it is the logical relationship between legal norms. Earlier empiri-cist positivists were less likely to use the language of norms given that it denotes both the ideal as well as the real (e.g. Austin, 1995). In contrast, the legal positivists of the twentieth century were much more amenable to locating legal obligation in social sources (Hart, 1994; Raz, 2009). Nonetheless, positivists claim a much clearer account of how the normative language of morality differs from the normative lan-guage of law: their source. Accordingly, while Hart admits the importance of a sense of obligation in order to avoid law becoming a variation on the threat of a gangster, he is eager to associate the *concept* of law with rules. While our sense of obligation is important it is the concrete, public, rules we are consenting to that are central to a legal system being a system.

Natural law theorists, conversely, do not require that the normativity take a real, concrete form. Reasonableness or the common good are the drivers of law, and these do not need to be empirical rules, enforced by sanctions, to be binding. Nor do natural lawyers draw a clear division between moral and legal norms. Natural law's deontology – its account of morality as a system of duties – and its valida-tion of legal systems by moral standards, means that there is a mutually supportive relationship between legal and moral norms. While Finnis and others concede that positivism is useful in identifying different *classes* of legal and moral norms, to the extent that they are prescriptive norms they have equal and indistinguishable status (Finnis, 2011: 297f). Distinguishing the *sources* of prescriptive norms does not entail that they have a different status *as a norm*.

It may be that there is no clear way to distinguish legal norms moral norms, *or* the social expectations and 'normal' behaviour that we find in a social life as a whole. This position, close to that of the Scandinavian realists (below), can be construed as a denial that there are prescriptive norms in the sense that positivists or natural lawyers would want to assert. On the contrary, legal and moral prescrip-tions resemble the descriptive norms of manners, sports and polite social behav-iour (Posner, 2000). We expect people to act in certain ways, and we can, by virtue of those norms, seek to persuade people to act in a particular way, but there is no special force to norms beyond *what people do* and what people can be persuaded to do. This is a diametrically opposed position to Kelsen's positivism, where law is *nothing but* a set of prescriptive norms having no relationship with the world of facts. A middle-ground is provided by American realism. Here 'law' is nothing more or less than the prescriptive norms generated by the Courts (Frank, 2009). For American realists, if we accurately *describe* the norms found in Courts then we have sufficiently explained law's *prescriptions*.

Clearly there is much at stake for the jurisprudential schools in the meaning and function of norms, more than in analysis of the formal properties of rules. Certain rules possess an authoritative pedigree; some rules are not commands but instructions to officials concerning the adjudication, modification or recognition of rules. This, however, leaves unanswered the question of *why* these rules can be said to have a binding force – and what this binding force consists of – in the absence of a threat or when there is disagreement over the nature and existence of a rule of recognition. The question of normativity pushes each school of thought to give a clear answer to why *anything* should be considered compulsory other than on the basis of the hypothetical imperative 'do this or risk a penalty'. For this reason the schools of jurisprudence, where they are concerned with the binding nature of law, often reveal their fundamental commitments when considering international law. Clearly the command theory cannot be reconciled with the plurality of sovereigns found in the international arena. However, Kelsen's more nuanced account of normativity, while broadly speaking a positivist one, has to presume continuity between national and international norms (normative 'monism'). Ross, a Scandinavian realist, lies at the other extreme, tying law's normativity to the marriage between national practices and a national legal system (normative 'pluralism').

EXAMPLE

R (on the application of Corner House Research) v *Director of the Serious Fraud Office* [2008] UKHL 60

Is a state prosecutor entitled to drop criminal investigations after having received a threat from a foreign government that the investigation 'jeopardises cooperation in national security issues'? It is suggested that the obligation to protect lives may be more binding than the rule of law. What is the most basic normative force at work in the decision: legal rules or the threat of force by terrorists?

[T]he right of a state to protect its security in the sense of protecting the lives of its citizens against terrorism is fundamental. As the Permanent Court of International Justice put it in the Case of the *SS Wimbledon* (1923) [. . .]: 'The right of a state to adopt the course which it considers best suited to the exigencies of its security and to the maintenance of its integrity, is so essential a right that in case of doubt, treaty stipulations cannot be interpreted as limiting it, even though those stipulations do not conflict with such

➡

an interpretation.' [. . .] Associated with the right of a state to take those measures which it considers necessary to protect its citizens, is the importance of those international norms which protect human rights and, in particular, the right to life. Some norms have a special or privileged status because of their content [. . .]. The obligation of a government in a democratic society to protect and safeguard the lives of its citizens was, as we have already recalled, described [. . .] as essential to the preservation of democracy.

1c Classifying norms

We have encountered the difference between prescriptive and descriptive norms. Norms can also be categorised in other ways. Some draw a distinction between social, legal and moral norms, some do not. First, norms can be described as *valid* or *invalid*. While rules are generally treated as *applicable* or inapplicable, and (deontological) moral norms face a test of *universality*, legal norms alone share with logic the test of *validity*. Validity depends on whether norms are structurally defensible, or whether they have the correct source, rather than whether they apply here or do not apply here. Thus, legal norms can be tested by the validity of their source (legal obligations are valid norms because they arise from a sovereign not a gangster), or their validity on the basis of their relationship with other norms (a legal decision is valid because it is derived from other valid norms within the system).

Another way of classifying norms in law is as 'peremptory' or as 'defeasible' (see Simmonds, 2008). Peremptory means 'admitting no debate'; an action, decision or statement is peremptory if it is intended to end debate without any further discussion. Many elements of law could be considered to be peremptory, for instance the decision of a highest Court of appeal, and Austin's sovereign commands are peremptory norms (commands that admit of no counter-argument). But peremptory norms – that cannot be contracted out of and cannot be temporarily suspended – are rare in law. Law is more often characterised by defeasible norms: norms that draw a limit to the use of other norms, without claiming any kind of universality or lack of exceptions. The notion of the peremptory norm captures the idea of certainty and rigidity we expect from law; but defeasible norms are more commonly found among a legal system's primary rules.

EXAMPLE

Committee of U.S. Citizens Living in Nicaragua v Reagan (1988) 859 F.2d 929 United States

Jus cogens *norms (literally 'compelling laws') are peremptory norms that cannot be derogated from, even by sovereign states. Following an International Court of Justice (ICJ) decision that the US was in contravention of international law in funding Contras in Nicaragua,*

> a group of US citizens brought claims within US Courts asserting that the US had failed to abide by the ICJ decision and (unsuccessfully) arguing that such a legal decision by the ICJ was itself a jus cogensnorm binding the US administration.
>
> > [T]he United States may have violated peremptory norms of international law. Such norms, often referred to as *jus cogens* (or 'compelling law'), enjoy the highest status in international law and prevail over both customary international law and treaties. Appellants' contention that the United States has violated *jus cogens* [norms] forms their primary argument before this court. They contend that the obligation of parties to an ICJ judgment to obey that judgment is not merely a customary rule but actually a peremptory norm of international law. [From the decision:] The Vienna Convention on the Law of Treaties, which reflects the common understanding of the term, defines *jus cogens* only in relation to international law: 'A treaty is void if, at the time of its conclusion, it conflicts with a peremptory norm of general international law . . . [which] is a norm accepted by the international community of States as a whole as a norm from which no derogation is permitted' [. . .].

2 Kelsen

Introduction

For positivists the question of 'normativity' is both crucial and problematic. It is crucial because positivists seek to find and isolate the normativity unique to law. It is problematic because normativity is sought in a particular set of facts, only secondarily in the perceptions and ideas that make certain things normative *for us* as individuals. The *sense* of obligation that is generated by particular sources – rules or society – is analytically separable from those sources. Rules are posited – promulgated and publicised – but obligatory 'force' is something that we see or feel.

An important exception to this empiricist positivism is found in the work of Hans Kelsen (1881–1973). His focus is on the normativity of law as the *ideal*, rather than the real, character of legal norms. He is a positivist to the extent that he accepts the sources thesis, and accepts the separation thesis, and therefore treats analysis as a form of scientific enquiry. However, he is poles apart from logical positivism and its reduction of knowledge to the verifiable and observable. Rather, a legal science is possible because the study of law can be freed from other areas of enquiry. In addition, once its subject matter has been isolated, law can be found, analysed and logically validated on entirely independent grounds. This project is a purification of legal enquiry, and its subject matter is law as a set of norms.

2a Kelsen's critical project

Kelsen's idiosyncratic position should be contextualised within the German philosophical environment in which he worked. First, German philosophy can be characterised as pursuing *Wissenschaft*. This is often translated as 'science', but should be thought to indicate any unified body of knowledge, be it in the hard and natural sciences or the arts and humanities. In the background of Kelsen's work is, therefore, the philosophical assumption that law is not characterised by disconnected facts but by its being a unified system. This means, amongst other things, that he wholly endorses the separation thesis which treats law and morality as different domains of enquiry. Second, like other scholars working in the German philosophical tradition, Kelsen is interested in 'axioms', unassailable first principles. Axiomatic for Kelsen is the division between facts and values. Kelsen is unusually consistent in this, making his work consonant with other forms of positivism and giving his account of law a claim to a certain kind of 'purity'.

Third, in Kelsen's intellectual environment Kant's philosophy was central, and Kelsen considered himself a continuator of Kant's 'critical project'. This is the project of rejecting dogmatic assumptions in philosophy, and discovering the *a priori* conditions of any knowledge, i.e. the truths presupposed or necessary for any kind of truth, knowledge or certainty. Kant's project led him to identify the structures of consciousness that shape our knowledge of the world; the approach is 'critical' because it looks for the most fundamental structures of reality, accepting neither rationalism nor empiricism but looking at the basis of both (Kant, 1929). Kelsen transfers this to law by asking, 'What must be assumed for a legal system to be possible?' Kelsen's answer is that there must be a system of normative claims and normative deductions which do not depend upon any other social facts. We can find *rules* in any walk of life; legal norms are, conversely, a completely distinctive set of obligations.

Kelsen's argument that the very possibility of law presupposes wholly distinctive *legal* norms is based on two related moves. First, law concerns a body of 'ought' propositions, norms that are prescriptive in the absence of any threat of coercion by the sovereign. Agreeing with Hart, these prescriptions are distinguishable from moral prescriptions because of the system within which they are contained – a legal system constituted by norms that themselves are the gauge of validity and invalidity (as opposed to a legal system constituted by norms validated by a morality external to the system).

> The validity of a legal norm cannot be questioned on the ground that its contents are incompatible with some moral or political value. A norm is a valid legal norm by virtue of the fact that it has been created according to a definite rule and by virtue thereof only. (2005: 113)

Second, the isolation of a system of distinctively legal norms relies upon treating the division of facts and norms as complete and unbridgeable. If there is a complete chasm between the two, then legality must be among prescriptions rather than social facts: 'Whereas an "is" statement is true because it agrees with the reality of sensuous experience, an "ought" statement is a valid norm only if it belongs to [. . .] a valid system of norms' (2005: 111). Accordingly, legality proper is characterised – crucially – by a normativity that is not dependent on any facts, be they facts about consequences or about legal institutions. Legal norms are unique, self-contained and also distinct from other kinds of norms. In this way, following Kant, Kelsen offers us an account of law that is purified of any empirical 'intrusions' from morality, politics or society.

EXAMPLE

'The Reich Constitution of August 11th' (Weimar Constitution, Germany 1919)

Kelsen was at the heart of the Weimar Republic period of German history (1919–1933). The ill-fated Weimar Constitution is principally remembered as a democratic constitution which allowed (through Article 48 concerning emergency powers) anti-democratic forces to take control of Germany. More widely, its blurring of general constitutional principles and social norms seems to render a 'science of legal norms' difficult, if not impossible.

[Preamble:] The German people, united in its tribes and inspirited with the will to renew and strengthen its Reich in liberty and justice, to serve peace inward and outward and to promote social progress, has adapted this constitution. [. . .] ['Second Chapter: Life within a Community'] Article 119: Marriage, as the foundation of the family and the preservation and expansion of the nation, enjoys the special protection of the constitution. It is based on the equality of both genders. / It is the task of both the state and the communities to strengthen and socially promote the family. Large families may claim social welfare. Motherhood is placed under state protection and welfare. / Article 120: It is the supreme obligation and natural right of the parents to raise their offspring to bodily, spiritual and social fitness [. . .].

2b A pure theory of law

Kelsen was concerned with separating the domain of law from other disciplines and social practices, but this does not mean that he was looking to *create* a 'pure law'. Kelsen knew that law and laws have a complex relationship with the reality from which they arise and help to create. What he was seeking to assert is that legal norms – i.e. truly legal obligations and not just political, social or other contingent obligations – are identifiable and can be isolated. Law is a system of 'oughts', of normative obligations. Purified of contingent social facts and moral claims, law is a self-contained system of normative obligations that are binding *because* they are legal norms, not because they are associated with social or political coercion.

One consequence of this is that identifying legal obligations is a question of isolating those norms and the relationships between those norms. Legal science is not an empirical science that looks only for those rules flowing from a particular source. Rather it looks for the relationships behind and between legal rules. 'Law is an order of human behaviour. An 'order' is a system of rules. Law is not, as it is sometimes said, a rule. It is a set of rules having the kind of unity we understand by a system' (2005: 3). Lawyers are those trained in looking past the materials generated by legal systems to the ways in which obligations flow from higher or more general obligations: i.e. finding *valid* legal norms deduced from other, valid legal norms. This validation of legal norms through their deduction from other legal norms is labelled 'imputation' by Kelsen. A legal rule always gains its validity (is imputed) from a higher norm, which in turn is imputed from another norm. If we want to know the obligations that are generated by contract law we need to find a valid norm which governs that area; finding that valid legal norm is not a question of its source, it is a question of imputing its validity from higher, more general, norms of contract law. These norms may have been imputed from even more general constitutional norms, and as such any legal system has to be seen as a network of norms and imputations (2005: 113f).

The merit of portraying law in this way is clear. It isolates and describes law in terms of distinctive obligations, obligations that are in no way dependent upon the contingencies of different sovereigns and their will, nor changing social practices, nor legal institutions and their functioning. We have no need at all to appeal to empirical sources. Rather, we are solely focussed on obligation, thereby making sense of why law resembles morality more than it resembles the threats of gangsters, but also showing how it is different from the categorical prescriptions found in morality. In short, the distinctively binding nature of law is derived from a unique web of normative claims.

EXAMPLE

R (on the application of Al-Saadoon) v Secretary of State for Defence [2009] EWCA Civ 7

International law depends upon an unusual kind of positivism – like Kelsen's – because it has no single sovereign. This case turned on the extent to which the jurisdiction of the English Courts encompassed the activities of English nationals in Iraq. The UK and other states had effective control over parts of Iraq following invasion in 2003; problems arose concerning prosecution and punishment of war crimes committed during and immediately after the invasion. Here the Court grapples with a complex question. There can be no simple imputation of norms in Kelsen's terms. Nonetheless, certain principles, such as 'sovereign legal authority', are treated as axiomatic.

Conclusion on the Jurisdiction Question: It is not easy to identify precisely the scope of [. . .] jurisdiction where it is said to be exercised outside the territory of the impugned State Party, because [. . .] its scope has no sharp edge; it has to be ascertained from a combination of key ideas which are strategic rather than lexical. Drawing on the *Bankovic* judgment and their Lordships' opinions in *Al-Skeini*, I suggest that there are four core propositions, though each needs some explanation. (1) It is an exceptional jurisdiction.

(2) It is to be ascertained in harmony with other applicable norms of international law. (3) It reflects the regional nature of the Convention rights. (4) It reflects the indivisible nature of the Convention rights. The first and second of these propositions imply (as perhaps does the term jurisdiction itself) an exercise of sovereign legal authority, not merely *de facto* power, by one State on the territory of another. That is of itself an exceptional state of affairs, though well recognized in some instances such as that of an embassy. The power must be given by law, since if it were given only by chance or strength its exercise would by no means be harmonious with material norms of international law, but offensive to them; and there would be no principled basis on which the power could be said to be limited, and thus exceptional.

2c The *Grundnorm*

One question which this purified picture of law gives rise to is where the system of norms has its beginning and *ultimate* normative force. We might agree that all legal obligations stem from other, more general, obligations, but this line of justification has to end. To avoid an infinite regress of norms – a ceaseless referring to higher and higher norms – Kelsen posits a *Grundnorm* (basic norm) from which all other norms gain their validity. 'The basic norm [*Grundnorm*] of a legal order is the postulated ultimate rule according to which the norms of this order are established and annulled, receive or lose their validity (2005: 113)'. The nature of this norm is unclear within Kelsen's writing; nonetheless, it must logically have certain qualities. It must be a *norm* not a state of affairs. It is a norm that those within a legal system implicitly assume (officials see their system as ultimately *valid* and not just effective). And it *must exist* in order for law to be a normative system (as opposed to a set of facts about behaviour).

The *nature* of the *Grundnorm* is clear to the extent that all norms within Kelsen's view of law must be norms, so the *Grundnorm* is not, and cannot be, a fact or set of facts. This distinguishes it from Hart's rule of recognition, which is based on whatever is perceived to be the basic *factual*, institutional, foundations of a constitution. The nature of the *Grundnorm* must be something like an 'ought' proposition that is free from empirical content and gives rise to all other legal obligations.

> The basic norm is not created in a legal procedure by a law-creating organ. It is not – as a positive legal norm is – valid because it is created in a certain way by a legal act, but it is valid because it is presupposed to be valid. (2005: 116)

One way of giving expression to this norm might be to say 'the norms of this system should be seen as obligation generating'. The *Grundnorm* must be a simple normative proposition, and this proposition does indeed *insist* (it is a prescriptive norm) that the norms found within the legal system are binding or have authority. Conversely, it is misleading to see such a norm as anything like a regulative rule. It is closer to a constitutive principle that makes other norms possible:

I would say [. . .] that the *Grundnorm* in Kelsen is a sort of 'logical' closure of his system[,] so to speak, a closure of convenience. It is a little like the idea of the absolute sovereignty of the nation-state. The idea of sovereignty as 'power of powers' is a closure of convenience, no different from the *Grundnorm* conceived of as a 'norm of norms'. Nothing verifiable corresponds, nor can correspond, to these notions. (Bobbio and Zolo, 1998: 358)

The *scope* of the *Grundnorm* is a different question concerning the extent to which different legal systems possess different *Grundnorms* validating the norms within their system, or rather (and this is more in keeping with Kelsen's Kantian assumptions) that there can only be one *Grundnorm* which serves to validate any and all legal norms. Much of Kelsen's writing does point to the conclusion that we should perceive domestic and international law in a monistic relationship where there is no boundary between the two or, indeed, any fundamental division between any legal systems. This monistic position is contrary to the assumptions within the majority of legal systems which consider themselves in a dualistic relationship with international law and would assume that they had to make conscious step to include international law within their jurisdiction. At the same time, Kelsen's position sits better with much international legal scholarship and the assumption that the customary norms of international law are binding unconditionally on all states. To presume there is a plurality of such realms would seem to be a suspiciously empirical assertion flowing from the fact that there is a plurality of legal systems. For Kelsen those obligatory norms that we call legal norms are not tied to contingent social or political facts, nor are they tied to effective control over a territory: they are a species of pure obligation.

Since a norm is no statement of reality, no statement of a real fact can be in contradiction to a norm. Hence, there can be no exceptions to a norm. The norm is by its very nature inviolable. To say a norm is 'violated' by certain behaviour is a figurative expression (2005: 46)

EXAMPLE

'Human Dignity and Liberty [Basic Law Number 1]', Passed by the Knesset on the 12th Adar Bet, 5752, 17 March 1992

The Israeli constitution has a number of Basic Laws – fundamental instruments with a constitutional status – which set out the legal principles by which the state and its organs should function. Like similar constitutional structures, some provision is made for suspension of basic principles in the event of emergency. Does this support or negate the idea of a Grundnorm *validating law universally and at all times?*

1. The purpose of this Basic Law is to protect human dignity and liberty, in order to establish in a Basic Law the values of the State of Israel as a Jewish and democratic state. / 2. There shall be no violation of the life, body or dignity of any person as such. / 3. There shall be no violation of the property of the person. / 4. All persons are entitled

to protection of their life, body and dignity. / 5. There shall be no deprivation or restriction of the liberty of a person by imprisonment, arrest, extradition or otherwise. [. . .] 12. This Basic Law cannot be varied, suspended or made subject to conditions by emergency regulations; notwithstanding, when a state of emergency exists [. . .] emergency regulations may be enacted by virtue of said section to deny or restrict rights under this Basic Law, provided the denial or restriction shall be for a proper purpose and for a period and extent no greater than is required.

3 Law and social norms

Introduction

Positing a distinction between legal norms and social norms is difficult, and potentially misleading. It is difficult because we cannot treat social norms – from the rules of courtship and manners, to the implicit or unconscious expectations involved in waiting for a bus – as pure descriptions of regularities in human behaviour. They are seen by their participants as obligations (MacCormick, 1988), certainly not obligations that are routinely accompanied by state coercion, but obligations nonetheless. Some social norms fall between legal and social obligations. Marriage rituals are both legally recognised contracts and socially significant events. The two aspects of the ritual are distinct, but we cannot understand the legal dimension of the ritual without reference to the social dimension. Marriage is contract formation in a very specific sense; it can only be understood in the context of long historical patterns of human relationships, familial relationships and social expectations. In other words, the social world and social expectations both pre-date, and are essential to understanding, the legal dimension of marriage.

This does not present an immediate challenge to formalists or Kelsenian positivists. While the social practices are one thing, the legal norms that arise out of them are another. These can be isolated and validated without reference to historical rituals and social norms. If, however, we want to account for why law has concerned itself with some social norms and not others, then we have to consider the less formal, and more 'impure', world of individual interests and social practices.

It is also the case that the formalist or Kelsenian accounts of law can be turned on their heads and recast as accounts of the rituals, the social expectations and the relationships that we find in a legal system. While lawyers concern themselves with rules and norms, their behaviour can be described through a set of objective, behavioural, norms. Like a marriage ritual, a legal process is also a social event with distinct historical origins, predictable ritual behaviour and any number of 'expectations' from the etiquette of Courts to the use of certain rules in certain ways. If this account of legal practices is sufficiently rich, the 'internal point of view' on rules, 'pure legal norms' and 'distinct legal obligations' could drop out of the picture to be replaced with a description of the norms that we see in legal institutions. If we want to isolate what is real, rather than ideal, in law we should look exclusively at what happens and what is likely to happen in legal institutions.

We can articulate this possibility in the language of formalism and anti-formalism. The formalist sees law as a system of rule-following wherein decisions are (using Kelsen's term) imputations from wholly distinctive – non-social and non-moral – legal norms. The anti-formalist denies this picture, drawing attention to both the regularities and idiosyncrasies of applying rules in Courts. They exhibit regularity: there is no doubt that we have a *system* of laws and not arbitrary commands. However, they are also idiosyncratic: because law involves the *selection* of facts and the *selection* of rules, and judges themselves are not wholly predictable. Law is best understood through prediction of the decision-making of judges. Legal norms and social norms therefore not only have the status, but require the same methodology: attention to what people *do*.

There are a number of ways in which this denial of the division between descriptive social norms and prescriptive legal norms can be articulated. Here we will look at historical, sociological and economic accounts of how social norms give rise to law.

3a Law and history

The example of a marriage ritual illustrates one of the many formalised social practices which pre-date state-based legal institutions. Indeed, many legal practices could be thought to build upon established historical antecedents. The modern state has taken social, cultural and commercial practices and formalised them to apply uniformly. The fields of modern law, from crime to family law, are undoubtedly foreshadowed by practices with social, not bureaucratic, origins. Freud offers an explanation of how certain legal norms can be said to have psychological and anthropological roots. We will also briefly consider Maine and Marx's wider historical reflections on law.

Sigmund Freud (1856–1939) applied a model of human psychological development in children to the formation of societies in 'humanity's infancy'. His model of infancy – where the human personality is formed through a conflict between biological drives and socialisation – remains provocative. Rejecting the prevailing view of childhood as a period where the 'blank slate' of the mind is filled with experience, early infancy is where strong fundamental drives for survival, for growth and pleasure do battle with the environment that they encounter; namely, their parents and the ways in which their parents interact with, allow, or frustrate those basic primitive drives. The negotiation between primitive drives and the authority exercised by parents is the central way in which the personality is formed.

Freud later sought to expand the scope of his analysis to look at the primitive drives that have served to shape social life and social being. Prohibitions (the frustration and control of drives) have been a perennial feature of social life, and from these ideas Freud attempts to reconstruct the earliest beginnings of human society. He suggests that natural drives posed a threat to early human social groups; in particular the drive for pleasure and for control lead to instances of incest and patricide (the killing of fathers). 'One day the expelled brothers joined forces, slew and ate the father [. . .]. This violent primal father had surely been the envied and feared model for each of the brothers' (Freud, 1938: 218). These crimes led to the earliest laws: the prohibition of incest and the prohibition of murder within one's own familial and social group. While there is more to Freud's account of the intertwined development of the human psyche and human society, this emphasis on the centrality of *crime* in the formation of human societies does give support to both positivist command theories and natural law theories that see the prohibition of certain acts as foundational to law.

Freud's analysis is controversial, but does offer a tempting account of how legal norms can be traced not only to social practices but to psychological processes. A rather less psychological, but no less sweeping, account of the evolution of legal systems is found in Henry Maine's (1822–88) historical jurisprudence. Maine's work *Ancient Law* not only attempts to chart the origin and evolution of all of the main species of legal system, but derives from this an account of the 'natural' evolutionary trajectory of legal systems (Maine, 1931). This natural evolutionary process is best exemplified by the changes found in Roman law and its movement from status to contract. 'Primitive' legal systems attribute powers, immunities and claims of right, on the basis of an individual's *status* within a social order; such social orders are hierarchical and patriarchal. The association of law with status undergoes a positive evolutionary shift when status is progressively replaced by *contract* as the foundation of legality. Under contracts, individuals enter into legal relations with one another as equal contracting parties and have their own rights and obligations as individuals recognised; such rights are independent of family, caste or group:

> The notion that persons under a contractual engagement are connected together by a strong *bond* or *chain*, continued till the last to influence the Roman jurisprudence of Contract; and flowing thence it has mixed itself with modern ideas. (1931: 261)

This movement is not driven by deliberate social engineering but is, for Maine, part of the organic development of any healthy society. While the evolutionary dimension of this should give us grounds for suspicion (by what objective standard is social evolution to be judged natural or progressive?), the descriptive aspects of Maine's account are powerful to the extent that they draw a distinction between types of law *in context*. That is, different ways in which social contexts can give rise to distinctive patterns of legal relations and legal rights.

Maine offers a suggestive description of how legal systems have changed their character over time, but Marx, following Hegel, provided explanation of the *sources* of historical change. Marx's materialist position represents a rejection of idealism (that ideas are the only reliable source of knowledge) in favour of the diametrically opposed position: that the material of the world, and the processes which emerge from our relationship with the material world, are the origins of our ideas. Combining the historical analysis of ideas undertaken by Hegel with the fact that human life depends upon the resources of the material world, Marx proposed an opposing historical materialism (see also Chapter 7). Sometimes labelled dialectical materialism, this is a dynamic materialism which encompasses ideas of conflict, change and, ultimately, progress.

Marx accepted the basic materialist assumption that material conditions are the basis of our ideas. He added to this a belief that our relationship with the material world and our ideas will evolve as we grapple with and overcome the contradictions found in our social lives (Marx, 2000: 419). Such contradictions arise from the fact that those most closely related to the appropriation of the material world, and its processing into something with exchange value, are those who profit least from it. Workers – those harnessing and refining the resources of the material world – are the least politically powerful class, and (through the translation of raw material into exchangeable commodities) alienated from the very thing they work with (Easton, 1961). The barrier to a more efficient and just harmony between the material and human is this irrational and exploitative relationship between the large class of productive individuals and those who employ them for profit.

Within historical materialism, historical change is not the consequence of arbitrary power or the evolution of forms of governance, it is driven by class struggle: the tension between those creating wealth and those holding wealth. This entails, on the one hand, that the role of law in society is secondary to changes in the relations of production (law is, in Marxist terms, only 'super-structural', a by-product of more fundamental economic structures). On the other hand, this offers a critical diagnosis of law and legal relationships. Law contributes to legitimising an unjust system; material *inequalities* are maintained through the conservative *equality* of constitutional and contractual legal relationships protecting property and wealth (Hunt, 1986). To an extent this also offers a project for reform. To see the basis of any wealth creation in a state as the product of working people not wealth holders, and to seek the eradication of inequalities between classes to ensure that working people are granted sufficient rights to immunise them against exploitation.

EXAMPLE

Constitution of the Republic of Cuba, 1976 (amended 1992): Preamble

The Cuban constitution is one of the few remaining constitutions committed to Marxist principles. It has a stirring preamble setting out the positive basis of the constitution (life without degradation) and its negative foundations (freedom from slavery and imperialism).

> We, *Cuban Citizens*, heirs and continuators of the creative work and the traditions of combativity, firmness, heroism and sacrifice fostered by our ancestors; by the Indians who preferred extermination to submission; by the slaves who rebelled against their masters; by the patriots who in 1868 launched the wars of independence against Spanish colonialism and those who in the last drive of 1895 brought them to victory in 1898, a victory usurped by the military intervention and occupation of Yankee imperialism; by the workers, peasants, student and intellectuals who struggled for over fifty years against imperialist domination, political corruption, the absence of people's rights and liberties, unemployment and exploitation by capitalists and landowners; by those who promoted, joined and developed the first organizations of workers and peasants, spread socialist ideas and founded the first Marxist and Marxist-Leninist movements; [. . .] / *Aware* that all the regimes based on the exploitation of man by man cause the humiliation of the exploited and the degradation of the human nature of the exploiters; that only under socialism and communism, when man has been freed from all forms of exploitation – slavery, servitude and capitalism – can full dignity of the human being be attained [. . .].

3b Law and sociology

Historical accounts of the origins of law provide a sense of the social practices which antedate but inform state-based legal institutions; they reveal historical patterns that legal systems share; and they can reveal the forces which drive historical change, including legal systems. Sociology is much more closely focussed on the structure of *modern* society and culture. This can be said to include Marx's work, and other work like it, which concerns the social groupings that we find in modern society and the patterns of governance under which they live.

The classic sociological works of Weber and Durkheim, as well as the more controversial work of Foucault, each contain insights into the function of law in modern society. What unites each of them is ambivalent view of modern society as characterised by both rationality in social processes and oppressive norms enforced or strengthened by law. In Max Weber's (1864–1920) work, the birth of modernity is characterised by a 'disenchantment' of the world: the substituting of magic or superstitious conceptions of the natural and social world for scientific forms of thought (Weber, 1978: 226f). Law is crucial in this process:

> For Weber, formal legal rationality symbolized the height of this disenchantment process, as it manifests a detachment from substantive value judgments; is based on general rules rather than on *ad hoc* assessments; and strips the adjudication process (as well as lawmaking) from any remains of sacredness, magic, and charismatic authority. (Blank, 2011: 640)

At the same time, the 'rationalisation' – the efficiency and professionalisation – of the management of social affairs forms part of the 'iron cage of modernity', a technocracy (rule by experts) that has stifled or destroyed more organic forms of community (Weber, 1978: 138–73).

This is a theme echoed by Emile Durkheim (1858–1917), for whom modernity is characterised by an experience of 'anomie' – literally 'being without law' – wherein a sense of meaning in people's lives has been lost (Clarke, 1976). In both Durkheim and Weber we see the deterioration of 'community' wherein people have a role and a sense of meaning and purpose, and a movement towards 'society' in its modern incarnation which is characterised by bureaucratic management. In other words, the movement from community to society, while allowing greater rationality in public affairs, severs social norms that are essential for a sense of meaning and purpose. The more regulated or rationalised structure of contemporary society manages us, but does not give us meaning.

Michel Foucault's (1926–84) work accentuates the negative dimension of modernity's drive to rationalise, emphasising the reduction of politics to 'management' of a populace and complicity between knowledge, technology and power (Foucault, 1977). This complicity has particular importance in his understanding of law, norms and punishment. Criminal law and normativity have a close, but not straightforward, relationship. Criminals are people who have deviated from 'normal' or at least 'generally approved' behaviour. To be law-abiding is to demonstrate adherence to prevailing norms; to act criminally is to deviate from those norms. This picture is, however, misleadingly simple. We can talk of deviating from the prescriptive norms of the law, but it is not always the case that those norms match social norms. It might be quite *normal* for people to want to engage in criminality, or at least engage in it and not get caught. Furthermore, there is always the potential for norms to become tools of oppression, particularly in criminal and penal law. If criminality is treated as an abnormality, this authorises us to use forms of punishment or therapy ensuring that law-breakers have such abnormalities subdued or reformed. But at what point does simple deviation from social norms become abnormality; and who is authorised to decide this? Such a use of norms and normality is, argues Foucault, the modern world's most widespread and insidious form of power and violence (1977).

It was Weber who first drew attention to the importance of the modern state's claim to a monopoly over legitimate use of violence (1978: 349) and nowhere is this more in evidence than in the use of punishment. From the seventeenth century onwards, through the diffusion of military forms of discipline to social action and education, the prison took on a more 'regulatory' role in disciplining the offender to act in particular ways that were 'normal'. The characteristics Foucault attributes to the 'technologies' of punishment have spread to other aspects of contemporary Western society (Luker, 1998; Oldfield, 2003). The norms that are appealed to when prisoners are rehabilitated in prison, and the processes by which a model of normality is prescribed through technologies of regimentation and social uniformity, are the basis of a more general movement towards 'normalisation'. Normalisation suggests that sovereign force and sovereign power no longer aim at brute control over citizens. A model of 'normal behaviour' and 'normal identities' has become the principal means by which we are controlled. Through our 'internalising' these expectations (see below) and through scientific disciplines such as penology, psychology and psychiatry, a standard of normality is enforced. Lest we think that these disciplines only reflect social reality or therapeutic practices meant to liberate us, Foucault cautions us to look closely at the assumptions about what is normal. Without exception they enforce ideas of self-control, and self-repression that are both convenient for society *and* bear similarities to the self-discipline demanded by prisons (Foucault, 1977). Whether or not this is a fair diagnosis of the managerial style of the contemporary state, it accords with the pessimistic tenor of much sociological thought.

EXAMPLE

Crime and Disorder Act 1998 (Part I Prevention of crime and disorder)

Is there a point at which criminal justice blurs into social ordering or social engineering? Anti-Social Behaviour Orders and Parenting Orders are means by which civil powers can be used over 'problematic' individuals such that their actions are constrained and they are placed in a position just short of criminal remedies. Should a non-convicted individual be 'normalised'?

Parenting orders. (4) A parenting order is an order which requires the parent – (a) to comply, for a period not exceeding twelve months, with such requirements as are specified in the order, and (b) [. . .] to attend, for a concurrent period not exceeding three months, such counselling or guidance programme as may be specified in directions given by the responsible officer. [. . .] (7) The requirements that may be specified under subsection (4)(a) above are those which the court considers desirable in the interests of preventing any such repetition or, as the case may be, the commission of any such further offence. / (7A) A counselling or guidance programme which a parent is required to attend [. . .] may be or include a residential course [. . .].

■ 3c Law and economics

The central concern of the law and economics movement is the application of economic principles and models to law itself and to relationships with a legal dimension. Relationships, not only business relationships but also many social relationships, generate costs. Maintaining friendships demands sacrifices, maintaining business relationships often involves hospitality, and maintaining the respect and trust of those around us can depend upon a whole series of socially approved actions from the way we speak to what we wear. The introduction of law to those relationships is itself a cost – it is expensive to make a contract, and even more expensive to litigate a dispute – but may also be an alternative to more costly ways of maintaining relationships, certainly in business contexts, where non-legal solutions to a problem are uncertain.

Moreover, legal processes and policies themselves can be explained or generated with economic models. With enough data about preferences and interests, individuals' actions can be made statistically predictable. Their economic behaviour demonstrates how much they are likely to pay to sustain legal relationships or prevent liability for losses; these 'revealed preferences' can be used to predict risk-taking, and used to tailor law to incentivise non-risky behaviour (Katz, 2011). For these reasons, the law and economics movement is concerned with descriptive norms: how we are likely to act, given that our preferences are statistically predictable. It also generates prescriptions about the forms and practices of law: how law should be used to distribute risk and apportion burdens through legislation (Posner, 2000). In both ways, it takes the pursuit of *efficiency* to be an explanation of our behaviour and an ideal for our legal institutions.

The analysis of social and legal practices can benefit from the models and assumptions used by economists. The assumption of most economic theories is that we are self-interested rational actors, who will seek to achieve our preferences by the most efficient means possible. We can, then, predict patterns of behaviour through modelling how it is that individuals are able to maximise their preference-satisfaction. This, alone, would not be a rich analytical framework for social science or legal scholarship. However, Eric Posner (b. 1965) and others have presented a deeper analysis of how law's functioning depends on social norms, norms that themselves can be captured by economic models. Thus, patterns of social etiquette reflect predictable patterns of cost and exchange. We behave in certain ways in public, potentially at some cost to ourselves, because of our need for social exchanges. 'Costly' social practices, such as showing 'good manners', can maximise the likelihood of our fulfilling a greater range of preferences. Clearly not all rules of social etiquette become legal norms. But it is the case that behind many effective legal rules, social norms are at work. '[M]any legal rules are best understood as efforts to harness the independent regulatory power of social norms' (Posner, 2000: 8). Thus, criminal law does not have to be explained in terms of neutralising or normalising dangerous individuals; criminalisation is also related to the deterrence of 'anti-social behaviour'. Many social norms centre on demonstrating that we are trustworthy, practices that individuals (consciously or unconsciously) adopt and which the anti-social criminal flouts. Effective criminal law is built upon reinforcing these existing social expectations.

In prescriptive terms, economic analyses can translate into policy recommendations, policies to ensure that efficiency is maximised in legal rules. Policy should distribute costs and benefits in such a way that rational decision-makers are not penalised, and so that people have incentives to act legally. This is often applied to the rules of tort, where the threat of punishment is absent but where recklessness and negligence can be costly to both individuals and for society as a whole (Katz, 2011: 203f). Through well structured legal regulation, laws can become social norms which minimise risks and costs. For example, penalties for risk taking (e.g. not wearing seatbelts in cars), can become social norms at relatively little cost. Taking risks with property can be deterred when, through systematic use of legal penalties, the cost of prevention becomes less than the cost of accidents. Economic analysis can also be used to prescribe more general public policies. This is true of environmental law where 'externalities' – costs, such as pollution, which do not immediately fall on private actors but on society more generally – can be shifted by law to those who generate the externalities.

EXAMPLE

Regina v *Ghosh* [1982] 3 W.L.R. 110

A case concerning the law of theft and the role of dishonesty in theft. The case provides a test for dishonesty requiring a decision on the part of the jury as to whether something was dishonest by the 'ordinary standards' of 'reasonable honest people'. Such a standard is necessary but variable. What may look unreasonable in normal social settings may look ordinary in certain business or commercial environments. The fact that the test is initially 'objective' suggests that dishonesty is a socially recognised phenomenon being harnessed directly for legal purposes.

> In determining whether the prosecution has proved that the defendant was acting dishonestly, a jury must first of all decide whether according to the ordinary standards of reasonable and honest people what was done was dishonest. If it was not dishonest by those standards, that is the end of the matter and the prosecution fails. [. . .] If it was dishonest by those standards, then the jury must consider whether the defendant himself must have realised that what he was doing was by those standards dishonest. In most cases, where the actions are obviously dishonest by ordinary standards, there will be no doubt about it. It will be obvious that the defendant himself knew that he was acting dishonestly. It is dishonest for a defendant to act in a way which he knows ordinary people consider to be dishonest, even if he asserts or genuinely believes that he is morally justified in acting as he did. For example, Robin Hood or those ardent anti-vivisectionists who remove animals from vivisection laboratories are acting dishonestly, even though they may consider themselves to be morally justified in doing what they do, because they know that ordinary people would consider these actions to be dishonest.

---

4 Realism

Introduction

'Realism' has a range of competing meanings in philosophy, including legal philosophy. To generalise, legal realists are often empiricists, concerned with verifiable facts, and therefore focus on *behavioural* responses to legal language and on the *decisions* of judges. Judicial decisions are shown to reflect the 'logic of experience' – what in practice is just, fair, equitable or justifiable – rather than logical 'imputations' derived from rules. Legal realists are also often philosophical pragmatists. They exhibit a degree of scepticism, not only about knowledge and truth claims, but about the reality of 'law' as it is conceived by other theories of law. The other schools of legal thought are seen as deploying questionable assumptions about the reality of law as a kind of social or normative 'substance' that can be distinguished from other substances in the world. The more sceptical conclusion favoured by certain realists (and shared with logical positivists) is that there is no such substance, that law can only be known by its effects on our action.

Despite convergence around these kinds of ideas, the American and Scandinavian schools of realism have distinct origins and perspectives. American realism originated in law schools and in the need to prepare law students for legal practice. Their perspective on law can be summarised as, first, a suspicion of abstraction, and second, treatment of legal adjudication as no different to other, non-institutionalised, forms of problem-solving. When any social or practical problem arises, some people – with more experience or more interest – have instincts about the right outcome. Whether we are dealing with a domestic disagreement or a Supreme Court case, decision-makers have a 'hunch' about what the right outcome should be. Facts and rules are secondary to that moment of insight.

Scandinavian realism arose from scholarly research on Freud's psychology and the work of the logical positivists. Their perspective on law can be summarised as treating legal and social norms as emotive statements which have a psychological impact on the recipient. Cast in the language of 'emotivism', this gives legal norms the same status as any other normative expressions: they are intended to persuade and exercise rhetorical force.

These are, therefore, two different 'realisms' perhaps best distinguished by what they are opposed to. American realism takes a realistic perspective on legal processes, opposing the *unrealistic* claims about legal processes made by other legal theorists. Scandinavian realism is a philosophical realism opposed to the *idealism* – the ideals, and certain kinds of rationality-focussed perspectives on law – often relied upon by other schools.

4a Realism and normativity

Realism is both practical and sceptical. Realists encourage us to refocus our attention on the functioning of legal language in Courts and in society. When we focus on what is normal in these contexts we discover that, while the language of law and legal rules has great 'potency', the reality of law is much less impressive than the ideal. Legal actors see themselves as problem-solvers rather than scientists discovering norms. Legal rules sometimes govern behaviour, and sometimes do not.

The normal functioning of law has its own logic, particularly in common law systems where rules and practices have been honed through the trial and error of casework. This view of the evolutionary 'wisdom' of the common law could be grounds for supporting formalism: the clarity and logic of rule application. However, when conjoined with philosophical pragmatism, it can also support the view that law is not a web of rules but the – culturally and historically contingent – *practices* of legal institutions. In reorientation towards legal practice and the everyday decision-making processes of law, we discover the real source of legal normativity: the traditions and expectations of the legal profession. Normativity does not have coherence, correspondence, logic or any other such stable foundation. In the words of Oliver Wendel Holmes, 'The life of the law has not been logic: it has been experience' (quoted in Bix, 2004: 92).

This is not to say that all realists reject theorising in favour of the description of legal judgment. Many realists would see themselves as part of a 'science of prediction', looking to combine accurate descriptive of the normal functioning of law with a prescriptive analysis of where and how 'good' or 'right' decisions are achieved. The practice of law does create normative standards of good decision and right judgment, and it is the distinctive contribution of realism to try to expose how such standards arise within general legal activity. Namely, through the insight and wisdom of individual judges, rather than the scientific application of rule to fact.

What this also entails, more sceptically, is an exposure and puncturing of the mythology of 'autonomous' rules. There is a tendency within positivism to treat rules 'governing' legal decisions. Realism associates that normative force with expectations; expectations legal actors are expected to fulfil. This anti-formalism insists that law is not reducible to mechanical application of rules, and it denies that law can be treated as a deductive system allowing the imputation of rules from a set of first principles. The real normativity of law lies in practices and expectations that surround legal decision-making. This means that norms vary frequently and illogically. Legal practices, and the societies that give rise to legal practices, will naturally vary over time and legal normativity will vary accordingly. Any more uncompromising view of legal norms is guilty of being *un* realistic: 'law must be more or less impermanent, experimental and therefore not nicely calculable. *Much of the uncertainty of law is not an unfortunate accident; it is of immense social value*' (Frank, 2009: 7, emphasis in original).

EXAMPLE

United States v Kirby 74 U.S. 482 (1868) United States Supreme Court

An Act of Congress prohibited 'wilfully and knowingly' obstructing the movement of post within the United States. Kirby and a number of others did precisely this by stopping a steamboat in Kentucky; they were, however, law enforcement officers apprehending a known criminal. Their actions fell clearly within the Act: should they be convicted? A realist and realistic answer is that we must rely on the 'common sense' of judges, not the rules of the law which were clearly contravened.

There can be but one answer, in our judgment, to the questions certified to us. The statute of Congress by its terms applies only to persons who 'knowing and wilfully' obstruct or retard the passage of the mail, or of its carrier; that is, to those who know that the acts performed will have that effect, and perform them with the intention that such shall be their operation. When the acts which create the obstruction are in themselves unlawful, the intention to obstruct will be imputed to their author, although the attainment of other ends may have been his primary object. The statute has no reference to acts lawful in themselves, from the execution of which a temporary delay to the mails unavoidably follows. [. . .] All laws should receive a sensible construction. General terms should be so limited in their application as not to lead to injustice, oppression, or an absurd consequence. It will always, therefore, be presumed that the legislature intended exceptions to its language, which would avoid results of this character. The reason of the law in such cases should prevail over its letter. [. . .] The common sense of man approves the judgment mentioned by Puffendorf, that the Bolognian law which enacted, 'that whoever drew blood in the streets should be punished with the utmost severity,' did not extend to the surgeon who opened the vein of a person that fell down in the street in a fit.

4b Scandinavian realism

Scandinavian realism represents a radical anti-metaphysical move in legal theory; a rejection of law as a unique normative system as well as a rejection of foundations in accounting for the normativity of law. Its view of law can be best summarised in its reductive view of legal language. Legal language is one, among others, type of persuasive social discourse. The 'oughts' and 'shoulds' of legal discussion have reality only to the extent that they have that persuasive psychological effect.

The school has its origins in psychological and psychiatric research in the early twentieth century, research exploring individuals' relationship with authority and the 'internalisation' of social norms (Ross, 2004: 70–4). We can be compelled to act through threats and coercion, but the authority of law (like other sources of such authority such as parents, politicians and officials) relies on the rhetorical force of their instructions and, to be fully effective, on our acceptance of those arguments and authorities as part of our *own* will and identity ('internalisation'). This psychological research, drawn upon by the founding figure of Scandinavian realism, Axel Hagerstrom (1868–1939), treated legal language as nothing more than a language able to empower the speaker and elicit feelings of compulsion on the part of the hearer. The potency of legal language, its 'magical' capacity to both compel us to act and to *accept* its compulsion, is completely explicable in psychological terms.

Consequently, the Scandinavian realists encourage us to reject any normative explanation of law other than the description of behavioural patterns. Our behavioural patterns demonstrate the extent to which we have accepted and internalised certain forms of behaviour as authorised. All the prescriptive normative claims that we attribute to law should be reduced to descriptive claims about what we do.

> The word 'ought' and the like are imperative expressions which are used in order to impress a certain behaviour on people. It is sheer nonsense to say that they signify a reality. Their sole function is to work on the minds of people, directing them to do this or to refrain from something else – not to communicate knowledge about the state of things. (Olivecrona, quoted in Spaak, 2011: 172)

Through these minimal explanatory commitments, the analysis of law can be made consistent with the verificationist demands of logical positivism: meaning should only be afforded to *behaviour* not normative claims *per se* (Ayer, 1970).

Some variations within the school are significant and rest on what kinds of non-psychological factors could also be considered significant. For Karl Olivecrona (1897–1980), the cause of obedience to law is a combination of internal factors (will, fear and compulsion) combined with external factors, particularly the respect afforded to law-makers and law's symbols of authority. The documented psychological capacity to internalise authority – to treat laws as arising from within us – is reinforced by being associated with the special rituals, displays and symbolism of law. For example, in English culture the police are sometimes referred to as 'The Law' reflecting our association of law not with abstract rules but with the physical presence of law enforcement agents on our streets (see Stolleis, 2009). Alf Ross links this with the wider, ideological and psychological, foundations of law:

> The force exercised by the police and executive authorities is not based solely on physical factors, such as the number of men at their disposal, their training and weapons, but on ideological factors as well. Were all citizens to conspire together, they would undoubtedly be stronger than the police. But this does not happen. The law-abiding citizen respects the police. The power of the police is based for the most part on this respect in conjunction with the feeling the police themselves have as exercising their authority 'in the name of the law'. To generalise, one may say that the physical means of compulsion must always be operated by human beings. (Ross, 2004: 56)

While the ultimate 'reality' of norms must be seen as psychological, legal norms are distinguishable from moral norms because they are seen to be more effective than moral norms. Legal ideas give rise to social practices and social phenomena which show us that law is *predictably* associated with force. This predictability marks out a special class of (legal) norms, those most likely to be considered binding or authoritative.

In sum, Scandinavian realism stresses the centrality of descriptive norms and argues that explaining 'law' is explaining what is likely to happen in *predictive psychological terms*. Thus the school seeks to be 'scientific' in the sense that law must be explained through behavioural observations, but not 'pure' in Kelsenian terms. Kelsen separates legal norms from the rest of the world; Scandinavian realism embeds them in our lives. While this overcomes the abstraction that is characteristic of Kelsen's position, the Scandinavian realists are less able to explain the subtleties of legal decision-making.

After all, judicial decisions are not fully explained as the result of internalised conceptions of authority but aspire to a particular kind of *consistency* (see Ross, 2004: 128f).

EXAMPLE

'The Protection of Civil Rights Act', 1955 [India] Section 7, 7A

Scandinavian realism encourages us to look at the whole range of social norms and the means by which they are enforced. Religious norms (which often involve various types of 'inclusion' of religious believers and 'exclusion' of non-believers) can become social and legal norms sanctioning social and economic marginalisation. This was especially pronounced in India's caste system. Here we see a legislative effort to remove the general discriminatory assumptions and the economic practices associated with discrimination.

[A] person shall be deemed to incite or encourage the practice of 'untouchability' if he, directly or indirectly, preaches 'untouchability' or its practice in any form; or if he justifies, whether on historical philosophical or religious grounds or on the ground of any tradition of the caste system or on any other ground, the practice of 'untouchability' in any form. / [7A. Unlawful compulsory labour to be deemed to be a practice of 'untouchability':] Whoever compels any person, on the ground of 'untouchability', to do any scavenging or sweeping or to remove any carcass or to flay any animal or to remove the umbilical cord or to do any other job of a similar nature, shall be deemed to have enforced a disability arising out of 'untouchability'.

4c American realism

American realism shares with Scandinavian realism a distrust of metaphysics and an interest in descriptive norms. Originating in US law schools, it combines aspects of rule scepticism, of positivism, and above all a parsimonious (the minimum necessary) approach to explaining law and legality. The latter point is significant. American realism attempts to explain law and legality by the least complex, least metaphysically extravagant, means possible. Eschewing appeal to anything other than the hard materials of case law, the constitution and day-to-day legal decision-making, American realism suggests that we can have a philosophy of law that is also recognisable and attractive to practitioners of law. That does not, of course, ensure that it is a good theory of law, but it is one that avoids exaggerated philosophical claims.

American realists would agree with positivism in its account of how law is distinguishable from other social institutions, namely through its being a set of obligations generated by rules that have a particular kind of pedigree. However, positivism can become formalism: the assumption that the answers to all legal questions can be discovered through the use and application of rules. For the American realists, rules are much less important than what legal officials do with them. There are a multitude of legal rules, rules can always generate contradictory answers, and there is always need for judicial discretion in deciding on what basis, and in which way, rules should be used. The most important dimension of the 'life of the law' is not the rules themselves, but the practices whereby judges make selection among rules (and among the facts to be brought under rules) in order to reach a conclusion.

The work of Karl Llewellyn (1893–1962), concentrated on law as the arbitration of disputes in Court and is associated with 'rule scepticism'. Judges make decisions about which facts to include and exclude in order to construct, not discover, a decision. With different exclusions and inclusions cases could have been decided otherwise (Ingersoll, 1966). For these reasons we should pay close attention to the style of reasoning found in judicial decisions and the rhetorical moves by which they harness the facts and rules to a solution. Such studies show us that the facts and rules are not the basis of a logical deduction: judges are professional decision-makers who make intuitive choices supported by the materials at hand.

Jerome Frank (1889–1957) also emphasised the choices that judges make among rules, and particularly their choice of facts; his work is associated with 'fact scepticism'. Each and every legal decision is 'under-determined' by legal rules, leaving the choice of relevant *facts* to the judge. This construction of legal answers through selection of facts and rules means that a legal decision is always a decision for a particular case, not the discovery of 'the' right answer. A legal decision is a 'hunch' to which rules are fitted, *after* the hunch, as justification. Facts themselves are always filtered, arranged and interpreted by a (fallible) judge:

> If his final decision is based upon a hunch and that hunch is a function of the 'facts', then of course what, as a fallible witness of what went on in his courtroom, he believes to be the 'facts', will often be of controlling importance. (Frank, 2009: 119)

It is this kind of analysis that allows the realists to insist that law is exclusively 'the decisions of the Courts': law is *only* law when a Court has made a decision about the application of a rule:

> For any particular lay person, the law, with respect to any particular set of facts, is a decision of a court with respect to those facts so far as that decision affects that particular person. Until a court has passed on those facts no law on that subject is yet in existence. (Frank, 2009: 50)

Undoubtedly, there are strong forces working on judicial decision-making, both rational and irrational, and it is the distinctive merit of the American realist school to concentrate on the institutional demands made on judges (for example the desire not to have a decision overturned) as opposed to the emphasis on behavioural cause and effect in social life (as per the Scandinavian realists). There are, nonetheless, limits to this style of analysis (see Gilmour, 1961). First, there is a danger of parochialism. While it works well to analyse a legal system (the United States) which has an influential and long-lived constitution, this foundation this does not necessarily exist elsewhere. Second is a more general failure to account for the importance of justice in our view of law. Judges are trained problem-solvers, and the attractiveness of legal processes is expert, and consistent, solutions to problems. However, the ends of law, including the common good and the rule of law, are more than the sum of law's parts. They are the ideals with an unclear, but nonetheless irreducible, role in our understanding of law. Emphasis on the judicial arm of government places too little stress on the wider relationship between law, politics and the common good.

Finally, a defence of rule indeterminacy is not without its problems. Certainly, hard cases seem to demonstrate that legal rules are *under*-determined. The scope of a rule may not be able to encompass every situation and it may be ambiguous. This does not entail that all rules are *undetermined*, i.e. capable of any interpretation (Solum, 2011). In simple cases, where law and facts are not disputed, the rules may give rise to the *right answer*. Moreover, the social norms underlying legal norms have a degree of stability which allows for the right understanding and right interpretation of rules. Such criticisms notwithstanding, the American realists' orientation of legal theory towards the norms of judicial practice can explain why law is used as a route to problem-solving: because the judiciary itself exhibits predictable behaviour and represents a class of problem-solvers with training and experience in complex problems.

EXAMPLE

Roth v *United States* 354 U.S. 476 (1957) United States Supreme Court

Obscenity is an area where considerable judicial latitude is granted and Roth *is an influential US case. It created a test of obscene material: 'whether to the average person, applying contemporary community standards, the dominant theme of the material taken, as a whole, appeals to prurient interest.' There are important questions to ask about the normativity (indeed the reality) of 'contemporary community standards'. We should also ask realist questions about whether judges are equipped to make estimations of such attitudes or whether we are happy to for them to use their judgment in these matters.*

[I]f 'obscenity' is to be suppressed, the question whether a particular work is of that character involves not really an issue of fact, but a question of constitutional judgment of the most sensitive and delicate kind. Many juries might find that Joyce's 'Ulysses' or Bocaccio's 'Decameron' was obscene, and yet the conviction of a defendant for selling either book would raise, for me, the gravest constitutional problems, for no such verdict could convince me, without more, that these books are 'utterly without redeeming social importance.' In short, I do not understand how the Court can resolve the constitutional problems now before it without making its own independent judgment upon the character of the material upon which these convictions were based. I am very much afraid that the broad manner in which the Court has decided these cases will tend to obscure the peculiar responsibilities resting on state and federal courts in this field, and encourage them to rely on easy labelling and jury verdicts as a substitute for facing up to the tough individual problems of constitutional judgment involved in every obscenity case.

5 Force and power

Introduction

We have talked throughout our analysis of 'the force' of rules and norms. At times this sounds merely metaphorical. A rule or obligation does not force us in the same way that a strong wind or a gunman forces us into acting. However, while normative accounts of the 'force of law' seek to dissuade us from thinking of law as command or violence, it may be that even by appealing to a 'sense of obligation' or the 'compulsory nature of law' or law 'binding us' we are obscuring a very real relationship between law and power. This relationship need not take the form suggested by command theories – such theories clearly over-simplify the nature of legal obligations – but power takes many other forms than commands and threats.

There is certainly something appealing in Hart's belief that a theory of law is not defensible if it cannot distinguish the demands of the sovereign and the demands of a gangster. Also, following Alexy, we might say that there is something necessary, but innocuous, in linking law and force:

> It seems to be quite natural to argue that a system of rules or norms which in no case authorizes the use of coercion or sanction – not even in case of self-defence – is not a legal system, and this is the case owing to conceptual reasons based on the use of language. Who would apply the expression 'law' to such a system of rules? (2004: 163)

Conversely, Scandinavian realists in particular, emphasise the compulsory force that legal discourse exerts upon us through its relationship with the symbols of authority, and our own psychological capacity to 'internalise' law: 'In law, fear of sanctions and a feeling of being bound by what is valid work together as integral motive components of the same action' (Ross, 2004: 61). In this sense, law forces us to act in certain ways through its 'conspiring' with our psychology to compel us. This is more than having an 'internal point of view on legal rules' whereby we 'accept' or 'acknowledge' the binding force of rules. With its hint of 'indoctrination', the internalisation of law points towards the conclusion that the social activities and institutions we see as making compulsory demands are ultimately activities and institutions capable of exercising force and violence. In other words, the command theory does not give us a complete account of legal rules and their functioning, but it is correct to assume that in the background of what we gently describe as law's 'efficacy' or its 'obligatory force' are coercive social institutions and threats. Even when we understand law as 'reason-giving' or 'action-justifying', this is against a backdrop of a sovereign state's force, power and violence.

Before moving any further it is important to distinguish force, violence and power. These terms have different meanings in different contexts; force and power in particular are often synonymous, but we can certainly draw distinctions between the predominantly *real* and the predominantly *ideal*. The use of violence, namely physical threat or physical harm, is undoubtedly real. This can be distinguished from 'force' which is often something ideal; the 'force of law', like the 'force of an argument', is more frequently related to *ideas* rather than real violence (Fish, 1988). Power can be both real and ideal: the use of violence, or rhetorical and argumentative force. While these categorisations may be contestable – Hannah Arendt's *On Violence* (1970) proposes a slightly different categorisation – they should sensitise us to the range of physical and mental events that can be associated with the 'force of law'. All three – force, power and violence – will be our concern.

5a Norms and repression

Is there something repressive about law and what does repression mean? Nietzsche's *Genealogy of Morals* is an account of the emergence of morality (Nietzsche, 1998). At its heart is an inversion of Hobbes' account of our emergence from a state of nature. It rejects benign notions of freedom from fear and the consent of the people, in favour of the emergence of forms of repression associated with law. Nietzsche centralises legal ideas of responsibility, contract and punishment in our expulsion from the state of nature. Its significance for our purpose is that many of the ideas found in Scandinavian realism are given an anthropological basis, it explains why the 'force of law' has such potency, and suggests why law should be seen as intimately tied to power.

Nietzsche's account of the genealogy (origins) of morality is intended to be provocative. Morality is treated throughout the text as a biological response to our environment, not a set of eternal truths. Nietzsche adopts a 'state of nature' narrative to show how it is that morality, as a form of human self-repression, could have emerged. This narrative does not chart our liberation from nature, but treats the emergence of morality as a point of decline in the vitality and happiness of humans. While Hobbes treats our emergence from nature as a positive step – that any law provided by a sovereign is better than a situation without law – Nietzsche treats the change from a natural state to one governed by laws as disastrous for the human as an animal. We could rely on our instincts in a natural environment. In a world governed by social expectations and norms the natural instincts have to be suppressed: 'One burns something in so that it remains in one's memory [. . .] only what does not cease to give pain remains in one's memory' (1998: 37). The suppression of instincts is not a simple product of societies deliberately repressing certain behaviours, but a millennia-long process of the emergence of social ideas (right and wrong) and social institutions (law and religion) which seek to justify and celebrate the suppression and taming of the human animal. On this account, our subjection to norms is not a process of those more powerful than us threatening us with *violence* lest we fall short of those norms. It is a long process of our learning to see suppression, self-denial and self-subjugation as natural and valuable. Such is the basis of real *power*.

This account depends upon Nietzsche's 'biologism': a tendency to judge human practices against standards more usually applied to the natural world. This is unsatisfactory on a number of levels given the multiplicity of ways in which we assess both human actions and human institutions (see Chapter 2). However, it does provoke us to understand power in a more complex way than many other models of social existence. Violence is one small part of how norms are created and enforced. As feminist scholarship shows (Chapter 2), the 'natural' has ideological force and can be used to justify injustice. Nietzsche is more radical than this. The suppression of our instincts is a central element of social norms and laws, and law helped to make this unnatural suppression natural. Moreover, the idea of 'power' is thereby given a much more nuanced meaning because we can be subject to both *real* violence and the force of *ideas*, both of which shape our social world and shape our self-perception.

Finally, Nietzsche places ideas of contract and responsibility close to the heart of all social practices, from law itself to wider moral ideas. This inversion of natural law's account of the origin of law (i.e. that morality precedes law) is also provocative and depends on a 'state of nature' model. The natural human animal, like other animals, would *react* to the world. The socialised human animal is compelled to *remember*, i.e. develop a complex relationship with its own past actions and those of others. The capacity to remember is essential to humans' social being because it is the basis of making other, repressive, norms effective. Without memory of what we have done we cannot be made to feel guilty about it, and without the capacity for guilt there is no effective way for people to repress themselves.

> Precisely here there are promises made; precisely here it is a matter of making a memory for the one who promises [. . .]. In this sphere, in contract law that is, the moral conceptual world of 'guilt', 'conscience', 'duty', 'sacredness of duty' has its genesis. (1998: 40–1, emphases removed)

Put another way, while an animal that is punished will refrain from doing that action again, a human that is punished is encouraged to see themselves, their past actions, and their identity in a new light: to devalue themselves and their past actions. Thus, memory is essential for this process of self-devaluation, a process that we now take for granted in the context of punishment. Society hopes that the punished individual will disown their own past selves and past actions. And such devaluation is, for Nietzsche, at the heart of law, society and power (1998: 35f). To remember that we are responsible for our actions, to remember that we owe a debt to others or to society, and to remember our own past errors, is the psychological structure that makes other social practices and social norms possible: 'for this, man himself must first of all have become *calculable, regular, necessary,* [. . .] in order to be able to vouch for himself *as future,* as one who promises does!' (1998: 36, emphasis in original). Accordingly, the social practices and social institutions, such as law, that we take to be the index of a positive progress in humanity, depend upon the unnatural demand that we remember, and hold ourselves responsible for, the entirety of our past actions. The force of law arises from the capacity to remember, and the capacity to remember is essential for power to be exercised over us.

EXAMPLE

Bowman and Others Appellants v *Secular Society, Limited Respondents* [1917] A.C. 406

This blasphemy case represents a conflict between the rules of 'public policy' and the rules of a 'secular society'. It required consideration of whether 'secular' also means 'immoral', and whether one could enter into a contract with such an 'irrational' organisation. The willingness of the judiciary to treat Christianity and public policy as synonymous is questionable and would certainly be challenged by Nietzsche, who identifies Christianity with powerful forms of repression.

[I]f the judges of former times have always regarded attempts to undermine Christianity as contrary to public policy, what ground is there for changing that policy? It is said that public policy is a dangerous principle, but every consideration against introducing new rules of public policy applies equally to abrogating old rules. [. . .] I have perused the rules of the society for the purpose of considering the force of this objection, and although I am of opinion that the society is based upon irrational principles, and seeks to realise a visionary and unattainable object, it is not, I think, to be considered as founded for the purpose of propagating irreligious and immoral doctrines in the ordinary and proper sense of those words. It is not such a society as that a person dealing with it could not acquire the right to enforce a contract entered into with him by the society. [. . .] This implies that if the result of the examination of the rules had been to show that the society was formed for irreligious purposes the decision might have been the other way.

5b The force of law

Hannah Arendt characterises violence as instrumental: it is a means to good or bad ends (1970: 46). This position has intuitive appeal because while violence is often a dreadful occurrence it cannot be denied that it sometimes aims at, and achieves, good ends. Just wars, liberation struggles and self-defence are all ends to which violence can be deployed and all forms of violence that law authorises. However, in his essay *Critique of Violence*, Walter Benjamin (1892–1940) attempts to analyse violence *purely as a means* and not in the light of its possible ends (1979). In an unconventional analytical move, he separates this entirely from the question of what ends violence might serve. He asks what *structure* violence possesses regardless of the ends it serves. His answer is that violence – if it is used functionally at all, and is not purely pathological behaviour – is always a means of generating or preserving law. The state uses violence to maintain law and order; the individual, through violence, is capable of establishing themselves as 'law-maker' or sovereign within a particular context. In the latter sense, 'law' appears to become merely metaphorical, but whosoever uses violence is claiming the power to decide what should happen in a particular context. This is only metaphorical sovereignty if we presume a positivist understanding of law as emanating exclusively from the state. In opposition to this, the *Critique* is avowedly an attack on positivist readings of law (and, by extension, legitimate violence) as arising only from the state. He is, ultimately, seeking to make sense of how a violent revolution could be law-*creating*.

Most violence, whatever its source, is 'law-preserving'. Violence is not a rupture in the fabric of law which needs to be remedied. It can always be understood within a legal framework with violence serving to trigger *legal* responses. Some violence may be 'law-creating', i.e. when through invasion or revolution a new legal order is initiated. In either case, however, violence entails the beginning or the maintenance of law:

> For the function of violence in law-making is twofold, in the sense that law-making pursues as its end, with violence as its means, *what* is to be established as law, but at the moment of instatement does not dismiss violence; rather, at this very moment of law-making, it specifically establishes as law not an end unalloyed by violence, but one intimately and necessarily bound to it, under the title of power. (Benjamin, 1979: 149)

Note that this is not a way of saying that states are necessarily violent, or necessarily respond to violence, but rather that law is never threatened by violence because law is the one thing that always accompanies violence. Furthermore, this does not serve as a justification or a celebration of either law or violence. On the contrary, it should lead us to a pessimistic conclusion that the relationship between the state and the use of violence is *not* a contingent one, but a very intimate and inescapable one.

In his essay 'The force of law', Jacques Derrida (1930–2004) draws upon Benjamin's critique of violence in an attempt to unpack two questions arising from Benjamin's position (Derrida, 1990). The first is how we should understand the 'force of law' and, second, where this leaves the relationship between law and *justice*. Derrida uses the work of Montaigne to articulate law's force as something more than violence: 'And so laws keep up their good standing, not because they are just, but because they are laws: that is the mystical foundation of their authority, they have no other' (1990: 942). The force of law can be seen as something 'mystical' in the sense that it has to be assumed but can be neither discovered nor proved. To that extent, the Scandinavian realists are correct in seeking to work on the assumption that there is an ideal, purely mental, normative force for law, but this can be used to lead away from Benjamin's conclusion that violence always accompanies law to an assumption about the importance of justice. The fact that the force of laws is *that they are laws* implies we are dealing with something more than a system of coercive threats; law, despite its relationship with violence, is an ideal. Put differently, the raw violence of law is not a sufficient explanation of why law can be treated as an ideal. Rather, law's compulsory force has precisely that property we have attributed to norms more generally: they are always ideal and real. The reality of law's normativity is its relationship with violence; the ideal aspect of law's normativity is that the imposition of law always brings with it a sense of the need for justice.

EXAMPLE

'Draft Articles on the Responsibility of States for Internationally Wrongful Acts' International Law Commission, UN Doc A/56/10 (2001), Article 23

Both Benjamin and Derrida were concerned with the significance of strikes as forms of force that may be instances of exceptional 'law-destroying' violence: where one legal system is destroyed but not replaced with another. The International Law Commission presented draft articles concerning state responsibilities, including situations force majeure: literally a 'greater force', like a natural event or massive upheaval which makes the normal functioning of life and law impossible. Law-destroying violence would have to be something like force majeure, an act of God.

Article 23:

Force majeure: 1. The wrongfulness of an act of a State not in conformity with an international obligation of that State is precluded if the act is due to *force majeure*, that is the occurrence of an irresistible force or of an unforeseen event, beyond the control of the State, making it materially impossible in the circumstances to perform the obligation. / 2. Paragraph 1 does not apply if: (a) the situation of *force majeure* is due, either alone or in combination with other factors, to the conduct of the State invoking it; or (b) the State has assumed the risk of that situation occurring. [From the International Law Commission's Commentary on the Article] Material impossibility of performance giving rise to *force majeure* may be due to a natural or physical event (e.g. stress of weather which may divert State aircraft into the territory of another State, earthquakes, floods or drought) or to human intervention (e.g. loss of control over a portion of the State's territory as a result of an insurrection or devastation of an area by military operations carried out by a third State), or some combination of the two.

5c Critical legal studies

Critical legal studies (CLS) is that school of legal philosophy most sensitive to the varieties of force and power at work in law. Whether it takes an 'external' critical perspective, looking at law's role in its wider social context, or an 'internal' critical perspective, analysing how legal processes and institutions betray ideological patterns of reasoning, the complicity between law and power-holding groups is central. In essence, law is said to reinforce social norms that are either unjust (law is discriminatory) or have the potential to be unjust (law can be used to challenge certain forms of discrimination, but at the expense of reinforcing *other* problematic social norms). This school, more than any other, is willing to identify precisely those social norms law *should* be challenging or maintaining.

The historical origins of the CLS group lie in the United States, the political upheavals of the 1960s, and in particular opposition to the Vietnam War (Tushnet, 1991). However, the philosophical origins of the movement lie in both American realism and in continental 'critical theory'. CLS scholars take from American realism opposition to formalism, but they offer an ideological diagnosis (rather than in Jerome Frank's work, psychological diagnosis) of formalism. The very existence of formalism reflects something more than the professional pride of judges claiming to be able to impute legal norms logically and without extra-legal intrusions. It reflects widespread patterns of thinking whereby social injustice can be ignored on the basis that 'rules are rules' and that law is always 'impartial'. Rules are the creation of a particular class and their interests, and law is not impartial in its basic assumptions (Hunt, 1986). Law assumes that property is more important than other basic goods, and it assumes that it should ignore the private sphere, the most important dimension of human life, in favour of the formalised contractual relationships found in the public sphere.

The influence of critical theory (of which Walter Benjamin is an example) is found in CLS' understanding of how social norms, and thereby legal norms, are created and maintained. Critical theory has Marxist origins, but rather than seeing culture and law as 'super-structural' by-products of economic relationships, law and culture are held to have a crucial impact on how economic systems are maintained. While culture and society certainly exhibit the influence of ideology, it has to be assumed that this is something more insidious than the poor being 'persuaded' to accept a subservient social and economic status. Rather, social systems exhibit complex patterns of indoctrination: what might be called 'internalisation' in the language of the Scandinavian realists or 'normalisation' in Foucault's terms (Hunt, 1987). Inequalities are not only legitimised, but treated as cause for pride (e.g. America is a 'land of opportunity' despite its deep inequalities; 'an Englishman's home is his castle' despite England being under the ownership of the Crown and land-owners).

Law has a close relationship with the maintenance of these fictions. It provides authoritative justification for the existing unequal distribution of wealth; it centralises the economic actor in the public sphere while ignoring the labour that takes place in the private sphere; it treats certain (scientific or economic) experts as authorities in order to reach legal conclusions that reflect dominant conceptions of 'normality'. In short, CLS draws together many of the negative ways in which law is based on or reflects social norms (Unger, 1986; Hunt, 1987). The basic responsibility for CLS scholars, therefore, is to work on exposing ideology and demonstrating the inseparable relationship between law and politics. This involves conventional political analysis and campaigning; it can also involve 'deconstruction' of legal decisions to show their internal tensions and faults (Douzinas and Gearey, 2005; see below). This is a noteworthy conclusion. Our early reflections on the justice sought to separate legal and political ideas of justice, a task that could not easily be achieved. CLS gives us the clearest answer to why this might be the case: law and politics are not related, law *is* politics.

EXAMPLE

A Tale of Two Cities, Charles Dickens [1859] (Dickens, 2003: 137–8)

CLS has encouraged a multi-disciplinary approach to law, including analysis of literature. In A Tale of Two Cities, Dickens provides one of the earliest 'courtroom dramas'. Two critical points are at work: Courts are not necessarily the route to justice, and legal language can mask political motives.

> Silence in the court! Charles Darnay had yesterday pleaded Not Guilty to an indictment denouncing him (with infinite jingle and jangle) for that he was a false traitor to our serene, illustrious, excellent, and so forth, prince, our Lord the King, by reason of his having, on divers occasions, and by divers means and ways, assisted Lewis, the French King, in his wars against our said serene, illustrious, excellent, and so forth; that was to say, by coming and going, between the dominions of our said serene, illustrious, excellent, and so forth, and those of the said French Lewis, and wickedly, falsely, traitorously, and otherwise evil-adverbiously, revealing to the said French Lewis what forces our said serene, illustrious, excellent, and so forth, had in preparation to send to Canada and North America. This much, Jerry, with his head becoming more and more spiky as the law terms bristled it, made out with huge satisfaction, and so arrived circuitously at the understanding that the aforesaid, and over and over again aforesaid, Charles Darnay, stood there before him upon his trial; that the jury were swearing in; and that Mr. Attorney-General was making ready to speak.

Questions

Section 1

- What kinds of normative claims do we commonly encounter?
- Is everything that is 'normal' an obligation? Does 'obligatory' admit of degrees?
- Is law binding in a way that is different from the obligations found in morality? If they are binding in the same way is this because they serve the same ends (regulation of conduct) or have the same form (generalisation)?

Section 2

- What is the relationship between prescriptive and descriptive norms? Does the fact/value distinction require that there is no possible relationship between the two, or rather that for descriptive norms to become prescriptive norms additional justification, or additional force, is needed?
- Is analysis of law through the imputation of norms applicable in common law systems with their emphasis on judges' identification and application of rules?
- Could a *Grundnorm* have content? That is, rather than being a purely formal constitutive norms, could the *Grundnorm* assert, for example, that 'law should realise the good'?

Section 3

- Are descriptive norms reducible to prescriptive norms (and *vice versa*)? Note that description of normality or regularity in human conduct could be seen as testifying to underlying laws (prescriptive norms) governing that normality or regularity.
- Should law *reflect* social norms; would it be effective if it did not? Should law *change or shape* social norms; would it be – morally or socially – justified if it did not?
- Should economic models inform the creation of policy and legislation? Does economic theory provide the right assumptions about the rationality of persons?

Section 4

- Are realists right to neglect discussion of *foundations* in favour of description of the *functioning* of the law?
- If we could accurately predict the outcome of legal processes to a high degree of certainty, would this give credence to a formalist defence of the priority of legal rules, or a realist emphasis on the importance of legal practitioners and their virtues?
- Is 'lawyering' ultimately about prediction? Are lawyers those who are best able to predict whether someone will do something (in court or in the course of a legal relationship)? If this is the case, does it mean that a good lawyer could predict the outcome of a case but fail to explain how a field of law is structured?

Section 5

- Is self-control always unnatural and is law, therefore, always non-natural? If so does this effectively refute all natural law philosophy?
- If we conceded that the force of law is somewhere between the threat of violence and the 'force' of rhetoric, would the best account of law be a realist one, or would positivism and natural law also have an explanative role?
- Does 'justice' mean 'criticism of law'?

Concepts and methods: Critique

Critique

Evaluation and criticism of law and laws has been a recurrent theme throughout our conceptual survey. Concepts such as good, right, justice etc. are critical not only in the sense that they serve important roles in jurisprudence, but also because they offer means to criticise law, and criticise claims about law. Criticism of law can be specific ('this is a poor law') or, more commonly in jurisprudence, general: that a legal system as a whole lacks certain essential qualities or fails to meet a fundamental goal.

Specific criticism of laws, by lawyers, is a kind of 'internal critique': it uses means internal to the system – rules or principles – to criticise other parts of the system. *General* criticism of laws and legal systems can be understood as 'external critique': it stands outside the system using tools of analysis that are non-legal. American realism – to the extent that it is critical – offers a kind of internal critique of legal theory and legal training showing that legal processes fall short of the formalist model. Critical legal studies represents a form of external critique using tools from the social sciences and political philosophy to challenge illegitimate assumptions in legal thinking.

In philosophical terms, there are three main strands of critique used in contemporary philosophy, and each is present in legal philosophy. The first is Kantian or 'transcendental' critique. This seeks to find certainty at the most fundamental level possible, i.e. the basic certainties possible in epistemology (knowledge) and metaphysics (reality). This is critique in the sense that all claims to knowledge from the senses (and certainly the received truths of tradition) are treated with suspicion unless they are founded upon basic truths about the conditions under which knowledge is possible.

The second strand of philosophical critique is 'genealogical' critique associated with Nietzsche. This is a critical approach concerned primarily with values. It shows that values are at work in even ostensibly objective enquiries into knowledge and reality. It seeks to show the presence of these values within *all* of our activities, implicitly and unconsciously supporting our claims to science, knowledge and certainty. These are often *bad* or *unsupportable* values that arise from human need, or human self-delusion, rather than insight into truth.

A third might be termed 'therapeutic' critique. This is associated with philosophers as diverse as Socrates and Wittgenstein. It suggests that the essence of philosophical enquiry is criticism of philosophy's *own* traditions and assumptions. That the basic philosophical responsibility is to show either that we are all ignorant of the truth (Socrates) or that philosophical problems are the result of confusions in thought and language (Wittgenstein). In either case, philosophy is a kind of 'therapy' for curing misapprehensions in our thought.

Genealogies, genealogical fallacies and *ad hominem* arguments

The origin of ideas is rarely crucial to understanding how they are used in debate. For instance, we can discuss the function of legal sovereignty without caring about its origin in religious thought. Nonetheless, sensitivity to the origins of an idea or argument can alert us to ambiguities in its use. The idea of a 'genealogy' suggests that the ideas we use today may not have the kinds of origins that we assume, and that they may have mutated or evolved from very different kinds of ideas and institutions. A genealogy of 'good' is provided by Nietzsche, who charts the change between good as antonym of 'bad' and then of 'evil'; he suggests the opposition between good and evil has questionable psychological origins (1998). Genealogical analysis entails that we should not assume that ideas, concepts and principles used in discussion have had a simple origin or beginning. Ideas such as the 'good' may have mutated over time, and it may be of particular significance if the idea's antonym has changed.

A common move in debate, but a debased kind of genealogy, is an '*ad hominem* argument' asserting that a claim should be judged on the basis of the person who makes the argument or their character. Avoid *ad hominem* arguments: ideas need judging by their content, not the character of the person who makes them. This is an instance of a genealogical *fallacy*. The fallacy is judging the value of something by its origins. Because certain things began life as repressive practices (punishment, or arguably law itself) does not mean that they are now repressive or illegitimate.

Deconstruction

Deconstruction is one of the most radical philosophical approaches. While the name is often associated with the general thrust of 'critique' (i.e. analysing why things are possible at all), deconstruction is a specific term of art. It concerns the analysis of texts (including philosophical writing and legal decisions) with the intention of exposing implicit oppositions within the text: mutually constituting oppositions which are unstable and which undermine the coherence of the text as a whole (see Hunt, 1987; Douzinas and Gearey, 2005). The opposition at the heart of Western philosophy is said to be between presence and absence (we generally prioritise what is here and now, though that cannot be understood without reference to what is absent). The opposition between speech and writing is often crucial in philosophy (we prioritise speech as an immediate and present thing, but speech presumes distinctions that are only possible through writing).

This approach has been applied to legal texts (e.g. Goodrich, 1990). Legal decisions draw upon a range of different classifications, but many of these are ultimately reducible to the 'universal *versus* the particular' and the 'necessary *versus* the contingent'. A deconstructive approach would see these as reducible to more fundamental, and problematic, ideas: both the universal and particular are contained in the idea of 'classification', and both the necessary and contingent contained in the idea of 'possibility'.

Do not treat oppositions as absolute unbridgeable poles of debate. Very often, oppositions share hidden assumptions, or are so reliant upon one another as to make them inseparable. This is true of 'foundationalism *versus* constructivism': foundations can be constructed; constructions serve as foundations. Both could be captured in the idea of an 'origin'. Note that deconstruction emphasises 'texts' rather than truth. The importance of this is that, unlike critical theory, there is no assumption that we can get to the truth. Rather we are reliant upon language as a means of conceptualising the world, but language is always susceptible to attack in its use of classifications and oppositions.

● Interdisciplinarity and the interstitial

This chapter, in using social, historical and sociological theory, has strayed far from the legal materials commonly used in learning about law. However, legal institutions and legal practitioners draw upon the whole fabric of human life, and with it a panoply of ideas and texts. It has been said that 'law is a scavenger, feeding off the leftovers of other disciplines' (Elliott, quoted in Hoeflich, 1986: 96); legal scholarship is wide-ranging, and indeed has to be. Put more generally, G.E.R. Lloyd expresses why we should be critical about drawing neat disciplinary boundaries, including boundaries between law and other disciplines:

> Current academic boundaries evidently serve a dual role, both liberating and constraining. They liberate in that they enable the student potentially to reach the frontiers of knowledge in the field. But they constrain in that specialisation inevitably entails a narrowing in the focus of interest. Narrower and narrower specialisations are a phenomenon of twenty-first-century science especially, where interdisciplinary or cross-disciplinary interests are frowned upon as diluting the concentration on the specific problems at the cutting edge of research, when they are not condemned as evidence of hopeless superficiality. (Lloyd, 2009: 181)

Classification demands drawing clear and distinct boundaries. Such boundaries may be finely drawn, but any kind of classification is likely to be, to some degree, a falsification of reality. Reality itself does not exhibit difference and opposition: these are classifications we impose on reality, and this is especially applicable to law. Law demands the creation of classifications, and while these classifications are always challenged and refined by the demands of legal disputes, they can never hope to be perfect 'mirrors of nature'. Classification is useful, but it is a human practice, not an insight into reality.

Respecting difference, and avoiding over-hasty classification, are traits of a legal system founded on liberal principles. We cannot impose our assumptions on others, and nor should we seek to impose our classifications upon them. We respect difference first of all by acknowledging it: differences of class, race, gender or ability. Acknowledging such difference should not be a means of marginalising or criticising difference. It is the means by which difference is recognised and through which measures can be put in place to ensure equality. Nonetheless, however refined such categories become, they do not reflect human reality. There are degrees of membership of a class, race and gender. There are degrees of physically or mentally 'normal'. The classifications used by law may not fit the self-perception or lives who those who are classified. Moreover, individuals fall into multiple categories: race and gender, or disability and class. Accordingly, the movement in social theory emphasising the 'interstitial' seeks to draw attention to those lives and experience at the meeting-point of classifications (e.g. Roach Anleu, 1992). Law has trouble recognising such complex social experiences – it needs clear classification – but without recognition of them it cannot claim to classify in a way that will do justice.

Law and art

The relationship between law and art, like art itself, varies considerably between times and cultures. Different cultures not only have different legal systems, but engage in different representations of legal practices. In any context, such representations are influential in the wider cultural understanding of law. This has two consequences. It contributes to our awareness of law and, as the Scandinavian realists argue, it is our awareness and imaginings about law that are its salient characteristic, not its rules or its institutional practices (see Spaak, 2011), and much of that representation involves criticism and parody. This may be for a number of reasons, but its consequence is to reinforce the view that law is a *distinct* part of the social world, not part of its normal or every-day proceedings. This gives more support to those positions associated with the right and the good: law has as special moral responsibility that separates it out from other social practices (the good) or it has its own rules and standards of correctness (the right).

The merit of considering law's relationships with the arts – in film, literature or the visual arts – is not simply representation. Art does more than represent, indeed not all art is representative of social or natural reality. Art has a relationship with knowledge, albeit a complicated and perhaps destructive relationship. Art can cultivate our 'emotional intelligence' (as Aristotle would argue), it shows the limits of the knowledge provided by our senses (as Kant argued), and it can even be seen as disruptive of knowledge (as in Plato's defence of censorship). Accordingly, when we consider the relationship between art and law we are certainly considering the cultural and psychological impact of representation, and this is crucial to the Scandinavian realists and some CLS scholars (e.g. Stolleis, 2009). We are, however, also considering the limits of our knowledge and the potential for reality to be greater, or at least more complicated, than our cognitive capacities allow us to perceive.

Law itself can be treated as a field of literature. An approach explored most frequently by the CLS school but arguably a dimension of any legal education, legal materials demonstrate specific styles of writing and trends in what is acceptable, good or legitimate legal writing. In short, legal writing is a genre. It involves narratives: stories about chains of events expressed through the ideas and vocabulary of a distinctive tradition. Furthermore, it is not surprising to note that writing – common law judgments in particular – are characterised by rhetoric: styles of writing intended to persuade. Appeal to authority is, of course, important legally, and this has stylistic consequences in the centrality and deference afforded to authorities.

Stylistically, it is undoubtedly true that legal language is also 'dry', i.e. systematic, lacking in excessive ornamentation, and lacking in warmth. This too is a consequence of law's rhetorical dimensions and its need to return frequently to authority. However, it also means, more particularly, that there is a distinctive absence of interiority. The interior lives of the people involved in legal disputes (excepting the views and perceptions of some judges) are absent or conceptualised in such a way as to become unfamiliar. Criminal cases, for instance, are rarely interested in motivation, that is, a rounded and full narrative of how someone came to decide to do something and the personal experiences that informed that decision. Rather, criminal law is concerned with intent – intention to bring about consequences – and this is gauged through objective behavioural patterns, not personal testimony. In short, legal texts, and the genre of the legal decision, are in some respects unappealing, but attention to these aspects of law can alert us to where critical concepts such as the good, the right and the person are being used, and perhaps abused.

Further reading

MacCormick (1998) provides a complex combination of approaches to norms, one that is in keeping with Hart's *Concept of Law* but that is much more attuned to law's institutional practices. Important work on norms has been undertaken by Korsgaard (1996); an introduction to her work can be found in Del Mar's review of (2007). Sylvia Delacroix's has written generally on norms (2006) and has also written on Kelsen (2005). There is no simple introduction or approach to Kelsen's work, but Bobbio and Zolo's is among the most accessible (1998). Posner (2000) makes a range of interesting and challenging points about law and social norms. Tapp and Levine (1974) explore the idea of norms within legal institutions from an American realist perspective, while Ross (2004) offers the fullest account of Scandinavian realism. Stanley Fish (1988) gives sustained attention to the 'force' of law. The best recent work on critical legal studies is Douzinas and Gearey's (2005).

Visit **www.mylawchamber.co.uk/riley** to access tools to help you develop and test your knowledge of legal philosophy including Podcasts on leading thinkers and theories, discussion questions, diagrams showing interrelations between concepts, and weblinks

 mylawchamber

7 Law

Introduction

There are two reasons why discussion of this clearly crucial concept has been delayed. The first concerns the complexity of the idea of 'law'. It is only by having first analysed concepts intimately related to law that the multiplicity of perspectives on law becomes apparent. Through these concepts we have encountered law as an institution, as a goal and as a means. These concepts show law to be, variously, a source of truth, a set of rules and a by-product of social forces. From the perspective of these concepts law is something both ideal and all-too-human.

The second reason for deferral of direct analysis of law is a consequence of adopting justice as our starting-point. The idea of justice encourages us to pursue intuitive questions about law, namely its goals and its means. The complexity of law's goals and its means gives rise to philosophical questions which are both analytical (conceptual and linguistic) and normative (related to values and ideals). The idea of justice led us towards a range of questions concerning language, truth, morality, politics and social philosophy.

As a consequence of commencing with justice, we have resisted engaging in a purely analytical exploration of the concept 'law' and have, instead, engaged with both analytical and normative philosophies. More specifically, we have considered the formal characteristics of legal systems (rules); what law aspires to or should be judged by (justice, the good); the internal logic of law (right); and what might be said to give rise to, or sustain, legal practices (persons and norms). The contribution that these core concepts make to our understanding of law is enormous. However, deducing neat generalisations about law from them is difficult. The conflicting claims made about these critical concepts, along with the variety of legal practices putting them to use, illustrate the difficulty of giving law a simple characterisation.

This difficulty making generalisations is true even if we concentrate on analytical questions rather than normative questions. Conceptual and linguistic analysis requires, in the first instance, clarity about what is being analysed. However, at a conceptual level, it is not clear whether we should be concentrating on law's sources, its structure or its goals; at a material level, it is not clear whether we should prioritise law's rules, its institutions or its procedures; and at a linguistic level, it is not clear whether 'law', 'laws' or 'legal' should be the primary focus of our analysis. For these reasons, it is unclear whether we should be analysing the concept 'law' at all. Like the concepts 'society' or 'justice', 'law' can be said to serve as a useful, if general, term under which more specific ideas can sit. Worse, insistence on finding a correspondence between the word 'law' and a clearly delineated group of *things* would be to misunderstand meaning in Wittgensteinian terms: i.e. meaning as the various, and potentially contradictory, *uses* of a word.

Related to this tendency to demand a correspondence between word and thing, analytical approaches to law can fall prey to the hasty, and conceptually dangerous, assumption that Dworkin labels the 'semantic sting' (1998: 42–4). That is, to assume that despite various *philosophical* disagreements, those inside the legal profession *must* have a shared idea of law, or else their disagreements over matters of law become nonsense. That is, they must already implicitly agree on everything that *could be considered law*, or else use of the word 'law' by legal officials would represent an anarchic linguistic battle to make *any* claim about law fit their conclusions. On the contrary, says Dworkin, lawyers do not simply sort through an agreed category of facts labelled 'the law'. Legal professionals are required to be creative; judgment in difficult cases requires 'interpretative debate among rival conceptions of law' (1998: 99). In short, we should not assume that philosophical uncertainty over the meaning of 'law' obscures universal legal consensus over what should be considered 'legal'. Hard cases involve resolving *legal* uncertainty over the meaning of 'law' and 'legal'.

Assuming that, despite these pitfalls, unfolding or explicating the concept of law is nonetheless desirable, philosophy offers several examples of 'ideal types'. The label 'ideal type' is Max Weber's (1978: 23–5) and denotes the employment of an exaggerated and simplified version of reality for the purpose of analysis and comparison. In different ways, the philosophies of Hart and Finnis are powerful attempts to do just this. Hart's *Concept of Law* presents us with the ideal structural characteristics of a legal system. The merit of Hart's ideal type is its distinction between the obligatory, as opposed to compulsory, dimension of legal rules, and the governance of rules by other rules. One problem with this ideal type is that Hart seems to have isolated the characteristics of a 'mature system of governance' rather than law *per se*: the union of primary and secondary rules could be said to be an aspect of any carefully regulated social organisation.

Finnis presents us with an ideal type related to law's *purposive* character, and the need for individuals and societies to exercise practical reasonableness through the governance of rules. The ideal type of a legal system is a system that harmonises with, and uses, practical reasonableness in the governance of human affairs to achieve the common good. This picture captures many of the ideas that are most closely associated with what humans are, what humans need and how law should be tailored to human interests. It also constructs an 'ideal type' that downplays the autonomy we think important in legal systems: law generates *right legal answers* to legal problems and, to that extent, law is distinguishable from other means of finding *good* answers to problems.

Nonetheless, Finnis and Hart's ideal types provide illuminating conceptions of law. They do not intend to encompass all aspects of legal reality, only the core functions or forms. Moreover, they are not intended to be normative models by which a legal system can be gauged to have failed or succeeded. All real systems fall short of ideal systems. Rather they are intended to draw out basic, formal, characteristics to which systems approximate to a greater or lesser extent.

Rather than assert and defend an ideal type, the present chapter seeks to provide a general classificatory scheme. It discusses law's *formal* properties, law's *functions* and its *foundations*. This classificatory scheme reflects some fundamental philosophical questions and methods. To discuss the foundations of law we are employing the idea of ontology, analysis of how things can be said to exist. To capture the formal properties of law we turn to phenomenology, the science of appearances. To analyse the functions of law we have to return to ideas of value, reason and justice.

This philosophical framework shows all of the competing schools of legal philosophy – normative and analytical – to be useful. It also highlights a number of ways in which we have to augment, or go beyond, the traditional jurisprudential schools in order to make sense of the many forms that law takes and functions that law serves. This remains an analytical task: providing the basic classifications required for conceptual understanding of law. However, it also has a critical element in showing that the main schools of jurisprudence are not, alone, complete explanations of law. As such, this chapter is intended to be both a summary of the previous chapters and an argument concerning the usefulness, and limitations, of each of the schools of legal philosophy.

1 Foundations

Introduction

Philosophy is concerned with the foundations of knowledge. But 'foundation', as much as 'knowledge' itself, represents a philosophical *problem*. Can we find things – facts, human capabilities or basic mental intuitions – that are certain and reliable, on which we can build a body of knowledge? Furthermore, can we find those foundations without assuming the very things we wish to prove? In the context of law this requires us to show what law *is*, without already assuming that certain laws, or sources of law, or legal institutions, provide the best starting point for our enquiries.

Such a seemingly simple requirement – to provide an account of what law is without making a presumption about the priority of certain sources or ideals – leads us into fundamental questions about knowledge.

Knowledge can only be gained through the capacities with which the human being is equipped. Through either ideas or the senses. In either case, a foundation for knowledge is identified, a foundation from which other forms of knowledge can be securely derived. Sound use of the mind leads to well-founded *understanding*; the evidence of the senses is the bedrock of reliable *enquiry*. The sceptical philosopher is one who either denies that such foundations are reliable, or that the foundations can produce the other kinds of knowledge that were hoped for. Having a defensible starting-point is one thing. It is quite another to prove that reliable or incontrovertible knowledge is possible.

The foundations of knowledge about law are somewhat clearer but also contested. Public institutions and public practices are the *source* of legal rules, but the *justification* or *authority* of those rules and institutions can be questioned. This represents a shift between philosophical points of view. Not only between factual sources and normative justifications, but between ontologies: how law can be said to exist at all. By arguing that even acknowledged sources of legal rules (e.g. a government) lack authority (as in cases of civil disobedience) law is being identified as something separable from social sources and existing only on the basis of its possessing moral or other authority. The existence of law can, therefore, be said to depend upon real sources or ideal justifications.

However, we cannot *assume* that either is the best starting-point; we have yet to *prove* that one is more important than the other. We have to 'put the question marks deeper' (Wittgenstein, in Hacker, 1997: 7) and ask whether real sources, or ideal justifications, can be said to be better foundations for legal knowledge. Immediately prioritising real sources or ideal justifications would be over-hasty in the same way that choosing our minds or our senses as the foundation of knowledge would be over-hasty. Both certainly lead to knowledge, but there are wider frames of analysis within which the two starting-points can, themselves, be assessed. We can ask in philosophy what it is for knowledge to exist at all (Kant's critical project), and, by extension, ask *what is necessary for law to exist at all?* This question is critical: it demands putting aside the knowledge we already have in order to explore the preconditions of knowledge. It is also ontological: it asks for the necessary conditions for something to be said to exist.

Three basic ontologies of law are possible: law is transcendent, it is immanent or it is self-subsisting. These treat the existence of law as (respectively) wholly outside human life, wholly inside human life or depending only upon itself for existence. These will be explored more fully below, but the importance of considering ontology and not just *sources* can be illustrated by returning to, and problematising, the positivist's 'social thesis' and in particular Raz's variation on this, the 'sources thesis'.

The sources thesis is not only concerned with insisting that particular social institutions are the sources of laws, but with emphasising 'that the existence and content of every law is fully determined by social sources' (Raz, 2009: 46). Laws exist because of societies and social practices. Nothing else is necessary for a law's existence, no external validation or justification. This can be contrasted with a weaker separation thesis claiming 'that the identification of the existence and content of law does not require resort to any moral argument' (Raz, 2009: 296). That is, law is always *found* in social practices and socially created laws, although it may be the case that certain spheres of law contingently contain (but do not *necessarily* contain) ideas found in morality. To this can be added a third, even weaker, claim about social sources and the meaning of 'law': ordinary language dictates that the word 'law' denotes something arising from human affairs unless we choose to stipulate otherwise. That is, 'law' generally denotes something with a social source, though it is also used in other ways (Raz, 2009: 316).

On these three accounts, the *sources* of law are certainly social. However, the sufficient conditions for the existence of law shift: social rules, social institutions or socio-linguistic practices. The common-denominator is something social, but what is meant by 'social'? Rules, practices and institutions themselves depend upon different kinds of things: generalisations, behaviour and language. These dimensions of the social themselves change over time; they depend upon norms which have no single, sustained, presence in the social world. On this basis we could conclude that *law is a set of norms possessing no stable content and no stable continuity through time*. This conclusion would be congenial to Scandinavian realists, but it is not the analytical conclusion, dividing law from non-law, intended by the positivist social thesis.

Nonetheless, we can describe the common-denominator in these positions as their having an understanding of law's foundations as *immanent*: found exclusively in the social world around us. This might be thought to encompass those meta-theories of justice offered by Rawls and Nozick (see Chapter 1). These theories of justice rely on extra-legal accounts of justice, but that extra-legal justice is an aspect of the human world, not another 'normative realm'. Indeed, many contemporary natural lawyers could be said to be interested in the values immanent in human life and human needs rather than treat values as having origins beyond the social world (see Chapter 3). The sources thesis is, of course, directly challenged by classic natural law. Early natural lawyers relied upon the claim that law originates in something that *transcends* human activity. Equally, however, some positivists, such as Kelsen and Simmonds, are also concerned with transcendent, Platonic or Kantian, claims about law's ultimate origin or source.

Both transcendent and immanent accounts of law's existence depend upon substantial philosophical underpinnings. They have to account for how law has stability and continuity through time (in the immanent account) and how it is that we could know law at all (in the transcendent account). A realist and pragmatist response might be that such philosophical underpinnings are neither discoverable nor useful. They are not discoverable in *practice* because the 'life of the law' is decision-making not 'foundation-finding'. They are not *useful* because they make no difference whatsoever to how law is conducted. The only conclusion compatible with this attack on foundations is to adopt the sources thesis in a different form. To treat law as arising from society, but now independent of society and sustaining itself: it is self-subsisting.

1a Transcendent

The idea of transcendence indicates that which is beyond our senses and beyond our social world. This is often associated with religious ideas of the world as created or understood by God. It also has philosophical use designating the point at which knowledge and metaphysics meet. Transcendent truths are the basic truths – about the world or our nature – which must hold good for us to know anything with certainty. This kind of argument is in evidence whenever we ask whether there is 'more to law' than our society's creation and use of law, and 'more to law' than the procedures and decisions of legal institutions. There is an ideal law which we recognise, partially and imperfectly, in the law of the land. Without this ideal we would have no understanding of the true nature of law and have no grounds for criticising existing laws. Plato's radical idealism is one example of this; Kant's appeal to the 'moral law' is another. Each can be understood as offering ideal types: law as an ideal, immutable, structure of which reality is an approximation.

Plato's position is that law has a transcendent foundation, namely justice. Such idealism, wherein law has an ideal template towards which the real aspires, continues to feature within legal philosophy long after the metaphysics associated with Platonic 'forms' has been abandoned. It is found in the assumption that there is a correct form that law should take and which legal systems approximate in 'the here and now'. Law 'proper' is a form towards which legal systems should move, and an unchanging standard with which to combat complacency about existing legal institutions (Simmonds, 2007). In many respects, the language of justice alone sustains this Platonic ideal (as in Derrida's work, see Chapter 6). Through justice, we criticise law for being imperfect, or as yet incomplete, without necessarily being able to articulate what justice would be in each and every case. *Real* law continues to generate ideas of *ideal* justice, and it is the language of justice that is the underlying 'force of law'.

A transcendent source of law is also associated with religious traditions. Revealed religion promulgates laws originating in a non-human realm. Not only does law have its existence secured by something beyond the social world, but also the proper shape and conduct of human lives. Religious views of law share with Ancient philosophy the assumption that law should make people good, ensuring that humans fulfil their function or destiny. If modern states (i.e. those centralising freedom) do not subscribe to this teleology, we nonetheless still think of law as something that speaks of the best in human endeavour and that reflects our potential as a species.

This teleology is partly secularised in Kant's idea of the 'moral law', the universalis-able duties binding the rational subject (1948: 67f). While insight into the moral law is achieved through human reason, reason itself transcends the individual: 'a purely rational belief is the signpost or compass by means of which the speculative thinking can orientate himself on his rational wanderings in the field of supra-sensory objects' (Kant, 1991: 245). Reason is the structure required for any intelligible perspective on the world, and obedience to duty is nothing more or less than conformity to rational laws as binding as those governing the universe. The moral law gives rise to ethical and legal obligations that are universal, basic commandments providing the foundation of all other laws. While the complexity of social life prevents this from being easily translated into a legislative programme (hence Kant's need to provide both a 'doctrine of virtue' and a 'doctrine of right', see Chapter 4) the underlying assumption remains attractive. There are not only local laws but also universal laws, and these are universal on the basis of their necessity, not their contingent social value.

EXAMPLE

Sophocles, *Antigone* (from The Three Theban Plays) (1984), pp. 81–2

This work of Ancient Greek drama remains a touchstone for theorists defending transcendent foundations for law. Antigone transgresses the law laid down by her monarch, Creon, which forbade burying a traitor. She appeals to a higher law that demanded respect for a relative: a transcendent justice that always supersedes or takes precedence over human laws.

Creon: And still you had the gall to break this law? / Antigone: Of course I did. It wasn't Zeus, not in the least, who made this proclamation – not to me. Nor did that Justice, dwelling with the Gods beneath the earth, ordain such laws for men. Nor did I think your edict had such force, could override the Gods, the great unwritten, unshakable traditions. They are alive, not just today or yesterday: they live forever, from the first of time, and no one knows when they first saw the light.

1b Immanent

The opposite of transcendence is immanence. This limits knowledge to what is immediately known of the world around us. On these grounds, the existence of law is located exclusively in the social and psychological existence of humans. While prohibiting appeal to anything transcendent, immanence encourages us to explore the fact that law permeates *every* aspect of the world around us. Law is not a distinct social institution: it is part of the fabric of our lives. We equate law with rules, but law is, more importantly, the 'glue' which binds society together. Our social lives could not take the form that they do without being regulated by law.

One way in which this can be articulated is that 'the people' are the foundation of law. That 'we' are the origin and justification of law finds expression in Rousseau's social contract theory. Another route, pursued by the Scandinavian realists and others, is to identify law with language, explaining law's existence through the ubiquity of the language of law.

The idea that 'we, the people' are in some sense the origin or foundation of law has its origins in the Revolutionary era, but this does not have to be narrowly construed as meaning that law *functions* to serve the interests and welfare of the many. It can be a more fundamental claim that law exists in or through the 'will of the people'. This echoes social contract theory, and Jean-Jacques Rousseau's (1712–78) work is part of that tradition. Rousseau wrote for a particular context, pre-Revolutionary France, and two elements of this context shape his thinking about law (see Solomon, 1988). First, the 'divine right' of monarchs, as a transcendent source of legal authority, is questioned. Second, there is a search for a replacement for the authority of the monarch. Finding a replacement is hampered by both the attractiveness of placing legal authority in the hands of one individual, and the diversity of interests among the populace.

In the background of Rousseau's social contract narrative is a view closer to the Biblical, rather than the Hobbesean, picture of the pre-legal world. The natural ease and plenty of the natural world was disrupted by the divisive intrusion of private property (Rousseau, 1968: 192–4). With the creation of society, along with law to protect property, humans were compelled to engage in commerce and competition, and conflict naturally arose from this. Thus the principal characteristic of the modern the state is loss of freedom, captured in Rousseau's famous maxim 'man is born free; and everywhere he is in chains' (1968: 3; see also Morrison, 1997: 153–6). However, amidst this conflict and competition, the sovereign represents the total, collective, will of a populace and is able to pursue the underlying demands of social existence: the 'general will'. Rousseau's social contract is the recognition of, and bringing to life through law, of the general will. The basic, natural, desire for peaceful co-existence. Law is the 'register of the general will' (Rousseau, 1968). Law is the underlying spirit, and underlying rationality, of a populace when the conflict of acquisitive competition is put aside in favour of the natural unity of human interests.

Law, as the register of the general will, supersedes individual freedoms. The loss of freedom necessary for social existence is replaced by the freedom associated with government by the people and for the people. Potentially repressive consequences flow from this: 'whoever refuses to obey the general will shall be compelled to do so by the whole body. This means nothing less than he will be forced to be free'

(1968: 15). Nonetheless, the movement towards legality is in accordance with the *spirit* shared by humans, even if individual humans are self-serving: 'equality of rights and the idea of justice which such equality creates originate in the preference each man gives to himself, and accordingly in the very nature of man' (1968: 25). Also, legality is perpetually justified – is necessarily just – in spite of the fallibility of humans and institutions: 'the general will is always right and tends to the public advantage [. . .]' (1968: 23).

Rousseau, with his idea of law existing in and through the people, gives an immanent foundation to law. He identifies law with our fundamental (though superficially diverging) interests. However, the idea of immanence also discourages us from identifying law's existence in the *ideal,* and from seeking foundations in terms of *essences.* Rousseau is encouraged to talk of a general will because this serves to replace the unity of law and legality provided by a monarch; the general will replaces this with a no less powerful 'body politic'. Such essentialism is problematic. As we found in discussion of 'humanity' (Chapter 2), attributing agency or interests to humans as a whole is difficult to defend. A return to Scandinavian realism and Wittgenstein's idea of a 'form of life' are useful at this point to show that immanence does not have to involve essentialism, i.e. attribution of an underlying unity to humanity.

Our language pushes us into essentialist assumptions; we assume that a word must correspond to a 'thing'. Is it possible to understand law as a purely immanent, social, phenomenon without falling into such essentialism? Certainly the presence of law in our lives can be gauged by our relationship with the word 'law'. Any competent English language user can use the word. Competent language users share a great deal of agreement over what this word is intended to mean, even if they had little or no direct knowledge of particular laws. We use the word 'law', and it is rarely confused with the homonym 'lore'; we engage in a meaningful, successful, conversation about 'the law' without having to read any legal instrument. This does not show that use of the word 'law' has an essential meaning; it demonstrates that law has a 'presence' in our lives. This rejection of meaning as *correspondence* in favour of meaning as *use* (see Chapter 5) serves useful analytical purposes.

It is significant that, for the most part, English language users cannot use the words 'law' and 'morality' interchangeably. Compare 'there is a law against speeding' and 'you have a moral obligation not to drive at speed'. The first has an immediate sense and force, while the second is an invitation for further discussion. These words have different meanings, which is to say they are used for different purposes. As such, the two things are, in one respect at least, not the same thing. There is a stability and predictability in our use of 'law', and its use marks a distinction (however opaque) with other words. Furthermore, this stability and predictability arises from our shared practices, our 'form of life' in Wittgenstein's terms (2001: 75). Thus, to the extent that 'law' has a stable and constant presence in our lives, it is because of our *practices* and our *language,* not because of its essence or ideal form:

both the idea of the state's divine omnipotence and the idea of a will of the people prevailing evaporate in a sober-minded consideration of the real state of things. It is because of the respect for an established system of rules that the always relative authority of the state exists. (Olivecrona, quoted in Spaak, 2011: 182)

EXAMPLE

'Decision of the State Council Regarding the Question of Rehabilitation through Labour' (Chinese National People's Congress on 1 August 1957)

Chinese law encompasses legislation, 'people's courts' where administrative decisions can be challenged, and various guifanxing wenjian (normative documents) issued by government departments and officials. Here, criminal legislation is tied to the general will; the measures allow rehabilitation, and therefore reintegration into the whole.

The following decision regarding the question of rehabilitation through labour is made [. . .] with a view to reforming those persons who are able to work but insist on leading an idle life, violating law and discipline, or will not engage in honest pursuits, into persons who are able to support themselves through their own labour, and to further maintaining public order, thus facilitating socialist construction: (A) Persons of the following categories shall be interned for rehabilitation through labour: (1) Those who will not engage in honest pursuits, involve themselves in hooliganism, commit larceny, fraud or other acts for which they are not criminally liable or violate public security rules and refuse to mend their ways despite repeated admonition; (2) Counterrevolutionaries and anti-socialist reactionaries who commit minor offences and are not criminally liable and who have been given sanctions of expulsion by government organs, people's organizations, enterprises or schools, and as a result have difficulty in making a living [. . .].

1c Self-subsisting

Whatever our understanding of the word 'law', its use denotes 'order'. Be it the ordered structures of the natural world, or the order found in any structured, 'law-governed', human practice. A legal order is a social and institutional arrangement exhibiting, and providing, predictability or regularity. More than that, law can be said to be an institution characterised by *self*-ordering: an autonomous process of developing its own basic assumptions, putting these into practice and then revising its assumptions. Law can also be said to be society's self-ordering: it is not through the decision-making of politics, but through subjecting itself to law that a society *creates*, and not just *manages*, itself. Law is the ongoing effort of society to create good order for itself. We have seen how, through rules and through the enforcement or amendment of social norms, law orders our society. Here we consider law's self-ordering and, with it, the idea that law depends only on itself for its existence.

Law's self-ordering can be understood as a circle:

> There is thus a characteristically legal 'circle', a sense in which the system (as the inter-related rules and institutions are significantly but loosely called) 'lifts itself by its own bootstraps' – a sense captured by the more scientific but still literally paradoxical axiom that 'the law regulates its own creation'. (Finnis, 2011: 268)

This explains the preoccupation of many theorists with 'hard cases' (Freeman, 2001: 1391–2), i.e. where law does not have the resources to answer a question or seems to generate contradictory answers about a question. In these instances, law it-self allows judges to make an intuitive decision about justice (Hart) or requires judges to make a decision about what would be most coherent given the underlying political commitments of a community (Dworkin). For Hart, legal systems are self-regulating because certain officials are authorised to 'fill the gaps' in the rules (1994: 134–5). For Dworkin, legal systems are self-regulating because those officials are required to show law in its 'best light' as possessing coherence, continuity and integrity (1998: 225f). This goes some way towards explaining the 'paradox' (in Finnis' terms) of law's self-regulation: it is not only constituted by malleable rules, but has the structure and resources necessary to develop or augment those rules in a non-arbitrary way.

Both Dworkin and Hart's positions can be expressed differently in terms provided by Niklas Luhmann's (1927–88) theory of 'autopoiesis'. For Luhmann, law is a sys-tem, but the idea of a system often involves 'reification': taking something abstract and treating it as a real or concrete thing. This is to obscure the fact that systems depend upon *relationships*, not tangible objects. Drawing upon research in biology, Luhmann approached law as a kind of organic system characterised not by its institutions but by the communication between its parts. Biological entities such as animals have physical elements, but their claim to be a system lies in the fact that the parts work together, reacting to one another and contributing to the functioning of the whole. Biological entities are thereby said to be 'autopoietic', meaning that while they func-tion in a wider environmental context – a context on which they depend and to which they react – they interact with the environment through their own, distinct, systemic processes. By extension, a legal system is part of a wider society – it depends upon and reacts to social needs and individuals' activities – but it is distinct and self-contained.

> This is what Luhmann calls the legal system's normative (or operative) closure. Normative closure denotes that norms do not change merely on the basis of factual conditions. Normative change occurs on the basis of autopoietic reproduction: the superimposition of norms onto norms. (Philippopolous-Mihalopoulos, 2010: 71, emphasis removed)

Social conflicts are drawn into a legal system and processed – analysed, classified and adjudicated – by the distinctive practices of that system. In this sense, a social conflict does not 'enter' the legal system; rather a conflict is 'processed' within a system and a distinctively legal answer is produced: 'legal' or 'not legal', 'legal win-ner' or 'legal loser'. Law's unique ability to distinguish lawful and unlawful is more than a function: it is the defining characteristic of law as a system. It 'determines the systemic boundary in relation to other social systems: law's monopoly on deciding between lawfulness/unlawfulness is at the same time the law's limit' (2010: 73). In this way we can respect the distinctive practices and meanings that are characteristic of a legal system (law has its own language, institutions and processes) and acknowledge law's relationship with other social forces (law reacts to its environment and reorganises itself in response to that environment), but still see law as an *independent* and *dynamic* system of communication.

There are a number of merits to this model. First, it is both dynamic and organic; legal systems are closely related to the 'soil' in which they grow and the problems they encounter, but their growth and change is the product of law's own internal resources. Second, it specifies the systemic aspect of law – a system of communication – without reducing the 'system' to particular institutions which are prone to change through time. It also means that we can refuse commitment to either transcendent or immanent accounts of law's existence. Law is not beyond the social world; nor is it reducible to the social world. It is a distinctive, dynamic, communicative practice within the social world.

Law, as a communicative system, contributes to the self-ordering of a community or society. The Greeks had a word for this phenomenon, *eunomia*, meaning 'good self-ordering through law'. The idea of *eunomia* encompasses both the basic assumption that law contributes to the ordering of the state, and the ontological assumption that law is a self-contained and self-regulating system. Societies can manage their own creation through law. They do not have to be created through the force of command or violence.

Philip Allott developed a contemporary theory of *eunomia* after the end of the Cold War (Allott, 1990). For Allott, like Hegel, law represents society's coming to consciousness, in this instance the coming to consciousness of the international community *as* an international community and not a collection of mutually antagonistic sovereign states. The driver of such a consciousness is not deliberate commitment to co-existence under law (it is not utopian), but rather the ongoing development of the existing rule of law in the international arena. Through processes of self-subjection to law – under international treaties and in the European Union – it is becoming clear that legality can now exist without the will of a single, dominant, sovereign power and can exist without coercion and force (1990: 264f). Law has emerged out of the self-regulating of a *community*, not of states. As this process continues, we will be become more aware of our social bonds and less committed to the fiction of the sovereign state, the dangerous fiction that sovereigns *are* the law and therefore cannot be governed by law.

Accordingly, Allott's *eunomia* is a theory of change on the basis of existing social and legal processes and one which represents a shift in our consciousness towards an international constitution.

The ideal constitution is the constitution as it presents to society an idea of what society might be. In the ideal constitution, society organises desire and obligation with a view to its own becoming. [. . .] The ideal constitution is not a fixed star towards which a society steers a fixed course. It is constantly being remade as society's words and ideas and theories and values alter society's idea of its potential self through all the intensive activity of the total social process. (1990: 136–7, emphasis removed)

Admittedly, such a shift in consciousness is difficult. It is often difficult to accept the idea that abandonment of the sovereign state is not a desire for anarchy but a desire for legality; it is difficult to see the 'international community' as more than an analogy with 'real, organic, communities'. But this shift in consciousness allows us to see that law is more than the will of sovereigns; law is a self-subsisting system which governs globally. Law is society's self-ordering through the self-ordering of law.

EXAMPLE

The Charter of the Arab League (March 22, 1945)

Is eunomia an ideal of universality, particularity, or both? Good self-ordering within and among societies is applauded by Allott. Would this include groupings of states founded upon racial or ethnic particularity? Established to ensure harmonisation on legal matters within Arab states, the Arab league identified core goods in its constituting charter. It also adds that the prevention of the use of force is high among its priorities.

Article II: The League has as its purpose the strengthening of the relations between the member-states, the coordination of their policies in order to achieve co-operation between them and to safeguard their independence and sovereignty; and a general concern with the affairs and interests of the Arab countries. It has also as its purpose the close co-operation of the member-states, with due regard to the Organisation and circumstances of each state [. . .]. **Article V:** Any resort to force in order to resolve disputes between two or more member-states of the League is prohibited. If there should arise among them a difference which does not concern a state's independence, sovereignty, or territorial integrity, and if the parties to the dispute have recourse to the Council for the settlement of this difference, the decision of the Council shall then be enforceable and obligatory.

---

2 Forms

Introduction

The form that law takes is not singular. It is not solely the decisions of courts, or the commands of sovereigns, or rules, or norms. It takes the form of classifications, rights, relationships and expectations. To reduce law to any one of these forms is not only culturally and historically narrow but also conceptually inadequate. The set 'classifications, rights, relationships and expectations' contains both the real and ideal; both descriptions of, and perspectives on, reality. The question, then, is whether we can analyse 'the formal characteristics of law' without theoretical presuppositions about the properties law must have.

Of course, to adopt a perspective without presuppositions is not only difficult but contradictory. We always make a judgment from a perspective. We bring presuppositions to bear in determining what 'law' is, namely our foundational assumptions about the sources and nature of law. Even turning this line of enquiry around, and insisting that certain formal arrangements are the defining mark of law (e.g. Hart's union of primary and secondary rules), is no less problematic. It begs a question as to whether this is enough for *law* to exist, beyond the presence of certain formalised activities within our society.

For this reason the starting assumption made here is that there are ways of categorising law's *appearances* which neither demand that 'law must take a particular form' or 'there is an essence of law underlying our different perceptions of law'. The present approach is therefore phenomenological, i.e. it seeks to chart different kinds of appearances without proposing an underlying essence behind those appearances. The phenomenological school of philosophy accepts sceptical conclusions about the limitations of 'truly' knowing the nature of reality, and exchanges this for a 'science' of appearances, of how reality appears to us. The methods used by phenomenologists have differed (see Moran, 2000). However, the basic insights – the importance of our perceptions and scepticism about finding essences – provide a fruitful approach to social practices such as law which take a variety forms and take on different appearances from different perspectives.

The most general set of categories within which to encompass law's appearances concern law's relationship with time, space and change. Regardless of the origins of law, where there is law it is ordered in a way that is intelligible to human beings. Law is structured by time and space, and it is susceptible to change.

2a Historical and territorial

Along with law, our social world is made up of countless complex systems, behaviours and perceptions, but our lives appear to us to have structure or stability. How do we find order in our complex social worlds? *Any* aspect of human life must be structured according to time and space. These are the basic preconditions of any activity or thought. It is these basic structuring principles that mean our perceptions have unity and meaning (Kant, 1929).

Law has its own distinctive relationships with time and space. It is territorial: tied to a particular geographical location, and it is historical: law changes through time, but it preserves its past through archives and through the use, and re-use, of legal rules and norms. These points, while seemingly trivial, draw out the fact that law is dependent on the raw facts of space and recording the past. This encourages us to look again at the insights of historical jurisprudence and its charting of the growth of different kinds of legal system. It also calls into question the nature of 'territory' and how space can take on legal qualities.

There are a number of lines of historical enquiry which see law as having an 'organic' relationship with the culture within which it functions. Be they schools of historical jurisprudence, or sociological theories such as Luhmann's, such historical and sociological narratives describe the ways in which law arises from, and is inexorably associated with, a particular cultural context. The originator of this kind of approach could be said to be Edmund Burke (1730–97) whose defence of the English constitution against revolutionary ideologies stressed the organic relationship between the British constitution and British culture. In opposition to calls for 'rationalisation' of legal systems (the project of Enlightenment philosophers and reformers such as Bentham), such organic relations are said to have a superior 'fit' with the spirit of the people.

In some instances we find this kind of assumption leading to speculation, as in the work of Maine, about the primitive origins of legal systems (Chapter 6). It can also lead to the 'spiritual', and perhaps nationalistic, understanding law found in Friedrich Von Savigny (1779–1861). As an 'expression' of culture, law is tied to the people and practices from which it emerges. For Von Savigny, law cannot be codified or rationalised without violence to the culture from which it emerged and the spirit of the nation transmitted through law.

> Savigny viewed the development of law as a part of the historical development of the common consciousness of a society. Law, he wrote, is developed first by custom and by popular belief, and only then by juristic activity. As a people becomes more mature and its social and economic life becomes more complex, its law becomes less symbolic and more abstract [. . .]. The professional or technical element should not, however, Savigny wrote, become divorced from the symbolic element or from the community ideas and ideals that underlie both the early and later stages of legal development (Berman, 1977: 1711, n. 161).

More rigorous historical research does not necessarily evidence an organic or systematic relationship between a state and its legal system (e.g. Foucault, 1977; Stolleis, 2009), but historical research does offer a strong counter-weight to the temptation to posit ideal types or 'grand narratives' about progress and change in legal systems. For instance, there has been a tendency in Marxist theories of law to assume that law is the by-product of more fundamental economic processes. Closer historical research paints a more complex picture of law's relationship with social life beyond its economic determinants and, indeed, beyond repressive ideology (see Thompson, 1975; Cole, 2001).

The idea of territory parcels the world into spaces where sovereigns exercise effective control over the lives and actions of a population. The discrete parcelling of the world into territory could not take place without law. Territory not only concerns land boundaries, but authority and the limits of authority. As such, territory has real and ideal components. Territory is real in so far as states literally mark and control space: they plant flags, manage public spaces through policing and exercise violence to repel invaders. It is also ideal: it concerns the *recognition* of certain authorities (governments or states) as having legitimate claim to that territory.

The idea of cosmopolitanism challenges this understanding of the necessary relationship between territory and authority. Cosmopolitanism is the pursuit of a single law or legal system that holds universally. The *cosmopolis* is an ideal, global, state of which all humanity is a citizen. The cosmopolitan ideal has roots in Roman legal thought and a body of Roman laws, the *jus gentium,* applicable to the whole Roman Empire (Berger, 1953). This body of laws partly codified, and partly created, legal uniformity across disparate lands. This was premised on the philosophically appealing idea (related to Stoicism) that common laws could be found in existence across different societies and nations, and good governance is a matter of enforcing these consistently and rigorously (Nussbaum, 1997). Conversely, this was a rather more oppressive ideology insisting that uniformity could be and should be enforced on nations whether they were willing or not.

The origins of modern cosmopolitan theory lie in Kant's work. As we have seen, Kant is one the pre-eminent theorists of the right as a moral and legal notion, and his position is one that pushes frequently towards identifying the necessary and universal in politics. For Kant, the cosmopolitan ideal is a universal rule of law that binds states and sovereigns regardless of territorial boundaries (Kant, 1991). This does not mean the destruction of the sovereign state, only universal values being re-spected by states. Kant's idea, which he talks of in terms of 'perpetual peace', a peace among nations without recourse to warfare, is in part narrow. It is an international rule of law, premised on the equality of sovereign states, which leaves the integrity of existing states as they are. Conversely, it is a potentially radical idea to the extent that, unlike Hegel, Kant does not accept the absolute primacy of the state, but rather the existence of a law higher than the state itself: 'The rights of man must be held sacred, however great a sacrifice the ruling power may have to make. [. . .] For all politics must bend the knee before right' (1991: 125).

Kant provokes us, as he provoked his contemporaries, into thinking about the basis and the goals of law, particularly international law. Our present international legal system is 'Westphalian', it flows from the Peace of Westphalia that ended the Thirty Years' War in 1648 and maintains there is no legal authority higher than the sovereign state, and that the sovereignty stems from the successful use of violence ('effective control') over a territory (Steinberg, 1966). Kant's ideas, conversely, point to a 'global' legal consciousness, because all territories on our planet, our globe, are ultimately interconnected. The moral bonds between states may be unclear, but there is no denying that territories have some *de facto* connection in sharing bounda-ries and ultimately sharing the earth. Kant was the first philosopher of law to fully grasp the fact of (actual and potential) globalisation, and his perpetual peace is the first analysis of the phenomenon of political and legal globalisation.

> ## EXAMPLE
>
> ### 'Draft Amendments to the Rome Statute of the International Criminal Court' (7 November 2010)
>
> *The Parties to the International Criminal Court statute are working on a new statutory definition of the 'Crime of [state] Aggression'. At present there is a working text (based on a UN General Assembly Resolution from 1974). This would make the seizure of territory illegal, but it would also leave in place the recognition of sovereignty on the basis of 'effective control', i.e. defensive force and the right of the Security Council to authorise the use of force.*
>
> #### Article 8 *bis*:
>
> > Crime of Aggression: 1. For the purpose of this Statute, 'crime of aggression' means the planning, preparation, initiation or execution, by a person in a position effectively to exercise control over or to direct the political or military action of a State, of an act of aggression which, by its character, gravity and scale, constitutes a manifest violation of the Charter of the United Nations [. . .]. Any of the following acts [. . .] qualify as an act of aggression: (a) The invasion or attack by the armed forces of a State of the territory of another State, or any military occupation, however temporary, resulting from such invasion or attack, or any annexation by the use of force of the territory of another State or part thereof; (b) Bombardment by the armed forces of a State against the territory of another State or the use of any weapons by a State against the territory of another State; (c) The blockade of the ports or coasts of a State by the armed forces of another State; (d) An attack by the armed forces of a State on the land, sea or air forces, or marine and air fleets of another State [. . .].

2b Atemporal and atopic

We see law tied to a particular time and space. It is closely related to societies and cultures; it changes as societies and cultures change, but law also appears to us as one of the most conservative dimensions of social life. Not only are its institutions characterised by preservation of the past, by tradition and repetition, but its use of rules (with their apparent categorical inflexibility) give the impression that law is a strongly conservative force in society. Law can be perceived to be a barrier to change, and dependent upon the maintenance of traditional ideas, principle and institutions.

Moreover, while law's formal characteristics reflect particular places and historical epochs, if we look at how legal rules are structured it becomes clear that law often aspires to be neither territorial nor historically conditioned. Statutes do not claim temporary validity, validity until such time as they are repealed. They claim indefinite authority into the future. And, while their application can be limited to parts of a territory (e.g. 'England and Wales, but not Scotland') they do not claim any origin in a particular place (e.g. Westminster) but claim to hold good *everywhere* that they apply.

Thus, the formal characteristics of law are paradoxical. We know that they have specifiable historical origins (their point of creation, where they were first recorded, and how they have changed over time). But the main material form in which we find laws – cases and statutes – deny these historical and geographical characteristics. Statutes express the law in such a way as to suggest that they only state the law; they are 'enacted' from a particular time and source, but thereafter their force applies at all times everywhere with no concern for their point of origin. Equally, legal decisions do not claim to speak from the point of view of the judges themselves: they are expressions, not of opinions here and now, but of the law. They claim a final, 'perspective free', statement of law in that case. In this way, the form of law may be said to be denial of its own historical and geographical roots. This is an important aspect of the phenomenology of law, its ability to give the impression of timelessness. We will also explore the possibility that law is no longer dependent upon territory.

The ahistorical character of law is a consequence of legal language. Law is a linguistic phenomenon found in written rules and the language of those qualified to profess the law. This language is perceived to be dry, dull and pedantically precise, a stereotype with a degree of truth: governance through law requires careful generalisation. Such is the distinctive 'aesthetics' of legality. This spare, generalising, language of the law is a reflection of law's functions, its need to classify and to justify (see below). But legal language can also be construed as a 'genre'. Legal language is characterised not only by generality, but by its being deliberately ahistorical and atemporal. Put another way, for laws to generalise about obligations they must *appear to be* categorical imperatives binding everywhere at all times, even if, as we have seen, legal rules are better characterised as defeasible rules, not categorical commands.

The CLS movement, with its interest in law as literature, draws upon the work of the novelist Franz Kafka (1883–1924) to understand how law is experienced in modernity (Luban, 1986; Douzinas and Gearey, 2005). For Kafka, the existence of law is immanent, rather than transcendent. It is omnipresent and all-pervasive, and as such oppressive. Law is experienced as the limitless potential to be judged and held guilty. But law's immanent nature gives rise to the formal character of law as countless categorical imperatives: limitless, potentially contradictory, obligations. That is, the *manifestation* of law in Kafka's writing is as something *omnipresent* but nevertheless *timeless* and therefore inaccessible. It is always unclear when a law is made, when a law is applicable, when a legal process begins or ends, or when a law ceases to be in force. This perception that laws have an inaccessible quality is captured in Kafka's parable 'Before the law' (Kafka, 1994: 59):

> 'Everyone strives to reach the Law,' says the man, 'so how does it happen that for all these many years no one but myself has ever begged for admittance?' The doorkeeper recognizes that the man has reached his end, and, to let his failing senses catch the words, roars in his ear: 'No one else could ever be admitted here, since this gate was made only for you. I am now going to shut it.'

This intimates, among other things, that the law is always there, and always there for us to use, but without knowing *when* the law exists – when all of its contradictory promises are in force or not in force – it remains inaccessible. This is an important, though rarely emphasised, characteristic of law: legal language denies its own historical contingency, even when we know that law is historical in nature and subject to change (see Goodrich, 1990).

Law's appearance with respect to space is complex, and globalisation has clearly disrupted the relationship between law and place. A characterisation of law as 'atopic' – without a place – runs contrary to the positivist demand that law be tied to territory. That is, as requiring either a single sovereign governing a territory, or as a system of rules requiring a definable set of institutions governing the rules and their recognition. Such links between legality and place are potentially undermined by transnational legal networks. Transnational law is distinguishable from public international law. The latter represents the contractual relationships between states. Transnational law is the network of legal relationships created by economic globalisation, networks which do not depend upon states.

> Transnational commercial law consists of that set of rules, from whatever source, which governs international commercial transactions and is common to a number of legal systems. Such commonality is derived from international instruments of various kinds, such as conventions and model laws, and from codification of international trade usage adopted by contract [. . .]. [Harmonisation is also driven by] 'soft law' restatements [. . .] which though not binding are regularly resorted to [. . .]. Underpinning these is the *lex mercatoria*, consisting of the unwritten customs and usages of merchants and general principle of commercial law. (Goode *et al*, 2007: lix)

These are networks of relationships, characteristic of contemporary global economic practices, which aim to by-pass many of constraints imposed by the territorial state. This is driven by a distinctive class of actors and their relationships. 'Transnational actors' are any actors whose activities involve investment, commerce or trade in two or more states. This can include multi-national firms, corporations, non-governmental groups or wealth fund managers, all of whom can be characterised as 'strategic actors' looking to build economic relationships which have the stability that we would expect from state-governed legal relationships, but without having recourse to the legal systems of particular states (Likosky (ed.), 2002).

Such strategic actors can be said to form legal 'networks' – as opposed to a distinctive system – and they depend upon norms rather than rules. These norms can be existing norms: 'best practice' in commercial and scientific conduct, or norms of adjudication found in alternative dispute resolution. They can be emerging commercial norms, including expectations about how litigation can be avoided, or expectations about minimising labour and other costs. These emerging norms are referred to as *lex mercatoria*, a law of merchants, suggesting continuity with ancient practices of localised dispute settlement using commercial norms (Teubner, 1997). Such networks can be supplemented by state law. For instance, in agreements over which jurisdictions contractual disputes will be heard in, usually the jurisdiction most attractive to the stronger bargaining party whether or not this is their 'native' state. Their essence, however, is the generation of regulatory networks that do not depend on, and deliberately by-pass, the territorial state in order to ensure economic efficiency and profit.

Even if we were to deny (on positivist or natural law grounds) that these networks have the status of law, they nonetheless constitute the most prevalent manifestation of 'global governance': the regulation of economic activity at a global level. They are also the best explanation of why activities that, from a legal perspective, have no single territorial focus – from contracting with a multinational corporation to using the internet – are nonetheless governed by predictable, rule-governed, practices of arbitration and regulation. Globalisation entails the disruption of the relationship between law and place. However, this does not entail the absence of law, only the increased importance of *norms* rather than rules.

EXAMPLE

Charles Dickens, *Bleak House* [1853] (Dickens, 1971: 74)

Reflecting the perception of law as 'outside time', this novel has a never-ending legal dispute at its heart. Dickens attacks both the unobtainable nature of legal justice and the legal profession which sustains it.

Equity sends questions to law, Law sends questions back to Equity; Law finds it can't do this, Equity finds it can't do that; neither can so much as say it can't do anything, without this solicitor instructing and this counsel appearing for A, and that solicitor instructing and that counsel appearing for B [. . .]. And thus, through years and years, and lives and lives, everything goes on, constantly beginning over and over again, and nothing ever ends.

2c Diachronic

The idea of the diachronic stresses that law is perceived as something *dynamic* characterised by change through time. There is a danger in seeking an 'ideal type' behind the many manifestations of law because, among other things, this neglects the fact that law is always characterised by change. Law's encounters with social reality, and its reaction to dynamic social processes and trends, might suggest that law exists primarily as a reaction to social processes, thereby accounting for law's conservative and reactive appearance. It may also be, more controversially, that law 'progresses', teleologically, on a path towards an ideal state. We will consider the possibility that law changes because it is subject to forces – logical and material – outside law. First, we return to Niklas Luhmann's *autopoiesis* theory, which provides an account of law's dynamic formal properties.

Law creates itself through communication, but this does not fully account for patterns of change within a legal system. To understand the stable processes and patterns of change found in a legal system Luhmann appeals to the idea of 'feedback' (Luhmann, 1988). A legal system 'absorbs' a conflict or dispute by categorising and analysing the conflict by its own, internal, concepts; it then generates a decision about the compatibility of the parties' claims with its own assumptions. Where complex or seemingly irresolvable problems arise, solutions are not simply 'chosen' by those within a system (through judicial intuition or creative interpretation). Law, as a system, is restructuring its own, internal, assumptions to make sense of the problem. Change is not achieved through the importation of something external to the system: a decision is the rearrangement of existing components of that system. This helpfully accounts for law's paradoxical appearance as simultaneously dynamic *and* ordered. Its rules change, but change is governed from within the system.

In contradistinction to Luhmann, we can attribute change to something external to law. Understanding the bases of *social* change – cultural, historical and technological changes in human societies – might well offer a way of understanding changes in law and legal institutions. However, social change is an area of extensive debate and uncertainty (Winch, 1958). It has to presume, first of all, that social change has a pattern and is not simply anarchical mutation of social practices. It also presumes that societies themselves – as entities or stable practices – have a distinct reality of their own explaining their endurance through time. The existence of an authority in a territory may be enough to attribute some basic unity to a society, but the existence of 'an authority in a territory' is surely distinguishable from wider social practices – moral, technological or cultural – which have their own logic of change and progress.

There are two ways of understanding the forces behind social change which, while related, have very different characters and offer different kinds of explanation of social and legal change. The idea of 'dialectics' arises from Greek philosophy and refers to a quality found in discussions, namely that they are characterised by a relentless process of argument and counter-argument (see Morrison, 1997: 26–33). Nineteenth-century German philosophy developed this idea of dialectics, with competing accounts offered by Hegel and Marx.

Hegel (using ideas taken from Johann Gottlieb Fichte, 1762–1814) used dialectical processes to analyse the evolution of human thinking (Hegel, 2008). The importance of this for law lies in the expansion of rationality, not as a project (as in the 'Enlightenment project'), but as the unfolding of legal ideas as they interact with reality. Our ideas may well sit uneasily with reality: legal rules often fail to find a fit with what is possible or desirable for a certain society. Nonetheless, the tensions between social practices and legal regulation will produce something new: new laws and new social practices. Those new laws and social practices will in turn produce new tensions and problems which themselves will be superseded by newer practices. In sum, when reality and law clash tensions and problems will arise. Nonetheless, in the sense of dialectics propounded by Hegel, such clashes and changes will, progressively, lead to more rational law and a more rational society (see Fine, 2001: 24f). The clash of the real and ideal leads towards something more logical, necessary, and universal.

Marxist accounts of the dialectical structure of change have, as can be anticipated (Chapter 4), the material world as their basis rather than the evolution of the ideal and rational. It is the material world, and the use of the material world for our survival and our profit, that drives social change and legal change. Technological changes in the way that we control and manufacture the material world have been changes in terms of speed, efficiency and ownership. With this has come change in the management of social affairs, including greater levels of management, and greater levels of profit for single individuals. It has also meant changes in our experience of work and of each other. We are no longer in a close relationship with the material of the world; we work in more specialised and mechanical ways, and the specialisation of work, along with the flow of profit to a few people owning the means of production, has the consequence that we are 'alienated' both from the fruits of our labour and from the profits that we generate (Easton, 1961). In this Marxist account, law can be portrayed as a peripheral phenomenon, significant only because it helps to maintain the *status quo* and bolster the power of the capital-holding class. However, it also sharpens our understanding of law as irreducibly tied to the processes of manufacture, exchange and nature itself. Law can be seen as a way of justifying inequality and the division of society into different (profit-creating and profit-holding) classes, or it can be seen as part of the process whereby we are alienated from the world and from each other. Either way, changes in law are not the product of internal processes of logic (formalism) or judicial wisdom (realism). Changes in law are symptomatic of inescapable forces outside law: the material world and our relationship with the material world.

EXAMPLE

'Turkey: Restrictions on Imports of Textile and Clothing Products' World Trade Organisation (1999) AB-1999–5

Trade disputes, particularly international disputes, are not easy to settle through the application of legal rules. In the face of power, wealth and vested interests, a combination of law and pragmatism is usually called for. Here protectionist practices are considered in the light of the General Agreement on Trade and Tariffs (GATT) and the rules of the World Trade Organisation (WTO). An intimate, perhaps dialectical, relationship between rules, profit and pragmatism is at work.

> This appeal relates to certain quantitative restrictions imposed by Turkey on 19 categories of textile and clothing products imported from India. Turkey adopted these quantitative restrictions upon the formation of a customs union with the European Communities. The Panel found these quantitative restrictions to be inconsistent with [the GATT agreement]. The issue raised by Turkey in this appeal is whether these quantitative restrictions are nevertheless justified [. . .]. [The WTO holds that] the purpose of a customs union is 'to facilitate trade' between the constituent members and 'not to raise barriers to the trade' with third countries. This objective demands that a balance be struck by the constituent members of a customs union. A customs union should facilitate trade within the customs union, but it should not do so in a way that raises barriers to trade with third countries.

3 Functions

Introduction

The identification of a single function, many functions, or even changing functions for law, is to provoke a number of vexatious debates. First of all, law no doubt serves many functions, but does this mean it has *a* function? To isolate a single function – i.e. a single goal or purpose – would be to lose sight of the reality of law in an over-arching ideal. Conversely, attempting to describe its many functions might be (conceptually or historically) incomplete: given the many formal changes in law and laws, to prioritise certain functions would be to neglect others. It would also threaten conceptual parsimony, finding the simplest possible explanation. So, it is not easy to decide in advance what the scope of an enquiry into law's functions would be. Raz describes three possible ways approaches:

> [First,] the functions that all legal systems necessarily fulfil [because of] certain universal facts of human nature. [Second, those functions] fulfilled by some or most [legal systems]. [. . .] Finally, theorists are interested in claims that legal systems in general or under certain circumstances ought to fulfil certain functions in certain ways. (Raz, 2009: 165)

Each of these approaches will have a role to play in what follows.

Brian Tamanaha's description of law as a 'multifunctional tool' (2008: 15) serves to emphasise that law does have a functional character, that it has many functions rather than one function, and it encourages us to think about a great many things which are routinely, but wrongly, excluded in discussion of law. Paradigm cases of law in action – mediation between two parties in contractual dispute for example, or governing the actions of a number of people through criminal law – distil law's functions into *mediation* and *governance*. Both of these are important functions served by law, but consider law's role in keeping us safe from our own actions, for example wearing a seatbelt in cars. Or law's function to change the way we *think*, and not only the way we act, through race relations or discrimination legislation. These are related to, but not reducible to, ideas of mediation (in an adversarial sense) and governance (in a policing sense). Law is a multi-functional tool for changing our thinking as well as our acting.

Law does not have unlimited functions. On the one hand, 'law does not concern itself with trivialities' meaning, among other things, that law is not a tool for fulfilling our fleeting preferences. On the other hand, there are certain functions that law could not serve and still maintain a relationship with what we commonly take to be *justice*. Using law as a tool to destroy a state and its population would look like a political act achieved through *quasi*-legal means. Law is intended to fulfil certain ends, captured by the idea of justice, which cannot be squared with wholly destructive, or wholly inhumane, objectives. This is not to say that law cannot serve undesirable ends. It suggests that such actions will always generate opposition and resistance pointing to the *misuse* of law (Derrida, 1990).

While law functions in various ways, it is generally associated with positive social functions rather than destructive functions. The challenge of analysing law's function is, therefore, to consider some basic *descriptive characterisations* of how law functions, and some *normative limits* to how law should function. This should clarify some of the questions concerning justice raised in the first chapter. Those debates – whether and how justice is a standard external to law, what it is for law to serve to the common good and whether justice is meaningful at all – challenged us to think about law's functions in the sense of the ends it serves and the means that it deploys. Here, then, we must take account of the values, and not only the facts, of law. We need to find what positive role law plays in our lives.

We consider three functions here: constituting, regulating and justifying. By finding where law fails to fulfil these positive functions, we are in a better position to understand justice and injustice. To *regulate* poorly and allow disparities of power, or irrational principles, to become acceptable in social life, is the most common way for law to fail to fulfil its functions. To *constitute* an unstable state, or fail to constitute defensible conceptions of personhood, is to make poor use of law's creative powers. To *justify* actions that are irrational or unreasonable is an attempt to make normal what cannot be made normal. While these three functions are different, and therefore do not necessarily point to a single function or objective for law, they represent widespread uses law, and widespread uses of law where ideas of justice, good, right, person, norms and rules commonly intersect.

3a Constitute

Analysis of legal rules demanded that we divide those rules which directly regulate our conduct from those prior rules that constitute legal institutions and processes, but the constitutive function of law is more potent than its ability to create legal practices and institutions through constitutive rules. It is the creative power of ideas, practices and expectations. In short, *law is constructive and creative*. It constructs principles to aid problem-solving, it constitutes the legal person, it constitutes the state and it creates ideals that we would not otherwise have. We would not have the idea of citizenship, or of the equality of individuals, or of just retribution, without law. As a society, we could not engage in complex endeavours such as progressive taxation, party politics or social welfare, without law. At the most basic level, the constitution of the state, and the constitution of the person, are among law's most important functions.

The power to constitute the state was evident in discussion of justice. The (corrective) justice of law and the (distributive) justice of politics are difficult to divide completely; law also distributes, and politics also corrects. However, a shared responsibility lies in creating and maintaining the conditions of social coexistence: i.e. law and politics always work together to create the state. Law and politics create the social and economic world that we inhabit; both law and politics are preconditions of the common good and individual rights. Fundamentally, there is a creative relationship between law and politics which allows us to distinguish them, but also adds to the complexity of their relationship. Constitutional law constitutes the state. But the state also constitutes law. The executive, judiciary and legislature are each drivers of law, and each organs of the state. It is this creative, constitutive, relationship between law and politics that allows human coexistence.

The relationship between law and politics is not only the shared responsibility of allowing human coexistence, but also a relationship of mutual constitution. We can understand politics by showing where it differs from law; we can understand law by distinguishing it from politics. Politics without law is brutal; law without politics is socially blind. Without this contrast we would have no sense of what is distinctive about legality. This mutually constitutive relationship is perhaps best understood in the CLS school. While this position is caricatured as reducing all law to politics, in fact it pushes us to understand how what we think of as normal and natural – the norms of social world – are the product of the interplay of law and politics. They shape our very understanding of what it is to coexist, and with this they shape the (ideologically malleable) idea of what is 'natural':

> Most people in the legal academy agree, albeit often with some reluctance, that law is politics in the superficial sense that we can talk about identifiably liberal and conservative positions on various issues in the law [. . .]. The indeterminacy argument and the critique of social theory led CLS to a different understanding of the proposition that law is politics. We saw law as a form of human activity in which political conflicts were worked out in ways that contributed to the stability of the social order ('legitimation') in part by constituting personality and social institutions in ways that came to seem natural. (Tushnet, 1991: 1526)

However, Finnis' centralisation of the common good also captures well the constitutive function of law. The idea of the common good is useful precisely because it is the creative project shared by law and the state: to purposely create a social world where the good can be realised. Extending this, there are ideas of the human, and of human relationships, that could not exist without law. Law not only serves to support a certain kind of good social life, but creates and promotes forms of human life. The 'person' is precisely that understanding of the individual human that most closely reflects our relationship with, and need for, law. That individual humans are recognised as having value, are to be immunised against being treated like animals, and are to be treated equally. This is the implicit normative content of law denoted by the idea of a person. This does not prevent laws being used to abuse individuals, nor does it prevent controversy concerning where personhood begins and ends and what interests personhood can be said to protect (Dayan, 2011; Ohlin, 2002). There is, however, a common-denominator among ideas of justice, human rights, the 'minimum content of natural law', the right, and the good, which limits the functioning of law. Law creates and protects personhood. Where it has been used to diminish or deny personhood it is met with claims concerning justice: something transcendent, immanent or self-contained, in the foundations of law which demands that it be constructive, not destructive, or personhood.

EXAMPLE

Salomon v Salomon & Co Ltd House of Lords, 16 November 1896 [1897] A.C. 22

Here the 'personality' of companies in English law is confirmed. The ability of law to give a single personality to groups of persons in a common endeavour is treated as 'self-evident' provided the criteria established by statute are fulfilled.

My Lords, the important question in this case [. . .] is whether the respondent company was a company at all – whether in truth that artificial creation of the Legislature had been validly constituted in this instance [. . .]. My Lords, the learned judges appear to me not to have been absolutely certain in their own minds whether to treat the company as a real thing or not. If it was a real thing, if it had a legal existence, and if consequently the law attributed to it certain rights and liabilities in its constitution as a company, it appears to me to follow as a consequence that it is impossible to deny the validity of the transactions into which it has entered.

3b Regulate

Many things drive social change – economics, politics, science – and law governs these drivers of change. In fact, law appears more as a *regulator* of social change than a driver of social change.

[Law] enables past, present, and predictable future to be related in a stable though developing order; it enables this order to be effected in complex interpersonal patterns; and it brings all this within reach of individual initiative and arrangement, thus enhancing individual autonomy in the very process of increasing individuals' obligations. (Finnis, 2011: 303)

Social and economic developments take place within a legal system, under the governance of rules, and their impact on society can be altered or managed through law. Accordingly, law 'regulates' not only in the sense of imposing obligations, but law *mediates* between society and the forces that act on society. Understanding this role requires considering the historical context in which legal systems were distinguished from other forms of authority as an independent and authoritative means of social mediation. We will consider how and why regulation is best understood as a normative, rather than specifically *rule*-governed, phenomenon. We will also consider how, in a related vein, law regulates the relationship between different spheres of human life.

It is telling that 'mediation between parties' can be distinguished from 'legal litigation of a dispute'. The former is a semi-formal 'umpiring', the latter a formal process of decision-making, but this is a difference in degree but not kind. The fact that a legal decision can be enforced is (as we have seen with reference to the command theory) not a sufficient condition for something to be legal. The rules by which the decision was reached have to be *recognised* as legal rules. It is the normative background of a mediation process that ensures it is legal: the public practices and mental attitudes that mark off certain rules and decisions as distinctive.

Legal decision-making offers to 'close' disputes more decisively than any other means. This is for various social, economic and psychological reasons, i.e. for reasons related to social *norms* not simply the pedigree of legal rules. Law has a distinctive and respected social status as a means of dispute resolution. Law provides reasons not found elsewhere (Raz, 1994); and because of the force of law – in the sense of force shared by the Scandinavian realists, Derrida, and others – we see law exercising a decision-making power that is distinctive and authoritative. Law neither merely commands, nor merely mediates: it regulates in that it *makes regular*, it provides the underlying stability for social norms. While law is less frequently a direct creator of social norms, it is the strongest social force for stabilising social forces. In sum, law's regulative function is best understood as a normative phenomenon, rather than as a coercive process.

'Regulation' should also be understood on a much larger, social and historical, canvas. The distinction between *de facto* and *de jure* authority is not simply a conceptual division but one with specific roots in European culture. The Medieval period, a high-water mark of natural law thought, grappled with the separation of the legal spheres of Church (*sacrum*) and state (*saeculum*) (Berger, 1953). This was of practical and philosophical significance. Practically, it concerned division of authority between kings and Church in a period where a state system was not in force and many kinds of authority could be claimed over territory. Philosophically, it weighed the authority of the conscience against the authority of the law. Freedom of conscience was by no means as valued or as protected as it is in the modern world, yet the stirrings of a sense of its importance and value was emerging. In short, the autonomy of secular law gave impetus to a view of the individual as autonomous; an independent secular sphere allowed a free-thinking individual to emerge.

The separation of secular and sacred hastened the more general 'separation of powers' that we expect to see in a modern state. The separation of courts and politics allows law to mediate between the individual and the political structure that they inhabit. Thus, put in a wider historical context, the function of law is mediation between spheres of *authority*. This can be illustrated through law's regulation of the public and private spheres. Law's governance of space, particularly its governance of public and private spaces, might be said to be among law's formal properties. Law certainty takes the form of 'territories'. However, it can be argued that this division depends upon values: law's *responsibility* to draw a dividing-line between the public and the private. The public–private division is something *regulated by law* rather than something dependent on space.

The division between public and private has long been articulated in the language of 'spheres'. There are a number of variations of this metaphor, but in essence they point to the existence of a space of choice, self-realisation and preference for the individual (the private), which is excluded from political (public) processes and decision-making. The public sphere is associated with the actions of the state and the governance of state and economy. The private sphere – associated with family, choice, preference and recreation – is (especially in liberal states) insulated from the intrusion of the public (Alldridge and Brants (eds), 2001). This negative prohibition against intrusion is essential to the priority of the right. The good – associated with the fulfilment and flourishing of the individual – is relegated to the private sphere of activity where (while held as valuable) it is not allowed to determine social and political decisions. To allow the good to dominate public life would be to endorse a project of social engineering.

Thus, a division between public and private allows autonomy and consistency. Autonomy is maximised in the private sphere, while the public sphere is characterised by the consistency provided by rights and legislation. In other words, it is essential to the priority of the right. In this sense, the two spheres are mutually regulating: encouraging private autonomy demands limiting the power of the public (i.e. the state and other public bodies); prioritising consistency in the public sphere demands the exclusion of private interest.

This classic, liberal, statement of the public–private divide (often associated with Mill's harm principle) has come under sustained attack from a number of quarters. Feminist criticisms in particular chart how this divide has been used to shield or hide domestic abuse and labour found in the private sphere in order to protect the interests of men (Kruks, 2005). There is also a question of how a 'division' can be said to exist at all. Because of the regulation of our private conduct, and because private bodies can discharge public duties, it is clear that the division is more than the difference between two geographical places (homes and public spaces); it is value-laden, and concerns the duties of both the state and the individual. This can expressed in Lon Fuller's terms as a division between the 'morality of aspiration' (personal excellence) which is the responsibility of the private individual, and a 'morality of duty' (minimum public virtues) which are certainly the concern of the state and legal system. 'There is no way by which the law can compel a man to live up to the excellences of which he is capable. For workable standards of judgment the law must turn to its blood cousin, the morality of duty' (Fuller, 1969: 9). The division between public and private can, in these terms, be understood as a division between different kinds of morality, not spaces. There is an important division between (more or less) 'purely' private places such as the home, where aspiration and even personal excellence are appropriate, and the public places, where the basic rules of public order are applied. Law's dual role is regulating activity in public and private, but also regulating the 'division' itself.

EXAMPLE

In the Matter of A Petition of Right, Court of Appeal, King's Bench Division, [1915] 3 K.B. 649

Private rights can sometimes become the victim of 'public necessity'. Such necessities can include general concerns for social welfare, but also include pressing considerations of national safety in a time of warfare. The present case concerns prerogative powers and the possession of land during the First World War.

It cannot, I think, be disputed, and the suppliants do not in fact dispute, that the King, as the supreme executive authority, was and is now by virtue of the prerogative entitled in certain circumstances of national emergency to take and use the property of a subject or otherwise interfere with private rights in order to provide for the safety of the public and the defence of the realm. [. . .] But it is said that the right is confined to the doing of what is necessary for the conduct of actual military operations against an enemy on the soil of this country. I cannot think that this can be so. So to limit the prerogative would in these days be to render it practically useless for the purpose for which it is entrusted to the King. The circumstances under which the power may be exercised and the particular acts which may be done in the exercise thereof must of necessity vary with the times [. . .].

3c Justify

It is through the ideas of reason, giving reasons and the reasonable that law functions to *justify* individual and collective actions. Reasons – in the general form of explanations, or in the specific form of rules – are important because they justify actions. We can only justify our actions if we have reasons for them: action without reason is action that is irrational, criminal or simply animal impulse. Law's ability to justify is crucial to understanding the functioning of law. However, we will also be concerned with the ways in which justification requires classification, and requires identifying the rational and reasonable, and the fact that this entails a problematic relationship with truth, knowledge and power. In sum, the relationship between law, justification and classification hinges crucially on what can be considered *rational* or considered *reasonable*, and the tension between the two.

Law, as reason-giving, allows us to justify our actions, but law's reason-giving processes also justify law itself. The 'self-justification' of law is not a simple assertion of its authority. Law justifies itself through its use of generalisations, classifications and rules. These lend order and stability to its decision-making. Judgments must involve stable points of reference and cannot be justified if they are the fleeting instincts of a judge. Law cannot justify the actions of individuals, or its own institutional practices, without such stability.

Stability is not the same as predictability of outcomes. Perfect predictability is neither discoverable nor desirable in law. Rather, the means law uses are stable. It is the stability that comes from law's imposition of reasonable rules and categories on life in order to reach a decision. The importance of law as a rule-based system is less the judgments that this allows it to reach, more the fact that classification of the world, and thereby the justification of action, has taken place in a rigorous, public and systematic way. We have encountered the relationship between rules and categorisation, and with it the problems of 'indeterminacy' and over- or under-inclusiveness. While this can be explained in terms of the nature of rules themselves, we should consider some deeper problems generated by law's need to classify and justify.

Classifications allow legal judgment – most fundamentally, as lawful or unlawful – but classifications are also creative. By creating new categories of relationships and responsibilities law is not only constituting new aspects of social reality but also justifying new forms of action and justifying new remedies and penalties related to those categories (Dayan, 2011). The creation of new categories of harm (e.g. environmental damage) has justified new forms of action and new remedies. The creation of new categories of perpetrator (e.g. the 'unpriviledged belligerent' of international humanitarian law) has justified new forms of criminal responsibility. The creation of new legal entities (e.g. the European Union) has justified the exercise of freedoms across territorial borders. In sum, the relationship between law, justification and classification hinges crucially on what can be considered *rational* or considered *reasonable*, and the tension between the two. Law encompasses and uses the reasonable as a test of what is normal or legitimate. It also provides reasons for action that are not found in any other sphere: it is a distinct source of justification.

This is not to say that there is a simple, binary, relationship between classifications and justifications. Law is justified in coming to decisions that emerge from the entirety of a legal system and culture. Our 'civil liberties' are a broad group of legal and cultural assumptions justifying many actions without explicit legal categorisation. Law is justified in coming to decisions in hard cases where a simple application of rules is impossible. In this sense justification encompasses both the norms that a legal system is intended to uphold and the authority we invest in our legal institutions. Law's justification is always more than the application of rules. It is the justification associated with law's overall institutional authority (see Raz, 2009).

The classifications found in our legal system therefore have a dual quality: we can expect them to be reasonable, and because of this, they give us a reason to act where other norms may be unclear.

> People often know what is morally the right thing to do, but just cannot bring themselves to do it, for one reason or another. That explains why there might be some practical point in superimposing a legal requirement over and above the moral one. Far from merely telling people to do something they would have done anyway, backing morality with the force of law gives people extra incentives (legal rewards and punishments) to do what is morally prescribed. Legalizing morality is, alas, far from redundant. (Goodin, 2010: 625)

Thus, saying that our actions are 'lawful' gives justification to our actions in a way that saying our actions are 'moral' does not. The lawful is clearly more difficult to contest, not only because it involves public rules associated with penalties, but because public rules are careful classifications clearly intended to justify in as specific a way as possible. Classification is one of the most powerful and distinctive human capacities and essential for giving reasons. But on what basis can we treat our classifications as reliable, meaningful or rational? The structures that we 'find' in the world, particularly those identified by the sciences which seem both reliable and powerful, are nonetheless of human origin.

Poststructuralism is a radical attempt to call such classifications into question (see Solomon, 1988; Morrison, 1997). Poststructuralism is characterised by suspicion about the promises made by modernism, i.e. many of the ideas that can be traced to the Renaissance and the Enlightenment. 'Enlightenment' suggests we should have the courage to use our own rational capacities to judge, accept and reject ideas received from the past and our cultures. Poststructuralism argues that this Enlightenment goal is more problematic than it appears because our classifications, and with it what we hold to be rational or reasonable, are always temporary, artificial or culturally determined. We cannot treat rationality as the route to a timeless and universal realm of truths, but have to see our identities and cultures, including what we see as *justified*, as culturally and historically determined.

This gives rise to two trains of thought encompassed by, but not exclusive to, poststructuralism. The first is a suspicion of claims about the timelessness of rationality and truth in our scientific and legal categories. Claims about rationality and truth need to be seen in their historical context as temporary, and problematic, assumptions. Our classifications of the world and of action always betray underlying assumptions about what our classifications *should* look like or achieve. There is no 'theory-free observation': we always bring assumptions to bear in our scientific or legal enquiries (Winch, 1958).

A second, more radical, conclusion can be drawn about the human sciences and law. Not only are these practices misleading as to what is objective, but they represent a drive to control human actions by determining certain things as 'normal' and others 'abnormal'. The human sciences are fundamentally a means, an instrument, of ordering and controlling, laying down standards for being human that are not necessary in any metaphysical or moral way but because they fit efficient, orderly, convenient scientific categories (Foucault, 2002).

One of the clearest examples of this can be found in the complicity between science, law and 'social values' with respect to sex, gender and sexuality. An ideology of 'natural', 'essential' human qualities posits changeless, natural, divisions between the sexes and also insists upon a universal, binary division between the biological sexes. This binary division, itself falsified by countless physiological variations among people, was used to obscure variations in gender and identity (because our physiological classification and our gender self-perception may not 'match') and in sexuality (because sexual attraction is not always for the opposite ('hetero') sex) (Roach Anleu, 1992). The social sciences remained under the spell of the biological sciences and thereby blind to real differences between persons. Treating as deviant those who do not fit biological categories is no longer a part of legitimate social scientific enquiry. Nonetheless, its historical presence in the 'purely descriptive' endeavour of social science is grounds for suspicion concerning its isolation from prevailing social attitudes and power.

Reason in the fullest philosophical sense, what is universally or timelessly rational, if it exists at all is something that we have neither definitively found (as a culture or civilisation) nor that law has an authoritative claim over. Whether we are suspicious concerning all claims to truth and reason, or merely accept the present limitations on human knowledge, law has not and cannot claim definitive insight into the rational. Law's deployment of the reasonable, and law's contribution to the creation of what is rational, serves the purpose of justification, justifying the actions of the state and the individual. But humans, and perhaps the state, may well be fundamentally irrational entities, pursuing goals, actions and experiences that cannot be understood as either reasonable or rational. Law is in constant tension with the irrational in human life. Not only the unreasonableness of the criminal. The unreasonableness that may well be a constant component of the human condition.

EXAMPLE

FM (FGM) Sudan CG [2007] UKAIT 00060 (UK Asylum and Immigration Tribunal)

Female genital mutilation (FGM) or female circumcision is a cultural practice explicable either as a rite of passage or institutionalised cruelty. Those differences in description can be cast as a debate between 'cultural relativists' (often social scientists seeking to record

➡

but not judge cultural practices) and 'universalists' (often politicians and lawyers seeking to change practices). The following passage was submitted as evidence in the trial; the author is a Dr Gruenbaum writing in an anthropology journal. The issue of methodology in the human sciences is as much at issue here as the practice of FGM itself.

Such responses [criticising FGM] strike many African women scholars as arrogant, especially because western culture has its own aesthetically motivated medical disasters such as silicone breast implants and useless cosmetic surgeries. The ethnocentric views of outsiders fail to recognise the dynamic nature of cultural patterns, imagining 'the other' perhaps as frozen in time, bound by 'traditional' ways of doing things, and as 'prisoners of ritual' who are not rational makers of their own history. But as Edgerton makes clear in his discussion of customs such as Sati in India as well as female circumcision in Africa, insiders to such cultures often have widely differing opinions and disagreements about them [. . .]. Culture, in fact, is far from static, as the cultural debates now raging in Sudan over the issue of female circumcision illustrate.

Questions

Section 1

- Is it possible to offer a definition of law which is neither local nor temporary? Is our use of the word 'law' always dependent upon the context in which it is used?

- Do we have to presume that law has foundations beyond our social and cultural history? If we were to deny law any foundation beyond our social and cultural history would this challenge the authority of law as *independent* of politics?

- Is it possible to combine the ideas that 'law is a system characterised by communication' and 'legal systems are always changing'? Does 'system' always presuppose static institutions?

Section 2

- Do trends in the formal characteristics of law evidence progress? For example, does the increased quantity of statutory law created in the last century mean that society is better – more rationally or more fairly – governed?

- Can a regulatory framework be classed as law? For example, do professional standards create legal relationships? Compare realist and positivist responses.

- Is the practice and study of law ahistorical? Does law demand that we ignore the past, or does law demand that we treat the past as present?

Section 3

- Is law a multi-functional tool or do the functions of law, together, serve a single function?

- Does the idea of 'law's function' refer to its institutions or its ideals? Are these separable?

- Is using law in a *just* way reducible to law being reasonable? Does reasonable always mean *rational*?

Concepts and methods: Knowledge

Knowledge and belief

What we know and what we believe can be demonstrated to be different things. We *know* that we exist (we have to exist in order to know anything). But we can only *believe* that, for example, the last train leaves at midnight. Our memory might be faulty or the last train may get cancelled. Much philosophical effort has been expended considering the relationship between knowledge and belief. Some of it considering the reliability of the senses and the human mind, much of it turning on the words 'knowledge' and 'belief' themselves.

The relationship between knowledge, belief and law has its own, complex, history. Law rarely aspires to absolutely certain knowledge. Rather, different levels of certainty ('proof') are appropriate in different contexts. In most jurisdictions we find a different standard of proof for different areas of law. Certainty in criminal cases is much more important – because liberty is at stake – but nonetheless, this is not certainty in terms of infallible knowledge, but to a level as high as is humanly possible.

Law is concerned with what beliefs people hold where this is important to determine their responsibilities (e.g. whether they understood the terms of a contract) or their desert (e.g. whether their intention to harm was premeditated). 'Belief' generally has a narrow meaning in law, isolating a narrow range of expectations within a narrow field of activity, e.g. 'did someone hold belief *x* during activity *y*'? Given that beliefs are subjective (and therefore defy direct examination), this will often be ascertained through their objective actions, or through a 'reasonable person' test determining what a person would be *justified* in believing in that context. Unlike philosophy, law much more rarely seeks to take a stand on people's 'personal beliefs', i.e. those ideas that are personally important to them, but which may not be held by everyone.

Appearance and reality

The difference between appearance and reality is the staple division at the heart of Western philosophy. By positing a difference between how the world appears to us and how it is in reality, we are articulating suspicion (the world is not as it seems) and a difference between epistemology and ontology (what we know and what actually exists). Simple suspicion is a useful philosophical tool. We should be suspicious of the evidence of our senses; there is no guarantee that they are suitable for apprehending reality. We should also be suspicious in the sense that we should not settle for simple answers to difficult questions. Suspicion about the relationship between epistemology and ontology fueled criticisms of transcendent accounts of law's existence: why should we believe anything exists beyond our social world? Equally, immanent accounts of law give rise to suspicions about the law's claim to authority: why should we invest authority in something that is only the product of human practices?

Scepticism about ontology itself – enquiry into the underlying structures of reality – does not entail scepticism about knowledge. Appearances themselves can be the route to predictable knowledge about the world. As phenomenologists and others have argued, appearances can always be mapped, and appearances can be manipulated with the use of our imagination. Imagination is the capacity whereby our intellect can be used to come to judgments (Kant, 1929). Without imagination we could not decide which of our appearances should be brought under general rules, and it is imagination that allows us to turn appearances into reasons for action and the bases of decision-making. In sum, appearances and imagination are – as realists might argue – not peripheral to law but central to its need to constitute, justify and regulate.

Epistemology and ontology

We have been concerned with knowledge – truth, certainty, justified belief – throughout our engagement with critical concepts in law. Knowledge and certainty, while crucial, are contested in philosophy and in law. We can seek the absolute and unchanging (Plato) or make more modest claims about law being made real in the practices of the courts (American realism). The former is a tempting but extravagant view of knowledge; the latter is a limited but parsimonious approach to what we should aim for when we seek 'the truth about law'.

This chapter has demanded a better sense of the relationship between epistemology and ontology. Ontology – the study of what exists and how it exists – is an eminently metaphysical branch of philosophy: it asks what structures underlie reality in order to allow things to exist and make them intelligible to us as humans. But ontology does not have to be understood as a metaphysical form of enquiry. We engage in ontology whenever we ask where something – particularly something non-physical – has come from or how it is that something can be said to exist. For example, how an institution exists (despite being characterised by people, processes and physical spaces), how a nation exists (despite being a conglomerate of disparate persons) or an ideology exists (despite being a non-physical system of ideas). These things exist in different ways but, nonetheless, exist (see Winch, 1958).

Discussing the 'ontology of law' sounds like abstract philosophical enquiry, but it can be understood in terms of what needs to be the case for law to exist at all. We can pinpoint where much law *comes from*, i.e. law-making sovereign bodies, but this is not the same asking 'what must be the case for there to be law at all'? For *legal institutions* to exist there must be both real practices (shared ways of doing things) and ideal standards (agreement on what should or should not be done). For law as a *practice* to exist there must be something that distinguishes legal rules from other rules (namely the conjunction of primary and secondary rules). For law as an *ideal* to exist there must be certain kinds of ideas that we share and which retain their meaning through time: that there should be good order, that there should be justice in human conduct and human affairs, or simply the idea that we have obligations rather than simply having preferences and interests. In sum, there must be both real activities and shared ideas for law to exist at all. Therefore, how we *know* law is also a question of *what* we are trying to know and how it exists.

Foundationalism

The use of the term 'normativity', which is relatively uncommon in general legal discourse, reflects an effort to consider the fundamental basis of obligations and rules. Sometimes appealing to a party's obligations is not enough: we have to turn the origins or justifications of those obligations in order to assess the 'force' of the obligation. Not only that, normativity can be used to explore the origins of justification of legality *per se*, giving us a language to articulate the fact that *law* is perceived as binding *aside from* the fact that individual laws are binding. As such, the language of normativity allows discussion of 'foundationalism'.

The term foundationalism has a number of different philosophical meanings, and while it is most closely associated with epistemology and the foundations of knowledge (Sartwell, 1992), it is applicable in legal contexts. Rules need a particular foundation or origin in order to be legal rules. Such a foundation might lie in the nature of, or relationship between, rules. However, to avoid an infinite regress in this analysis – there must be a point at which appeal to other rules ceases – rules must have a foundation that is extrinsic to rules, even if this is the authority of a legal constitution.

Note that the foundation of laws or legality may well be something different to a constitution or constitutional settlement. The modern preoccupation with constitutions can distract us from the fact that systems of law and law-making long pre-date the modern constitutional state. To argue that 'law' proper only begins with the constitutional state ignores the historical relationship between social and legal norms which pre-date the emergence of the sovereign state in the seventeenth century.

The meaning of foundationalism turns on the philosophical opposition between 'foundationalism' and various forms of 'constructivism' (Alexy, 1989). The latter suggests that institutions, processes and ideas that seem to demand foundations are, in fact, constructed through human agency and activity. This position is not necessarily a sceptical one, it simply denies that foundations are always as necessary – timeless or unchanging – as we assume. Note that this opposition is susceptible to deconstructive challenge (see Chapter 6).

Grammar

Law is a structured phenomenon. It has rules governed by institutions, and has institutions structured by constitutive rules of recognition, modification and adjudication. Even those systems dismissed as 'primitive' have structuring principles: expectations about how disputes should be mediated and what kinds of remedies are appropriate. Norms *and* rules give structure to legal institutions and legal rules.

One way to stress the ideal – rather than real or concrete – dimensions of the structure of law is to say that law has a grammar. That is, law has structuring principles that determine what can and cannot be said, or be meaningful, within the system. This captures part of what is being expressed in Luhmann's systems theory. It is part of the CLS criticism of law's ideological dimension (Unger, 1986). It is also related to Wittgenstein's understanding of rules as public practices; our social lives have a grammar, a structure, which determines what should and should not be done (Wittgenstein, 2001). Like grammar in linguistics, there are systematic rules for determining what is right or wrong in all of our social systems. However, these rules are not written into the fabric of reality, nor are they necessarily explicable in rational, formal, terms. The grammar of social life, including legal practices, depends upon our witnessing public practices and testing our own actions against public practices.

The term 'grammar' is useful to avoid the reification (artificial concretisation) of a legal *system*. A legal system has real, physical, components: people, buildings, rules written in books, but these are unified by a structure that is not part of our physical world. The structure unifies by providing public rules for rightness and wrongness – a grammar – which is not real but nonetheless has real effects.

Further reading

Many, if not all, of the classic texts in the jurisprudential canon give an account of what law is or how questions concerning its definition should be approached. For works more focussed on how the definition of law should be approached, Tamanaha (2008) gives a broad functional approach, while Twining (2009) and Walker (2003) contrasting foundational accounts. Goodrich (1990) offers a powerful CLS analysis of the formal characteristics of the common law; a philosophical overview of other kinds of legal systems can be found Twining (2009). The emergence of new networks of governance at a global level is discussed in Likosky (ed.) (2002); a more general introduction to law, regulation and networks can be found in Morgan and Yeung (2007). The relationship between law and space is analysed by Delaney (2001).

Visit **www.mylawchamber.co.uk/riley** to access tools to help you develop and test your knowledge of legal philosophy including Podcasts on leading thinkers and theories, discussion questions, diagrams showing interrelations between concepts, and weblinks

Glossary of philosophical terms

Analytical jurisprudence The study of those concepts crucial to understanding law as an institution and law as a social practice. The aim of analytical jurisprudence is to achieve conceptual clarity: to distinguish the concept, and the practice, of law from other social practices and ideals. Contrasted with normative jurisprudence (see below).

Antonym The opposite of a term. Understanding a concept demands understanding both the meanings attributed to the word and how it can be held to be the opposite of something else.

Autonomy To be a 'law unto oneself'. Autonomy designates the human *capacity* for rational action and decision-making. It can be contrasted with 'freedom' which is a more general *absence* of barriers to action and decision-making.

A priori Truths or principles existing prior to knowledge gained through the senses; of particular concern to rationalists. If there is any knowledge *a priori* – prior to the information received by our senses – it is either of a formal nature (logical or mathematical truths, or the existence of a perceiving subject) or of a metaphysical nature (the existence of God).

A posteriori Knowledge gained through the senses; the principal concern of empiricists. *A posteriori* knowledge is any 'raw data' about the world received by a human subject.

Causation A relationship of cause leading to effect. Causation and causality apply at both a micro level (e.g. particles) and a macro level (e.g. 'social forces'). Hume insisted (1975) that there is no 'thing' or 'power' that is 'causation' *per se*. When we label something as the cause of an effect, any kind of process or power could be at work. This presents problems for any *scientific* attempt to give a meaning to causation – science presumes, so cannot prove, causation – although it remains a useful term of analysis.

Conditions (necessary and sufficient) A condition is that which has to be fulfilled or in place for an outcome. Necessary conditions are multiple conditions. A number of causal forces may have to be in place in order to bring about an effect; each of these individual causes may be needed (necessary) but not sufficient. Sufficient conditions are those causes which are, in themselves, enough to bring about an effect.

Consequentialism Any moral theory (including, but not exclusively, utilitarianism) is consequentialist if moral worth or value is determined purely on the outcome of the actions. Compare deontology.

De facto / de jure *De facto* refers to the fact that power has been exercised (often the power to make a decision); *de jure* identifies the fact that power has been exercised lawfully. The difference between the two depends upon one's philosophical starting-point: positivists point to sources, natural lawyers to external validation, and critical legal studies would deny that there is any stable division at all.

Deontology Claims concerning duties. Deontological theories of morality are concerned with identifying obligatory or prohibited actions without reference to the consequences of actions, often on the basis of what can be made universal.

Determinism The belief that everything is the product of causation, including human action.

Empirical Generally meaning discovered or verified by the senses, empirical is often used to mean anything discovered by scientific investigation.

Empiricism The claim that everything that can be considered knowledge can be traced to the immediate evidence of our senses.

Epistemology Theorising about knowledge. Epistemology is generally concerned with distinguishing 'mere belief' from knowledge. Knowledge is often understood as belief that is – additionally – both justified and true.

Foundationalism Claims about the sources, or basic cause, of a phenomenon. Foundationalism is needed to show that any set of beliefs, norms, or rules must have a source outside themselves (in order to avoid infinite regress in explanation).

Ideology Strictly, any system of ideas. More commonly, a system of ideas that seeks to gain power, or maintain inequality, through misrepresentation of reality or misrepresentation of human interests.

Immanent Arising from the immediate human and social world; not depending upon any explanation beyond the human and social world.

Imperatives Claims – taking the form 'ought' or 'should' – which either demand or encourage a course of action. In Kant's terms, hypothetical imperatives encourage adoption of specified means to ends; categorical imperatives bind unconditionally.

Indeterminacy The characteristic of rules to be either under- and over-inclusive, or fail to guide judgment at all. Indeterminacy can be attributed to the nature of legal judgment, the structuring of facts in legal contexts, or uncertainty in language itself.

Infinite regress The endless expansion of justifications or explanations. A consequence of trying to explain something by positing a prior explanation that itself needs explanation.

Metaphysics Literally 'after nature', this is the field of philosophical enquiry that looks for the first causes, the structure or the fundamental laws of the universe. It can be used more broadly to label (and often criticise) claims about the world that are not verifiable through scientific means.

Monism Explanation based on a single property, process or substance. In metaphysics it can be contrasted with dualism (i.e. there is more than one substance in the world, namely bodies and minds). In ethics it can be contrasted with pluralism (i.e. there are many sources of moral obligations rather than one).

Morality A system of norms or 'mores' governing individual conduct. Morality is partly distinguishable from *ethics*, which centralises character and virtue. However, in modern thought, ethics is associated less with character and virtue and more with universal obligations and therefore morality. Arguably distinguishable from law via the positivists' separation thesis.

Naturalistic fallacy The error of assuming that facts (i.e. what is 'natural') directly or automatically give rise to values; a violation of the fact/value distinction.

Normative jurisprudence Analysis of the content laws and legal systems should have, or the functions a legal system should serve. Often involving the denial of a distinction between legal, political and moral philosophy.

Ontology Discussion of being. That is, how things can be said to exist; what conditions make it possible for something to exist.

Phenomenology The science of appearances. Taking its inspiration from the work of Descartes and Kant, phenomenology grants that certain kinds of knowledge are unobtainable (namely pure, objective, insight into the workings of nature). Nonetheless, the presentation of reality to human subjects can be carefully analysed and yield truths about how reality is structured for that perceiving subject.

Proposition An assertion, in language, of a fact or relationship between facts. Propositions are similar to, but distinguishable from, a sentence. A sentence is an utterance or assertion whose meaning can be context-specific. The statement of fact, or relation of ideas, expressed by a proposition should not be context-specific.

Rationalism The claim that for anything to be considered knowledge it must have arisen from or be validated by the mind.

Reason Used as a noun, reason is an idealisation and generalisation of the human capacity for thought. As a generalisation, reason denotes the rational capacities possessed by all humans. As an idealisation, it suggests that human reasoning – wherever it is found, and if stripped of error – allows insight into the functioning of the world and the functioning of reasoning itself.

Reification Illegitimately treating something ideal (mental) as real (empirical or concrete).

Scepticism Denial of the reliability of human knowledge; denial of the capacity for human thinking to gain insight beyond what is immediately known to the senses.

Teleology Discussion of ends or goals. In a general sense it denotes the pursuit of goals. In a metaphysical sense it denotes the claim that entities, including humans, have a predetermined form of completion or fulfilment.

Transcendent Beyond the knowledge of the senses but potentially accessible through reason.

Verificationism An epistemology associated with logical positivism. Broadly, it suggests that the title 'knowledge' can only be attributed to facts gained through verified, or verifiable, observation. Strictly, it is the claim that propositions only have *meaning* if they can be associated with a method of verification or falsification.

Bibliography

Alexy, R. (1989) *A Theory of Legal Argumentation*, Oxford: Oxford University Press.

Alexy, R. (2004) 'The Nature of Legal Philosophy' *Ratio Juris* **17** (2) pp. 156–67.

Alldridge, P. and Brants, C. (eds) (2001) *Personal Autonomy, the Private Sphere and the Criminal Law: A comparative study*, Oxford: Hart Publishing.

Allott, P. (1990) *Eunomia*, Oxford: Oxford University Press.

Aquinas (2002) *On Law, Morality, and Politics*, Indianapolis, IN: Hackett Publishing.

Arendt, H. (1970) *On Violence*, Orlando, FL: Harcourt Books.

Arendt, H. (1998) *The Human Condition*, Chicago, IL: University of Chicago Press.

Aristotle (1987) *A New Aristotle Reader*, Oxford: Oxford University Press.

Arrigo, B.A. (2003) 'Justice and the deconstruction of psychological jurisprudence: The case of competency to stand trial' *Theoretical Criminology* **7** (1) pp. 55–88.

Augustine (1963) *St. Augustine's City of God*, Oxford: Oxford University Press.

Austin, J. (1995) *The Province of Jurisprudence Determined*, Cambridge: Cambridge University Press.

Averroës (1998) 'On the harmony of religions and philosophy'. Available at: www.muslim-philosophy.com/ir/art/ir100.htm. Accessed 30 January 2012.

Ayer, A.J. (1970) *Language, Truth and Logic*, London: Victor Gollancz.

Baggini, J. and Fosl, P.S. (2007) *The Ethics Toolkit: A compendium of ethical concepts and methods*, Chichester: John, Wiley and Sons, Ltd.

Baggini, J. and Fosl, P.S. (2010) *The Philosopher's Toolkit: A compendium of philosophical concepts and methods* (2nd edn), London: Wiley-Blackwell.

Barnes, J. (1987) *Early Greek Philosophy*, Harmondsworth: Penguin Books.

Barnes, J. (ed.) (1995) *The Cambridge Companion to Aristotle*, Cambridge: Cambridge University Press.

Bayles, M. (1986) 'Principles for legal procedure' *Law and Philosophy* **5** (1) pp. 33–57.

Benjamin, W. (1979) *One Way Street*, London: Verso.

Bentham, J. (2007) *An Introduction to the Principles of Morals and Legislation*, Mineola, NY: Dover Publications.

Berger, A. (1953) 'Encyclopaedic Dictionary of Roman Law' *Transactions of the American Philosophical Society* **43** (2) pp. 333–809.

Berman, H.J. (1977) 'The origins of Western legal science' *Harvard Law Review* **90** (5) pp. 894–943.

Bix, B.H. (2004) *A Dictionary of Legal Philosophy*, New York: Oxford University Press.

Blackburn, S. (2006) *Plato's Republic: A Biography*, London: Atlantic Books.

Blank, Y. (2011) 'The reenchantment of law' *Cornell Law Review* **96** (4) pp. 633–670.

Bloch, E. (1986) *Natural Law and Human Dignity*, Cambridge, MA: MIT Press.

Bobbio, N. and Zolo, D. (1998) 'Hans Kelsen, the theory of law and the international legal system: A talk' *European Journal of International Law* **9** (2) pp. 355–67.

Bridgeman, J. and Millns, S. (1998) *Feminist Perspectives on Law: Law's engagement with the female body*, London: Sweet & Maxwell.

Cain, P. (2010) *The Hart-Fuller Debate in the Twenty-First Century*, Oxford: Hart Publishing.

Campbell, T. (1999) *Legal Positivism*, Aldershot: Ashgate.

Campbell, T. (2001) *Justice*, Basingstoke: Macmillan.

Carey, C. (2012) *Trials from Ancient Athens* (2nd edn), Devon: Routledge.

Caudill, D.S. and Gold, S.J. (1995) *Radical Philosophy of Law: Contemporary challenges to mainstream legal theory and practice*, Atlantic Highlands, NJ: Humanities Press.

Chloros, A.G. (1958) 'What is natural law?' *The Modern Law Review* **21** (6) pp. 609–22.

Cicero (1998) *The Republic and The Laws*, Oxford: Oxford University Press.

Cicero (2008) *On Obligations*, Oxford: Oxford University Press.

Clarke, M. (1976) 'Durkheim's sociology of law' *British Journal of Law and Society* **3** (2) pp. 246–55.

Cleveland Metro (2011) 'Identifying photo-copy machine poses, problem for Cuyahoga County Official', http://blog.cleveland.com/metro/2011/03/identifying–photocopy–machine.html (accessed 8 July 2012).

Cole, D.H. (2001) 'An unqualified human good: E.P. Thompson and the rule of law' *Journal of Law and Society* **28** (2) pp. 177–203.

Copleston, F. (2003) *A History of Philosophy Volume 3: Late Medieval and Renaissance Philosophy*, Cornwall: Continuum Books.

Coval, S.C. and Smith, J.C. (1982) 'Rights, goals, and hard cases' *Law and Philosophy* **1** (3) pp. 451–80.

Coyle, S. and Morrow, K. (2004) *The Philosophical Foundations of Environmental Law: Property, Rights and Nature*, Oxford: Hart Publishing.

Davies, T. (1997) *Humanism*, London: Routledge.

Dawson, G. (1981) 'Justified true belief is knowledge' *The Philosophical Quarterly* **31** (125) pp. 315–29.

Dayan, C. (2011) *The Law is a White Dog: How legal rituals make and unmake persons*, Princeton, NJ: Princeton University Press.

De Beauvoir, S. (1963) *Nature of the Second Sex*, Surrey: New English Library.

De Beauvoir, S. (1988) *The Second Sex*, London: Picador.

Delacroix, S. (2005) 'Schmitt's critique of Kelsenian normativism' *Ratio Juris* **18** (1) pp. 30–45.

Delacroix, S. (2006) *Legal Norms and Normativity: An essay in genealogy*, Oxford: Hart Publishing.

Delaney, D. (2001) 'Making nature/marking humans: Law as a site of (cultural) produc-tion' *Annals of the Association of American Geographers* **91** (3) pp. 487–503.

Del Mar, M. (2007) 'Legal norms and norma-tivity' *Oxford Journal of Legal Studies* **27** (2) pp. 355–72.

Del Mar, M. (ed.) (2011) *New Waves in Philosophy of Law*, Croydon: Palgrave Macmillan.

D'Entreves, A.P. (1957) *Natural Law: An introduction to legal philosophy*, London: Hutchinson University Library.

Derrida, J. (1990) 'Force of law: The mystical foundation of authority' *Cardozo Law Review* **11** pp. 919–1045.

Descartes, R. (1968) *Discourse on Method and the Meditations*, Harmondsworth: Penguin Books.

Dickens, C. (1971) *Bleak House*, Harmondsworth: Penguin Books.

Dickens, C. (2003) *A Tale of Two Cities*, Harmondsworth: Penguin Books.

Dillon, J. and Gergel, T. (2003) *The Greek Sophists*, London: Penguin Books.

Douzinas, C. and Gearey, A. (2005) *Critical Jurisprudence: The political philosophy of justice*, Oxford: Hart Publishing.

Dworkin, R. (1975) 'Hard cases' *Harvard Law Review* **88** (6) pp. 1057–109.

Dworkin, R. (1977) *Taking Rights Seriously*, London: Duckworth.

Dworkin, R. (ed.) (1977) *The Philosophy of Law*, Oxford: Oxford University Press.

Dworkin, R. (1998) *Law's Empire*, Oxford: Hart Publishing.

Easton, L.D. (1961) 'Alienation and history in the early Marx' *Philosophy and Phenomenological Research* **22** (2) pp. 193–205.

Eberle, E.J. (2002) *Dignity and Liberty: Constitutional visions in Germany and the United States*, Westport, CT: Praeger Press.

Fernandez, J. (2009) 'An exploration of the meaning of truth in philosophy and law' *The University of Notre Dame Australia Law Review* 11 pp. 53–83.

Fine, R. (2001) *Political Investigations: Hegel, Marx, Arendt*, London: Routledge.

Finnis, J. (2011) *Natural Law and Natural Rights* (2nd edn), Oxford: Oxford University Press.

Fish, S. (1988) 'Force' *Washington and Lee Law Review* 45 (3) pp. 883–954.

Flew, A. (ed.) (1979) *A Dictionary of Philosophy*, London: Pan Books.

Foucault, M. (1977) *Discipline and Punish: The birth of the prison*, Harmondsworth: Penguin Books.

Foucault, M. (2002) *The Order of Things*, London: Routledge.

Frank, J. (2009) *Law and the Modern Mind*, New Jersey: Transaction Press.

Freeman, M.D.A. (2001) *Lloyd's Introduction to Jurisprudence* (7th edn), London: Sweet & Maxwell.

Freud, S. (1938) *Totem and Taboo*, Harmondsworth: Penguin Books.

Fuller, L.L. (1969) *The Morality of Law*, New Haven, CT: Yale University Press.

Gerry, K. (2011) 'On the nature of law: Philosophical anarchism and the function of law'. Available at: http://ssrn.com/abstract=1937437. Accessed 23 February 2012.

Gilmore, G. (1961) 'Legal realism: Its cause and cure' *Yale Law Journal* 70 (7) pp. 1037–48.

Glover, J. (2001) *Humanity: A moral history of the twentieth century*, London: Pimlico.

Goode, R., Kronke, H., McKendrick, E. (2007) *Transnational Commercial Law: Text, cases and materials*, Oxford: Oxford University Press.

Goodin, R.E. (2010) 'An epistemic case for legal moralism' *Oxford Journal of Legal Studies* 30 (4) pp. 615–33.

Goodrich, P. (1990) *Languages of Law: From logics of memory to nomadic masks*, London, Weidenfeld & Nicolson.

Gray, J. (1996) *Mill on Liberty: A defence*, London: Routledge.

Hacker, P.M.S. (1997) *The Great Philosophers: Wittgenstein*, London: Weidenfeld & Nicholson.

Hamilton, A. (2012) 'The Federalist No. 78: Saturday, June 14, 1788'. Available at: http://www.constitution.org/fed/federa78.htm. Accessed 27 February 2012.

Hampson, N. (1968) *The Enlightenment*, Harmondsworth: Penguin Books.

Hart, H.L.A. (1994) *The Concept of Law* (2nd edn), Oxford: Clarendon Press.

Hegel, G.W.F (2008) *Outlines of the Philosophy of Right*, Oxford: Oxford University Press.

Hendrickson, N. (2008) *The Rowman and Littlefield Handbook for Critical Thinking*, Plymouth: Rowman & Littlefield.

Hobbes, T. (1996) *Leviathan*, Oxford: Oxford University Press.

Hoeflich, M.H. (1986) 'Law & geometry: Legal science from Leibniz to Langdell' *The American Journal of Legal History* 30 (2) pp. 95–121.

Hogg, J.E. (1908) 'French and English land law' *Journal of the Society of Comparative Legislation* 9 (1) pp. 64–8.

Hohfeld, W.N. (1913) 'Some fundamental legal conceptions as applied in judicial reasoning' *The Yale Law Journal* 23 (16) pp. 16–59.

Holmes, O.W. (1897) 'The path of the law' *Harvard Law Review* 10 pp. 457–78.

Honneth, A. (1995) *The Struggle for Recognition: The Moral Grammar of Social Conflicts*, Cambridge: Polity Press.

Human Rights in China (2010) 'Sichuan activist sentenced to five years for 'Inciting subversion of state power''. Available at: http://www.hrichina.org/content/377. Accessed 26 February 2012.

Hume, D. (1975) *Enquiries Concerning Human Understanding and Concerning the Principles of Morals*, Oxford: Clarendon Press.

Humm, M. (1992) *Feminisms: A Reader*, London: Longmans.

Hunt, A. (1986) 'The theory of critical legal studies' *Oxford Journal of Legal Studies* 6 (1) pp. 1–45.

Hunt, A. (1987) 'The critique of law: What is 'critical' about critical legal theory?' *Journal of Law and Society* **14** (1) pp. 5–19.

Hunt, L. (2007) *Inventing Human Rights: A history*, New York: W.W. Norton & Company.

Husik, I. (1909) 'Averroës on the metaphysics of Aristotle' *Philosophical Review* **18** (4) pp. 416–28.

Husserl, G. (1937) 'Justice' *International Journal of Ethics* **47** (3) pp. 271–307.

Hutchinson, A.C. (1995) 'A postmodern's Hart: Taking rules sceptically' *The Modern Law Review* **58** (6) pp. 788–819.

Ingersoll, D.E. (1966) 'Karl Llewellyn, American legal realism, and contemporary legal behaviorism' *Ethics* **76** (4) pp. 253–66.

Kafka, F. (1994) *The Trial*, Harmondsworth: Penguin Books.

Kant, I. (1929) *The Critique of Pure Reason*, London: Macmillan Press.

Kant, I. (1948) *The Moral Law*, London: Hutchinson University Library.

Kant, I. (1991) *Political Writings*, Cambridge: Cambridge University Press.

Kant, I. (1996) *The Metaphysics of Morals*, Cambridge: Cambridge University Press.

Katz, L. (2011) *Why the Law is so Perverse*, Chicago, IL: University of Chicago Press.

Kelley, D.R. (1990) *The Human Measure: Social thought in the Western legal tradition*, Cambridge, MA: Harvard University Press.

Kelsen, H. (2005) *General Theory of Law and State*, London / New Jersey: Transaction Press.

Korsgaard, C. (1996) *The Sources of Normativity*, Cambridge: Cambridge University Press.

Kramer, M.H. (1999) *In Defense of Legal Positivism: Law without trimmings*, Oxford: Oxford University Press.

Kruks, S. (2005) 'Beauvoir's time/our time: The renaissance in Simone De Beauvoir studies' *Feminist Studies* **31** (2) pp. 286–309.

Landers, S. (1990) 'Wittgenstein, realism, and CLS: Undermining rule scepticism' *Law and Philosophy* **9** (2) pp. 177–203.

Laughland, J. (2008) *A History of Political Trials: From Charles I to Saddam Hussein*, Oxford: Peter Lang.

Lee, R.W. (2007) *The Elements of Roman Law* (4th edn), London: Sweet & Maxwell.

Lester, A. (1976) 'Fundamental rights in the United Kingdom: The law and the British constitution' *University of Pennsylvania Law Review* **125** (2) pp. 337–63.

Likosky, M. (ed.) (2002) *Transnational Legal Processes*, London: Butterworths.

Lloyd, G.E.R. (2009) *Disciplines in the Making: Cross-cultural perspectives on elites, learning, and innovation*, Oxford: Oxford University Press.

Locke, J. (1960) *Two Treatises of Government*, Cambridge: Cambridge University Press.

Locke, J. (1975) *An Essay Concerning Human Understanding*, Oxford: Clarendon Press.

Luban, D. (1986) 'Legal modernism' *Michigan Law Review* **84** (8) pp. 1656–95.

Luban, D. (1989) 'Difference made legal: The Court and Dr. King' *Michigan Law Review* **87** (8) pp. 2152–224.

Lucy, W. (2009) 'Abstraction and the rule of law' *Oxford Journal of Legal Studies* **29** (3) pp. 481–509.

Luhmann, N. (1998) 'The third question: The creative use of paradoxes in law and legal history' *Journal of Law and Society* **15** (2) pp. 153–65.

Luker, K. (1998) 'Sex, social hygiene, and the state: The double-edged sword of social reform' *Theory and Society* **27** (5) pp. 601–34.

MacCormick, N. (1988) 'Norms, institutions, and institutional facts' *Law and Philosophy* **17** (3) pp. 301–45.

MacCormick, N. (2007) *Institutions of Law: An essay in legal theory*, Oxford: Oxford University Press.

Maine, H. (1931) *Ancient Law: Its connection with the early history of society and its relation to modern ideas*, London: Murray.

Marmor, A. (2004) 'The rule of law and its limits' *Law and Philosophy* **23** (1) pp. 1–43.

Marx, K. (2000) *Karl Marx: Selected writings* (ed. McLellan), Oxford: Oxford University Press.

Mill, J.S. (1991) *On Liberty and Other Essays*: Oxford: Oxford University Press.

Monroe, K., Martin, A. and Ghosh, P. (2009) 'Politics and an innate moral sense: Scientific evidence for an old theory?' *Political Research Quarterly* **62** (3) pp. 614–34.

Moore, G.E. (1959) *Principia Ethica,* Cambridge: Cambridge University Press.

Moran, D. (2000) *Introduction to Phenomenology,* London: Routledge.

Morgan, B. and Yeung K. (2007) *An Introduction to Law and Regulation: Texts and materials,* Cambridge: Cambridge University Press.

Morrison, W. (1997) *Jurisprudence: From the Greeks to postmodernism,* London: Cavendish Publishing.

Murdoch, I. (1970) *The Sovereignty of the Good,* London: Routledge & Kegan Paul.

Nietzsche, F. (1998) *On the Genealogy of Morality,* Indianapolis, IN: Hackett Publishing Company.

Nozick, R. (1974) *Anarchy, State, and Utopia,* London: Blackwell.

Nussbaum, M. (1986) *The Fragility of Goodness: Luck and ethics in Greek tragedy and philosophy,* Cambridge: Cambridge University Press.

Nussbaum, M. (1997) 'Kant and stoic cosmo-politanism' *Journal of Political Philosophy* **5** (1) pp. 1–25.

Nussbaum, M. (2000) *Women and Human Development: The capabilities approach,* Cambridge: Cambridge University Press.

Ohlin, J.D. (2002) 'Is the concept of the person necessary for human rights?' *Columbia Law Review* **105** (1) pp. 209–49.

Oldfield, K. (2003) 'Social class and public administration: A closed question opens' *Administration & Society* **35** (4) pp. 438–61.

Paine, T. (1969) *Rights of Man,* London: Pelican Books.

Patterson, D. (ed.) (1996) *A Companion to Philosophy of Law and Legal Theory,* Oxford: Blackwell Publishing.

Philippopoulos-Mihalopoulos, A. (2010) *Niklas Luhmann: Law, Justice, Society,* London: Routledge.

Plato (1997) *Complete Works,* Indianapolis, IN: Hackett Publishing Company.

Posner, E.A. (2002) *Law and Social Norms,* Cambridge, MA: Harvard University Press.

Price, D.A. (1989) 'Taking rights cynically: A review of critical legal studies' *Cambridge Law Journal* **48** (2) pp. 271–301.

Quinton, A. (ed.) (1967) *Political Philosophy,* Oxford: Oxford University Press.

Radbruch, G. (2006) 'Five minutes of legal philosophy' *Oxford Journal of Legal Studies* **26** (1) pp. 13–15.

Rawls, J. (1999) *A Theory of Justice* (Rev. edn), Cambridge, MA: Belknap.

Raz, J. (ed.) (1978) *Practical Reasoning,* Oxford: Oxford University Press.

Raz, J. (1994) *Ethics in the Public Domain: Essays in the morality of law and politics,* Oxford: Clarendon Press.

Raz, J. (2009) *The Authority of Law* (2nd edn), Oxford: Oxford University Press.

Roach Anleu, S.L. (1992) 'Critiquing the law: Themes and dilemmas in Anglo-American feminist legal theory' *Journal of Law and Society* **19** (4) pp. 423–40.

Rosati, C.S. (2004) 'Some puzzles about the objectivity of law' *Law and Philosophy* **23** (3) pp. 273–323.

Ross, A. (2004) *On Law and Justice,* Clark, NJ: Lawbook Exchange.

Rousseau, J.-J. (1968) *The Social Contract* (trans. Cranston), Harmondsworth: Penguin Books.

Rucker, D. (1966) 'The moral grounds of civil disobedience' *Ethics* **76** (2) pp. 142–5.

Sadurski, W. (1988) 'The right, the good and the jurisprude' *Law and Philosophy* **7** (1) pp. 35–66.

Said, E.W. (1978) *Orientalism,* London: Routledge & Kegan Paul.

Sanders, T.C. (1962) *The Institutes of Justinian* (7th edn), London: Longmans.

Sartre, J.-P. (2007) *Existentialism is a Humanism,* New Haven, CT: Yale University Press.

Sartwell, C. (1992) 'Why knowledge is merely true belief' *The Journal of Philosophy* **89** (4) pp. 167–80.

Schauer, F. (1991) *Playing by the Rules: A philosophical examination of rule-based decision-making in law and in life,* Oxford: Clarendon Press.

Schmitt, C. (2006) *Political Theology*, Chicago, IL: University of Chicago Press.

Sen, A. (1999) *Development as Freedom*, Oxford: Oxford University Press.

Shklar, J. (1986) *Legalism: Law, morals and political trials*, Cambridge, MA: Harvard University Press.

Simmonds, N. (2007) *Law as a Moral Idea*, Oxford: Oxford University Press.

Simmonds, N. (2008) *Central Issues in Jurisprudence: Justice, law and rights*, London: Sweet & Maxwell.

Skorupski, J. (1993) *English-Language Philosophy 1750–1945*, Oxford: Oxford University Press.

Smart, J.J.C. and Williams, B. (1973) *Utilitarianism: For and Against*, Cambridge: Cambridge University Press.

Solomon, R.C. (1988) *Continental Philosophy Since 1750: The rise and fall of the self*, Oxford: Oxford University Press.

Solum, L. (2011) 'Legal theory blog'. Available at http://lsolum.typepad.com/legaltheory/. Accessed 26 February 2012.

Sophocles (1984) *The Three Theban Plays: Antigone, Oedipus the King, Oedipus as Colonus*, Harmondswort: Penguin Books.

Spaak, T. (2011) 'Karl Olivecrona's legal philosophy: A critical appraisal' *Ratio Juris* **24** (2) pp. 156–93.

Spragens, T.A. (1993) 'The antinomies of social justice' *The Review of Politics* **55** (2) pp. 193–216.

Stanford Encyclopedia of Philosophy (2011) Available at: http://plato.stanford.edu/. Accessed 26 February 2012.

Steinberg, S.H. (1966) *The 'Thirty Years War' and the Conflict for European Hegemony 1600–1660*, London: Edward Arnold.

Stolleis, M. (2009) *The Eye of the Law: Two essays on legal history*, London: Birkbeck Law Press.

Sun Tzu (1994) *The Art of War* (trans. Giles), Project Gutenberg. Available at: http://www.gutenberg.org/files/132/132.txt. Accessed 13 February 2012.

Tamanaha, B. (2008) 'Law' (St. John's Legal Studies Research Paper No. 08–0095). Available at: http://ssrn.com/abstract=1082436. Accessed 10 January 2012.

Tamanaha, B. (2010) *Beyond the Formalist-Realist Divide: The role of politics in judging*, Princeton, NJ: Princeton University Press.

Tapp, J. and Levine F. (1974) 'Legal socialization: Strategies for an ethical legality' *Stanford Law Review* **27** (1) pp. 1–72.

Taylor, C. (1992) *Sources of the Self: The making of the modern identity*, Cambridge: Cambridge University Press.

Teichmann, R. (2002) 'Explaining the rules' *Philosophy* **77** (302) pp. 597–613.

Teubner, G. (1997) 'The king's many bodies: The self-deconstruction of law's hierarchy' *Law and Society Review* **31** (4) pp. 763–88.

Thompson, E.P. (1975) *Whigs and Hunters: The origins of the black act*, London: Allen Lane.

Tuck, R. (1999) *The Rights of War and Peace: Political thought and the international order from Grotius to Kant*, Oxford: Oxford University Press.

Tur, R.H.S. (1978) 'What is jurisprudence?' *Philosophical Quarterly* **28** (111) pp. 149–61.

Tushnet, M. (1991) 'Critical legal studies: A political history' *Yale Law Journal* **100** (5) pp. 1515–44.

Twining, W. (2009) *General Jurisprudence: Understanding law from a global perspective*, Cambridge: Cambridge University Press.

Twining, W. and Miers, D. (2010) *How to do Things with Rules: A primer of interpretation*, Cambridge: Cambridge University Press.

Unger, R. (1986) *The Critical Legal Studies Movement*, Cambridge, MA / London: Harvard University Press.

Walker, N. (ed.) (2003) *Sovereignty in Transition*, Oxford: Hart Publishing.

Weber, M. (1978) *Max Weber: Selections in Translation*, Cambridge, Cambridge University Press.

Weinreb, L.L. (1978) 'Law as Order' *Harvard Law Review* **91** (5) pp. 909–59.

West, R. (1998) 'Toward humanistic theories of legal justice' *Cardozo Studies in Law and Literature* **10** (2) pp. 147–50.

Whitehead, A.N. (1979) *Process and Reality*, Doncaster: Free Press.

Wieacker, F. (1990) 'Foundations of European Legal Culture' *American Journal of Comparative Law* **38** (1) pp. 1–29.

Wilkins, D.B. (1990) 'Legal realism for lawyers' *Harvard Law Review* **104** (2) pp. 468–524.

Winch, P. (1958) *The Idea of a Social Science and its Relation to Philosophy*, London: Routledge & Kegan Paul.

Winthrop, D. (1978) 'Aristotle and theories of justice' *American Political Science Review* **72** (4) pp. 1201–16.

Wittgenstein, L. (1974) *Tractatus Logico-Philosophicus*, London: Routledge & Kegan Paul.

Wittgenstein, L. (2001) *Philosophical Investigations*, Oxford: Blackwell Publishing.

Wollstonecraft, M. (1997) *Vindication of the Rights of Women*, Ontario: Broadview Press.

Index